Sovereignty Across Generations

Sovereignty Across Generations

Constituent Power and Political Liberalism

ALESSANDRO FERRARA

Great Clarendon Street, Oxford, OX2 6DP,
United Kingdom

Oxford University Press is a department of the University of Oxford.
It furthers the University's objective of excellence in research, scholarship,
and education by publishing worldwide. Oxford is a registered trade mark of
Oxford University Press in the UK and in certain other countries

© Alessandro Ferrara 2023

The moral rights of the author have been asserted

First Edition published in 2023

All rights reserved. No part of this publication may be reproduced, stored in
a retrieval system, or transmitted, in any form or by any means, without the
prior permission in writing of Oxford University Press, or as expressly permitted
by law, by licence or under terms agreed with the appropriate reprographics
rights organization. Enquiries concerning reproduction outside the scope of the
above should be sent to the Rights Department, Oxford University Press, at the
address above

You must not circulate this work in any other form
and you must impose this same condition on any acquirer

Public sector information reproduced under Open Government Licence v3.0
(http://www.nationalarchives.gov.uk/doc/open-government-licence/open-government-licence.htm)

Published in the United States of America by Oxford University Press
198 Madison Avenue, New York, NY 10016, United States of America

British Library Cataloguing in Publication Data

Data available

Library of Congress Control Number: 2022945706

ISBN 978–0–19–287107–7

DOI: 10.1093/oso/9780192871077.001.0001

Printed and bound by
CPI Group (UK) Ltd, Croydon, CR0 4YY

Links to third party websites are provided by Oxford in good faith and
for information only. Oxford disclaims any responsibility for the materials
contained in any third party website referenced in this work.

For my grandchildren Clementina and Michele

Preface

This book builds on and carries forward two endeavours that have deeply shaped my intent to revisit John Rawls's paradigm of 'political liberalism'—as distinct from the comprehensive liberalism of *A Theory of Justice*—and make it engage concerns not directly central to its original context and formulation. The first leg of my journey towards an expanded political liberalism led to *The Democratic Horizon* (2014). Among several inhospitable conditions for liberal democracy at the end of the millennium, I singled out 'hyperpluralism' as a major challenge for the capacity of a political conception of justice, and a constitution inspired by it, to bridge divides between the rival visions held by opposed constituencies in the democratic arena. New additions to the toolbox of political liberalism included: rethinking the democratic ethos (and adding the virtue of openness to it); making pluralism reflexive and using conjectural arguments to include the 'partially reasonable' among the addressees of political justification; remedying the possible failure of conjectural arguments through the multivariate polity; and, finally, de-Westernizing the democratic ethos. Symposia and debates on *The Democratic Horizon* confirmed that political liberalism can incorporate new concepts. When in tune with the paradigm's normative bent, these notions accrue to its exceptional potential to outline in detail what is presupposed by the notion, evoked today from all philosophical quarters often as an empty slogan, of equals living together in diversity without oppression.

The second, more recent endeavour consisted of co-authoring, with Frank Michelman, *Legitimation by Constitution* (2021). I could not have met a more attentive, inspiring, and challenging partner than Frank for an extended, passionate conversation on the core of political liberalism, conducted with the intention of drawing out, reflecting on, and elucidating the implications of Rawls's constitution-centred view of legitimation in three areas: the tension between democratic sovereignty and the ideal of government under law, then judicial review, and finally the difficulties of applying 'legitimation by constitution' to supranational governance. As we rewrote past exchanges and explored untried paths, both sometimes felt—as we facetiously noted in our frequent emails—like two moths buzzing around a flame. Rawls's paradigm attracted us because its normative but non-foundationalist perspective, centred around the twin standards of the 'reasonable' and the 'most reasonable', casts light onto the whole spectrum of questions connected with the oppression-free coexistence of differently minded free and equal citizens.

On the encouraging spur of these two experiences, the project of this book began to shape up. During the mid to late 2010s, the challenge of hyperpluralism seemed to pale when compared to the populist questioning of liberal democracy—a seemingly irresistible tide that culminated with Brexit, the election of presidents Trump and Bolsonaro, and the rule of prime minister Modi. That tide brought to centre-stage a new theme, on which political liberalism has a lot to say in an innovative way, but which is only tangentially addressed in Rawls's book: constituent power, its different forms, the conditions of its legitimate exercise, and its elusive bearer, 'the people'.

Thus, a new step in the updating and revisiting of political liberalism has become the object of this book: to reconstruct Rawls's implicit view of constituent power beyond the scant three pages dedicated to it in *Political Liberalism* and to bring that view into dialogue with major constitutional theories of the twentieth century. The *sequential* understanding of democratic sovereignty that undergirds Rawls's constitutionalism offers the best antidote to the populist empowerment of the electorate, attributed the same constituent power as 'the people' and considered the sole pro-tempore owner of the constitution, in a *serial* understanding of democratic sovereignty. Over and beyond reconstruction, the *expansion* of the Rawlsian paradigm, here pursued, consists in tracking the normative core of sequential sovereignty to a *vertical reciprocity* that binds all the generations of a democratic people, considered as *demos*.

Acknowledgements

This book has grown out of dialogues conducted in many venues on lots of stimulating and challenging occasions. On a couple of those the manuscript has been discussed if not in its entirety at least concerning most of its chapters. The first such occasion was the Book Manuscript Workshop held on 25 and 26 January 2021 at the Centre for Ethics, Politics, and Society (CEPS) of the Institute of Arts and Humanities at the University of Minho, Portugal. My gratitude for the generous feedback received during those sessions goes first of all to Daniele Santoro for having organized the workshop and for his insightful remarks; then to Giuseppe Ballacci, Cristina Lafont, David Rasmussen, Benjamin Schupmann, and Camila Vergara for having commented on several chapters; and to all the participants who took the floor with their questions. That workshop then gave rise to a fruitful collaboration within CEPS's project on 'The Public Interest' (EXPL/FER-ETC/1226/2021).

The other occasion was a one-day session of the Proseminar of the Doctoral Curriculum in Philosophy and Social Science of the University of Rome Tor Vergata, held on 3 February 2021, during which the whole argument of the book was the focus of passionate discussion. Warm thanks are due to my friends and colleagues Tonino Griffero, Giovanni Dessì, Valerio Fabbrizi, Claudia Hassan, and Marco Tedeschini, and to post-docs Leonardo Fiorespino and Celestino Mussomar.

I am also very grateful to Johan van der Walt for having organized two engaging seminars, at the Faculty of Law and Economics of the University of Luxembourg, to discuss Chapter 3—'Transcending an Ossified Binary: Political Liberalism on Constituent Power' on 23 September 2020, and to discuss Chapter 7—'Amending Power: Vertical Reciprocity and Political Liberalism' on 27 April 2022. His comments have been very helpful to me and I wish to thank all the participants in those seminars. I learned much from the points raised specifically by Frank Michelman, Hans Lindahl, Marco Goldoni, Neil Walker, Emilios Christodoulidis, Ricardo Spindola Diniz, Steve Winter, and David Rasmussen.

Equally stimulating discussions have helped me to refine the ideas of Chapter 1. Under the title 'The Revolution of the "Most Reasonable". Rawls's Legacy in the Twenty-First Century', preliminary versions of the argument were discussed at the Centennial Lecture celebrating the 100th anniversary of Rawls's birth, held at the University of Mumbai, India, and at the Conference 'What Justice? The Legacy of John Rawls 100 Years after His Birth' on 16 and 17 December 2021, at Luiss University Guido Carli, Rome. My gratitude goes to the organizers and especially to Kanchana Mahadevan, Elisabetta Galeotti, Sebastiano Maffettone, Valentina Gentile, Gianfranco Pellegrino, Luigi Caranti, and Rainer Forst for their questions and comments.

Concerning the argument on populism outlined in Chapter 2, I am indebted to Reset-Dialogues on Civilization for the seminar on 'The Populist Upsurge and the Decline of Diversity Capital', held in Venice on 8–10 June 2017, and to Giancarlo Bosetti, Volker

Kaul, Albena Azmanova, and Akeel Bilgrami for their comments. The workshop on 'The Nature and Transformation of Contemporary Political Regimes: Sino-European Perspectives', held at the Centre for Political Thought, University of Exeter, on 13–14 February 2020, has also been very helpful in this respect. I owe thanks to Dario Castiglione and the other colleagues of the Centre for having organized it and for their questions, as well as to Yves Sintomer, Richard Bellamy, Stephen Skinner, Emilie Frenkiel, and the other participants for their comments.

Over the nearly three years of writing this book I have benefitted from continuous and less formal discussions, sometimes in person and sometimes online, with many friends and colleagues who have generously read more or less extended parts of the manuscript. I am very much indebted to Mariano Croce, Andrea Salvatore, and Benjamin Schupmann for invaluable discussions on Schmitt and Rawls, and to Hans Lindhal, Seyla Benhabib, David Rasmussen, once again Leonardo Fiorespino and Valerio Fabbrizi, Ricardo Spindola Diniz, Francesco Maiolo, Joel Colón-Ríos, Dario Castiglione, and Steven Winter for their often quite detailed comments and insightful responses on various parts of the manuscript.

I wish also to acknowledge the very helpful suggestions offered by two anonymous reviewers for Oxford University Press. My sincere thanks to them for having contributed significantly to the improvement of my manuscript, the surviving shortcomings obviously to be attributed only to me.

I am no less grateful to Alex Flach, editor at OUP, for having supported this project and having scrupulously accompanied it along the path from submission to contract.

Finally, I would like to mention previously published work, from which some ideas and passages in the chapters that follow are drawn.

Chapter 1
'The Revolution of "The Most Reasonable": Rawls's Legacy in the Twenty-First Century' (2021) *Sambhashan,* special issue on John Rawls (1921–2021) 21.
'Social Freedom and Reasonable Pluralism: Reflections on Freedom's Right' (2019) 45/5 Philosophy and Social Criticism 665.
'Sideways at the Entrance of the Cave: A Pluralist Footnote to Plato' (2019) 45/4 Philosophy and Social Criticism 390.
'Authority, Legitimacy, and Democracy: Narrowing the Gap between Normativism and Realism' (2020) 27/4: 655.
'How to Accommodate *Modus Vivendi* Within Normative Political Theory' in (2018) 53/2 BDL-Biblioteca della Libertà 9.
'The Dual Paradox of Authenticity in the 21st Century' in T Claviez, K Imesch, and B Sweers (eds), *Critique of Authenticity* (Vernon Press 2019).

Chapter 2
'Can Political Liberalism Help Us Rescue "the people" from Populism?' (2018) 44/3 Philosophy and Social Criticism 463.
'Capitalism in Neoliberal Times: Rethinking the Left' (2021) 11/2 Philosophy and Public Issues (New Series) 19.

Chapter 4
'Unconventional Adaptation and the Authenticity of a Constitution' in R Albert (ed), *Revolutionary Constitutionalism* (Hart 2020) 155.

A Ferrara and F Michelman, *Legitimation by Constitution: A Dialogue on Political Liberalism* (Oxford University Press 2021).

Chapter 6

'The People and the Voters' (2021) 47/1 Philosophy and Social Criticism 45.

A Ferrara and F Michelman, *Legitimation by Constitution: A Dialogue on Political Liberalism* (Oxford University Press 2021) 92–95.

Alessandro Ferrara
Rome, May 2022

Contents

Introduction ... 1
1. The People and the Electorate: Serial and Sequential Conceptions of Democratic Sovereignty ... 1
   a. Constituent power as always 'under law': under which law? ... 2
   b. Constituent and amending power ... 3
   c. Two additional liberal principles of legitimacy ... 4
   d. A political conception of the people ... 5
   e. The mandate to represent the people, and its relation to democracy ... 8
   f. Evaluating the execution of the mandate to represent the people ... 9
   g. Vertical reciprocity, sequential sovereignty, and the limits of amending power ... 11
2. Plan of the Book ... 14

1. Why Political Liberalism? ... 19
   1. Three Breakthroughs of Political Liberalism ... 21
      a. Normative democratic dualism: Rawls's constitutionalism ... 21
      b. The liberal principle of legitimacy, or 'legitimation by constitution' ... 23
      c. The revolution of the 'most reasonable' ... 25
   2. Political Liberalism and Its Main Competitors ... 31
      a. Habermas's discursive approach to deliberative democracy ... 32
      b. Dworkin's rights-foundationalist approach to democracy ... 35
      c. Republican approaches to democracy: Pettit and Bellamy ... 39
      d. Agonistic conceptions of democracy: Mouffe and Tully ... 45
      e. Modus-vivendi and 'political-realist' liberalism: Gray and Williams ... 49
      f. Starting up where many leave off: a Hegelian approach to justice, post-deconstructionist views of community, and political liberalism ... 56
   3. Political Liberalism beyond *Political Liberalism* ... 60

2. Populism and Political Liberalism ... 63
   1. How Not to Define Populism: Six Conceptual Dead Ends ... 64
   2. A Three-Pronged Definition of Populism ... 66
   3. Populism and Democracy ... 69
   4. The Populist Stream and Its Tributaries ... 72
      a. The people and the electorate ... 72
      b. Full and unlimited constituent power ... 75
      c. Presumptively justified intolerance ... 80
   5. Is Left-Wing Populism Significantly Different? ... 84
   6. What the Definition Highlights and Some Questions It Leaves Open ... 90

3. Transcending an Ossified Binary: Political Liberalism on
   Constituent Power   93
   1. Rawls and Kelsen on Constitutionalism: Three Points of Discordance   94
      a. Political realism in normative disguise   97
      b. Law and 'the reasonable'   100
      c. The groundlessness of the basic norm   102
   2. Schmitt's Existential Constitutionalism and Its Relevance for Political
      Liberalism   103
      a. The state *is* a constitution   103
      b. Why Schmitt's constitutionalism is relevant for political liberalism:
         three points of interest   108
      c. Schmittian themes in political liberalism?   113
      d. Seven dissonances between Rawls and Schmitt on the nature of
         'the political'   116
   3. Transcending the Kelsen–Schmitt Binary: Constituent Power within
      Rawls's Constitutionalism   123
   4. The Liberal Principle of Constitutional Legitimacy   126
      a. Constituent power as 'always under law'   127
      b. The 'most reasonable' as the normativity constituent power is under   130
      c. The liberal principle of constitutional legitimacy   134

4. Political Liberalism and 'the People'   137
   1. A Self-Constituting People? Lindahl's Paradox of Constituent Power   139
   2. A Political Conception of the People   142
      a. The two political capacities of a people   143
      b. Dispelling the conceptual ambiguity of 'the people'   145
      c. Rousseau's riddle reformulated: *ethnos* and *demos*   148
      d. Excursus on self-constitution   152
      e. Rousseau's riddle solved: the commitment to share commitments   155
   3. Four Manifestations of Constituent Power   156
      a. Regime change and constitutional authenticity   157
      b. *Demos* and secession   163
      c. Turning a *demos* into an *ethnos*   170
      d. Reigniting the radical democratic embers: the self-correcting *demos*   174

5. Sequential Sovereignty: On Representing 'the People' and the Electorate   177
   1. Understanding Political Representation: Pitkin's Paradigm   178
      a. Descriptive representation and its limitations   178
      b. Symbolic representation   181
      c. Two kinds of formalistic representation   182
      d. Substantive representation   184
      e. The trustee version of substantive representation   186
      f. The delegate version of substantive representation   188
      g. Political representation, reasonable pluralism, and public reason   191

2. Rethinking Representation after Pitkin   193
     a. Mansbridge's fourfold typology of representation   193
     b. Saward's 'representative claim'   196
     c. Rehfeld's eightfold typology of representation   199
  3. Grounding Sequential Sovereignty: Time and Representation   201
     a. Representing 'the people' and the electorate   201
     b. Judicial review as representing the transgenerational people   206
     c. Three flaws of serial sovereignty   210

6. Representing 'the People' by Interpreting the Constitution   217
  1. The Democratic Legitimacy of Judicial Review Revisited   217
  2. Interpreting the Constitution: the Mandate of the Interpreter   224
     a. Reconciling the tension between two versions of the interpreter's mandate   225
     b. Living originalism as 'political originalism'   229
     c. Modulating constitutional interpretation: strictures and amplitudes   232
     d. The contribution of judicial review to constitutional authenticity   234
  3. The Normativity of the Most Reasonable and the Line between *Interpreting* and *Transforming*   237
     a. The standard of the most reasonable applied to adjudication   238
     b. The red line between interpretation and transformation   242
     c. Correcting the highest interpreter: author and interpreter of the constitution in conversation   244

7. Amending Power: Vertical Reciprocity and Political Liberalism   247
  1. The Concept of Amending Power   248
     a. The function of amending power for democratic legitimacy   248
     b. The specificity of amending power   250
  2. Four Facets of the Exercise of Amending Power   252
     a. Time for a change: when is amending needed?   252
     b. Corrective and ameliorative amendments   255
     c. Who is to amend what?   256
     d. The institutional venues of amending power   258
  3. The Limits of Amending Power   259
     a. What can amending power *not* change?   261
     b. Why are implicit unamendables unamendable?   265
     c. Vertical reciprocity and implicit unamendability   272
     d. Amendments, permissible and impermissible: how to sort them?   275
  4. The Liberal Principle of Amending Legitimacy   280

Bibliography   283
Index   299

Introduction

Every cohort of voters may dream of being 'the people', under the sway of serial views of sovereignty; or it may understand itself more modestly, as co-author of a constitutional project in a cross-generational sequence rooted in the past and extending into the future. The aim of this book is to articulate a theory of democratic sovereignty and constituent power grounded in John Rawls's political liberalism. Embedded in his political philosophy and implicit constitutional theory lies an unsurpassed capacity to offer a normative, yet non-foundationalist, account of the justness and legitimacy of political and legal orders.

Neither exegetic nor abstractly analytic, my argument takes as its inception the realization that 'political liberalism' is broader than Rawls's *Political Liberalism* of 1993. Constructed by its author as an answer to the question 'How is it possible for there to exist over time a just and stable society of free and equal citizens, who remain profoundly divided by reasonable religious, philosophical, and moral doctrines?',[1] the paradigm outlined in *Political Liberalism* enables us to address facets of that question that the historical context of the time induced Rawls to sideline.

In response to insidious populist threats to democracy, still latent in the early 1990s, this book focuses on a hitherto neglected two-word phrase within Rawls's question: 'over time'.[2] That inconspicuous phrase signals the urgency of clarifying the proper relation of 'the people', understood as the transgenerational author of the constitution in force in the polity, to its pro-tempore living segment in its dual capacity as electorate—a constituted power among other constituted powers—and as co-author of the constitution. An elucidation of that relation brings 'constituent power' into the picture and requires *seven steps*, the conceptual backbone of this book.

1. The People and the Electorate: Serial and Sequential Conceptions of Democratic Sovereignty

The people is the bearer of constituent power. In contrast to like-minded normative political and legal philosophers Ronald Dworkin and Jürgen Habermas, Rawls does not eschew the concept of 'constituent power'. In the footsteps of John Locke—the only political philosopher quoted by him on this topic—Rawls attributes the exercise of this power to 'the people', distinguishes constituent power from 'the ordinary power

---

[1] John Rawls, *Political Liberalism* (expanded edn, Columbia University Press 2005) 4. *Political Liberalism* was first published in 1993. Hereafter, this book will be cited as Rawls, *PL*.
[2] In 'The Idea of Public Reason Revisited', Rawls explicitly brings in a transgenerational perspective: he qualifies liberal-democratic citizens as reasonable 'when, viewing one another as free and equal in a system of social cooperation *over generations*, they are prepared to offer one another fair terms of cooperation according to what they consider the most reasonable conception of political justice', *PL* 446 (emphasis added).

Sovereignty Across Generations. Alessandro Ferrara, Oxford University Press. © Alessandro Ferrara 2023.
DOI: 10.1093/oso/9780192871077.003.0001

of officers of government and the electorate', and attributes to constituent power the function of inscribing in a constitution 'the political ideal of a people to govern itself in a certain way'.[3]

Constituent power is further distinguished from 'ultimate constituted power', or the constituted power that has the last word—a notion rejected by Rawls, under the twin headings of parliamentary and judicial 'supremacy', in favor of an equi-influence of all the three separated powers, each responding to 'the people' *qua* bearer of constituent power.[4]

a. Constituent power as always 'under law': under which law?

Distinct from sovereignty, of which it is a mere component, constituent power is not unbound for Rawls, but operates—to use Frank Michelman's felicitous expression—'always under law'.[5] However, considering how inconsistent it would be to introduce any reference to natural law, natural rights, or any other foundationalist normative notion into the paradigm of political liberalism, the *first* step, for those who wish to further elaborate Rawls's largely implicit conception of constituent power, consists of specifying what law constituent power might then possibly be under that does not collide with constituent power's being exercised by a subject—the people—supposedly *sovereign*. This first step will be taken in Chapter 3. To anticipate, the normativity that constituent power is under, for the later Rawls, cannot emanate from any objectively or antecedently valid notion of justice, not even from justice as fairness as the outcome of a decontextualized thought experiment (as in *A Theory of Justice*). Consistently with the political, not metaphysical, framework of political liberalism, such normativity can only originate from justice as fairness as *the most reasonable political conception of justice for us*,[6] where 'most reasonable' means that, among the 'at least reasonable' conceptions, it is the one that realizes the best fit—tested through reflective equilibrium—between its free-standing principles and the historical, political, and cultural features salient for the to-be-constituted people. Constituent power is under the normativity of a reflective judgment that brings principles and situated identity into optimal equilibrium. Anticipated by Rousseau's figure of the legislator, the innovative quality of Rawls's normativity of the 'most reasonable' will be illustrated by reformulating Plato's allegory of the cave. Assuming that not just one, but several philosophers ventured outside the cave and had reasonable disagreements about what they saw, they can be imagined to agree, when they re-enter the cave and begin to rule its population, on banning the use of legal coercion in support of the contentious parts of their reports. The normativity of that ban, to which the constituent power of the philosophers submits itself, rests on what Rawls would call *the most reasonable principle of conduct for ruling the cave*—a principle that the philosophers do not *discover* as binding on them, but reach through

---

[3] Rawls, *PL* 231–32.
[4] ibid 232.
[5] See Frank I Michelman, 'Always Under Law?' (1995) 12 Constitutional Commentary 227.
[6] See *PL* xlvi and 28. See also Chapter 1, n 39.

their common public reason. The irrecusability of this 'most reasonable' principle *for them* does not detract from the Platonic philosophers' sovereign autonomy. The same context-sensitive normativity applies, as we shall see, to the democratic sovereignty of a transgenerational people. However, the constituent power to bring a political and legal order into existence does not simply stand over against the constituted powers entrusted with applying, implementing, and executing the constitutive rules thus enacted. In between is an intermediate form of power, namely the amending power to revise, as time, circumstances, and historical evolution may suggest, those constitutive rules. The *second step* consists then of clarifying how the primary constituent power of a democratic sovereign should ideally relate to the subordinate constituent power to *amend* these rules. Their relation can be understood in terms of a *serial* or *sequential* view of popular democratic sovereignty.

b. Constituent and amending power

Amending power is usually vested in the separated powers entrusted with proposing and ratifying constitutional amendments, as well as directly in the living segment of the people, involved through participation, elections, and referendums. In *Political Liberalism*, Rawls acknowledges that amending power can only operate legitimately within the tracks established by the superordinate, yet also 'under law', constituent power vested in 'the people'. Constituent and amending power respond to two different forms of normativity: while primary constituent power responds to the political conception of justice most reasonable for its bearers, amending power responds to the normativity of constitutional essentials *already in force* and supposedly willed by the whole people and not just by its living segment.

Why should constituent and amending power be constrained by two diverse kinds of normativity? Because, contrary to an ambiguity that political philosophers such as Rousseau, Locke, and Sieyès, along with icons of democracy like Thomas Jefferson, left unresolved (and that contemporary populism reaches back to), the single part cannot be on equal footing with the whole, and thus the living segment cannot be on equal footing with the transgenerational people. Consequently, the essentials of the constitution, imputable to the will of the transgenerational people, are *implicitly* unamendable by its living segment. But if the power to amend the constitution ranks higher than the constitution itself (otherwise it would not be legitimately authorized to change it), why should these essentials be beyond its reach? The distinction of the whole and its parts cannot, in and of itself, be exhaustive of the answer to that question. As Émile Durkheim noted about the perception of the sacred, a part of the relic of a saint—when detached from the whole—counts as no less sacred than the whole. The fragments of the Holy Cross, housed and exhibited in the Basilica of the Holy Cross of Jerusalem, in Rome, are certainly not regarded by Catholic believers as less sacred than a relic of the entire cross would be. Why couldn't then one segment of the entire people, namely the present electorate, be as sovereign as the whole transgenerational people?

When addressing this question, we gain a better grasp of why political liberalism is broader than *Political Liberalism*. Rawls's best answer, as it will be argued in Chapter 7, is not his explicit one—namely, placing constituent and amending power on the same plane would allow amending power to contradict the promise embedded in the constitution (a prerogative of dubious legitimacy if that initial promise has progressively unfolded in a long and successful democratic practice). Rather, Rawls's best answer can be derived from the notion of *reciprocity* posited by him as integral to 'the reasonable' and at the core of the fair scheme of cooperation that undergirds a just and stable society of free and equal citizens. Alongside his notion of horizontal reciprocity among free and equal citizens, a new notion of *vertical reciprocity* can be introduced and posited as the normative criterion that undergirds the proper relation among free and equal generations of the same people and, derivatively, the proper relation of each segment to the whole.

The reference to or neglect of this notion of vertical reciprocity, applicable to all generations insofar as the (constitutionally fixed) scheme of cooperation remains in place 'over time', marks the difference between a *sequential* exercise of popular sovereignty (inclusive of the proper distinction of constituent and limited amending power) and the dubious idea of *serial* ownership of the constitution, consisting of an exclusive exercise of sovereignty (and full constituent power) on the part of each living generation. Serial sovereignty—authoritatively endorsed, among the most illustrious classical authors, by Rousseau and Jefferson who kindled the project of periodical constitutional conventions meant to offer each generation a separate chance to confirm or thoroughly change 'the form of government'—in our times is hijacked by populist forces that misattribute constituent power to the electorate.

Serial sovereignty, more closely explored in the concluding section of Chapter 5, generates three problematic consequences. First, it fails to detect the deficit of legitimacy of a 'wanton republic' prone to changing its basic structure in opposite directions at each new generation, with a consequent collapse of the transgenerational regulatory function of the constitution. Second, it fails to sustain the *political*, as opposed to ethno-cultural, uniqueness of the polity, insofar as it obscures why, with regard to the basic structure and the key political values, the living citizens should consider previous generations of *their own* people as their forerunners. Finally, serial sovereignty cannot rule out as illegitimate the intentional curtailing of the freedom and rights of future generations for the benefit of the present ones.

c. Two additional liberal principles of legitimacy

If constituent and amending power arguably respond to different forms of normativity, then it makes sense—in a *third step*—to articulate specific principles for evaluating the legitimacy of their exercise on the part respectively of the transgenerational people and the pro tempore living segment of the people or its representatives. Such evaluation rests on a reflective judgment oriented respectively by (i) a 'liberal principle of *constitutional* legitimacy' and (i) a 'liberal principle of *amending* legitimacy'. Both build on Rawls's 'liberal principle of legitimacy'. The articulation of separate, additional principles for assessing the legitimate exercise of constituent and amending power has been preferred to the alternative of simply modifying one of Rawls's formulations of the liberal principle of legitimacy.[7] This strategic choice is supported by two reasons.

On one hand, a modification of Rawls's own principle in order to accommodate the specifics of constituent and amending power would introduce an (at least for me) prohibitive complexity of subordinate clauses in the formulation. On the other hand, such choice would risk blurring two differences, which by themselves warrant the articulation of distinct principles. Crucial for the legitimacy of exercises of ordinary, *constituted* power is their consistency *with the whole of a constitution*, including its details. Their compatibility with a political conception of justice (through their being included in a supposedly justice-reflecting constitution) only *indirectly* contributes to their legitimacy. Instead, exercises of *constituent* power are legitimated by the constitutional essentials' *direct* responsiveness to a political conception of justice, 'most reasonable' for the bearers of constituent power—a direct responsiveness that sets a constitution apart from an 'instrument of government' based on a modus vivendi. The 'liberal principle of amending legitimacy', in turn, is distinct from the other two principles of legitimacy insofar as vertical reciprocity is more crucial when the constitution is being amended than when the whole constitution functions as a benchmark for the legitimacy of acts of government, or when, at the founding moment, constituent power orients itself only to the present and future generations, unconstrained by the past, for example because a regime change has occurred. These two additional principles of legitimacy are discussed in Chapters 3 and 7.

d. A political conception of the people

A discussion of how constituent and amending power should be exercised and should relate to one another cannot but presuppose a reflection on their bearers. While a lot has been said in political and legal theory about the electoral body and the constituted powers that represent it, 'the people', as bearer of constituent power, has remained more the object of ideological construction than of conceptual analysis. This persisting lacuna needs to be filled, as a *fourth step* towards outlining a political liberal theory of constituent power. *Political Liberalism,* along with most classical and contemporary political and legal philosophy, is silent on the subject. Although the people is constantly evoked within Rawls's 'five principles of constitutionalism', no definition is offered and no solution is outlined to Rousseau's famous riddle of popular sovereignty, recently revived as 'the paradox of constitutionalism'.[8] One contemporary reformulation of Rousseau's riddle could run: 'How can a people constitute itself by adopting a constitution if in order to adopt a constitution it must already exist?' Rawls even speaks of a 'democratically ratified constitution'[9] as if democracy, in *legal* terms,

---

[7] On the different formulations of the liberal principle of legitimacy, see Chapter 1, n 22.

[8] The people is claimed to possess a power that 'can only be exercised through constitutional forms already established or in the process of being established', Martin Loughlin and Neil Walker (eds), *The Paradox of Constitutionalism: Constituent Power and Constitutional Form* (Oxford University Press 2008) 1 (hereafter Loughlin and Walker, *Paradox of Constitutionalism*).

[9] Rawls, *PL* 232.

didn't actually begin *after* the enactment of a democratic constitution. In this area, political liberalism is urgently in need of further elaboration.

Thus, a 'political conception of a people', designed to supplement Rawls's political conception of a person, is propounded in Chapter 4. Possessed of the two capacities (i) to act politically (ie to prioritize, on the basis of decisions affecting most or all participants, ends that cannot be simultaneously pursued)[10] and (ii) to act politically in accordance with self-posited *constitutive rules*, a people can be described as a *demos* that has emerged from (at least) an *ethnos*, understood as a human grouping brought and kept together primarily by non-political characteristics. Whilst not all *ethnoi* give rise to *demoi*, a *demos* can include and, in a world in which *ethnoi* vastly outnumber *demoi*, normally does include several *ethnoi*.

A *demos* emerges when an agent (a single leader, a movement, or a party) offers to an *ethnos* (or a plurality thereof) not a cognitive rendition of who the members collectively *are* and who *is* included (as in the essentialist versions of the self-positing of a *demos*), but a new set of normative *commitments* concerning the purpose and terms of the members' association henceforth. Thus, according to a political conception of a people, the *demos* need not 'already exist' in order to choose a form of government or a basic structure and to inscribe it in a constitution. Rather, a *demos* emerges from an ethnic collectivity, whose individual members are aware to various degrees and in various ways of their 'common distinctiveness', through jointly making certain commitments.[11] A constitution makes the people, no less than the people makes the constitution, which is possible without paradoxical implications because the people is intended as *demos* in the first phrase, as *ethnos* in the second.

The two modes of existence of a people, as *ethnos* or *demos*, are connected via the rise, within an ethnos, of a 'commitment to share commitments'. That condition is empirical; no normativity can mandate it. Only after a 'commitment to share commitments' materializes and becomes widely accepted within a population—due partly to unintentional factors (territorial contiguity, mutual linguistic and cultural understanding, shared orientations) and partly to conscious effort—can the population's generic willingness to 'commit to joint commitments' morph into the acceptance of no longer generic, but *specific* joint commitments in the form of a constitution that ideally embeds *the most reasonable terms of cooperation for the participants* as holders of constituent power. At that point, a *demos* is created through that act and the former *ethnos* is simultaneously transformed too.

To be sure, the process whereby out of a multitude with merely ethnic ties a politically autonomous, self-governing demos self-constitutes—at first through the preliminary step of accepting a commitment to share commitments and then through constitution-making proper—is little more than a construction aimed at updating the classical conversation of contract theory about the creation of a commonwealth. In a world where no 'unconstituted' multitudes exist which are not—willing or unwilling—part of a polity, a transition in those terms is nowhere to be observed.

---

[10] See Alessandro Ferrara, *The Democratic Horizon: Hyperpluralism and the Renewal of Political Liberalism* (Cambridge University Press 2014)13, 25.

[11] Along similar lines, see Hans Lindahl, 'Constituent Power and Reflexive Identity: Towards an Ontology of Collective Selfhood' in Loughlin and Walker, *Paradox of Constitutionalism* (n 8), 22.

In its lieu, four actual manifestations of constituent power are observable, and will be analysed, in Chapter 4, from the angle of the normative challenges that they raise for political liberalism. To anticipate that discussion, these four forms comprise: (i) regime change, or the transition *from demos to demos*; (ii) secession, or the transition *from an embedded ethnos to a new, autonomous demos*; (iii) merging, or the transition *from demos to ethnos*, the most common manifestation of constituent power on the scale of human history; and (iv) constitution-amending, or *intra-demos transformation*. In the remaining chapters, the book focuses on this fourth manifestation of constituent power, by and large the most usual one *today* (albeit involving the less far-reaching modality of amending power), in the age of constitutions.

A political conception of the people is only one building block of the theory of sequential sovereignty, and needs to be supplemented by answers to such questions as: 'Who represents the transgenerational people?', 'What does it mean to represent it properly?', and 'When can the will of the voters legitimately vaunt the title of "will of the people"?'.

Rawls's rejection of the serial model, derivable from his discussion of the implicit entrenchment of the First Amendment of the Constitution of the United States,[12] presupposes that the will of the voters, in order to legitimately amend the constitution, be consistent—at least as far as the constitutional essentials are concerned—with that of the transgenerational people. For the purpose of ascertaining that consistency, the past and future generations of 'the people', no longer or not yet endowed with agency, must be *represented*. If the *nemo judex* principle is to be honored, these no-longer- and not-yet-living generations must be represented by an agent different from the potentially self-interested electorate and its representatives. Although no conceptual necessity imposes that the people be represented by a judicial institution, it is beyond the scope of this book to explore alternatives to the usual entrusting of that function, in Western democracies, to a high, constitutional, or supreme court. While legislators and presidents or prime ministers *may* represent the people and not just the voters, and certainly have done so at various historical junctures, they cannot be blamed for not living up to that exceptional standard. Instead, a constitutional or supreme court is defined by that mandate: should it represent only the will of the present voters and not that of the transgenerational people, it would fail its mandate.

A political liberal constitutional theory is then confronted with a further challenge: to explicate, from a normative angle premised on Rawls's twin standards of the 'reasonable' and the 'most reasonable', the nature of that court's mandate and the benchmark against which its successful execution must be assessed. A constitutional or supreme court's mandate to represent the will of the entire transgenerational people concretizes in the mandate to *interpret* the constitution as reflecting that will over time and, upon request, to *review* ordinary legislative, administrative, or lower judicial acts of the constituted powers in the name of that will.

---

[12] Rawls, *PL* 238–39.

e. The mandate to represent the people, and its relation to democracy

The *fifth step* within the project of developing a political liberal constitutional theory concerns the elucidation of the interpretive mandate to represent the people, that is: (i) the exact nature of that mandate, (ii) its relation to democracy, and (iii) the quality of the mandate's execution. The quality of the execution of the mandate will have to be submitted to a threefold assessment: What makes an interpretive judgment *sound* and *proper*? How can the *interpretation* and the *transformation* of the constitution be distinguished? How can a fallible interpretive judgment be prevented from becoming unduly final?

A vast literature exists on the nature of a supreme or constitutional court's mandate to 'represent the people'. Two of the most interesting accounts are offered by Frank Michelman and Jack Balkin. According to Michelman, the mandate can be understood as directed either at remedying an endemic shortfall of consensus in societies pervaded by reasonable pluralism or at remedying an equally endemic occlusion, due to the institutional complexity of contemporary polities, of the democratic will of the voters. The first understanding of the mandate inevitably inclines the judicial interpreter to focus on what the transgenerational people *should* will, thus towards a more philosophical or constructivist propensity. The second understanding of the mandate inclines the judicial interpreter to focus instead on what the people *did actually will* and thus towards a more *originalist* propensity.[13] Along roughly similar lines, Balkin distinguishes a *restrictive* or and an *expanded* way of understanding the interpretive mandate, but points to 'fidelity to the constitution' as an inescapable frame of reference undergirding both.[14] Using a Rawlsian terminology, I have renamed this modicum of unavoidable originalism, emphasized by Balkin and Michelman, 'political originalism'. In turn, the fidelity to the constitution built into the court's mandate can be understood either along the lines of a 'framework originalism' (ie as aimed at fidelity to the intended meaning but not to the originally expected applications of the constitution's rules, standards, and principles) or along the lines of a 'conservative originalism' based on the dubious intent to align contemporary legal interpretation with the originally expected *applications* of the same meanings.[15]

In the attempt to bridge the gap between these parallel polarities illustrated by Michelman and Balkin, I spell out 'political originalism' as entailing a 'reflective fidelity' to the original *normative* commitments embedded in the constitution but not to the original *cognitive* assumptions in light of which those commitments were made or to the views of the living segment of the people. The stance of reflective fidelity internal to political originalism tries to ascertain whether it is rational and reasonable to recast these contemporary views as a reformulation, relative to the contested issues, of the commitments scripted in the constitution by the whole transgenerational people.

---

[13] See Alessandro Ferrara and Frank I Michelman, *Legitimation by Constitution: A Dialogue on Political Liberalism* (Oxford University Press 2021) 84–87.
[14] See Jack M Balkin, *Living Originalism* (Harvard University Press 2011) 39.
[15] ibid 7–12.

'Political originalism', guided by 'reflective fidelity', is designed to ensure the continuity of the regulatory function of the constitution and thus to buttress the sequential sovereignty of the people. Yet, the democratic credentials of judicial review have often been questioned by 'political constitutionalists' and fervent democrats of many stripes, who often reach back to Alexander Bickel's famous countermajoritarian objection.[16]

Concerning its relation to democracy, judicial review is defended, in Chapter 6, against the accusation of detracting from the democratic quality of the polity on the basis of four distinct arguments. First, the argument against the questionable implications of serial sovereignty, which vests exclusive sovereignty in the living segment of the people. Second, the untenability of the thesis that judicial review thwarts the will of the electorate, given that the legal contestation that activates judicial review attests that the electorate's will is already divided. Third, the advantage connected with the court's reframing of political debate in terms of principle as opposed to bargaining and compromise.[17] Fourth, judicial review contributes to 'constitutional authenticity' by valorizing the uniqueness of the constitution, and its integrative function (Grimm),[18] as opposed to its merely providing a technique for living together with a manageable conflict.

The fourth argument in favour of judicial review is worth further specification. Three ways by which judicial review sustains the authenticity of a constitution can be distinguished. *First*, the court's constant revisiting of the constitution's key normative terms enhances their salience in public discourse. *Second*, by articulating new meanings for older standards and principles the court indirectly evidences the *vitality* of the constitutional project and its potential for bringing together the normative past, present, and future of the polity. *Third*, judicial review enhances constitutional authenticity by reducing the opposite risk of the constitution's giving in to pressures coming from special interests and transient ideologies.

To recap: within judicial review, a constitutional or supreme court represents the transgenerational people by interpreting the constitution along the lines of 'reflective fidelity', and in so doing it fosters constitutional authenticity and enhances *sequential* sovereignty. The quality of the court's execution of the mandate, however, needs to be evaluated.

f. Evaluating the execution of the mandate to represent the people

To outline the guidelines of such evaluation is our *sixth step* in reconstructing the sequential view of democratic sovereignty embedded in political liberalism. The point of evoking Hanna Pitkin's theory of representation, in Chapter 5, for the purpose of describing the relation of the highest court to the transgenerational people, is that

---

[16] See Alexander Bickel, *The Least Dangerous Branch. The Supreme Court at the Bar of Politics* (first published 1962, 2nd edn, Yale University Press 1986) 16–17.

[17] The second and third arguments in defense of the democratic credentials of judicial review are drawn from Cristina Lafont, *Democracy Without Shortcuts. A Participatory Conception of Deliberative Democracy* (Oxford University Press 2020) 227–28.

[18] See Dieter Grimm, 'The Basic Law at 60—Identity and Change' (2010) 11 German Law Review, 2010, 33.

'substantive representation' allows us to assess the quality of the act of representing. In this case, given that the representing takes place primarily by way of interpreting the constitution, the quality of the representing is coextensive with the quality of interpreting. As Pitkin once put it, 'in a democracy where all agencies of the government are servants of the sovereign people, the judge might be said to represent the people'.[19] Whereas the voters can be represented by their elected representatives in many ways, constitutional interpretation is the only way in which a constitutional court can represent the transgenerational people. In this case, then, to assess the quality of the representing also requires an assessment of the quality of the interpreting that occurs in the context of adjudication. To tell whether the court's mandate has been well executed, however, amounts not only to telling whether the court has offered the best interpretation, but also whether the court has adjudicated the subject matter without overstepping the limits of *interpreting* the constitution and unduly *transforming* it, and whether enough institutional leeway remains for the people to subsequently correct the court's interpretation through a formal amendment to the constitution. What standards should be applied here? Three standards, applicable to each facet of this complex evaluation, will be discussed in Chapter 6.

To anticipate, let me start with the benchmark for assessing the *soundness* of the court's interpretation: drawing on Rawls's dual normative standard of the 'reasonable' and the 'most reasonable', when a constitutional court acts as an exemplar of public reason, its (re)-interpretation of a constitutional provision commands consent not just because it is one of the reasonable conclusions of public reason, but because it is arguably *the most reasonable*. That expression, when applied to the interpretation of a contested constitutional standard or principle, signals that the majority of the court understands such interpretation—for example, interpreting 'equal protection' as excluding segregation or allowing same-sex marriage—as an 'irrecusable' commitment that 'the people', including its presently living segment, within which the matter is contested, *cannot but make*, lest its permanence as the self-same people which authored the constitution be endangered. Calling one interpretation of a constitutional clause the 'most reasonable', in other words, is equivalent to the court's addressing the entire transgenerational people by saying '*we* can do no other than interpret the controversial constitutional matter in this way, if we want to continue to pursue the constitutional project that regulates our political life'. Dissenting justices and other public voices, instead, when they dispute that claim of 'non-cognitive necessitation', maintain that the 'most reasonable' interpretation is at best 'just reasonable' and is being pushed further up on the scale of normativity out of the court majority's arbitrary preference.

Concerning the *interpretive*, as opposed to *transformative*, quality of the court's judgment, when a pronouncement is understood to refer to a commitment that the people *cannot but respect* in order to remain faithful to its constitutional political identity, we are in the domain of *interpretation*. When instead a pronouncement is understood (or alleged) to refer to a commitment that the people *may want* to make in order to improve, update, or simply revise their constitutional project, there we enter the domain of *transformation*, thereby leaving the jurisdiction of a constitutional court.

---

[19] Hanna F Pitkin, *The Concept of Representation* (University of California Press 1967) 117.

Finally, representing the people adequately includes leaving enough *leeway for correction* of the court's interpretive judgment. The people and the court relate to one another as an author (in this case: of the constitution) and its interpreter when they debate the meaning of a text. Presented with judicial interpretations, the living segment of the people, being a generational co-author, may: (i) tacitly *accept* the interpretation offered; (ii) *dispute* it by raising legal cases that could lead to modify it; or (iii) reject the interpretation altogether and amend, *qua* generational co-author, the constitution in such a way that the rejected judgment is corrected. These three responses can be detected only via the observation of indicators.

In the case of a tacit acceptance of the court's interpretation, no voices are raised in the public sphere against the pronouncement. When aspects of the court's interpretation are disputed, segments of the citizenry bring new constitutional cases to the attention of the court, which may or may not modify its stance, thereby leading the conversation back to the first case or on to the third case. When the co-author of the constitution wishes to reject the interpreter's interpretation, citizens or their representatives activate the formal procedures for *amending* the constitution in the desired direction. This is also the entry point for correctly assessing whether judicial occlusion of the democratic will is at risk of occurring. In lieu of questioning the democratic standing of judicial review on the basis of a dubious conflation of the will of the voters and the will of the people, the relevant question is: 'Under the present conditions, is the prospect for the living segment of the people to correct the pronouncement of the highest judicial interpreter of the constitution becoming more and more dismal?' The work of Bruce Ackerman is exemplary in addressing this question with reference to the United States of the New Deal era and afterwards.[20]

g. Vertical reciprocity, sequential sovereignty, and the limits of amending power

The eventuality that in order to amend the constitution the voters might proactively mobilize, directly or through their representatives, *motu proprio* or in response to a pronouncement of the supreme or constitutional court, leads to the *seventh step* of our elucidation of the sequential view of democratic sovereignty; namely, to define amending power and the conditions of its legitimate exercise from the standpoint of political liberalism.

The electorate's entitlement to amend the constitution (directly or through its representatives) derives not from its representing or impersonating the people, but from being a co-owner of the constitution, along with all the other generations. As part of the larger people, the electorate is by definition possessed of the two political capacities to (i) engage in intentional political collective action, and (ii) self-regulate its action via constitutive rules. However, the constitutive rules through which an electorate acts politically are not of its own making, but are already embedded in the script that

---

[20] See Bruce Ackerman, *We the People*, vol 2, *Transformations* (Harvard University Press 1998) and *We the People*, vol 3, *The Civil Rights Revolution* (Harvard University Press 2014) (hereafter Ackerman, *Civil Rights Revolution*).

charters the political life of *all* the generations of the people. In any structured practice, constitutive rules can certainly be amended, through proposals for change advanced by some participants and the acceptance of these proposals on the part of the rest of the participants. In the case of constitution-amending, however, the consent that validates a proposal for transforming the rules must come not from the voters, but from a subject—again, the people—*not* physically present. If so, the legitimacy of amending the constitution must be closely scrutinized. The electorate can never be considered *fully sovereign* without thereby generating a risk of incurring the problems of serial ownership.[21] But then, how can the constitutive rules of politics ever be transformed, if the living segment of the people is not fully sovereign and the real democratic sovereign, the people, is not present but is only a construction? Can the 'will of the voters' ever be legitimately considered the 'will of the people'?

Two conditions, one necessary and the other sufficient, warrant a positive answer to this question. First, the will of the voters must not contradict, as far as constitutional essentials are concerned, the will of the people as registered in the constitution. The validation of a formally approved constitutional amendment by a court that represents the entire transgenerational people is the necessary condition that must be satisfied if the amendment is contested by some as unconstitutional. But a further and sufficient condition must be satisfied for the legitimacy of an exercise of amending power. That condition concerns *temporal continuity*: the amendment must not be rejected and then repealed by subsequent generations of the people, as exemplified by the case of the Eighteenth Amendment to the Constitution of the United States (establishing 'prohibition', in 1919), repealed by the Twenty-First Amendment in 1933.

Little can be said on the sufficient condition. It owes its fulfilment to historical contingencies that lie beyond the reach of political and constitutional theory. On the contrary, a view of amending power rooted in political liberalism has a lot to say concerning the necessary condition for the will of the electorate to count as the will of the people. The single most important aspect of a legitimate exercise of amending power concerns *the limits of its use* and, more specifically, its respecting the *implicit* unamendability of the constitutional essentials. What aspects of the constitution are 'implicitly unamendable' and for what reasons? Five broad categories of implicitly unamendable elements are identified in Chapter 7: (i) *aspects of the basic structure* (in Rawls's sense); (ii) *general legal principles* and *general presuppositions of the rule of law*; (iii) *implicit principles of democracy*; (iv) provisions rooted in *binding international law and treaties*, elements of *global constitutionalism* and *regional supranational law* such as EU law in relation to member states; (v) *aspects of the life-world, lifeform, or background* necessary for the intelligibility of political practice.

The unamendability of these constitutional essentials has been prevailingly defended on the basis of *coherence* as an indispensable requirement of the constitution. Some variants of the coherence argument use the metaphor of the 'pillars' that sustain a building (as opposed to parts whose removal does not affect stability); others evoke the vital, as opposed to secondary, organs of a body. As Victor Hugo famously put it, a tree changes its leaves, not its roots. Other coherence theories of unamendability

---

[21] See Chapter 5, Section 3.c.

use the notion of *identity* as a normative core. Coherence arguments, however, are all affected by a blind spot. Designed to make regressive change illegitimate, they end up making progressive change (eg the democratization of an authoritarian constitution) equally difficult to justify. To avoid this pitfall, Rawls and others have introduced *teleological* versions of the coherence argument, designed to allow progressive change but to block degenerative change. However, these raise more problems than they solve, examples being the usually contested nature of progressive change or the dependency of entrenchment more on time than on the importance of the entrenched substance.

Another influential argument for the unamendability of constitutional essentials rests on the *principal–delegate relation* that supposedly connects the holders of constituent and amending power—the people and its pro-tempore living segments. This argument sometimes comes in a *moderate* version, according to which the holder of amending power, as 'trustee of the people', is only a *fiduciary power* to act for *certain ends*, in due alignment with the principal's will.[22] In a more *radical* version, found in the work of Akhil Amar[23] and William Harris,[24] the principal can always regain control over its delegate and amend the constitution (via referendum or other initiatives) beyond the limits applicable to officials vested with constituted power. The problem with the moderate version of the *principal–delegate* defence of implicit unamendability of the constitutional essentials is that the living segment of the people seems to lack an autonomous will of its own, and solely to represent the will of a larger subject. The problem with the radical version is that the will of the people, just as in serial conceptions of democratic sovereignty, seems to coincide with the will of the electorate.

Thus, in the conclusive seventh step an alternative argument for the unamendability of constitutional essentials is articulated, on the basis of the Rawlsian notion of *reciprocity*. Amending power, vested in the living citizens, should not alter the constitutional essentials in ways that would make it *putatively less than reasonable* for future (or, *counterfactually*, for past) generations of the people to be willing to live their political life within the new constitutional order. As a link in an intergenerational chain, and no differently from an individual citizen living in a *horizontal* scheme of fair social cooperation, the electorate is under the obligation to abide by *vertical reciprocity*, that is, by constitutionally defined terms of cooperation that *all* generations of the same people as free and equal can presumably accept.

A political-liberal conception of sequential sovereignty, aimed at improving Rawls's own explicit view, can then be summed up as follows: The will of the electorate can *never* be directly equated with the will of people, except at the inaugural stages of new polities, when the same generations have both ratified the constitution and do live under it. When instead a temporal gap separates the people as charterers and as chartered, the will of the electorate can vaunt the title of 'will of the people' only in the attested absence of inconsistency with the main commitments underwritten by the author of the constitution and if the subsequent living segments of the people do not

---

[22] See Samuel Freeman, 'Constitutional Democracy and the Legitimacy of Judicial Review' (1990) 9 Law and Philosophy 348–49.
[23] See Akhil R Amar, 'Popular Sovereignty and Constitutional Amendment' in Sanford Levinson (ed), *Responding to Imperfection: The Theory and Practice of Constitutional Amendment* (Princeton University Press 1995) 109.
[24] See William F Harris II, *The Interpretable Constitution* (Johns Hopkins University Press 1993) 199–200.

repeal the ratified amendment. As anticipated above, a 'liberal principle of *amending legitimacy*', at the centre of a political-liberal view of sequential sovereignty, can only aspire to account for when such absence of inconsistency holds, but must bow to historical contingency as far as the second condition is concerned.

With the completion of the seven steps specified above, the meaning and implications of the 'over time' phrase in the opening question of *Political Liberalism* can be said to have become less vague. In turn, that elucidation brings Rawls's constitutional theory, largely implicit within *Political Liberalism*, one step closer towards fulfilling its outstanding potential to reconcile respect for political plurality and a normativity respectful of that plurality. Advancing that reconciliation is, in my opinion, equivalent to advancing the cause of minimizing oppression in matters political.

2. Plan of the Book

Chapter 1, 'Why Political Liberalism?', makes good on the promise, implicitly stipulated above in the opening and closing paragraphs, to substantiate the claim that the Rawlsian paradigm is the one, among the many frameworks available in political and legal philosophy today, that offers the best account of the normativity binding on constituent power without falling back on foundationalist Archimedean points. The approach to normativity that undergirds *Political Liberalism* is argued to be best positioned for alleviating the tension between the democratic will and rights, for conceptualizing the normativity under which constituent power operates, and for rethinking legitimacy within a hyperpluralist context. Its superior potential in all these respects— if compared to the political and legal philosophical frameworks propounded by Jürgen Habermas, Ronald Dworkin, Philip Pettit, Richard Bellamy, Chantal Mouffe, James Tully, John Gray, Bernard Williams, and various theorists of difference and recognition—is claimed to rest on three major, game-changing breakthroughs: (i) the normative twist impressed by Rawls on the dualist conception of democracy that he borrows from Ackerman; (ii) an innovative understanding of legitimacy ('legitimation by constitution') fully adequate to the conditions of hyperpluralist societies; and (iii) a non-foundationalist anchoring of normativity in public reason's dual standard of the 'reasonable' and the 'most reasonable'. The magnitude of the latter achievement is reconstructed by using Plato's allegory of the cave, which has largely shaped the Western conversation of political philosophy, as a foil for highlighting the novelty of Rawls's view of the normativity of public reason on the plane of that general conversation. The chapter ends by taking stock of areas in which the paradigm of political liberalism remains in need of further elaboration, among which a response to the populist conflation of the voters and the people stands out as most urgent.

Chapter 2, 'Populism and Political Liberalism', uses the conceptual resources of political liberalism for making sense of populism—a complex phenomenon notoriously impervious to being univocally defined. After clearing away six dead-end strategies for defining populism, a three-pronged definition is offered. Populism is suggested to consist of (i) the conflation of the people, *qua* democratic sovereign, with the electorate, and of the will of the people with the will of the voters; (ii) the attribution of fully fledged constituent power to the electorate as embodiment of the people; and (iii) presumptively justified intolerance against all opinions that differ from what populist leaders posit as the general interest of the people. This definition, equally applicable to right-wing and left-wing populism, metaphorically pictures populism as a stream swollen by three major tributaries, corresponding to the three prongs of the definition, that flow through territories indeed quite distinct from populism. Among the points of continuity of contemporary populism with major thinkers of the canon of political and legal philosophy, serial sovereignty (traces of which are found in Rousseau and Sieyès) stands out as the most significant, along with the equation of judicial review (in its strong forms) with judicial supremacy (an equation suggested by political constitutionalists Waldron and Bellamy). Feeding into the populist stream, these tributaries account for its massive flow. After showing how left-wing populism is not so different, along the three dimensions of the proposed definition, from right-wing populism, the chapter ends by outlining the agenda for expanding the constitutional theory implicit in *Political Liberalism*. It calls for reflection: (i) on whether the constituent and constituted forms of power mentioned by Rawls in his capsule rendition of constitutionalism really exhaust all forms of political power; (ii) on the relation of the transgenerational people to its living segment, *qua* constituted power and co-participant in constituent power; (iii) on the limits of this intermediate power and on who will represent the transgenerational people, not endowed with direct agency, in what terms; and, above all, (iv) on the nature and prerogatives of 'the people' as the bearer of constituent power.

Chapter 3, 'Transcending an Ossified Binary: Political Liberalism on Constituent Power', begins to address that agenda. Rawls's account of the conditions for the stability of a just society of free and equal citizens embeds political philosophical insights that put him in a fruitful dialogue with major figures of twentieth-century constitutional theory. Although Rawls never cites Hans Kelsen or Carl Schmitt, his political liberalism is in the uniquely interesting position of cutting across the ossified polarity of Kelsen's paradigm of pure law and Schmitt's existentially tinged constitutional theory. Rawls's situated normativity of the (most) reasonable provides a vantage point from which Kelsen's and Schmitt's head-on-opposed paradigms appear respectively as a formalist and an existential-decisionist variant of legal positivism. Chapter 3 reconstructs a dialogue that never happened but *could* have taken place, with great advantage for constitutional theory. In such virtual dialogue, Rawls sides with Schmitt in affirming the existence of constituent power as the power of a subject (the people, in democratic theory) to articulate in a constitution its political ideal 'to govern itself in a certain way'; in assuming that such power persists, after founding a new regime, as the power to amend the original constitution; in presupposing that amending power cannot alter the basic design of the constitution; and in considering prudential reasons, reflected in compromises, an unacceptably weak basis for a constitutional order. However, he also deeply diverges from Schmitt: on the nature of the limits of amending power; on the institution entrusted with acting as the guardian of the constitution; and on the desirable basis for non-instrumental convergence (a comprehensive and holistic basis for Schmitt, a 'political' one for Rawls). In other areas, Rawls decidedly sides with Kelsen: in downplaying all reference to contentious truths in the democratic arena; and in vesting the power to protect the constitution in a constitutional court. In the end, Rawls take a position distinct from the diverse, yet concurring legal positivism of *both* Kelsen and Schmitt. In fact, neither Kelsen's 'normative' legal system crowned by the basic norm nor Schmitt's existential-political constitution-making claims validity on any basis other than mere (*legal* or *political*) facticity. For Rawls, instead, the original position (even if downscaled to a 'device of representation' in *Political Liberalism*) allows for a free-standing elucidation of why an overlapping consensus might be expected to hopefully coalesce around justice as fairness as the *most reasonable* political conception of justice available to 'us' for grounding constitutional principles. Political liberalism brings to fruition a situated normativity that turns a new page in contemporary constitutionalism and is captured by the 'liberal principle of *constitutional* legitimacy' with which the chapter concludes.

Chapter 4, 'Political Liberalism and "the People"', aims at filling a lacuna mentioned above: as with modern and contemporary liberal-democratic political philosophers, Rawls neglects to develop a theoretical account of the nature of the people, the bearer of constituent power. In the chapter, a 'political conception of a people' is outlined, then the distinction of *demos* and *ethnos* is introduced, and Rousseau's riddle—'It would be as well, before we examine the act by which a people elects a king, to examine the act by which a people is a people'—is reformulated as the challenge of clarifying how an *ethnos* turns into a *demos*. Drawing on analytic theories of *self-constitution* (to which a special excursus is dedicated) and in dialogue with Hans Lindahl's account of the 'paradox of constituent power', a *demos* is argued to emerge when an *ethnos* (or a plurality thereof), after having come to share a willingness to share commitments, embraces a specific set of normative commitments that specify the constitutive rules of its future political action and terms of association. The chapter then discusses four types of historically observable manifestations of constituent power: regime change, secession, merging, and the amending of the constitution.

Chapter 5, 'Sequential Sovereignty: On Representing "the People" and the Electorate', focuses on the action of *representing*. If legislative institutions and elected executive officers usually represent the voters, and only supererogatorily represent the transgenerational people, whereas representation of the latter is officially entrusted to a constitutional or supreme court, it remains to be determined whether in both cases the act of representing is the same, or whether the meaning of 'to represent', in the phrase 'to represent the voters', differs from its meaning in the phrase 'to represent the people'. I turn to Hanna Pitkin's standard-setting account of representation, as well as to the major developments that her account has undergone at the hands of Jane Mansbridge, Michael Saward, Andrew Rehfeld, and others over the next half-century. The gist of Pitkin's contribution is summed up as the proposition that while 'descriptive' and 'symbolic' representations are hard to reconcile with a normative perspective, for lack of a foothold that enables us to assess the *quality* of the *act* of representing, 'substantive' representation or 'acting for' (as opposed to 'standing for') someone does allow for such evaluation. At the same time, 'good representing' cannot be freed from the Goldilocks dilemma of perpetually oscillating between two extremes that equally undermine representation altogether. Representatives who always and consistently act contrary to their constituents' orientation appear as unresponsive oligarchs, representatives who just follow all oscillations of their constituents' opinions appear simply as their tools. However, even if the Goldilocks principle is satisfied and 'representing' takes place within the range of those extremes, there is conceptual leeway for differently nuanced notions of representation, located closer to either the trustee or the delegate version of 'acting for' someone, be it the people or its living segment. Then the relation between temporality and representation is shown to differentially impact on the meaning of representing in the case of the electorate and the people. The larger the temporal extension of the constituency, the more representation will approximate trusteeship. But different subtypes of trusteeship can be envisaged that, taking cue once again from Michelman, correspond to *active* or *quiescent*, *assertive* or *tolerant* dispositions of the (in this case judicial) representative, and to different institutional forms (*weaker* or *stronger*) of judicial review. On the other hand, members of parliaments usually operate on a different understanding of the temporality of their representing and may be more tempted, though by no means necessitated, to lean towards the delegate end of the spectrum, with elective heads of the executive branch (presidents) subjected to pressures from both polarities. After a critical discussion of Samuel Freeman's suggestion to uncouple the function of guardian of the constitution, and thus of representing the transgenerational people, from the judiciary, the chapter closes with a broader discussion of the difficulties incurred by all serial conceptions of democratic sovereignty.

Chapter 6, 'Representing "the People" as Interpreting the Constitution', builds on the assumption that the transgenerational people is represented by a supreme or constitutional court and is represented through the court-specific practice of adjudicating cases by interpreting the higher law authored by the people itself. If the court 'acts for' the people in pronouncing judgments about the constitution, then to assess the quality of its representing amounts to assessing the soundness of its interpretive practice. The chapter breaks up the evaluation of this institutional practice into three moments, respectively centred on: (i) how, drawing on the work of Michelman and Balkin, different understandings of the court's mandate can be distinguished and assessed; (ii) how the execution of the court's mandate enriches or detracts from the quality of the democratic process; and (iii) how the soundness of the court's judgment over the contested matters can be assessed. In addressing the third moment, the paradigm of political liberalism is found most relevant. It offers a non-foundationalist twofold standard of the 'reasonable' and the 'most reasonable', an equally non-foundationalist distinction of legitimate interpretation and abusive judicial transformation of the constitution, and a benchmark for assessing the lack of occlusive influence of the judicial pronouncement on the democratic process. What separates judicial review from judicial supremacy is the amplitude of the institutional leeway not just theoretically, but *actually*, available to the living segment of the people—the only cohort endowed with agency—to oppose the court's judgment and use its amending power to change the relevant constitutional provisions.

Chapter 7, 'Amending Power: Vertical Reciprocity and Political Liberalism', offers a political-liberal account of the nature, source, and limits of amending power—an account consistent with, purportedly ameliorative of, but not explicitly present in *Political Liberalism*. After introducing the concept of amending power and its twofold partaking of both constituted (insofar as it is exercised by officials and by the electorate) and constituent (insofar as it can amend the constitutive rules of the polity) power, its exercise is elucidated in relation to the questions, 'When is amending needed or to be avoided?', 'What can be amended?', 'Who is to amend what?', and 'In which institutional venues is amending to occur?'. The second part of the chapter addresses the limits of amending power: it identifies aspects of the constitution that are to be considered implicitly unamendable (independently of their being so qualified in specific 'eternity clauses') and then reviews different justifications that have been offered in support of implicit unamendability. A new justification, premised on the notion of *vertical reciprocity* among free and equal generations of the same people, is then introduced as an ameliorative addition to Rawls's own explicit argument for the implicit entrenchment of the First Amendment of the Constitution of the United States. In closing, a 'liberal principle of *amending* power' is propounded, illustrated and claimed to round out the reconstruction of the sequential conception of democratic sovereignty implicitly embedded in *Political Liberalism*.

1
Why Political Liberalism?

> The work of philosophical icons is rich enough to allow appropriation through interpretation. Each of us has his or her own Immanuel Kant, and from now on we will struggle, each of us, for the benediction of John Rawls. And with very good reason. After all the books, the footnotes, all the wonderful discussions, we are only just beginning to grasp how much we have to learn from that man.
>
> (Ronald Dworkin, *Justice in Robes* 261)

Why read Rawls on constituent power, today? During the first two decades of the twenty-first century the upsurge of populist parties, leaders, and movements, sometimes accompanied by phenomena of democratic backsliding, has confronted liberal-democratic regimes with unprecedented pressure. Presidents and prime ministers, legislatures, administrations, and cabinets often claim to represent *the will of the people* and in its name try to legitimate not just ordinary legislation but also constitutional amendments, projects for extensive constitutional revision, or landmark statutes of constitutional significance. This predicament makes it all too urgent to revisit the tension, at the heart of constitutional democracy, between popular sovereignty as the touchstone of legitimacy and the notion that even the constituent power exercised by the popular sovereign, far from absolute, must operate within normative tracks that call for specification.

Throughout this book, Rawls's 'political liberalism' is presented as the paradigm of political philosophy and constitutional theory that carries most promise for understanding and allaying, if not reconciling, democracy's inherent tension between popular sovereignty and rights. In full awareness that such a pronouncement in favour of *Political Liberalism* might sound to some as a belated extolment of the Ptolemaic system, this chapter aims to highlight the reasons that, on the contrary, support casting the mantle of the Copernican revolution on Rawls, rather than on his main competitors.

The superior potential of political liberalism for elucidating the relation of constituent power to normativity consists in its combining three breakthroughs not found in other contemporary conceptions of liberalism and democracy. These three game-changing breakthroughs are: (i) the normative twist impressed on the dualist conception of democracy that Rawls borrows from Ackerman, (ii) an innovative understanding of legitimacy, and (iii) a non-foundationalist view of normativity anchored in public reason's dual standard of the 'reasonable' and the 'most reasonable'.

Before elaborating on each of them, let me briefly recall the core of the paradigm.[1] In *Political Liberalism* Rawls offers the following answer to the question that opens and undergirds his book. A just and stable society of free and equal citizens who remain profoundly divided by reasonable religious, philosophical, and moral doctrines is possible *over time* insofar as an overlapping consensus of a wide majority of citizens coalesces, in spite of their persisting differences, around a 'political conception of justice'[2] whose overarching principles (i) would be selected in the original position, (ii) can inspire a suitable basic structure[3] and offer a shared benchmark when 'constitutional essentials and questions of basic justice are at stake' in the public forum,[4] and (iii) are reflected in a number of 'constitutional essentials' that provide the benchmark for judgments concerning legitimacy and secure a scheme of equal basic liberties.[5]

The 'just and stable society of free and equal citizens' is no normative template good 'for all seasons' and all latitudes. Based on political liberalism, a variety of concrete instantiations of the same basic liberties can be envisaged. Just as 'not everyone can speak at the same time, or use the same public facility at the same time for different ends',[6] so the basic liberties must be made compatible with one another in a 'scheme', constitutionally scripted, that secures that for each single liberty its 'central range of application' be respected. There is no single 'scheme' or blueprint for the basic liberties. As Rawls puts it, 'it is enough that the general form and content of the basic liberties can be outlined and the grounds of their priority understood. The further specification of the liberties is left to the constitutional, legislative and judicial stages'.[7]

This is, in a nutshell, Rawls's solution to the problem of stabilizing over time the oppression-free cohabitation of differently minded citizens. What is so innovative about it?

---

[1] The literature on the various aspects of the paradigm is immense. For essential readings, see Samuel Freeman, *John Rawls* (Routledge 2007) 324–415; Sebastiano Maffettone, *Rawls: An Introduction* (Polity 2010) 210–92; Burton Dreben 'On Rawls and Political Liberalism' in S Freeman (ed), *The Cambridge Companion to Rawls* (Cambridge University Press 2003) 316–46; Charles Larmore, 'Public Reason', ibid 368–93; Paul Weithman, *Why Political Liberalism. On John Rawls's Political Turn* (Oxford University Press 2010). Recently, for the centennial of Rawls's birth, a resurgence of interest in political liberalism has become manifest in *Justice and Public Reason: With Rawls and Beyond*, special issue of (2021) 2 Sambhashan Quarterly; Valerio Fabbrizi and Leonardo Fiorespino (eds), *The Persistence of Justice as Fairness: Reflections on Rawls's Legacy*. With a preface by Florian Çullhaj (UniversItalia 2022).

[2] 'Justice as fairness' is the proper name Rawls assigns to his own version of a political conception of justice, premised on two lexically ordered principles—the principle of equal liberties and the difference principle (*PL* 5–6)—but other 'political conceptions of justice' are admittedly possible. The possibility of competing, equally 'political', conceptions or justice is discussed in *PL* xlvi–xlvii.

[3] The term 'basic structure', much as the ancient term 'politeia', is designed to capture 'the way in which the major social institutions fit together into one system, and how they assign fundamental rights and duties and shape the division of advantages that arises through social cooperation' (*PL* 258). Examples of social institutions included in the basic structure are: 'the political constitution, the legally recognized forms of property, and the organization of the economy, and the nature of the family'.

[4] See Rawls, *PL* 44.

[5] Among these liberties are 'freedom of thought and liberty of conscience; the political liberties and freedom of association, as well as the freedoms specified by the liberty and integrity of the person; and finally, the rights and liberties covered by the rule of law', Rawls, *PL* 291.

[6] Rawls, *PL* 296.

[7] ibid 298.

1. Three Breakthroughs of Political Liberalism

The three innovations inherent in the paradigm of political liberalism jointly offer an adequate benchmark for comparing Rawls's constitutional theory with other legal- and political-philosophical accounts. In Chapter 3, the specific implications of the paradigm for theorizing constituent power will be foregrounded.

a. Normative democratic dualism: Rawls's constitutionalism

Acknowledging his debt to Ackerman, Rawls defines his view of constitutional democracy as *dualist*, in that 'it distinguishes constituent power from ordinary power as well as the higher law of the people from the ordinary law of legislative bodies' and rejects the doctrine of 'parliamentary supremacy'.[8] In the section of Lecture 6 entitled 'The Supreme Court as Exemplar of Public Reason', Rawls sums up his view of constitutionalism on the basis of five principles. The first principle is the distinction, taken from Locke, of constituent and ordinary power. The former is 'the people's constituent power to establish a new regime' for the purpose of regulating ordinary power 'and it comes into play *only when the existing regime has been dissolved*'.[9] Ordinary power, instead, is the power of 'officers of government and the electorate' and is exercised 'in day-to-day politics'.[10]

The second principle enunciates the distinction of higher and ordinary law: 'higher law is the expression of the people's constituent power and has the higher authority of We the People, whereas ordinary legislation has the authority, and is the expression of, the ordinary power of Congress and of the electorate'.[11]

Third, the democratic constitution, written or unwritten, reflects in the language of higher law 'the political ideal of a people to govern itself in a certain way':[12] this function and the correlated need for an ample consensus of the citizens make it desirable that higher law not be burdened 'with many details and qualifications' and have its essential principles embedded in the basic institutions. For better or for worse, this principle leads Rawls to exclude fair equality of opportunity and the difference principle from the number of the constitutional essentials.[13]

Fourth, 'in a democratically ratified constitution with a bill of rights' the citizens establish certain constitutional essentials—the basic liberties and equal rights (freedom of speech and association, freedom of movement and choice of occupation, and the protections of the rule of law)—which then become necessary conditions for an ordinary democratic will to count as legitimate.[14]

---

[8] ibid 233.
[9] Rawls, *PL* 231 (emphasis added).
[10] ibid.
[11] ibid.
[12] Rawls, *PL* 232.
[13] ibid.
[14] ibid.

Finally, constitutional democracy for Rawls is a regime in which no separate branch of constituted power wields ultimate authority. Rejecting the opposite views of 'parliamentary supremacy' and 'judicial supremacy', Rawls states that 'ultimate power is held by the three branches in a duly specified relation with one another with each responsible to the people'.[15] Even the authority of the Supreme Court as ultimate judicial interpreter of the constitution is not final: 'the constitution is not what the Court says it is. Rather, it is what the people acting constitutionally through the other branches eventually allow the Court to say it is'.[16]

At first glance, Rawls appears to remain in the footsteps of Ackerman's 'democratic dualism',[17] but a closer scrutiny reveals one crucial difference. Rawls supports the idea of a structural entrenchment of fundamental rights and, presumably, of the basic liberties that twists Ackerman's dualism in a normative direction. The question is 'whether an amendment to repeal the First Amendment, say, and to make a particular religion the state religion with all the consequences of that, or to repeal the Fourteenth Amendment with its equal protection of the laws, must be accepted by the Court as a valid amendment'.[18] This is a fundamental question concerning constituent power. Is the power to amend the constitution—to be exercised in accordance with the procedures provided by the constitution—on a par with the original constituent power to frame and enact a constitution? Or is it a kind of intermediate power, endowed with a superordinate regulatory function relative to ordinary legislation, but nonetheless subordinate to the fully fledged constituent power of the transgenerational people and legitimate only to the extent that it is exercised in accordance with the 'constitutional essentials'? The answers offered by different constitutional theorists and by Rawls in an explicit or implicit form will be discussed in more detail in Chapter 7.

To anticipate, Rawls's idea of an implicit unamendable core of the constitution, anchored in a long historical democratic practice, the subversion of which cannot be accepted as valid law regardless of the formally correct procedure followed for proposing and ratifying and amendment, departs, in a normative direction, from Ackerman's approach. In the three volumes of *We the People*, Ackerman sharply contrasts the public effervescence of popular mobilization during 'constitutional moments' and the 'lengthy periods of apathy, ignorance and selfishness that mark the collective life of the private citizenry of a liberal republic'.[19] According to his view, the political energy that animates the cycle of signalling, proposing, triggering, ratification, and consolidation is so bound up with the constituent power of the people that the substance of the new constitutional transformation cannot be legitimately invalidated by a constituted power, such as the Supreme Court. The only safeguard of the integrity of the Constitution consists for him of the usually more extended time frame, and rougher course, of the amendment process relative to ordinary legislation, on account of the necessary supermajorities and stages of ratification. Differently from Rawls, however, if a broad majority of the people, beyond the narrow majorities of partisan politics,

---

[15] ibid.
[16] Rawls, *PL* 237.
[17] See Bruce Ackerman, *We the People*. Vol. 1, *Foundations* (Harvard University Press 1991) 3–33 and 230–94 (hereafter Ackerman, *Foundations*).
[18] Rawls, *PL* 238.
[19] Ackerman, *Foundations* (n 17) 265.

over sometimes a long cycle of electoral confrontations, persists in endorsing a significant modification of one or other of the constitutional essentials, Ackerman denies that the ensuing outcome could be rejected by the Supreme Court as not valid.[20] This contentious point, once again, will be at the centre of our discussion of Rawls's conception of judicial review and of amending power, but for now suffice it to say that one of the original traits of 'political liberalism' is the combination of a *dualist* and a *normative* perspective.

b. The liberal principle of legitimacy, or 'legitimation by constitution'

The conception of legitimacy embedded in political liberalism constitutes nothing less than a philosophical revolution within the liberal-democratic tradition. Ever since Locke's *Two Treatises of Government* and Rousseau's *The Social Contract*, liberals and democrats have understood the legitimacy of legislation, governmental action, and the conduct of authorities as resting on the consent of the citizens. Legitimate government is defined by the consent of the governed also by the nineteenth-century liberalism of Constant, Tocqueville, and Mill.

This idea of a piecemeal consent of the governed has continued to be at the centre of subsequent conceptions of democratic legitimacy, much in the same way as Montesquieu's tripartite understanding of separated powers continues to hold sway in spite of the obvious gap in institutional complexity between contemporary societies and the societies of the mid eighteenth century. The 'liberal principle of legitimacy' sets Rawls's political liberalism apart not only from the classical liberal tradition but also from most other liberal-democratic paradigms of our time. Among the five formulations of this principle, offered by Rawls,[21] the first one runs: 'Our exercise of political power is fully proper only when it is exercised in accordance with a constitution the essentials of which all citizens as free and equal may reasonably be expected to endorse in the light of principles and ideals acceptable to their common human reason.'[22]

---

[20] ibid 13–14.
[21] See above, 'Introduction', n 7. The third formulation will be more extensively discussed in Chapter 7, Section 4.
[22] Rawls, *PL* 137. The *second* formulation runs: 'our exercise of political power is proper and hence justifiable only when it is exercised in accordance with a constitution the essentials of which all citizens may reasonably be expected to endorse in the light of principles and ideals acceptable to them as reasonable and rational', ibid 217. Both date back to 1993, the year of publication of the first edition of *Political Liberalism*, and were actually preceded a third version of the principle published in 2001 (John Rawls, *Justice as Fairness: A Restatement*, ed E Kelly (Harvard University Press 2001) 41, but actually written ten years earlier: 'political power is legitimate only when it is exercised in accordance with a constitution (written or unwritten) the essentials of which all citizens, as reasonable and rational, can endorse in the light of their common human reason'. On these vicissitudes of the liberal principle of legitimacy, see Erin Kelly, 'Editor's Foreword', in ibid xii; and Frank Michelman, *Constitutional Essentials: On the Constitutional Theory of Political Liberalism* (Oxford University Press 2022) Chapter 2.1.1, n 5. A *fourth* formulation, found in the 'Introduction to the Paperback Edition' (1996) introduces the theme of reciprocity and a somewhat problematic reference to (subjective) 'belief': 'our exercise of political power is proper only when we sincerely believe that the reasons we offer for our political action may reasonably be accepted by other citizens as a justification of those actions', Rawls, *PL* xliv. A year later, in 'The Idea of Public Reason Revisited', a *fifth*, almost identical formulation runs: 'our exercise of political power is proper only when we sincerely believe that the reasons we would offer for our political actions—were we to state them as government officials—are

This definition of the legitimate use of constituted power prompts a doctrinal, so to speak, and a contextual comment.

As to the doctrinal comment, Rawls's formulation speaks to us through what it does *not* say. The phrase 'in accordance with a constitution' stands over against alternative formulations used in the past and still on offer: for example, against the idea, endorsed by majoritarian, populist, and 'political constitutionalist' views, that political authority acts legitimately when it acts 'in accordance with the will of the majority of the voters as expressed in the latest elections'. It also stands in opposition to other understandings of legitimacy which at certain times have held sway: for example, authority as acting legitimately when it acts 'in accordance with what the public wishes, as attested by reliable polls', or 'in accordance with our political tradition', or 'in accordance with the Bible, the Qur'ân, or any other sacred text'. Furthermore, Rawls's formula requires that the constitution be endorsed, at least in its essential elements, by *all* the citizens *as free and equal*. Finally, the citizens' endorsement of the constitutional essentials must proceed *from principles and ideals acceptable to them as reasonable and rational*. Consent must be based on considerations of justice, as opposed to considerations of *prudence* such as the fear of the consequences of refusing to consent. A constitution accepted out of preoccupation for the political consequences of conflict can at best legitimize a *modus vivendi*, perhaps a Hobbesian stable society, but cannot legitimize the basic structure of a 'stable *and just*' society and the exercise of coercive power within it.

Concerning the historical context, matters are more complex. Although he intended to address conditions of 'reasonable disagreement' in free societies, Rawls's formula in fact can be taken as a broader response to adverse conditions for democracy typical of the late twentieth century: the immense extension of the electorates, which encourages 'rational ignorance'; the institutional complexity of contemporary societies, which negatively affects the accountability of authority; the increasing pluralism of contemporary publics; the anonymous quality of the communication processes whereby public opinion is formed.[23] In the light of these 'inauspicious conditions'—to which a new cluster of equally adverse tendencies have accrued[24]—the standard of legitimacy can less and less sensibly be interpreted as requiring citizens to endorse *all* details of the legislative, executive, and judicial activity of democratic institutions. It makes better sense to settle, under those conditions, for a less demanding criterion that exempts single outcomes of such activity from *direct* justification. There will always be groups of citizens to whom some verdict, statute, or decree appears unjust and coercive. And yet the 'consent of the governed' can duly remain the lodestar for assessing the legitimate exercise of democratic authority when properly reformulated as a judgment passed on the 'constitutional essentials' with which all the ordinary

---

sufficient, and we also reasonably think that other citizens might also reasonably accept those reasons', ibid 447.

[23] Frank Michelman, 'How Can the People Ever Make the Laws? A Critique of Deliberative Democracy' in James Bohman and William Rehg (eds), *Deliberative Democracy* (MIT Press 1997) 154.

[24] Among these additional inauspicious conditions, it is worth mentioning the financialization of the economy, the acceleration of societal time, the rise of supranational governance, the further transformation (and polarization) of the public sphere, and the impact of the extensive use of opinion polls. See Alessandro Ferrara, *The Democratic Horizon: Hyperpluralism and the Renewal of Political Liberalism* (Cambridge University Press 2014) (hereafter Ferrara, *Democratic Horizon*) 8–12.

legislative, judicial, and executive acts must *be consistent*. Frank Michelman has aptly renamed Rawls's principle 'legitimation by constitution' and has captured the gist of Rawls's theoretical innovation as the deflection, given the prohibitive conditions mentioned above, of

> divisive questions of legislative policy and value (does this law or policy merit the respect or rather the contempt of a right-thinking person?), to a different question (is this law or policy constitutional), for which the answer is to be publicly apparent, or at any rate ascertainable by means that are an order of magnitude less open to divisive dispute than are the deflected substantive disagreements.[25]

c. The revolution of the 'most reasonable'

The third breakthrough inherent in political liberalism relates to the understanding of pluralism. For political and legal philosophers of normative inclination, the notion of pluralism is one of the most impervious to elucidation. Relatively unproblematic if understood along the lines of political realism, as a shorthand signifier for the diversity of orientations found in the political field under observation, pluralism raises a dilemma for the *normative* political philosopher.

The dilemma does not concern the definition of pluralism, but its normative credentials. It is relatively unproblematic to characterize pluralism, for the purposes of political and legal philosophy, as the simultaneous presence within the same polity of broad, 'comprehensive' conceptions of society, of the human condition, and of what is desirable that are pervaded by and responsive to competing values not reconcilable within a shared hierarchy of priority. That pluralism so understood should count not as an unfortunate predicament to be remedied as urgently as possible, but as a permanent condition that legitimate institutions and authorities ought *not* to try to alter through the coercive force of law, is the claim which generates a difficult dilemma for the normative philosopher.

On one hand, one cannot cast this stance as one opinion among others—a Rortyan 'that's the way we do things here, in democratic contexts' or 'that's how we feel, in liberal progressive circles'—without thereby emptying it of all normative force and reducing it to a matter of 'political taste', as it were. On the other hand, one cannot claim that the obligation not to try to reduce or bring the predicament of pluralism to an end, through the coercive use of law and the agency of institutions, is *objectively* binding on us, as though it were part of the normative furniture of the universe. One would then instantly incur a performative contradiction: the plurality of perspectives predicated at one level would be implicitly denied at the meta-level of the justification offered for endorsing pluralism.

Plato's allegory of the cave offers an invaluable 'expository device' for illustrating this point. The allegory narrates of an underground cave where prisoners chained to their benches face a wall onto which shadows are projected by objects lit by a fire positioned

---

[25] Frank Michelman, 'Political-Liberal Legitimacy and the Question of Judicial Restraint' (2019) 1 Jus Cogens 65.

behind them. Shadows are all that the prisoners see and are misperceived as the whole of reality, a form of belief that symbolizes shifting and ungrounded opinion. One of the prisoners frees himself, succeeds in reaching the outside world, and painfully slowly acquires true knowledge of the objects and the sun, the source of all light. He decides to return inside and inform his fellow cave-dwellers, only to be derided for failing to discern the contours of the shadows, because his sight is temporarily impaired by the sudden transition from full daylight to the penumbra of the cave. He even risks being killed when he tries to unbind his comrades in order to enable them to take the same journey.[26]

The over twenty-four centuries elapsed since the time when Plato wrote *The Republic* have added a great number of substantive variations to the allegory's theme, while leaving the overall teaching basically unchallenged. The idea of the Good, symbolized by the sun, has over time been replaced by the revealed will of a monotheistic God, by insights into the desiring nature of man, by the laws of evolution, by Reason in history, by the dynamics of class struggle and revolutionary emancipation. Underlying all these expressions is the idea that true knowledge, a speculative knowledge which precedes intersubjective deliberation and sets the standard for sorting out good and bad deliberation, provides the foundations for the legitimate use of coercive power, for political obligation, and for all the normative concepts found in politics.

The latest reincarnation of such an epistemic approach to normative political philosophy is 'justice as fairness' as understood in *A Theory of Justice*. It is the weakest possible version of Plato's allegory, topographically located at the edge of his philosophical model, beyond which the construction undergoes radical transformation. In *A Theory of Justice*, the fact of pluralism is part of the 'circumstances of justice', the point of 'justice as fairness' being to enable us to build a just polity amidst conflicting conceptions of the good outside the cave, and ultimately it is the consensus of us inside the cave that can validate the philosopher's argument—a premise that Plato would never have accepted.[27] However, *A Theory of Justice* still lies *within* the bounds of Plato's line of thinking because it incorporates the expectation, later denounced as 'unrealistic' in *Political Liberalism*, that everybody in the cave will eventually recognize the superiority of 'justice as fairness' over all the rival accounts of what is outside the cave, and notably over utilitarianism—as though the 'burdens of judgment' could be fully neutralized by some philosophical argument.[28]

With a radical departure from this long-established tradition, public reason breaks free from Plato's spell.[29] It is a kind of *deliberative reason* which neither surrenders to

---

[26] Plato, *The Republic*, translated, with notes and an interpretive essay, by A Bloom (2nd edition, Basic Books 1991) 193–95 (514a–517b).
[27] See John Rawls, *A Theory of Justice* (1971) (revised edition Harvard University Press 1999) 129–30.
[28] See Rawls, *PL* 58.
[29] At three junctures the later Rawls takes explicit distance from *A Theory of Justice*. First, in footnote 7 of Lecture 2 of *Political Liberalism* (on which more will be said in Chapter 3, Section 4) he dismisses his own attempt, pursued in *A Theory of Justice*, to ground a justification of the principles of justice on the theory of rational decision as 'incorrect'. Second, in the text, on p 53, Rawls calls the idea of justice as fairness as embedding the attempt to derive the reasonable from the rational a 'misinterpretation' of the original position. Third, on p 489 of 'The Idea of Public Reason Revisited', Rawls admits that the kind of 'well-ordered society' envisaged in *A Theory of Justice*, namely a society whose members affirm justice as fairness as a comprehensive liberal doctrine, '*contradicts the fact of pluralism* and hence *Political Liberalism* regards that society as impossible' (emphasis added).

the world of appearances, as *doxa* does, nor presumes that normativity can originate from without, from subjecting politics in the cave to 'the whole truth' imported from out of the cave. As Rawls famously put it, 'the zeal to embody the whole truth in politics is incompatible with an idea of public reason that belongs with democratic citizenship'.[30] Public reason, instead, tries tenaciously to distinguish better and worse, the more and the less just, the more reasonable and what is less so, within the bounds of the cave. How to sum up Rawls's revolution of public reason and the reasonable using the allegory of the cave as a foil?

If we wish to translate the gist of Rawls's non-perfectionist liberalism into Plato's vocabulary, we must introduce a modification and imagine the scene of the cave *at a later stage* on the basis of a formulation occurring later in the dialogue. At 519d Socrates is undoubtedly speaking in the plural: 'our job as founders is to compel *the best natures* ... to go up that ascent; and when *they* have gone up and seen sufficiently, not to permit them what is now permitted'.[31] He and Glaucon are referring to a class of philosophers: 'consider that we won't be doing injustice to the philosophers who come to be among us', Socrates continues, 'but rather that we will say just things to them while compelling them besides to care for and guard the others'.[32]

Let us then recalibrate the temporal setting of the allegory at that subsequent point in time, not entirely beyond Plato's mindset: not just one single prisoner, as in the canonical version, but a number of them, say an expedition team of three or four philosophers, have made their way up to the outside world. On coming back, their accounts of what lies outside conceivably would *partly overlap and partly differ*, not because the returning philosophers lie or are individually blinded by prejudice, but simply because they are all-too-finite beings faced with an overwhelmingly complex, if not infinite, reality. Even allowing for the fact that they obviously come from the same milieu of the cave, some of the 'burdens of judgment' may be operative. Out there in the outside world, when trying to make sense of the relation of sunlight to objects and to shadows, our philosophers may legitimately converge on identifying the relevant aspects of reality, yet may assign a different weight to these single aspects due to their singular experiences in the cave, their specific location or point of observation in the outside world, and their propensities or personal charactcristics. *We need not imagine that their accounts be radically diverse*. All that a Rawlsian case for pluralism requires is the assumption that their accounts *are not identical*.

This assumption is enough for reinterpreting Plato's allegory of the cave in a *non-epistocratic* way. Imagine, as stipulated above, that the philosophers' accounts are discovered to be partly the same, partly different. What then? Should the operation of politics, within the cave, the ordinary workings of authority, of government, be suspended until it is determined which of the diverse accounts is the true one? Should authority be exercised according to what each official in charge deems the best account? Should the cave dwellers collectively decide, in a kind of populist referendum, to adopt one account to the exclusion of others? If oppression means to be forced, through the coercive power of law, to live according to principles one does not endorse, how can

---

[30] Rawls, 'The Idea of Public Reason Revisited', in *PL* 442.
[31] Plato, *Republic* (n 49) 198 (519d) (emphasis added).
[32] ibid (520a).

life without oppression take place under such conditions in the cave even if the philosophers are ruling? The allegory has now been reformulated in terms not too distant from the ones now made familiar by the opening question of *Political Liberalism*.

The political-liberal solution to the problem of avoiding oppression consists of dividing the public space into two areas, which Rawls calls the 'public forum' and the 'background culture'.[33] In the public forum legislative, executive, or judicial decisions binding for all are made. Their legitimacy, the legitimacy of legal coercion and of the exercise of power in order to secure compliance, and the corresponding obligation of every citizen to abide by these decisions, cannot but be justified, if oppression is to be avoided, on principles that derive or are somehow connected with the overlapping part of the reports on the outside world. Only if life in the cave is so ruled can no one lament being a victim of oppression.

This normative restraint, at the core of public reason, does not hold in the institutions of the 'background culture' and is not meant to suppress the desire that human beings share to find out which of the distinct and rival accounts better mirrors the order of the world out there. That natural impulse must only be relocated—in a non-epistocratic reformulation of the allegory of the cave—from the public forum to the 'background culture', the public sphere or any other segment of social life where passionate exchanges of reasons and ideas are at home, but no practical decision binding for all is expected to follow, and therefore no exercise of authority and legal coercion is linked with the prevailing of one or other view. Plato's just polis is premised on the primacy of *episteme* over *doxa*, but if we allow for a plurality of fugitive-philosophers venturing out of the cave and returning possessed not of a monolithic form of *episteme*, but of a plurality of partially diverging *epistemai*, then it follows that a polis where one controversial kind of *episteme* is imposed, through legal and institutional coercion, not over *doxa*, but over *rival versions of episteme*, is not a just polis.

We are at the last leg of our revisitation of Plato's allegory of the cave. Rawls's understanding of 'reasonable pluralism'—that is, pluralism as bona fide 'intra-epistemic' disagreement the coercive suppression of which inevitably generates oppression—has been translated into a modified version of the allegory, consistent with the original one. However, a normative blind spot affecting Rawls's view still needs to be addressed.

The normative blind spot concerns the *justification* of the pluralistic stance. The burdens of judgment are the keystone of a *descriptive* argument about why, in the absence of an oppressive matrix of positive and negative incentives, the expected outcome of the deliberation of finite and situated human minds over issues of broad scope and significance should be plurality and not unanimity. Not all of the six burdens are applicable to the cave setting, but for the sake of our argument some are fully relevant. For Rawls, the descriptive argument about the burdens of judgment serves as a premise for a complex *normative* argument to the effect that:

(1) the bona fide reasonable pluralism generated by the burdens of judgment should be preserved for the sake of avoiding oppression;

---

[33] Rawls, *PL* 215 and 220–22. On the relation of the 'background culture' to Habermas's 'public sphere', see Rawls, 'Reply to Habermas', in *PL* 382.

(2) coercion can be exercised legitimately in the cave only when it is used to enforce norms that everybody can endorse for principled reasons, thus only when it can be justified on the basis of the *non-controversial, overlapping part* of the accounts of the outside world;
(3) in order to reconcile the desire to avoid oppression and the legitimate aspiration to identify the one fully true account, the public space of the cave is best understood as divided into the two realms of the 'public forum' and the 'background culture'.

We need to take a closer look at the normative credentials of these three intimations. As Charles Larmore has rightly observed, why in the intra-cave public forum couldn't political actors dig in their heels and refuse to accommodate views that do not correspond to their favourite account of the external world? How can it be a virtue to accommodate what one considers less than adequate? Who said oppressing others by forcing them to comply with what one considers to be the only true principles is worse than compromising with error?

What answer to these questions could be gleaned from political liberalism? Two alternative answers seem to me equally problematic. The first, offered by Larmore, consists of pointing to a principle of *equal respect* operative underneath both the pluralism-respecting public forum and 'justice as fairness' as a political conception of justice. This principle—the 'moral heart of liberal thought'—is 'the idea that basic political principles should be rationally acceptable to those whom they are to bind'.[34] As Larmore points out, 'Respect for persons lies at the heart of political liberalism, not because looking for common ground we find it there, but because it is what impels us to look for common ground'.[35] Consequently, the principle of equal respect must be 'understood as having more than just *political* authority', indeed an authority 'that we have not fashioned ourselves' and that is 'binding on us *independently of our will as citizens*'.[36] This way of understanding the normative credentials of pluralism-respecting institutions forfeits the 'political' quality of our liberalism. Once again, out of the cave the sun symbolizes one unitary moral hyper-good, now reconceived as 'equal respect'. The philosophers are its exclusive interpreters and in its name select 'justice as fairness'. We are back to an epistocratic stance that singles out pluralism as the best means for realizing an overarching value antecedently discovered outside the cave.

The second answer essentializes pluralism as though it was part of the furniture of the world outside the cave. Isaiah Berlin is the champion of this view. Like Larmore's solution, 'metaphysical pluralism' à la Berlin also restores the epistocratic reading of the allegory of the cave, with all its authoritarian implications. The philosophers are the guardians of an ontological truth that happens to have pluralism as its content but incurs an ironic performative contradiction: it asserts pluralism but does not allow for a pluralist understanding of its claim. The alleged existence of a plurality of diverse values 'not structured hierarchically' is not open to plural interpretations.[37]

[34] Charles Larmore, 'The Moral Basis of Political Liberalism' (1999) 96 Journal of Philosophy 605.
[35] ibid 608.
[36] ibid 609 (emphasis added).
[37] Isaiah Berlin, *The Crooked Timber of Humanity* (Random House 1992), 79–80. In the same passage Berlin contends that this view of pluralism is distinct from relativism.

We are still in search of an adequate answer. How could the acceptance of pluralism be something other than one opinion among the many voiced in the cave and yet not an authoritative injunction coming from out of the cave? Rawls built his answer into the core of political liberalism under the heading of *the reasonable*, the standard of public reason. The reasonable is neither part of the normative furniture of the outside world (lest public reason be turned into the mouthpiece of practical reason within the cave) nor one preference or orientation among many others. Rawls did not explore the broader philosophical implications of his invention, which amounts to identifying a non-speculative, but fully *deliberative*, mode of reason—which of course draws inspiration from the transformative and critical powers of speculative reason, but remains anchored to a context where the best solution to a pressing communal problem must be found *before* consensus on the relevant normative questions has coalesced. According to my modified version of the allegory, life in the cave must be somehow regulated *before* the controversy concerning which of the philosophers' accounts truly matches the outside world is over.

The predicate 'reasonable' then applies to *all* positions that understand their own validity as something other than full-scale mirroring of the order of the outside world. Among all these positions, respect of pluralism and 'justice and fairness', qua *political* conception of justice equally endorsable by the supporters of all the complete accounts of the external world, can aspire to the status of 'most reasonable for us'. Not a second best, this is the idea of normativity that *we* can have if we wish to avoid the epistocratic interpretation of the allegory of the cave and at the same time to avoid embracing a *relativism* incapable of spelling out how one position or proposal could ever be better than another.[38]

Returning to the allegory of the cave: can that complex symbolic structure, so influential on our political imaginary, accommodate the new non-foundational normativity found in Rawls's political liberalism? The answer is positive.

Imagine that the group of philosophers—destined to rule the cave—are heading back from the outside world for motivations not different from the ones found in the canonical version. They want to report what they have seen and reform life in the cave. Wouldn't they also perhaps want to stop for a while, on their way back, at the entrance of the cave to exchange impressions and check if they can agree on a common story that one of them, as their spokesperson, would relate? And if upon conversing at the entrance of the cave, standing sideways, the conversation dragged on without coming to a close, and they came to the realization that their dialogue would not be likely to result in a common report: wouldn't they agree to keep their report to the observations and conclusions blessed by full overlap and to make them the only basis for exercising legitimate authority in the cave? As to the contentious conclusions and observations, wouldn't they agree to bar any factional, divisive enforcement of them, and to further explore their merit in proper venues, for the purpose of seeing if the area of agreement could be further extended in the future? And finally, would they describe the

---

[38] For an example of such relativist contextualism, see Richard Rorty, 'The Priority of Democracy over Philosophy', in R Vaughan (ed), *The Virginia Statute of Religious Freedom: Two Hundred Years After* (University of Wisconsin Press 1988) 257.

newly established prohibition, for those in charge in the cave, to enforce controversial portions of the accounts—so that none of the accounts could triumph or succumb because of the sheer contingency of the distribution of power—as just another 'opinion' like the ones exchanged in relation to the passing shadows? 'Certainly not', any twenty-first century Glaucon would concede. Could then the fugitive-philosophers describe that pluralism-affirming argument as something that they *found* in the outside world, as objectively as they found the light of the sun? 'Hardly so', a contemporary Glaucon again would have again to admit. Evidently the philosophers, during their conversation, *standing sideways at the entrance of the cave*, ground their pro-pluralism stance neither on *doxa* nor on *episteme*. That stance simply is *the most reasonable thing for them* to do. At that moment, they have given rise to *deliberative* or *public reason* and to its standard of reasonability.

This reconstruction of Plato's allegory of the cave helps us to grasp the magnitude of the philosophical breakthrough contained in Rawls's claim that

> What justifies a conception of justice is not its being true to an order antecedent to and given to us, but its congruence with our deeper understanding of ourselves and our aspirations, and our realization that, given our history and the traditions embedded in our public life, it is the most reasonable doctrine for us.[39]

In Chapter 3 this view of normativity will be put to use in order to make sense of Rawls's conception—unique within constitutional theory—of constituent power as not unbound, but responsive to an 'ought' that does not detract from the sovereignty of its bearer. Meanwhile, in the next section Rawls's three breakthroughs will be assessed against the foil provided by some of the leading contemporary approaches to political philosophy.

2. Political Liberalism and Its Main Competitors

Rawls's normative version of Ackerman's 'democratic dualism', his reformulation of the liberal standard of the consent of the governed as 'legitimation by constitution', and his non-foundationalist grounding of the acceptance of pluralism on public reason's standard of the 'most reasonable for us' place political liberalism in a position of competitive advantage over such influential paradigms of 'democratic theory' as Habermas's discursive paradigm of deliberative democracy, Dworkin's 'rights-foundationalist' approach to democracy, Pettit's republicanism and Bellamy's 'political constitutionalism', Mouffe's and Tully's varieties of agonistic democracy, Gray's and Williams's 'modus-vivendi' or 'political-realist' liberalism, as well as over philosophical proposals centred on 'difference' or 'recognition'.

---

[39] John Rawls, 'Kantian Constructivism in Moral Theory' (1980) 88 Journal of Philosophy 519.

a. Habermas's discursive approach to deliberative democracy

Jürgen Habermas's approach to deliberative democracy, based on a discursive view of justice and articulated in *Between Facts and Norms*, must be credited with two highly original contributions that qualify it as the most challenging competitor of political liberalism: (i) a conception of the co-originality of the sovereign democratic will and fundamental rights,[40] and (ii) a theory of the public sphere, more differentiated and richer than Rawls's understanding of the 'background culture'.[41]

However, Habermas's discursive paradigm is affected by three drawbacks: (i) a traditional view of the consent of the governed, (ii) an unrealistic normative requirement that rational consensus be based on the same reasons, and (iii) a traditional view of pluralism.

In *Between Facts and Norms*, the legitimacy of legal norms, legislation, and policies is connected with a hierarchically ordered variety of 'discourses'. At the bottom of the scale of normativity are *pragmatic* discourses—that is, communicative exchanges on the *expediency* of adopting some provision, norm, or policy. The assessment of the pragmatic advantageousness of what for brevity will be called norms rests on the assumption that such expediency does not clash with our sense of what is *good* for us, as ascertainable in *ethical* discourses. Should such a suspicion be raised, then the legitimating communicative exchange or discourse would have to step up to the level of ethical questions concerning our vision of the *good*. No norm can be legitimate if advocating it as advantageous in pragmatic discourse runs against our sense of the good for us. Visions of the good, in turn, can be acceptable only insofar as they do not violate our sense of *justice*, namely if their normative presuppositions and implications can withstand all possible objections in *moral* discourses about justice. A conception of the 'good for us' cannot defensibly be shared and endorsed if it does not pass the test of being compatible with justice for all the affected persons. The bulk of the legislative, administrative, and judicial activities occurring in a polity can then be said, according to Habermas, to take place under a routine presumption of legitimacy, unless objections are raised, either in the public sphere or in the institutional forum, that throw into question the pragmatic, ethical, or moral credentials of such activities: if no such questions are raised, it can be assumed that said activities would be vindicated by pragmatic, ethical, and moral arguments recognized as better than conceivable alternatives under idealized conditions of communication.

Within the discursive view of deliberative democracy, then, just as in traditional liberal-democratic accounts of legitimacy based on the 'consent of the governed', the object of consensus-worthy normative arguments are single acts of legislative, executive, and judicial authorities. From his extended dialogue with Rawls, no indication emerges that Habermas has ever engaged the liberal principle of legitimacy. Reading *Between Facts and Norms*, the closest approximation that we can find to 'legitimation

---

[40] See Jürgen Habermas, *Between Facts and Norms: Contributions to a Discourse Theory of Law and Democracy* (William Rehg tr, MIT Press 1996) 103–04 (hereafter Habermas, *Facts and Norms*), and 'Postscript to *Faktizität und Geltung*', in (1994) 20 Philosophy and Social Criticism 135.

[41] See Habermas *Facts and Norms* (n 40) 359–84.

by constitution' is the statement that 'the legal system as a whole has a higher measure of legitimacy than individual legal norms'.[42] That said, just one paragraph above the cited sentence Habermas had emphasized that 'the *legitimacy of statutes* is measured against the *discursive redeemability* of their normative validity claim'.[43] Thus, single statutes are presumably assessed, when contestation arises, via the discursive test of 'rational consensus'—where rational consensus *for the same reasons* represents a much more demanding, perhaps unrealistic, benchmark than Rawls's overlapping consensus.

To sum up, we get no clear sense, from *Between Facts and Norms*, that the discursive assessment of legitimacy in contemporary complex societies is any different from the traditional liberal view of the 'consent of the governed', as though social differentiation or cultural pluralism did not affect the likelihood of consensus to coalesce around the minutiae of policy making, legislation, and adjudication. All that can be gleaned from Habermas's texts is that the presumption of legitimacy of the whole legal system *routinely* redeems the legitimacy of the single statutes—so, rather than 'legitimation by constitution' (which pivots around constitutional *essentials*), in *Between Facts and Norms* we find a kind of 'legitimation by rule of law', so to speak. However, should the legitimacy of single statutes or other acts of government be questioned (as it often happens under today's 'inauspicious conditions' and 'hyperpluralism') then we are 'back to discourse' and to 'rational consensus' on the single, contested statute's validity as supported by 'the better argument'.

The second drawback of Habermas's view concerns the understanding of pluralism implicit in his discursive view of deliberative democracy. The difficulty is twofold. On one hand, controversial public issues and contested policies do not emerge in the public sphere with a convenient label that pre-assigns them to pragmatic, ethical, or moral discourses. That assignment is itself a matter of contestation. While such assignment, in fact, may concur in determining which argument will count as the better, no neutral meta-discourse on assigning contentious issues to the three types of discourse is anywhere in sight. On the other hand, Habermas seems to assume that, at least insofar as justice-tracking moral discourses are concerned, if certain idealized conditions of dialogic exchange hold, a consensus will coalesce around the argument that emerges as better than all the others. However, what makes us suppose that 'the force of the better argument' can silence the 'burdens of judgment'?[44] According to Habermas's renowned general formulation of the principle of discourse D: 'Just those norms are valid to which all those possibly affected could agree as participants in rational discourses'.[45] Furthermore, principle D supposedly applies not just to constitutional essentials, as we would expect in a discursive equivalent of Rawls's dualist scheme, but also to the single legal provisions, administrative measures, judicial verdicts, and sentences, should their legitimacy be challenged through acceptable and competent objections.

---

[42] ibid 30.
[43] ibid (emphasis added).
[44] For a contrastive appraisal of the philosophical underpinnings of Habermas's and Rawls's views of pluralism, see Alessandro Ferrara, 'What the controversy over "the reasonable" reveals: on Habermas's *Auch eine Geschichte der Philosophie*' (2022) 48/3 Philosophy and Social Criticism 313.
[45] Habermas, *Facts and Norms* (n 40) 107.

For Habermas, the 'better argument' that vindicates these provisions, measures, and judicial outputs becomes, under ideal conditions, the object of a 'rational consensus' among all the participants, where a 'rational consensus', as opposed to one resting on a fair compromise, should proceed *from the same reasons*. Whereas Rawls's distinction of overlapping consensus and modus vivendi revolves around the motivation for endorsing the two schemes of cooperation—a motivation based on considerations of principle in the case of overlapping consensus, on expediency or prudence in the case of a modus vivendi[46]—Habermas's functionally similar distinction of 'rational consensus' and 'compromise' revolves around the sameness of the reasons for supporting a given scheme—same reasons for 'rational consensus', different ones for compromises, regardless whether fair or unfair.

Habermas's criterion of legitimacy appears then significantly more demanding, more traditionally liberal-democratic than Rawls's, and of dubious applicability in complex societies: legitimacy remains piecemeal and fine-graded, geared to single details of the rule of law. Whereas the Rawlsian actors in the end come to agree on a fair scheme of oppression-free coexistence from different angles and for different reasons, anchored in their comprehensive doctrines, for Habermas the key to the rationality (not reasonableness) of 'rational consensus' on a system of rights or on an institutional order is that the participants agree *for the same reasons*, and they are able to do so because they recognize *the force of the better argument*.

Thirdly, if we unpack the requirement that the citizens' rational consensus be based 'on the same reasons' we find a quite traditional notion of pluralism underlying it. Assuming that under ideal conditions the burdens of judgment would never prevent the 'better argument' from emerging amidst all the rival positions, only then can citizens sensibly be expected to endorse a scheme of cooperation, a basic structure, an institutional regime *for the same reasons*. Only on that assumption does it make sense for Habermas to qualify Rawls's notion of the reasonable as an unfortunate second best, relative to the morally valid as tracked by autonomous practical reason. The price to be paid, however, is that Habermas's 'post-metaphysical reason', differently from Rawls's public reason, presupposes a very traditional understanding of pluralism, inherited from theology, indeed an unmetabolized residue of religious thinking. Pluralism exists only because the world is imperfect: the City of God will be immune from pluralism. People subscribe to different reasons and are unable to recognize the force of the reasons enunciated in the best argument because the idealized presuppositions of discourse are never empirically satisfied. However, in a world where the ideal presuppositions of discourse were satisfied, the best argument would prevail and 'the reasonable', an ambiguous benchmark designed to accommodate recalcitrant differences, would have no place.

Nothing could be more un-Rawlsian than this view of pluralism. As the author of *Political Liberalism* forcefully emphasizes, pluralism is a permanent condition even in an ideal world. It is the expectable outcome of the exercise of reason under conditions of freedom. If we now take the Rawlsian view that neither public reason nor 'better arguments'—destined to remain better only in the eyes of the beholder—can

---

[46] On prudential motivations and modus vivendi, see Rawls, *PL* 147.

ever neutralize the burdens of judgment, we are left with the need for a normative benchmark for preventing oppression among supporters of different doctrines, and that benchmark cannot evoke putative better arguments. Then the reasonable and the 'most reasonable for us', a variant unduly neglected by Habermas, constitute a normative benchmark, which can be disqualified as second best only at the price of rejecting 'reasonable pluralism' and retreating to old-time 'pluralism as the fruit of human imperfection'.

b. Dworkin's rights-foundationalist approach to democracy

Dworkin's view of democracy shares some aspects in common with Rawls's. It is antimajoritarian, for starters. It rejects the premise that the laws and policies resulting from the democratic process are legitimate insofar as they meet the approval of the majority of the citizens, and it rejects the ensuing implication that whenever some derogation from that principle is allowed, for example in order to safeguard fundamental rights at risk of being violated by certain decisions, then 'something morally regrettable has happened, a moral cost has been paid'.[47] When he denies that 'it is *always* unfair when a political majority is not allowed to have its way, so that even when there are strong enough countervailing reasons to justify this, the unfairness remains', Dworkin is on the same page as Rawls.

However, they propound ultimately different views of democracy. Dworkin's 'constitutional conception of democracy' rests on the premise that collective decisions should be 'made by political institutions whose structure, composition, and practices treat all members of the community as individuals, with equal concern and respect'.[48] Such a view overlaps with the standard view that decision-making officials are to be elected, but such majoritarian procedures as elections for Dworkin are justified 'out of a concern for the equal status of citizens, and not out of a concern for majority rule'. Should these on specific occasions prove less adequate than non-majoritarian procedures, then no moral regret would be proper in replacing them with non-majoritarian procedures. In other words, 'democracy means government subject to conditions of equal status for all citizens'.[49] His model of democracy, alternative to the majoritarian one, is later renamed by Dworkin 'the *partnership* model of democracy', described in the following terms: 'democracy means that the people govern themselves each as a full partner in a collective political enterprise so that a majority's decisions are democratic only when certain further conditions are met that protect the status and interests of each citizen as a full partner in that enterprise'.[50]

---

[47] Ronald Dworkin, *Freedom's Law: The Moral Reading of the American Constitution* (Harvard University Press 1996) 16.
[48] ibid 17.
[49] ibid.
[50] Ronald Dworkin, *Is Democracy Possible Here? Principles for a New Political Debate* (Princeton University Press 2006) 131 (hereafter Dworkin, *Is Democracy Possible Here?*). The forerunner of the partnership model can be found in the model of the orchestra, outlined by Dworkin in 'Liberal Community' (1989) 77 California Law Review 479 (hereafter Dworkin, 'Liberal Community').

Rawls would not dispute Dworkin's critique of the majoritarian assumption and his alternative view, but he would twist the idea of the proper functioning of the institutions of democracy in the direction of legitimation by constitution. Furthermore, the strategy adopted by Dworkin for grounding the legitimacy of democratic lawmaking and policies in the light of persisting disagreements seems to follow the method of avoiding, and, in ways not dissimilar from how public reason proceeds, to advocate backtracking from, the divisive issues until a firm ground of agreed premises is found. The similarity, however, is only superficial. In *Is Democracy Possible Here?* Dworkin suggests that such common ground be found as a convergence on two philosophical principles that jointly capture the meaning of human dignity. First, the principle of intrinsic value stipulates 'that each human life has a special kind of objective value'[51] and that such value be understood as potentiality: 'once a human life has begun, it matters how it goes. It is good when that life succeeds and its potential is realized and bad when it fails and its potential is wasted'.[52] This principle grounds the political value of equality as an irrecusable commitment. Second, the principle of personal responsibility stipulates 'that each person has a special responsibility for realizing the success of his own life, a responsibility that includes exercising his judgment about what kind of life would be successful for him'.[53] This principle grounds the political value of freedom.

Dworkin's strategy for addressing persistent disagreement in hyperpluralist complex societies thus consists in using the two principles of human dignity as a touchstone for assessing competing claims. On the surface this strategy seems close to Rawls's idea that a just and stable society of free and equal citizens who endorse conflicting comprehensive conceptions can exist insofar as an overlapping consensus on a political conception of justice materializes. At closer scrutiny, however, justice as fairness does not operate as a shared touchstone in the way Dworkin suggests the two principles of human dignity could. Justice as fairness directly inspires only the basic structure of society, constitutional essentials, and a scheme of basic liberties. The shared area on which citizens rely for bridging their disagreements on same-sex marriage, abortion, or free speech is therefore much more context-specific than in Dworkin's approach. Moreover, it reflects the historical specificity of each democratic polity in a much closer way than reliance on the very abstract two principles of human dignity. Dworkin's arguments in defence of abortion, same-sex marriage, and a tolerant secular society as opposed to a tolerant religious one, in the end, draw on one and the same set of basic principles supposedly cogent *for all liberal-democratic polities*.

Against public reason's requirement that interlocutors, whether officials or citizens, refrain from adopting controversial premises, Dworkin maintains that 'we must not try to exclude people's most profound convictions from political debate. On the contrary, we must try to achieve a genuine debate within civil society about those profound convictions'.[54] If by 'political debate' Dworkin refers to discussions in the broader background culture, then political liberalism implies no such exclusion. Insofar as due

---

[51] Dworkin, *Is Democracy Possible Here?* (n 50) 9.
[52] ibid.
[53] ibid 10.
[54] ibid 65.

respect is paid to the 'duty of civility', anything can be the object of public debate. That said, where binding legislative, administrative, or judicial decisions are made—that is, *in the public forum*—it is hard to see how decisions based on controversial assumptions could be legitimately backed up by the force of law. For all his scepticism concerning the separability of the public forum from the broader public arena, assumed by Rawls, it is hard to see how Dworkin could avoid, *malgré lui*, some version of the same separation. Furthermore, one wonders how Dworkin's dignity-based philosophical justification can ever bridge political disagreements without relying on substantive assumptions *unrelated* to the principles of dignity, but rooted in the constitutional and jurisprudential history of a given polity.[55]

Furthermore, Dworkin rejects the idea of public reason as superfluous. In his opinion, the notion of public reason ambiguously encompasses two distinct ways of accounting for the justifications that liberal authorities can legitimately adopt and back up with legal coercion. In its *first* mode, public reason resorts to the normative notion of reciprocity: under this interpretation public reason 'permits only those justifications that all members of the political community can reasonably accept'.[56] However, it is hard to see what, if anything, 'the doctrine of reciprocity excludes'.[57] If I am convinced of the rightness of a doctrine, how can I not suppose that others should be convinced as well? In its *second* mode, 'public reason requires officials to offer justifications that are based on the political values of the community and not on comprehensive religious or moral or philosophical doctrines',[58] but Dworkin rejects the Rawlsian distinction of political and non-political values.

According to Dworkin, the core values underlying justice as fairness are not above controversy. Two examples of the partiality of justice as fairness are offered by the second principle and by Rawls's position on abortion. The difference principle rests on the assumed, but disputable, 'moral irrelevance of effort and responsibility'.[59] The most disadvantaged are entitled to the position of beneficiaries of justified inequalities regardless of whether they themselves are responsible for their disadvantaged position. Second, Rawls's defence of a constitutional right to abortion within the first trimester of the fetus's life rests on a disputed lesser status of the fetus as a person. Equal protection does not apply until the third month of intrauterine life. Such a view 'that a fetus does not have interests and rights of its own', Dworkin argues, in unwitting consonance with Sandel,[60] 'is as much drawn from a comprehensive position as the view that it does, and we cannot reach a decision about abortion without adopting one of these two views'.[61] The remedy, according to Dworkin, is to jettison the notion of public reason altogether and to derive the necessary constraints on judicial reasoning from an 'interpretivist' approach to constitutional law: judges 'should not attempt to

---

[55] I'm grateful to an anonymous Oxford University Press reviewer for comments that have stimulated me to reflect on this point.
[56] Ronald Dworkin, *Justice in Robes* (Harvard University Press 2008) 252 (hereafter Dworkin, *Justice in Robes*).
[57] ibid.
[58] ibid.
[59] ibid 253.
[60] See Michael Sandel, 'Moral Argument and Liberal Toleration: Abortion and Homosexuality' (1989) 77 California Law Review 521.
[61] Dworkin, *Justice in Robes* (n 56) 254.

legislate as the legislature would, but should instead try to identify the law of the community as a whole and apply those principles to the new case'.[62] Starting from the principles that undergird a constitution, but also from the institutions provided for in the constitution and from the most important decisions made in those institutions, judges are supposed to adjudicate hard cases in the light of a principle of overall coherence or integrity of the legal system. 'Coherence is the best protection against discrimination', as suggested by the Equal Protection Clause of the Fourteenth Amendment.[63] Dworkin then argues that:

> Citizens are best protected from arbitrariness and discrimination when judges interpreting the law and elaborating it in hard cases are responsible for coherence, not simply with particular doctrines here and there, but, as best as it can be achieved, principled coherence with the whole structure of law.[64]

However, one of the problems with Dworkin's recourse to the two philosophical principles that define dignity is that they may not suffice for reconciling complicated reasonable disagreements. As Joshua Cohen put it,

> Consider people who are committed to human dignity but who endorse, for example, the ideal of a tolerant religious society rather than a tolerant secular society. Have they failed to notice the conflict between their deep convictions about dignity and their political principles? Is their judgment clouded by interest and divisive passion? What kind of mistake are they making?[65]

To conclude, Dworkin's rejection of public reason leads him to short-circuit two levels of political justification that in political liberalism are kept separate: namely, (i) the level of the assessment of *single, specific* legislative, executive, or judicial acts, and (ii) the level of *the most general* normative principles. This strategy binds Dworkin's model to an old understanding of the 'consent of the governed' as directed at every single act of government, forfeiting the advantages afforded by Rawls's liberal principle of legitimacy. Furthermore, this strategy deprives his 'democracy as partnership' model of the possibility of accounting for the specificity of single instantiations of a democratic order in diverse historical and cultural contexts: it is hard to see how one democratic polity would differ from any other as far as the judgment on the legitimacy of a given measure or provisions is concerned. The single measure or provision would be assessed against one and the same set of general principles, whereas in the Rawlsian model no such direct assessment in terms of justice as fairness is carried out. Even assuming that justice as fairness were accepted as the political conception of justice underlying *all* liberal-democratic polities, it would still be reflected in diverse versions of the basic structure typical of each society, or at least of groups of similar societies, and

---

[62] ibid 248.
[63] ibid 250.
[64] ibid.
[65] Joshua Cohen, 'Taking Democracy Seriously. Review of Ronald Dworkin, *Is Democracy Possible Here?*', at https://www.academia.edu/26733113/Review_of_Ronald_Dworkin_Is_Democracy_Possible_Here accessed 17 November 2021.

in diverse versions of the system of basic liberties, differently balanced, and this diversity would account for the unique institutional identity of each liberal-democratic polity. This institutional diversity, combined with 'legitimation by constitution', makes the legitimacy of single legislative, executive, and judicial acts assessable along lines that are overlappingly similar but in the end *specific to each society*. Political liberalism thus incorporates a level of societal individuation hard to recover in the Dworkinian model of democracy.

c. Republican approaches to democracy: Pettit and Bellamy

Contemporary republicanism tries to make the most of the ancient ideal of equal freedom of participation in, and influence on, the shaping of communal policies as the key normative notion, without buying into the glorification of *vita activa* found in Aristotle, Cicero, Machiavelli, and later in Arendt. Of the many representatives of today's republicanism, Philip Pettit and Richard Bellamy are of special interest in relation to Rawls's work.

Pettit maintains a constitutional dimension within his vision of democracy. Drawing on his previous distinction of 'freedom from interference' and 'freedom from domination'[66]—not equivalent to Berlin's 'negative' and 'positive' freedom, and questionably correlated with the liberal and the republican traditions[67]—Pettit articulates a republican notion of political legitimacy partly designed to compete with Rawls's approach to legitimacy. While the obtaining of freedom as non-domination can be ascertained through the 'eyeball test'—do citizens live in a polity that allows them to 'look others in the eye without reason for the fear or deference that a power of interference might inspire'?[68]—the *legitimacy* of an institutional order can be ascertained through the 'tough luck test'. Such a test, through measuring the degree and quality of resentment among the citizens, aims at ascertaining whether citizens 'have good grounds to think that any unwelcome results of public decision-making are just tough luck',[69] as opposed to the result of a deliberate ill-disposition on the part of authorities and institutions.

The difference between the two tests—(i) for detecting a 'horizontal' private domination of one citizen over another, and (ii) for detecting a 'vertical' domination exercised by institutions and authorities over citizens severally and collectively taken—is designed to track respectively justice and legitimacy.[70] As Pettit points out, a polity could be just in the distributive sense of giving everyone what is owed to him or her, or just in the sense of treating each citizen with equal respect, and yet could achieve

---

[66] Philip Pettit, *Republicanism: A Theory of Freedom and Government* (Clarendon Press 1997) (hereafter Pettit, *Republicanism*).
[67] For a critique of the correlation of freedom of interference and liberalism as such, see Alessandro Ferrara, *The Force of the Example: Explorations in the Paradigm of Judgment* (Columbia University Press 2008) 109–15 (hereafter Ferrara, *Force of the Example*).
[68] Philip Pettit, *On the People's Terms: A Republican Theory and Model of Democracy* (Cambridge University Press 2012) (hereafter Pettit, *People's Terms*) 84–85.
[69] ibid 177.
[70] 'Where the issue of social justice is a matter of the horizontal relations of citizens to one another, political legitimacy is a matter of their vertical relations to the state that rules over them', ibid 136.

this commendable state through legislative or administrative acts and policies that lack legitimacy. Conversely, the legislative and administrative output of a polity could meet all tests of legitimacy and yet result in a state of affairs that fails to be just.

Ultimately, and not too differently to Rawls's stance, according to Pettit, 'the question of whether a state is legitimate is best taken as the question of whether state coercion of citizens is consistent with their continuing freedom',[71] namely whether it is *justifiable*. And justifiable coercion is understood by Pettit as coercion over which the coerced subject retains a measure of control, in the sense of having been the creator of the scheme within which coercion is exercised and retaining the right to effectively orient its outcome—in the footsteps of Ulysses, ordering his crew to tie him at the mast of the ship and to disregard all orders to untie him during the time when he will be exposed to the sirens' song.[72]

This control, on the part of the potentially coerced citizens, over the wielders of coercion, namely state authorities and institutions, must be capable of steering the action of government and institutions in a direction consistent with the will of the citizens. Discarding all solutions that vest such function in an assembly coextensive with the citizenry in its entirety, on account of the paradoxes inherent in the aggregation of individual wills into a consistent pattern, Pettit's preference is for a 'mixed constitution': namely, for an elected representative assembly complemented with 'the separating of the many powers of government, the sharing of each of those powers by different authorities, and the recognition of popular acquiescence as the ultimate guarantor of the constitution'.[73] In the end, given the enormous differential of power between the state as ultimate possessor of the monopoly of the use of physical force and any partial association of citizens (whether a party, a congregation, or a social movement), the guarantee of a not purely nominal control on the part of the citizens lies, as Pettit argues, in the actual readiness of the citizens 'to resist measures that compromise their influence', in their being 'resistance-prone' and in the corresponding propensity of the government to 'back down' from any all-out confrontation with the citizenry, or in its being 'resistance-averse'.[74]

Aside from the pathos of resistance—so unspecific of republicanism as to be found, along with an emphasis on freedom as non-domination, in the liberal views of John Locke[75]—there is little in Pettit's republicanism not also present in political liberalism.

---

[71] ibid 301.

[72] Pettit reworks this example in terms of entrusting the key to a cupboard where alcoholic beverages are stored to another person 'with instructions not to heed a request for the key except at twenty-four hours' notice. When you suffer a rebuff to a request for the key now, then you will certainly endure interference and frustration; the element of consent, contrary to the freedom-of-contract idea, does not change the fact that you want the key now and I am refusing to hand it over. But you will not suffer any loss of freedom in the presence of such interference, for while I impose a will that is hostile to your current wishes, this imposition is subject to your control. The interference you endure, as it is traditionally phrased, is of a non-arbitrary form; it does not express my will and does not reflect my arbitrium', ibid 152.

[73] ibid 305.

[74] ibid 304–05.

[75] See John Locke's definition of the 'Freedom of Men under Government' as, among other things, the freedom 'not to be subject to the inconstant, uncertain, unknown, Arbitrary Will of another Man', *Two Treatises of Government* (1690), with an introduction and notes by Peter Laslett (New American Library 1965), *Second Treatise* (hereafter Locke, *Second Treatise*) § 22, 324. On the right of rebellion against a tyrannical government, see ibid § 212–43, 455–77.

Chapter 3 of *On the People's Terms*, entitled 'Political Legitimacy', directly engages political liberalism. Somewhat surprisingly, Pettit accuses Rawls of conflating justice and legitimacy and reducing legitimacy to justice.[76] In Pettit's words,

> Justice, in the new contractualist formulation, is easily confounded with this [legitimacy]. It is the ideal of having a social order that is imposed only insofar as it satisfies terms that people could have rationally endorsed, even if they didn't: in Rawls's (1995: 148) way of thinking, 'terms that all reasonable parties may reasonably be expected to endorse'. The difference in formulation is subtle but it may mark a deep divide. Even an order that is not suitably supported by its people, as they are actually disposed, might satisfy terms that they would endorse if they were properly rational or reasonable.[77]

This interpretation flies in the face of Rawls's extended discussion of the 'liberal principle of legitimacy', quoted by Pettit only in order to derive from it the obvious requirement that the 'basic structure and its public policies are to be justifiable to all citizens'. Legitimacy so understood 'depends only on the fact that the order imposed is such that it could be justified' to the citizens. According to Pettit, Rawls does not offer a conception of *legitimacy* proper, but a reformulation of the standard contract-theoretical conception of *justice*.

Another problematic element in Pettit's interpretation of Rawls consists in the fact that the liberal principle of legitimacy submits the institutions' acts to the test of consistency with the constitutional essentials (the underlying political conception of justice, the basic structure, and the system of the basic liberties and rights) *not* (as Pettit suggests) as they could have been rationally endorsed by the citizens in the original position, but rather as they may be endorsed by the citizens as free and equal (thus after Pettit's 'eyeballs test' has *already* been passed by the polity).

Furthermore, the liberal principle of legitimacy is distinct from assessments of justice on three other counts, all neglected by Pettit. First, discussions about legitimacy do not take place in the original position but in the actual political arena, and are conducted by actual citizens, under no veil of ignorance and in terms not of rationality alone, but combining considerations of *rationality* and *reasonableness*. Second, at stake within debates over legitimacy are not the principles that should inspire a political conception of justice, but the legitimacy of single legislative, administrative, and judicial acts or 'exercises of power', located on the vertical axis of the relation of office-holders to citizens and not on the horizontal axis of the relation among citizens. Third, Rawls's liberal principle of legitimacy offers a version of the 'tough luck test' that equates the test with consistency with the constitutional essentials and not, as Pettit's understanding of legitimacy requires, with the piecemeal independent justification of single exercises of legislative, executive, and judicial authority. In contexts of hyperpluralism and systemic complexity, to ground the legitimacy of single exercises

---

[76] A separate contention concerns then Rawls's view of justice. Pettit defends a view that revolves around an equivalent of the first principle and claims to derive the second principle from the notion of equal maximal freedom. See Pettit, *People's Terms* (n 68) 144 and 184–86.
[77] ibid 144.

of coercive authority on the consent of the citizens is likely to overburden the capacity of constituencies (and theorists alike) to bring these assessments to any form of consent-worthy coherence.

Finally, whereas Rawls's political liberalism offers an elaborate account of dualistic democracy, and of the attendant relation of constituent to constituted power, Pettit only pays lip service to a dualistic model of democracy. Drawing on the work of Oliver MacDonagh, he reconstructs the transformation of the British institutional order after the debates about the Great Reform Bill of 1832. Massive political pressure, inspired by the moral outrage stirred by the abysmal condition of the working class under nineteenth-century laissez-faire capitalism, led to the extending of the franchise and to legislation protecting labour and ensuring participation. The moral 'intolerability' of the living conditions of the working class propelled fine-grained activities of petitioning, canvassing consent, fundraising, and electoral pressure that in the end transformed the constitutive rules of the British polity. The 'reform' of the unwritten constitution emerged as though an invisible political hand had given direction to these distinct forces. As Pettit describes this process, major constitutional change

> was a by-product of debates that were focused on rather more specific, short-haul policies. Those norms had a slowly mounting impact, not because humanitarian norm-compliance was a target at which anyone aimed, but because it was a common, barely recognized constraint on the concessions and adjustments that politicians were forced to make under the pressures of day-to-day politics.[78]

The teaching to be drawn is that

> The citizens of a dual-aspect democracy control for their government's satisfaction of accepted norms ... in the same way that the consumers in an ideal market control for the competitive pricing of available goods. The dual-aspect democracy gives effect to the political wishes of citizens, as the ideal market gives effect to the economic wishes of consumers. Each mode of organization has an empowering effect, helping to ensure that the relevant desires of the parties, economic or political, get to be satisfied.[79]

Pettit then questionably maps this model of democracy onto classical constitutionalism, exemplified by Lincoln's famous triad of 'government of the people, by the people, for the people' and by the distinction of constituent and constituted power, in order to offer a 'political ontology' articulated in six principles.[80] The 'incorporated' or constituted people are distinguished from the 'civic' or constituting people, and the priority of the latter over the former is affirmed. Both the constituting people and the 'incorporated' or constituted one relate to the commitments embedded in a constitution, but in fundamentally different ways:

---

[78] ibid 273.
[79] ibid 276.
[80] See ibid 288–92.

The constituted people will be responsible for the shape of the constitution to the degree that they can change it under constitutional rules of amendment. The constituting people will be responsible for it to the degree that not only can they change it under those rules of amendment, they can also change it by non-constitutional means: they can replace the old constitution with a new one, thereby establishing a novel state and a novel constituted people.[81]

Then, Pettit argues, constitution change through non-constitutional means amounts to regime change—as best exemplified by the transition from the Articles of Confederation to the Philadelphia Constitution. One of the problems with Pettit's view is its entailing that *any* constitutional change that follows from an 'unconventional adaptation'[82] should count as regime change, and any amendment that satisfies the formal requisites stipulated in the constitutional provisions should count as legitimate, regardless of substance. Another problem is that on implicit or structural entrenchment of constitutional essentials Pettit appears to waver between the notion that 'every law must be capable of being amended', albeit on the basis of supermajorities in the case of constitutional provisions,[83] and the idea that certain rights (eg women's right to vote) and provisions that spell out a 'norm of norms' of discursive reciprocity should be 'exempt from the democratic proviso',[84] that is, beyond majoritarian approval or repeal.

An additional difficulty incurred by Pettit's account is that the constituting and the constituted people are embodied in the same set of individuals and no distinction is drawn between the temporal span of the constituting people—the author of the constitution and of its subsequent transformations—and the constituted people as a set of voters or an electorate. While the constituted people is duly represented by the legislature, it remains utterly unclear whether the constituting people is represented by the separated branches of power, is supposed to directly reform the constitution outside the formal legal procedure for amendment, or is represented by the highest judicial interpreter of the constitution.

Finally, his denial of a systematic role for judicial review leads Pettit to understand the constitution as a market-like result of political forces operating at a lower level. It is hard to recover, within his works, a sense of the written or unwritten constitution as a legal framework designed for regulating ordinary legislation or as having an author in the intentional sense of the term.

Richard Bellamy's republicanism is even further removed from the insights of political liberalism. From the perspective of his 'political constitutionalism', the

---

[81] ibid 292.
[82] On the notion of 'unconventional adaptation', see Bruce Ackerman, *We the People*, volume 2, *Transformations* (Harvard University Press 1998) 8–15. For a discussion of different kinds of unconventional adaptation, see Alessandro Ferrara, 'Unconventional Adaptation and the Authenticity of a Constitution', in Richard Albert (ed), *Revolutionary Constitutionalism. Law, Legitimacy, Power* (Hart 2020) 157–68.
[83] Pettit, *Republicanism* (n 66) 180.
[84] Pettit, *People's Terms* (n 68) 25 and 255. Thanks are due to Leonardo Fiorespino for having brought this point to my attention. See his enlightening discussion of Pettit's oscillation between two competing models of constitutionalism, Leonardo Fiorespino, *Radical Democracy and Populism: A Thin Red Line?* (Springer 2022) 138–42.

constitution takes on a function different to the strictly regulatory role of 'law of lawmaking'. In his words,

> the constitution represents a fundamental structure for reaching collective decisions about social arrangements in a democratic way. That is, in a way that treats citizens as entitled to having their concerns equally respected when it comes to deciding the best way to pursue their collective interests.[85]

From Bellamy's perspective, 'the democratic process *is* the constitution' in a fourfold sense. First, rather than being equated with a 'basic *law* or *norm*', the constitution should be understood as 'a basic framework for resolving our disagreements—albeit one that is also the subject of political debate'. Second, 'the constitution is identified with the political rather than the legal system, and in particular with the ways political power is organized and divided'. Third, the 'political constitutionalist' considers 'law as functioning as politically as democratic politics' and, fourth, offers 'a normative account of the democratic political system'.[86]

Bellamy's political constitutionalism forfeits the regulatory function of a constitution, which depends on the constitution's having a legally superordinate status equivalent to that of constitutive rules in any structured game. The constitution then becomes a *descriptive*, rather than normative, account of the 'politeia' or basic structure of a given polity. When equated with the democratic process as such, the constitution undergoes a complete self-destruction. As Aristotle once noticed in relation to Athenian direct, assembly-centred democracy, when the will of the participants ongoingly reshapes the constitution, 'there is no constitution': for 'no decree' of the assembly—and, for us, no legal provision legislated by parliamentary institutions that merely reflect the will of the voters—'can have general validity', that is, last beyond the time frame during which that assembly or electoral will lasts.[87]

In Bellamy's book, co-authored with Dario Castiglione, *From Maastricht to Brexit*, the prospect of a constitution for the EU in the formal sense of the term, as a written document, is presented as a hindrance to the ability of 'the EU institutions to check and balance each other' and to the 'contestatory power of ordinary citizens'.[88] Taking issue with the liberal view which, according to him, equates the rule of law 'with the upholding of rights by an independent judiciary', Bellamy spells out his republican political constitutionalism as grounding justice in the process of politics:

> political mechanisms not only ensure all are subject to the laws and that no one can be judge in their own case—the traditional tasks of the separation of powers—but also that the laws connect with the understandings and activities of those to whom they are to apply—the side benefit of dispersing power so that more people have a say in its enactment.[89]

---

[85] See Richard Bellamy, *Political Constitutionalism: A Republican Defence of the Constitutionality of Democracy* (Cambridge University Press 2007) (hereafter Bellamy, *Political Constitutionalism*) 4.
[86] ibid 5.
[87] Aristotle, *The Politics*, translated by TA Sinclair (Penguin 1992) 251 (1292a31).
[88] Richard Bellamy and Dario Castiglione, *From Maastricht to Brexit* (Rowman and Littlefield 2019), 66.
[89] ibid 81.

d. Agonistic conceptions of democracy: Mouffe and Tully

Under the heading of 'agonism' I include a group of political theorists,[90] who define themselves in opposition to an alleged liberal penchant for reconciliatory schemes aimed at neutralizing political and social conflict. As representatives for this strand, I will address the critiques of liberalism put forward by Chantal Mouffe and James Tully. Theorists of agonistic democracy emphasize the ineliminability and centrality of conflict and accuse *all* forms of liberalism, including political liberalism, of introducing a dubious distinction between 'acceptable diversity', which offers liberalism a window-dressing case for presenting itself as the epitome of toleration, and 'unruly diversity', to be contained and excluded in good conscience. Rawls is accused of preemptively screening out the really troublesome instances of diversity and immunizing overlapping consensus from serious challenges by way of distinguishing 'reasonable pluralism' and pluralism as such. In the words of a defender of 'agonistic pluralism',

> there is only a multiplicity of identities without any common denominator, and it is impossible to distinguish between differences that exist but should not exist and differences that do not exist but should exist. What such [liberal] pluralism misses is the dimension of the political. Relations of power and antagonism are erased and we are left with the typical liberal illusion of a pluralism without antagonism.[91]

According to Mouffe, political liberalism is not immune from indulging in such illusion of a 'pluralism without antagonism'—a truly inevitable illusion if Mouffe herself, in her latest work, comes to consider it crucial that in complex societies conflict 'not take the form of an "antagonism" (struggle between enemies) but of an "agonism" (struggle between adversaries)' and that confrontation 'take place within democratic institutions',[92] in other words within a constitutional framework shared by the conflicting parties.

Rawls, according to Mouffe, uses his notion of the reasonable person (*qua* loyal cooperator respectful of the burdens of judgment) in order to screen out the *full range* of diverse comprehensive conceptions: reasonable conceptions, admitted to the overlapping consensus and to 'legitimate pluralism', are those endorsed by people who, by being reasonable, have already embraced a liberal outlook. After conflating the reasonable person with the liberal person, Mouffe claims that admitted to the space of

---

[90] See Chantal Mouffe, *The Democratic Paradox* (Verso 2000) (hereafter Mouffe, Democratic Paradox), *Agonistics: Thinking the World Politically* (Verso, 2013), *For a Left Populism* (Verso 2018) (hereafter Mouffe, Left Populism); William Connolly, *The Ethos of Pluralization* (University Minnesota Press 1995), *Pluralism* (Duke University Press 2005); James Tully, *Strange Multiplicity: Constitutionalism in an Age of Diversity* (Cambridge University Press 1995) and *Public Philosophy in a New Key. Vol 1: Democracy and Civic Freedom* (Cambridge University Press 2008) (hereafter Tully, Public Philosophy); Edward C Wingenbach, *Institutionalizing Agonistic Democracy: Post-Foundationalism and Political Liberalism* (Ashgate 2011); Stephen K White, *The Ethos of a Late-Modern Citizen* (Harvard University Press 2009), *A Democratic Bearing: Admirable Citizens, Uneven Injustice, and Critical Theory* (Cambridge University Press 2017).
[91] Mouffe, Democratic Paradox (n 90) 20.
[92] Mouffe, Left Populism (n 90) 91–92.

legitimate pluralism are only those comprehensive conceptions that do not question liberal principles,[93] as though her own distinction of *acceptable* agonistic and *unacceptable* antagonistic confrontations (outlined in *For a Left Populism*) did not repeat the same scheme of reasoning. Be that as it may, Mouffe accuses Rawls of hiding his contingent and 'groundless' stance in favour of reasonability under a veneer of moral universalism, as though the exclusion of the unreasonable doctrines and persons were mandated by some moral intuition external to politics. In the end, according to Mouffe, Rawls denies that 'like any other regime, modern pluralist democracy constitutes a system of relations of power', and renders 'the democratic challenging of these forms of power illegitimate': political liberalism, no less than all other kinds of liberalism, tries to exclude its adversaries from the arena while pretending to stand on neutral ground.[94]

Mouffe's agonistic critique of Rawls fails any test of minimal interpretive accuracy. First, she equates reasonable people with liberals, and on this basis accuses Rawls of stacking the deck: reasonable, and as such admitted to the overlapping consensus, are only those doctrines, endorsed by reasonable people, that already are liberal. No passage in *Political Liberalism*, however, suggests that reasonability is a virtue only of people inclined towards liberalism. The ingredients of reasonability are (i) the acceptance of the burdens of judgment and (ii) the willingness to take part in a cooperation with others 'on terms all can accept'[95]—two qualities that people from all sorts of comprehensive conceptions, religious and secular, can possess. If 'epistemic humility' and a disposition towards reciprocity were possible only for those who move within the circle of liberalism, the whole point of moving from the comprehensive versions of liberalism (Kant, Mill, Constant) to political liberalism would become obscure. If an argumentative sleight of hand takes place, that is committed by Mouffe when she unduly interprets Rawls's phrase 'on terms that all can accept' as meaning 'on terms that all and only those who already are liberal can accept'.

Second, the idea of a 'moralization' of the exclusion of the unreasonable from overlapping consensus, as though such exclusion was mandated by a moral intuition external to politics, flies in the face of the distinction, drawn by Rawls, of *moral* versus *political* constructivism and of his idea of completing the autonomization of politics from 'metaphysical' positions.[96]

Third, in rejecting 'the very possibility of a non-exclusive public sphere of rational argument where a non-coercive consensus could be attained', because such a project allegedly includes a longing for 'oneness' and reconciliation, Mouffe forfeits all possibility of distinguishing between coercive and non-coercive forms of political authority. Consequently, she forfeits all possibility of identifying any foothold on which a critique of existing hegemonic practices, existing grammars of the political, existing patterns of exclusion could lay a claim to constituting anything other than an aspirational counter-hegemony.

---

[93] Mouffe, *Democratic Paradox* (n 90) 25.
[94] ibid 31–32.
[95] Rawls, *PL* 50.
[96] *PL* 93–101.

In her latest book, Mouffe reiterates her critique and through her distinction of 'antagonism' (ie revolutionary protest that calls into question the entire basic structure of the polity) and 'agonism' (ie radical contestation of policies, authorities, and institutions within the bounds of the constitutional frame)[97] proposes a crypto-liberal scheme: pluralism is acceptable only within the limits of 'agonism'. The agonistic perspective, advocated by Mouffe, just reduces itself to a rhetorical emphasis on the 'impossibility of a final reconciliation',[98] which adds little to the burdens of judgment. In her words, 'by envisaging the confrontation in terms of adversaries and not on a friend/enemy mode, because that might lead to civil war, it allows such a confrontation to take place *within democratic institutions*'.[99] The core of political liberalism remains unscathed by Mouffe's agonistic rhetoric of conflict and contestation. It is hard to see how Mouffe's own proposal for a left populism could escape the very same fate of liberalism, once she advocates adversarial agonistic relations and excludes antagonistic relations among partisans. Mouffe would be at pains to deny that agonistic, as opposed to antagonistic, relations are made possible by the parties' sharing a certain common ground of respect for diversity and plurality—a common ground which then logically must be immune from the us/them division.

James Tully's constitutional agonism fares somewhat better in terms of internal consistency and embeds a balance of difference and consensual normativity. Political freedom for him partakes of both. Drawing on Arendt, Wittgenstein, Foucault, and Skinner, Tully interestingly argues that 'no game is completely circumscribed by rules':

> If it is always possible to go on differently, if a consensus on the rules has an element of 'non-consensuality', then an important aspect of concrete human freedom will be 'testing' the rules and purported meta-rules of the current game, ensuring that they are open to question and challenge with as little rigidity or domination as possible, and experimenting with their modification in practice, so humans are able to think and act differently.[100]

This element of 'non-consensuality' in democratic freedom affects citizenship. Ingredients such as equal rights and duties, fundamental principles of justice, Rawls's 'constitutional essentials', shared procedures of validation and authorization, and our sense of political identity or of the 'we' are, according to Tully's version of agonism, to be complemented by *something else*. In a move indebted to Arendt, but somehow also to Saussure's distinction of 'langue' and 'parole', Tully calls these elements

> the 'elaborate framework', not the activity, of citizenship, of being a free people. To concentrate on them is to mistake the stage-setting for the play. More importantly, citizens (and theorists) disagree about them. They are always open to question,

---

[97] 'The agonistic confrontation is different from the antagonistic one, not because it allows for a possible consensus, but because the opponent is not considered an enemy to be destroyed but an adversary whose existence is perceived as legitimate', Mouffe, *Left Populism* (n 90) 91. A similar distinction was outlined earlier in *Democratic Paradox* (n 90) 13.

[98] Mouffe, *Left Populism* (n 90) 92.

[99] ibid (emphasis added).

[100] Tully, *Public Philosophy* (n 90) 144.

disagreement, contestation, deliberation, negotiation and change over time in the course of citizen participation, from discussing a municipal by-law to revolution. Principles, rights, goods and identities are thus constituents of the 'framework' in a special sense. Politics is a type of game in which the framework—the rules of the game—can come up for deliberation and amendment in the course of the game. At any one time, some constituents are held firm and provide the ground for questioning others, but which elements constitute the shared 'background' sufficient for politics to emerge and which constitute the disputed 'foreground' vary. There is not a distinction between the two that stands outside the game, beyond question for all time. Consequently, what citizens share is nothing more or less than being in on the dialogues over how and by whom power is exercised, which take place both within and over the rules of the dialogues.[101]

Saussure's distinction of 'langue' and 'parole' helps us grasp the strong complementarity of normativity and contestation in Tully's variety of agonism—a complementarity obscured in forms of agonism, such as Mouffe's, that denounce normativity as illusory and masking power relations. 'Parole' could not exist without the normativity of 'langue', yet 'langue' cannot draw its normative dimension from any other source than 'parole':

Agreement, when it occurs, is always non-consensual to some extent. At its best, free individuals and groups establish a certain provisional overlapping consensus as the result of a critical dialogue within and on the spatial-temporal field of power and norms in which they find themselves. But, for any number of reasons, the best of agreements remain potentially open to reasonable disagreement and dissent.[102]

Based on the doctrine of the burdens of judgment, the normativity of constitutional essentials need not be assigned any more essentialist status than that of the planks of the ship not to be moved about in our ongoing reconstruction at sea. Tully's remark, however, offers a possibility of correcting a blind spot of Rawls's view of the overlapping consensus. The transition from a modus vivendi to a 'constitutional consensus' (when citizens share a certain understanding of rights but contend over the application and implications of these rights) to a full overlapping consensus (when citizens come to largely agree also on the practical implications of rights) seems to be unidirectional. What is controversial across different comprehensive conceptions may at a certain juncture become 'political' through the work of public reason and the trust-building capacity of a democratic debate under the aegis of the principle of civility. However, in *Political Liberalism* it remains quite obscure how constitutional provisions, political values, as well as interpretations of rights—which were previously 'political' and thus part and parcel of the overlapping consensus—may over time cross the border in the opposite direction and 'return', so to speak, to be controversial. A reflection of this blind spot can be found in Rawls's argument for 'structural entrenchment', based on a progressivist view of the expansion of rights. In this argument a residue of the

---

[101] ibid 146–47.
[102] ibid 147 (emphasis added).

Enlightenment view of the cumulativity of knowledge and of history as progress can be detected, in the work of a theorist who has certainly gone to the greatest length in distancing his normative political and legal philosophy from the ideological elements of the Enlightenment.[103]

e. Modus-vivendi and 'political-realist' liberalism: Gray and Williams

Among the competitors of 'political liberalism', a kind of 'normatively minimalist' liberalism must be counted, whose champions are John Gray, Bernard Williams, Raymond Geuss, and others.[104] In spite of the diversity of nuances, philosophical agendas, and theoretical propensities, these defenders of what Judith Shklar named the 'liberalism of fear' incur similar difficulties. For brevity's sake, I will address only the work of Grey and Williams as representatives for the whole trend.

In a chapter of *The Two Faces of Liberalism* entitled 'Modus Vivendi', Gray highlights two 'philosophies' that struggle for the soul of liberalism:

> In one, toleration is justified as a means to truth. In this view, toleration is an instrument of rational consensus, and a diversity of ways of life is endured in the faith that it is destined to disappear. In the other, toleration is valued as a condition of peace, and divergent ways of living are welcomed as marks of diversity in the good life. The first conception supports an ideal of ultimate convergence on values, the latter an ideal of *modus vivendi*. Liberalism's future lies in its turning its face away from the ideal of rational consensus and looking instead to *modus vivendi*.[105]

The modus-vivendi liberalism propounded by Gray reaches back to Hobbes. Freeing ourselves from the letter of Hobbes's argument, he suggests that we reformulate his teaching in pluralist terms:

> The end of politics is not the mere absence of war, but a *modus vivendi* among goods and evils.... Amended in this way, Hobbes's thought implies that the most important feature of any regime is not how it succeeds in promoting any particular value. It is how well it enables conflicts among values to be negotiated. The test of legitimacy for

---

[103] This point is addressed in Alessandro Ferrara, *Justice and Judgment: The Rise and the Prospect of the Judgment Model in Contemporary Political Philosophy* (Sage 1999) (hereafter Ferrara, *Justice and Judgment*) 155–56.

[104] Representative of this strand are Bernard Williams, *In the Beginning Was the Deed: Realism and Moralism in Political Argument*, selected, edited, and with an introduction by G Hawthorn (Princeton University Press 2005) (hereafter Williams, *In the Beginning*); John Gray, *Two Faces of Liberalism* (Polity 2000) (hereafter Gray, *Two Faces*); Raymond Geuss, *Philosophy and Real Politics* (Princeton University Press 2008). For illuminating reviews and critical commentaries, see William Galston, 'Realism in Political Theory' (2010) 9(4) European Journal of Political Theory, 385–411; William Scheuerman, 'The Realist Revival in Political Philosophy, or: Why New Is Not Always Improved' (2010) 50(6) International Politics 798–814; Jonathan Floyd and Marc Stears (eds), *Political Philosophy versus History? Contextualism and Real Politics in Contemporary Political Thought* (Cambridge University Press 2011).

[105] Gray, *Two Faces* (n 104) 105.

any regime is its success in mediating conflicts of values—including rival ideals of justice.[106]

Gray's neo-Hobbesian rethinking of liberalism carries two methodological consequences. First, 'the trundling distinction between *de facto* and *de jure* authority', the pivot on which any and every normative view hinges, is now called 'less than helpful'. Second, 'the demarcation of reasons of principle from reasons of prudence' is declared untenable. According to Gray, such distinction derives from the illusion that morality overrides all other considerations and that its demands are 'normally self-evident to reasonable people'.[107]

It would be tempting to reject these formulations as gross misunderstandings of political liberalism. Countless times Rawls underscored that nothing, not even public reason, can miraculously make the burdens of judgment vanish and that the zeal to embody the whole truth in politics is ultimately incompatible with democracy. Although he acknowledges that political liberalism rejects the perfectionist idea of legitimacy as resting on a regime's responsiveness to some 'supreme virtue', Gray accuses Rawls of stopping halfway and still nurturing the illusory faith in an overlapping consensus on a political conception of justice. Furthermore, both Gray and political liberalism acknowledge that some 'primary goods' are indispensable preconditions for any worthwhile human life. Whereas Rawls, however, allegedly embraces the optimistic view that 'primary goods do not conflict with one another', Gray's neo-Hobbesian liberalism embeds the realistic view that these goods, including rights, do not form a 'consistent, harmonious system' but are often at war with one another.

Gray's interpretation of Rawls on primary goods is inaccurate on at least one account. Rawls's overlapping consensus on a political conception of justice is meant as an ideal-theory end-state to be striven for or used as a yardstick, but by no means as an account of the current predicament of democratic societies. Such a predicament is best described as a 'constitutional consensus'[108] on rights and constitutional essentials but *not on their implications*. For example, citizens in all walks of life, including justices, agree on 'equal protection of the laws' or 'free speech', but may disagree on what these formulae imply. Such disagreement obviously extends to the way the different primary goods and the basic liberties ought to be balanced and, if necessary, prioritized. In the next section, Gray attributes to Rawls the intent 'to formulate principles of justice which any reasonable person is bound to accept, or at any rate cannot reject, regardless of her conception of the good. The result is a liberal philosophy of right in which justice is meant to have priority over all other goods'.[109] Again, this interpretation is inaccurate: as stated above, as of 1980 the normative credentials of justice as fairness do not rest for Rawls on its being 'being true to an order antecedent to and given to us', as Gray would have it, but simply on its being the political conception of justice 'most reasonable for us'.[110]

---

[106] ibid 133.
[107] ibid.
[108] Rawls, *PL* 164–68.
[109] Gray, *Two Faces* (n 104) 135.
[110] See n 6, above.

Considering now the constructive part of modus-vivendi liberalism, Gray's priority of peace over justice leads to three counterintuitive consequences. *First*, in the absence of any screening of the 'ways of life' or 'conceptions of the good' susceptible of being party to a modus vivendi, *any* context could be the setting of a modus vivendi. Even in Syria then, a modus vivendi could be achieved among the Assad regime, Isis, and Al-Nusra, and such a modus vivendi would not differ in essence from the one that regulates the coexistence of different conceptions of the good in France or the UK. Of course, it would be different in the obvious sense that no two modi vivendi are identical, but not so different as to require that we come up with a different term. That questionable implication needs to be buttressed by a robust argument that is nowhere in sight.

Second, the idea that all human groupings have an interest in peaceful coexistence contributes little to explaining why human groupings that have wildly disproportionate stakes in the stability of an agreement (say, the United States of America and the Republic of San Marino) should equally abide by its terms. In the end, the explanation of stability comes to rely on the classical political-realist notion of balance of power, according to which an agreement has a chance for stability only when the parties have roughly equal power and stakes.

Third, Gray's questioning the distinction of reasons of principle and of prudence leads his liberalism to rest on a dubious moral phenomenology. The sense of justice plays no role distinct from the rational pursuit of one's advantage, as though no difference existed between the point of view of what is to my or our advantage and what is fair to *all* the parties concerned.

Were these not, in and of themselves, formidable difficulties, Gray's project of a liberalism of modus vivendi is affected by an internal tension between its underlying intent and the means through which such intent is carried out. Modus vivendi is the affirmation of the primacy of peace, of peaceful coexistence over all other political values: *primum vivere*. However, Gray recoils from accepting the implications of his own argument. Aware of the risk that the priority of peace might lead to the acceptance of the most horrible forms of injustice, Gray hastens to add that 'modus vivendi is far from the idea that anything goes.... There are limits to modus vivendi'.[111] These limits, as it somewhat surprisingly turns out, are set by 'universal human values'. These putatively universal values, earlier denounced as incapable of generating a view of justice,[112] are now invoked in order to 'set ethical limits on the pursuit of modus vivendi'.[113]

Furthermore, the limit-setting cogency of these values seems to be accepted not because it is prudent and expedient to do so, but because we recognize their intrinsic worth, their being 'just'. Gray's modus-vivendi liberalism, in order to avoid turning into a caricature-like idea of 'might makes right' or 'anything goes', in the end comes back full circle to presupposing non-prudential, actually even 'universally' cogent, values that set limits on legitimate forms of modus vivendi. It also surreptitiously reinstates the distinction between prudential and principled motivations. The 'universal

---

[111] Gray, *Two Faces* (n 104) 20.
[112] ibid 19.
[113] ibid 20.

52 WHY POLITICAL LIBERALISM?

values' that mark the red line between an acceptable and an unacceptable modus vivendi evidently cannot be endorsed for prudential reasons: so Gray needs, *malgré lui*, to presuppose that at least some normative contents are endorsed for reason of principle only, because they are *just*. Modus vivendi, the concept that should have emancipated us from the spell of universal normativity—to which Rawlsian liberalism falls prey hook, line, and sinker—now appears to presuppose 'universal values'.

To sum up, Gray's idea of modus vivendi as the only model for the polity suffers from the same weakness that affects pacifism as a philosophical position on war. Pacifism only makes sense as a radical outlook à la Gandhi that rules out any exception, *including self-defence*. The moment pacifists allow for any exception—taking arms in self-defence—they turn into theorists of 'just war'. Their position becomes indistinguishable from a very demanding and narrow theory of just war, which admits only 'war in self-defence'.[114] A similar flaw affects neo-Hobbesian liberalism. Modus-vivendi liberalism is consistent and coherent only as an extreme position, prepared to claim that any agreement whatsoever, insofar as it can secure any kind of peace, even a Hitlerian peace, is better than conflict. The moment modus-vivendi theorists reintroduce principled, value-based, normative *limits* to the kind of admissible modus vivendi, they fall back into a kind of normative theory, and a very poor one at that—because the invoked 'universal values' are ad hoc and come virtually from nowhere.

Many of the flaws of Gray's liberalism can also be found in Bernard Williams's sophisticated political realism. Differently from the theorists who, in the footsteps of Weber and Schumpeter, have enervated the critical dimension of legitimacy by equating it with a mere 'belief in legitimacy', Williams must be credited with challenging what he calls 'moralism'—the subordination of politics to a standard of legitimacy derived from moral principles or from a 'moral reading of the Constitution' (Dworkin)—by giving us a competing realist account of what can count as a *justified belief in the legitimacy of authority*.

Along Hobbesian lines, Williams identifies the 'first political question', on which the edifice of political philosophy rests, 'as the securing of order, protection, safety, trust, and the conditions of cooperation. It is "first" because solving it is the condition of solving, indeed posing, any others'.[115] While crude forms of political realism in the past failed to adequately distinguish between legitimate authority and arbitrary power, Williams vindicates political realism for the twenty-first century by building into it the normative assumption, rejected by Gray, that such distinction makes sense. To be sure, 'the first question' should be answered without reference to moral principles, but such an answer is only a first step towards meeting the 'basic legitimation demand'. Then for a polity to *meet the basic legitimation demand* (and thus for its authorities to be *legitimate*) means to provide an 'acceptable' solution to the first political problem—as opposed to its providing a solution that is merely de facto accepted by the subjects of that polity.[116] One even wonders why this view of legitimacy should be considered a political-realist one after all.

---

[114] For a more elaborated version of this argument see Andrea Salvatore, *Guerra giusta? Morale e politica dei conflitti armati* (Manifesto Libri 2016), 65–68. See also Andrea Salvatore, *Il pacifismo* (Carocci 2010).
[115] Williams, *In the Beginning* (n 104) 3.
[116] Williams comes very close to a normative account of legitimacy when he states that: 'The situation of one lot of people terrorizing another lot of people is not per se a political situation: it is, rather, the situation

The answer is that although all forms of political authority must answer the first question in order to be legitimate, not all need to meet the basic legitimation demand *in the same way*. In some parts of the world, people may place *additional* requisites on authority, over and beyond answering the first question: for example, the requisite that authority also meet certain liberal-democratic standards. This is the element of political realism that survives in Williams's account. Nothing can be said for liberal democracy, other than the fact that in some parts of the world—and 'for the time being', one should add—liberal-democratic credentials are taken as requisites for the legitimacy of authorities.

Two consequences follow. *First*, both democratic and *non*-democratic forms of authority may be legitimate, as Gray also emphasizes. *Second*, those who once posed additional liberal-democratic constraints on authority (in the guise of a bill of rights, or the presumption that political justification must be *equally* acceptable to *everyone* subject to the authority), in a changed historical constellation may cease to pose them. Now, if legitimate authority is required to satisfy liberal standards only after the onset of modernity, we have 'no ground for saying that all non-liberal states in the past were illegitimate, and it would be a silly thing to say'.[117] For a structure of authority to claim legitimacy within its own parameters means that 'it makes sense to us as such a structure',[118] where 'making sense' means something more than just the factual operation of a certain power structure. To 'make sense' is understood by Williams as a *descriptive* notion when applied to a political situation other than our own, but as a *normative* notion when applied to *our case*, insofar as the structure of authority confronting us is one that '*we* should accept'.[119] What exactly does the expression 'should' mean, from Williams's political-realist point of view?

Criticizing the 'moralism' of those who, like Rawls and Dworkin, allegedly locate such 'ought' in unsituated principles or in the moral significance of the constitution, Williams advocates a Weberian ethics of responsibility and a rethinking of 'the political'. We can consider legitimate certain contemporary non-liberal states. The notion of legitimacy used in this case is *normative* insofar as these non-liberal societies 'co-exist' with ours and thus 'cannot be separated from us by the relativism of distance'.[120] Discussions about legitimate authority, Williams contends, must proceed from realistic assumptions about the chances of these societies to achieve stability: in particular, 'if the current legitimation is fairly stable, the society will not anyway satisfy the other familiar conditions on revolt'.[121]

Williams's position incurs three difficulties. *First*, his adoption of a Hobbesian question as the fundamental one of political reflection cannot go unquestioned. Although

---

which the existence of the political is in the first place supposed to alleviate (replace). If the power of one lot of people over another is to represent a solution to the first political question, and not itself be part of the problem, *something* has to be said to explain (to the less empowered, to concerned bystanders, to children being educated in this structure, etc) what the difference is between the solution and the problem, and that cannot simply be an account of successful domination. It has to be something in the mode of justifying explanation or legitimation: hence the Basic Legitimation Demand', ibid 8.

[117] ibid 14.
[118] ibid.
[119] ibid 11 (emphasis added).
[120] ibid 14.
[121] ibid.

trust and the conditions of cooperation are mentioned, a residue of the old-fashioned political realism survives in Hobbes's 'priority of stability over justice'. For a different view, let us recall Locke's point that unjust political arrangements, such as absolute monarchy, may result in a *worse* predicament than the imperfect order of the state of nature:[122] the test of political legitimacy is then more demanding than the mere ensuring of order. The purpose of the Lockean commonwealth is to *avoid oppression*, where oppression certainly *includes* the deprivation of life, but also includes being deprived of one's property and being forced to live according to principles one cannot endorse. A just commonwealth is one in which not only life is protected, but rights are respected, authorities are subject to the law, and the principles of government are endorsed by the citizens: together these features define an alternative 'first question of politics' premised on 'the priority of justice over stability', all the way to authorizing rebellion against established authority. Williams's selection of a Hobbesian version of the first political question, posited as self-evident, biases the basic legitimation demand in a minimalist direction: 'Have you protected my life?' and 'Have you ensured order?' are the benchmark questions for testing authority's legitimacy. A Lockean version of the first political question would generate a different benchmark question, which does not reject but *expands* the Hobbesian one: 'Have you protected me from oppression?'. Williams's selection of a Hobbesian 'first question' leads his realism to question-begging. His anti-normative argument depends on his having *already* presupposed a political-realist understanding of how the question of legitimate authority must be approached.

The *second* difficulty is that while Williams concedes that several competing assessments of the legitimacy of authority—some critical, others apologetic—will seek public acceptance in the public forum, his rejection of a normative standpoint leaves him unable to specify the basis on which the factually prevailing narrative of legitimation could ever be challenged.

Third, like most authors discussed above, also Williams fails to acknowledge the significance of Rawls's turn from the framework of A *Theory of Justice* to that of *Political Liberalism*, and inaccurately attributes to Rawls a view of legitimacy as connected with a moral principle. In *Political Liberalism*, instead, the standard of legitimacy is harnessed to a political conception of justice endorsed by citizens who embrace *diverse* moral comprehensive conceptions. Rawls's declared goal is to investigate the conditions that enable a *stable and just* society to last over time despite broad moral disagreement among its citizens. This modified understanding of legitimacy is partially acknowledged by Williams in his review of *Political Liberalism*,[123] which contains important insights, but is overlooked in the chapter 'Realism and Moralism in Political Theory', within *In the Beginning Was the Deed*. The Rawlsian liberal principle of legitimacy is unduly ignored, along with fact that *Political Liberalism* completes the autonomization of politics by also outlining, over and beyond the autonomization of

---

[122] Locke, *Second Treatise* (n 99) § 13, 316–17.
[123] See Bernard Williams, 'A Fair State', Review of Rawls's Political Liberalism (1993) 15 London Review of Books, 7.

politics from morality theorized by Machiavelli, the autonomization of politics from theory.[124]

The case of Gray and Williams reveals an inability—on the part of 'political realist' critics—to grasp the difference between a normativity of principles and the exemplary normativity of the reasonable. Either disregarding, or paying only lip service to, the paradigm shift that separates *A Theory of Justice* from *Political Liberalism*, the neo-Hobbesian critics fail to notice that the justification of justice as fairness, now taken as 'the most reasonable doctrine for us', has shifted away from so-called moralism and instead brings together normativity and plurality in an innovative way. The reasonable and the 'most reasonable' remain rooted in the situatedness of the political subject to whom political justification is owed. If we want to spell out what 'most-reasonableness' means, we find the intuition—ultimately not alien to the advocates of modus vivendi—that most reasonable for us is the political conception of justice which best comports with the historical plurality of reasonable comprehensive conceptions found in our context and best enables everyone to abide by the common normativity without betraying their own comprehensive intuitions. What makes a political conception of justice most reasonable is not responsiveness to something beyond us, but its superior ability—relative to its competitors—for allowing each of us to remain in alignment or resonance with ourselves while abiding by its intimations.

What a normative political philosopher does, and realist critics of Rawls keep missing, is to bridge a gap between positions whose supporters are unaware of the common ground they share. The philosopher is to unravel that common ground, show how broader than suspected it is and how it can support institutional implementation. In Rawls's words, one of the tasks of a normative political philosophy is

> to focus on deeply disputed questions and to see whether, despite appearances, some underlying basis of philosophical and moral agreement can be uncovered, or differences can at least be narrowed so that social cooperation on a footing of mutual respect among citizens can still be maintained.[125]

This normative understanding of a 'stable *and* just' society shares with the modus vivendi propounded by Gray and the realism advocated by Williams a total independence from context-transcendent values. But Rawls does not need to inconsistently invoke unsituated standards from 'out of the cave' when it comes to blocking locally degenerated patterns of coexistence: these pacts are *suboptimal*—that is, less than 'most reasonable'—in their forcing some of the citizens to suffer misalignment from their own moral intuitions and comprehensive conceptions.[126] My point, however, is not simply that Rawls's view of a just and stable society is possibly more coherent

---

[124] On this interpretation of Rawls's contribution to political philosophy, see Ferrara, *Democratic Horizon* (n 24) 27–30.
[125] John Rawls, *Lectures on the History of Political Philosophy*, edited by S Freeman (Harvard University Press 2007), 10.
[126] The normativity of the 'most reasonable', differently to the normativity of the 'most rational', is connected with exemplarity and cannot be reduced to the dynamic of subsumptive determinant judgment, to use Kant's terminology. It is bound up with the exemplarity-tracking capacity of reflective judgment. On this point, see Ferrara, *Force of the Example* (n 67) 72–79.

and consistent than Gray's and Williams's neo-Hobbesian views, but that Rawls's view can—if appropriately expanded—also respond to one important challenge that these authors raise: namely, to clarify how a political-liberal view of legitimacy could possibly convince the non-liberal publics present in complex societies.

f. Starting up where many leave off: a Hegelian approach to justice, post-deconstructionist views of community, and political liberalism

Finally, in response to the challenge of reconciling justice and plurality political liberalism outranks the responses offered by a set of philosophers keen on belabouring the nexus of subjectivity and difference, or subjectivity and recognition. Some belong in the tradition of post-deconstructionist philosophy—for example, Jean-Luc Nancy, Jacques Rancière, Maurice Blanchot, Giorgio Agamben, and Roberto Esposito—and others, for example Homi Bhabha, Adam Seligman, and Thomas Claviez, militate in other academic subcultures but share a similar train of thought. From the different field of critical theory, Axel Honneth's theory of recognition and ambitious attempt to work out a Hegelian approach to justice wind up in a similar relation to political liberalism. After tortuous argumentative steps and turns, all these authors eventually lead their patient readers to a philosophical height identified as the raising of the question: 'How can individuals and groups live together in full respect of their difference and without oppressing each other?'. In a different vocabulary, the same question constitutes not the conclusion, but the opening gambit of *Political Liberalism*, and is then followed by a detailed answer, which is hard to find in these philosophers' work.

In *Freedom's Right*, Honneth aspires to offer an account of normativity and justice more adequate than the normative approaches that revisit the Kantian ethics either along discursive lines (Habermas) or as normative thought-experiments (Rawls in *A Theory of Justice*). While Kantian models understand justice as conformity of the institutional texture of a society to some antecedent and self-standing principle, according to Honneth a Hegelian theory of justice avoids all appeal to such abstract normativity. It draws on a normative reconstruction of the values and normative standards already embedded in the social practices and institutions 'indispensable for social reproduction'.[127] Underlying a Hegelian theory of justice is the principle that 'social practices and institutions are "just" to the extent that they are capable of realizing *generally acceptable values*',[128] where 'just' means that such social practices and institutions further values that *deserve* to be universally accepted: freedom, in the first place. The general difficulty, which affects Honneth's Hegelian model of justice and puts it at a disadvantage relative to the paradigm of political liberalism, is its limited ability to accommodate pluralism. The closer relation of what is rational to what is real is paid for at the cost of having the theory depend on *one correct view* of what is rational and, which is somewhat more perplexing, on *one correct reconstruction* of what is real. This 'perfectionist' bias is signalled, among other things, by the recurrent reference to normative

---

[127] Axel Honneth, *Freedom's Right: The Social Foundations of Democratic Life* (J Ganahl tr, Polity Press 2014) (hereafter Honneth, *Freedom's Right*), 6.
[128] ibid 10.

ideas embedded in competing accounts as 'pathologies' and to discordant facts as 'misdevelopments'.

This methodological flaw results in a *threefold pattern of selectivity*. *First*, Honneth chooses, along with Hegel, *freedom* as the keystone of normativity—'negative freedom' (revolving around *autonomy*) and 'expressive freedom' (revolving around *authenticity*) being two reductive versions along the evolutionary path to 'social freedom', that is, being with oneself within relations of reciprocal recognition. Had 'equality' or 'justice' been chosen, a different narrative would have resulted. However, it remains unclear what role should be reserved, in a democratic society where *legitimate* power will have to be exercised, for claims, proposals, projects, movements, and initiatives anchored in normative reconstructions that revolve around the primacy of justice, of equality, or of social utility. How will the key institutions of a Honnethian ideal society be justified to those who take such different views of 'the rational', or will these competing views be discounted as less than fully rational?

Second, an unaccounted selectivity also affects the selection of the institutional spheres of recognition against which the narrative of social freedom unfolds. Drawing on Hegel, Honneth expands the family into the larger realm of 'personal relationships', civil society into the sphere of relations mediated by the market, and the state into the sphere of democratic will-formation. Another kind of selectivity seems to be operative here. Why in our complex societies are these still the only three spheres where citizens are socialized to social freedom and mutual recognition? Two spheres that Hegel ignored and that today appear as equally formative, though excluded from Honneth's account for no discernible reason, are the educational system and the free churches. A clarification is needed of the criterion for including and excluding single institutions in the number of those conducive to social freedom, as well as for adjudicating contested inclusion or exclusion.

Finally, a *third* kind of selectivity operates not just *between* spheres of social action (eg including the family and excluding the educational system), but also *within* each of them. Leaving aside Honneth's accounts of the modern and contemporary development of the nuclear family and of industrial relations in general,[129] an unjustified selectivity again affects Honneth's narrative of the unfolding of social freedom in the democratic public sphere. He credits Durkheim, Dewey, and Habermas for a so-called third model of democracy, supposedly alternative to both representative and plebiscitarian democracy. The model is premised on the idea that in a properly functioning public sphere 'a constantly revisable consensus develops which can, if need be, come about by compromise; its directives are then transformed into binding resolutions made by the political authorities in charge'.[130] Honneth denounces as 'theoretical folly' the fact that 'contemporary theories of justice are guided almost exclusively by the legal paradigm'. Theories of justice should rather rely on 'sociology and historiography', because these disciplines are 'more sensitive to changes in everyday moral behaviour'.[131] No principle of legitimation is discussed, no awareness transpires

---

[129] For a discussion of Honneth's account of developments in the family and in industrial relations, see Alessandro Ferrara, 'Social freedom and reasonable pluralism: Reflections on *Freedom's Right*' (2019) 45 Philosophy and Social Criticism 639.
[130] Honneth, *Freedom's Right* (n 127) 305.
[131] ibid, 329.

of the need for rethinking the separation of powers in societies much more complex than those of Montesquieu's and Hegel's times, not a word is offered on the revolution brought about by the Ackermanian–Rawlsian dualistic model of democracy or on the struggle between an 'abstract' originalist understanding of the constitution and the idea of the 'living constitution' as capable of bringing the law in dialogue with the new visions of freedom elaborated during the Civil Rights Revolution.

To sum up, Honneth's idea that thick descriptions of processes of affirmation of social freedom would free us from the 'burdens of judgment' and the fact of reasonable pluralism may prove wishful thinking. At the end of a long journey through a reconstructed Hegel the reader is left with the question 'How should those who either identify different institutions as crucial for social reproduction or agree on which institutions are relevant for freedom, but endorse different accounts of their relevance, live together without oppression?'—repeating the question that Rawls in *Political Liberalism* starts from.

A similar philosophical trajectory is shared by Jean-Luc Nancy, Jacques Rancière, Maurice Blanchot, Giorgio Agamben, Roberto Esposito, Homi Bhabha, Adam Seligman, and Thomas Claviez.[132] These authors urge on us the idea that the self cannot be understood as a centre of unified agency. Internal heterogeneity, fragmentation of motives, impulses, and incompatible drives are the norm, and agency follows suit: agency unfolds under the sign of hybridity and fragmented, occasional motivation, at best under the aegis of shared rituals. They also urge on us the idea that community and the polity cannot be the locus of unified agency and homogenous self-representation either: these human collectivities are just the juxtaposition of irreducible singularities. Only difference exists. The unity of community, when we talk about it, is constructed from without, as an objectifying gaze that glosses over difference, and is a false unity.

Elsewhere I've addressed the internal difficulties that affect this view of subjectivity and, more specifically, of community.[133] On one hand, when defined through its members' shared exposure to finitude, community paradoxically loses its *difference* and becomes synonymous with the human condition, with *humanity*. There is no sense in which one community is different from any other, or in which its existence now differs from its existence one thousand years ago. For all their insistence on difference and singularity, Nancy, Agamben, Blanchot, and Esposito deactivate our capacity to connect human groupings with singularity. They merge community and the human condition

---

[132] Jean-Luc Nancy, *The Inoperative Community* (1986) (University of Minnesota Press 1991) 28–35 and *Being Singular Plural* (1996) (Stanford University Press 2000) 75–76; Maurice Blanchot, *The Inavowable Community* (1983) (University of Minnesota Press 1988), 11–18; Giorgio Agamben, *The Coming Community* (1990) (University of Minnesota Press), 10.1, 64.5, 85.6; Roberto Esposito, *Communitas: The Origin and Destiny of Community* (1998) (Stanford University Press), 1–2, 13–19; *Third Person. Politics of Life and Philosophy of the Impersonal* (2007) (Polity Press 2012), 14–15, 125–33, 142–46; Homi Bhabha, *The Location of Culture* (Routledge 1994), 175, 190; Adam Seligman, 'Ritual and Sincerity' (2010) 36 Philosophy and Social Criticism, special issue on Ritual and/or Sincerity, 11; Thomas Claviez, 'Traces of a Metonymic Society in American Literary History' in W Fluck et al (eds) *American Studies Today* (Winter 2014), 299–321 and 'A Metonymic Community? Toward a Poetics of Community' in T Claviez (ed), *The Common Growl: Toward a Poetics of Precarious Community* (Fordham University Press 2016) (hereafter Claviez, *Common Growl*) 39–56.

[133] See Alessandro Ferrara, 'The Dual Paradox of Authenticity in the 21st Century' in T Claviez, K Imesch, B Sweers (eds), *Critique of Authenticity* (Vernon Press 2019) 3.

to an extent unprecedented among the most universalist and formalist among their antagonists. On the other hand, these authors are unable to distinguish their variously called 'inoperative', 'inavowable', 'coming', and 'munus-connected' community from random and transient human groupings, such as those forming at the interstices of social life. 'Gate 22' is the nightmare of *communitas*. For at Gate 22 the crowd of people waiting to board the plane is all difference and no unity. They share nothing of their past and nothing of their future, of what they'll do at their destination once they will arrive. They only share a micro-segment of their life-course and exposure to the same vulnerability. The community without *immunitas* propounded by the deconstructionist is undistinguishable both from these random groupings and from the human community of those exposed to finitude—a dual flaw that in both cases severs the link between the deconstructionist community and *unique singularity*.

Recently, these features are found in the idea of a 'metonymic community', a community that juxtaposes differences without ranking them in a hierarchy. Thomas Claviez writes: 'the central question raised by Agamben—as well as by Maurice Blanchot's and Jean-Luc-Nancy's reflections on the topic of community—is, to put it rather simply, whether "being in common" necessarily implies "having something in common".[134] Claviez renames difference as 'contingency', and identity-based 'immunitary community' as the project of reducing difference to the sameness of a 'we'. As Claviez points out, 'attempts to exclude the other, the stranger, them, from "us" and our confines—our shared borders—not only fail to provide security from contingency, but also "close" or "wall us in" with strangers or wolves, and thus heighten rather than lower the potential contingencies within'.[135] Then, he adds, in order to stave off contingency Western political theory has posited consensus as 'the *sine-qua-non* of any community'.[136] This identity-thinking, keen on neutralizing contingency and difference, starts with Aristotle, traverses the whole of the Western conversation of political philosophy, and resurfaces in Heidegger's distinction of the passive fate or *Schicksal* and the active destiny or *Geschickt* of a community. A community can overcome the 'state of contingent possibility' only by creating a teleological narrative 'designed to overcome contingency by means of necessity'.[137] But even that proposition is flawed, according to Claviez. We live in a globalized world where our neighbours, far from being our neighbours out of necessity, are our neighbours accidentally, forced to live with us in what Butler has called 'unwilled adjacency'. Under these conditions, Claviez suggests that 'we start thinking of community as *metonymic*'.[138]

Claviez too misses the difference between metonymic communities that acknowledge finitude and contingency, and, in contrast, purely accidental groupings of people who happen to share space at a bus stop or train station, in a certain building, or simply happen to live during a certain historical time. Conflating these two kinds of groupings prevents us from making sense of collective agency and responsibility—both of which are needed in order for political action to be possible—and dedifferentiates our

---

[134] Thomas Claviez 'Introduction' in T Claviez (ed), *The Common Growl* (n 132) 5.
[135] Thomas Claviez, 'A Metonymic Community? Toward a Poetics of Contingency', in ibid 43.
[136] ibid.
[137] ibid 45.
[138] ibid 46 (emphasis added).

conceptual universe. Community and non-community come to coincide. Finally, it becomes unfeasible to envisage, from such deconstructionist perspective, legitimate partitions of the human population: the metonymic community has no boundaries and coincides with humankind. Its insubstantiality and fuzziness render it of limited use in political philosophy.

It is unfortunate that deconstructionism and its epigones within political philosophy have contributed to discredit the notion of a reflectively unified subject and of a reflective community. Their rightful critique of Tönnesian *Gemeinschaft* also ends up reverberating negatively on the pluralistic community prefigured by Dewey's 'Great Community', or the reflexive community envisaged by Ronald Dworkin as a 'liberal community',[139] two approaches to community as hospitable to difference as desirable and not liable to confusing political community with universal vulnerability, finitude, or ephemeral human groupings.

In the end, the deconstructionist plea for understanding community as 'different people living together in the same place', no less than Honneth's view of justice as a reconstruction of the values embedded in the institutions indispensable for social reproduction, raises the question *which specific arrangements* may ensure that different people living together do not oppress one another through the force of the law. Decades of deconstructionist critique of the authentic community thus lead us back to the proverbial square one, in this case to the initial question of *Political Liberalism* concerning the possible persistence over time of a stable and just society of free and equal citizens profoundly divided by reasonable religious, philosophical, and moral doctrines. Answers from a deconstructionist and a neo-Hegelian angle are still awaited.

3. Political Liberalism beyond *Political Liberalism*

The superior promise of political liberalism, unmatched by the competing approaches discussed above, should not mislead us to believe that Rawls's paradigm needs no refurbishing. *Political Liberalism* originated from a reflection stimulated during the 1980s, among other things by the communitarian and the feminist critique of *A Theory of Justice*. Although public reason and its dual normative standard revolutionized the previous understanding of 'justice as fairness', liberalism, and normative political philosophy, certain planks of the renovated boat remained in place. Thirty years after the publication of *Political Liberalism*, it is time to take stock and expand the paradigm in order to enable it to cast light onto areas that in the historical context of its elaboration had not yet appeared in need of immediate consideration.

The area which combines pressing urgency and the greatest prospect for a decisive contribution on the part of political liberalism lies within the precinct of constitutional theory. The challenge posed to democracy by the rise of populism and so-called illiberal democracy—a momentous tide inaugurated by the electoral gains of populist parties in many democratic societies and crowned by the twin 2016 occurrences of Brexit and the election of President Trump, now perhaps on a downward trend after

---

[139] See John Dewey, *The Public and Its Problems* (1927) (Swallow 1954), 126–27 and Dworkin, 'Liberal Community' (n 50).

the outbreak of the COVID-19 pandemic—will survive the political ups and downs of its protagonists. The populist challenge, in fact, touches the core area—and the raw nerve that sets off many radical democrats' sensibilities—of the proper relation of the sovereign people, as putative author of the constitution and of its subsequent transformations, to its pro-tempore living segment, which acts both as a constituted power, *qua* electorate, and as a sovereign *co-author* of the constitution. In this area, the contest of different theories of constitutionalism is vibrant. Political liberalism, once its implicit teaching is reconstructed and expanded beyond the 'five principles of constitutionalism' recalled above in Section 1.a, can bring a significant contribution to the debate on the different forms of constituent power, their relation to one another, and the normativity that binds their exercise.

As we move on to examine constituted powers, we will need to elucidate what it means to 'represent the people' as the subject of constituent power, as opposed to representing the electorate, the people's living segment. We will need to clarify how the two modes differ, if we assume that the meaning of 'representing' is not the same in both cases.

A further range of questions originates from the circumstance that historically the function of representing the people, as opposed to the electorate, has been entrusted to the highest judicial interpreter of the constitution. We need then to explore the distinction between interpreting the constitution and transforming it, and to spell out the notion of 'validity in constitutional interpretation' along lines consistent with the core political-liberal standard of the 'most reasonable for us'. Finally, we need to address from the angle of political liberalism the power of transforming or amending the constitution. What are its limits? How should the implicit entrenchment of constitutional essentials, including basic liberties and rights, be conceived on the basis of Rawls's standard of reasonability?

Before addressing these questions in the light of political liberalism, however, we need first to consider the phenomenon that propelled them to the top of the agenda for reconstructing and elaborating Rawls's constitutional theory: populism, the object of the next chapter.

2
Populism and Political Liberalism

> If the people of a Territory want slavery they have a right to have it.
> (Stephen Douglas, Seventh Debate with Abraham Lincoln, Alton, Illinois, 15 October 1858)

At first sight, it might seem counterintuitive to define populism, even tentatively, before having clarified what a people is.[1] At closer scrutiny, however, such attempt makes sense because populism, as a contemporary political phenomenon, may stimulate reflections that may contribute to outline a notion of 'the people' sharper and more stringent than those on offer. Furthermore, populism is an observable phenomenon in a way that a people is not.

Although several voices suggest that populism is a hopelessly muddled concept and perhaps should be sidelined or dropped,[2] I think complexity is no reason for theory to abdicate its role: the challenge is still entirely before us, to delimit our object, at least as an ideal type[3] distinct from neighbouring phenomena, such as authoritarianism and fascism.

Other political theorists incline to lend democratic credentials to twenty-first-century populist parties because they may attack important junctures of the liberal-democratic rule of law but, differently from fascism, never threaten to suspend elections or reject their results. Urbinati holds that 'populism pertains to the interpretation of democracy',[4] and Canovan urges that populist movements, bent on mobilizing 'the people as excluded part in the name of the people as sovereign whole', do have a point when they 'see in contemporary democracy a conspiracy to keep power from the people, and they are dangerous because they are right'.[5] Populism, in sum,

---

[1] This task will be the object of Chapter 4.
[2] Bruce Ackerman, *Revolutionary Constitutionalism: Charismatic Leadership and the Rule of Law* (Harvard University Press 2019) 2; Maria Pía Lara, 'The term "Populism" as a combat-concept and a catch-word' (2019) 9–10 Philosophy and Social Criticism, special issue on populism, 1144; Paul Blokker, 'Varieties of populist constitutionalism: The transnational dimension' (2019) 20 German Law Journal 343.
[3] For the strategy of outlining an ideal type of populism on the basis of ten criteria, see Jean L Cohen, 'Populism and the Politics of Resentment' (2019) 1 Jus Cogens 5, especially 3–14.
[4] See Nadia Urbinati, *Me the People: How Populism Transforms Democracy* (Harvard University Press 2019) (hereafter Urbinati, *Me the People*) 71.
[5] Margaret Canovan, *The People* (Polity Press 2005) (hereafter Canovan, *The People*) 85; see also Benjamin Arditi, 'Populism as an Internal Periphery of Democratic Politics' in Francisco Panizza (ed) *Populism and the Mirror of Democracy* (Verso 2005) 72; Thomas Claviez, 'Where are Jacques and Ernesto when you need them? Rancière and Laclau on populism, experts on contingency' (2019) 9–10 Philosophy and Social Criticism, special issue on populism 1132; Claudia G. Hassan, 'Populism, racism and scapegoat' in Alfredo Alietti and Dario Padovan (eds), *Clockwork Enemy. Xenophobia and Racism in the Era of Neo-populism* (Mimesis International 2020) 221.

would be *anti-liberal* but not *anti-democratic*.[6] In fact, as Mudde and Kaltwasser put it, populism 'exploits the tensions that are inherent to liberal democracy', especially the tension 'between majority rule and minority rights'. Because 'populists will criticize violations of the principle of majority rule as a breach of the very notion of democracy, arguing that ultimate political authority is vested in "the people" and not in unelected bodies', then 'populism can develop into a form of *democratic extremism or, better said, of illiberal democracy*'.[7] Others, with whom I find myself more in agreement, consider populist forces 'a real danger to democracy (and not just to "liberalism")'.[8]

In this chapter, drawing on the conceptual resources of political liberalism, an argument will be developed to the effect that populism is a highly complex phenomenon but not entirely impervious to being captured by a clear and univocal definition. I will begin by clearing away six dead-end strategies, fraught with shortcomings, for defining populism. Then a three-pronged definition that draws on political liberal premises, and equally applicable to right-wing and left-wing populism, will be outlined and subsequently put to use by propounding a metaphoric image of populism as a stream swollen by three tributaries corresponding to the three prongs of the definition. Finally, the advantages inherent in that definition will be discussed and the problems that it raises for a political liberal constitutional theory to address will be highlighted.

1. How Not to Define Populism: Six Conceptual Dead Ends

The idea that populism is an intrinsically blurry concept, perhaps to be jettisoned altogether, sinks its roots in the chameleonic nature of this phenomenon, which made its first appearance in the nineteenth century and underwent many transformations, including long decades of existence as an invisible undercurrent to mainstream political life in Western liberal democracies. Six alternative strategies for pinpointing populism seem, for different reasons, unfit for recovering the unchanging core that underlies such diversity of manifestations.

First, we would not capture what is distinctive of populism if we tried to pin it down as the political ideology of one specific social class. Embraced by rural populations in the nineteenth century in Russia and the United States,[9] populism then became

---

[6] See also Margaret Canovan, 'Trust the people! Populism and the two faces of democracy' (1999) 47 Political Studies 14 (hereafter Canovan, 'Trust the people').

[7] Cas Mudde and Cristobal Rovira Kaltwasser, *Populism: A Very Short Introduction* (Oxford University Press 2017) 82. On the positive effects of populist movement on democracy (offering voice to unrepresented groups, integrating excluding sectors of society, improving the responsiveness of the political system, increasing democratic accountability) alongside negative ones, see ibid 83. On the notion of illiberal democracy see also Fareed Zakaria, *The Future of Freedom: Illiberal Democracy at Home and Abroad* (Norton 2007); Yascha Mounk, *The People vs. Democracy: Why Our Freedom Is in Danger and How to Save It* (Harvard University Press 2018) and Steven Levitsky and Daniel Ziblatt, *How Democracies Die* (Crown 2018).

[8] Jan-Werner Müller, *What Is Populism?* (University of Pennsylvania Press 2016) (hereafter Müller, *What Is Populism?*) 104.

[9] The *narodnichestvo* movement in the 1870's in Russia started as an attempt, on the part of educated urban radicals, to mobilize sectors of the peasantry, recently freed from feudal bondage, to rebel against the Tsar and the new condition of wage labor. The attempt failed but a seed was sown that eventually contributed to the revolutions of 1905 and 1917. See Richard Wortman, *The Crisis of Russian Populism* (Cambridge University Press 1967) and Margaret Canovan, *Populism* (Junction Books 1981) 112–28. In the United States,

the preserve of the lower middle class (or *petite bourgeoisie*) in the aftermath of the First World War in continental Europe, leading eventually to reactionary totalitarian regimes,[10] and in the twenty-first century resurfaced as the outlook typical of a displaced and despondent working class and of urban self-employed classes previously seduced, and then disappointed, by the neoliberal ideology of globalism and self-entrepreneurship.

Second, we should be wary of defining populism primarily in socio-psychological terms, as the political expression of resentment against the elites and of anxiety for a prospect of downward mobility. A widespread anti-elite resentment may be a causal factor that, depending on other variables, favours the rise of populist movements, but we should be wary of turning it into the pivotal element of our definition of populism for two reasons. Final evidence is lacking about the association of this disposition with all forms of populism. Furthermore, a socio-psychological definition risks obscuring the specifically *political* message conveyed and the specifically *political* challenge raised by populism.

Third, it is impossible to associate populism with a distinctive set of substantive values and policies given the extreme variety of orientations that it can assume:[11] just think of the conservative *National Rally* in France, the *UK Independence Party*, the *League* in Italy, the *Dansk Folkeparti*, the *Sweden Democrats*, the *Finns Party* (previously the *'True Finns'*), the *Dutch Party for Freedom*, the *Vlaams Belang* or 'Flemish Interest' Party in Belgium, *Fidesz* in Hungary, *Law and Justice* in Poland, *Alternative für Deutschland*, *Vox* in Spain, and *Golden Dawn* in Greece; and then on the other hand *Podemos* in Spain, *Syriza* in Greece, the *Five Star Movement* in Italy, the Latin-American examples of Peron, Chavez, and Morales, and Modi in India or Duterte in the Philippines.

Fourth, populism cannot be understood as the preserve of oppositional movements in their anti-elite revolt. All too often populism resounds from the top. Some lines of President Trump's inaugural address, reminiscent of President Chavez's claim that with him in charge 'the people rule', leave no doubt as to the possibility of a populist administration: 'we are transferring power from Washington, DC and giving it back to you, the people', and 'January 20th, 2017 will be remembered as the day the people became the rulers of this nation again'.

Fifth, populism cannot simply be reduced to a vociferous indictment of the ruling elites for failing to attend the needs, interests, and political will of their constituents. Many critical voices that denounce inequality, the dismantling of welfare programmes, the precariousness of new labour contracts, and the privatization of public services, or that condemn the democratic deficit of supranational structures of governance, first

---

the People's Party grouped independent farmers who blamed 'the great magnates of the country, and Wall Street brokers, and the plutocratic power' (Lawrence Goodwyn, quoted in Canovan, *The People* (n 5) 73 for their dire economic plight and claimed to be representing 'the common people' against oligarchic privilege.

[10] See Peter Worsley, 'The Concept of Populism' in Ghita Ionescu and Ernest Gellner, *Populism: Its Meaning and National Characteristics* (Garden City Press 1969) 241.

[11] See Jan-Werner Müller, '"The People Must Be Extracted from Within the People": Reflections on Populism' (hereafter Müller, '"The People Must Be Extracted"') (2014) 21 Constellations 485–86. For a more extended analysis see his *What is Populism?* (n 8).

and foremost those of the EU of the institutions of financial regulation and governance, would then automatically have to be discounted as 'populist'.

Sixth, populism cannot be equated with the rejection of representative democracy in favour of direct democracy and referenda: although sometimes they convey this message, contemporary populist movements generally do accept elections and representative institutions, and struggle in order to conquer these institutions for the honest people and to wring them from the corrupt elite. To the extent that they accept elections and electoral politics, today's populist forces are different from the totalitarianism-prone forms of populism of the early twentieth century, though this acceptance, by itself, has now become insufficient to qualify them as fully democratic.[12]

Although the conduct of populist parties, leaders, and movements may show one or more of the above elements, none of them is by itself a necessary or a sufficient ingredient of populism. Populist movements, parties, and leaders may originate from rural or urban, lower- or middle-class backgrounds. They may lean to the right and coalesce around white-supremacist, racist, ethnocentric, and nationalist themes or adopt a leftist outlook centred on redistribution, social protection, and welfare themes. They may agitate religious issues and foster religious intolerance or they may lean toward secular values. They may challenge the powers that be or emanate from them or impersonate them. In the past, they used to reject representative democracy in favour or plebiscitary acclamation, but in the twenty-first-century populist movements, parties, and leaders seek to win elections and obtain a mandate.

If none of these traits counts as an indispensable ingredient of contemporary populism, though many of them can be found in populist forces, should we then not try to outline our definition of populism on a different conceptual plane, independent of those unpromising features and characteristics?

2. A Three-Pronged Definition of Populism

The choice of political liberalism as a paradigm in the light of which to define populism is motivated not only by its superior promise, relative to competing paradigms, but also by the superior clarificatory potential inherent in its five principles of constitutionalism as well as in its notions of public reason and reasonability.

Political liberalism and its standard of reasonability direct our attention to the following three constant aspects of *all* the forms of populism, which may otherwise differ on the above mentioned six dimensions (ie class composition, psychology of resentment and/or anxiety, value orientation, oppositional or apologetic rhetoric, anti-elite demagoguery, and radical democratic rhetoric):

(1) the conflation of 'the people' *qua* democratic sovereign with 'the electorate', and of the will of the voters with the will of the people;
(2) the attribution of *full constituent power* to the electorate as embodiment of 'the people'; and

---

[12] See Canovan, *The People* (n 5) 83–90; Nadia Urbinati, *Democracy Disfigured: Opinion, Truth, and the People* (Cambridge University Press 2014), 229–30.

(3) the postulation of only one legitimate interpretation of the general interest of the people and the fostering of *presumptively justified intolerance* against all opinions that differ from that interpretation.

As a general premise, it should be noted that while the six descriptive dimensions can be useful for distinguishing sub-types of political movements *already identified as populist*, it is primarily the three prongs of our proposed definition that can help us to distinguish genuinely populist movements from other forces that may share some ingredient (especially the first two features) but not the whole set and therefore are best understood in terms of either radical versions of democracy or secular and religious zealotry.[13] Having said that, some comments on each of the three components of our definition are in order.

Concerning the first aspect, 'the people' is a crucial element of all democratic order. It is a necessary construction, on which more will be said in Chapter 4, best understood along *formal* lines, thus breaking away from the eighteenth-century understanding of it as a 'nation'. 'The people' here simply means the *political subject* to which the enacting of a constitution, written or unwritten, can be imputed or, in other words, to which the setting of the 'terms' or 'rules' of politics in a given territorially bounded unit can be attributed.

Just like many tokens of the same type may exist, so every structured activity, including politics, rests on the assumption—broader in scope than the opposition of 'constituent' and 'constituted' power—that a distinction ought to separate the constitutive rules[14] of a practice and each specific move or unit *within* that practice. For example, different hands, sets, or instances of a game can be played according to the same rules, which are not supposed to change in the midst of a token-game and are to be known in advance. The people is then the political subject that—within the political practice called *democracy*—can be attributed authorship of the rules by which politics is played out in a bounded political space.

Another way to understand the nature of the people is by reference to the fact that every legal system can ultimately be conceived as an artificial device that coordinates the consociates' actions by determining 'who ought to do what, where, and when'.[15] No coordination of action, however, is conceivable without a *point*: just as with any other pragmatic structure, a legal order also has a *point*, a *finalité*. The point of the WTO is to bring about 'free global trade', the point of the ICC is to prosecute 'the most serious crimes of concern to the international community'.[16] This 'point' determines 'what is

---

[13] I'm indebted to an anonymous reviewer for having prompted me to clarify the relation of the six 'conceptual dead ends' for pinpointing the nature of populism and the three components of the definition here proposed.

[14] On 'constitutive rules', see John Searle, *Speech Acts: An Essay in the Philosophy of Language* (Cambridge University Press 1969) 33–42. The notion of a *definitional*, as opposed to 'summarizing' or descriptive, relation of certain kinds of rules to practices, and its long lineage deriving from Hume, Mill, and Austin, is best elucidated by John Rawls when he distinguishes a 'practice view' of rules, similar to Searle's constitutive rules, and a 'summary view', similar to Searle's notion of 'regulative rules', in 'Two Concepts of Rules' (1955) 64 Philosophical Review, 3.

[15] Hans Lindahl, *Authority and the Globalisation of Inclusion and Exclusion* (Cambridge University Press 2018) (hereafter Lindahl, *Authority*) 65.

[16] Hans Lindahl, 'Inside and Outside Global Law', *Julius Stone Address* (2019) 41 Sydney Law Review 6.

important to joint action' and thus worth including. As Hans Lindahl rightly suggests, this pragmatic approach to law sinks its roots in a narrative view of collective identity or 'difference', that is, 'in the process of telling a story about ourselves "as" being about this or about that'.[17] Then a people, as opposed to a king, a despot, an oligarchic elite (religious or secular), or the spontaneous order of the market, is the political subject to which, in a *democratic* polity, setting the point of joint political action can be imputed. Of course, the people so understood need not coincide with the 'population', and different theories of democracy do, to use Lefort's expression,[18] 'extract the people from the people', or tell who in the population counts as the people, in different ways.

Populist forces of all stripes, instead, conflate the people with the electorate and often, though not necessarily and only when they position themselves on the right-wing side of the political spectrum, *essentialize* the people as 'the nation': America, not 'the United States', was to be first in Trump's electoral slogan, as for Jean-Marie Le Pen the priority was 'aux *français*' and for Salvini '*Italians* come first'. Furthermore, over and beyond this ethnicization of the possessor of democratic sovereignty, two assumptions undergirding the populist conflation of the people and the voters need closer critical scrutiny. *First*, the assumption that the rules of the democratic game, no different to the rules of *any* game or structured practice, can be legitimately changed will be examined in Chapter 7, under the heading of amending power. *Second*, the consequences of assuming that the electorate, as the living segment of the people and the only one endowed with agency, owns the constitution and has the privilege to change it according to its unconstrained political will, will be addressed in the concluding section of Chapter 5, on the 'serial' model of democratic popular sovereignty.

Finally, the populist conflation of the people and the electorate beclouds two other meanings of the expression 'the people': (i) the 'participating people' composed of those who strike, demonstrate, and generally contribute to the shaping of public opinion through 'voice'; (ii) 'the people' as the sum total of the respondents to polls, whose opinion has come to exert increasing influence over contemporary politics, though not through voice but in a more passive yet often no less influential way.[19] In other words, populist forces not only reduce the people to its living segment, the electorate, but also often fail to do full justice to several other dimensions of the living segment of the people—for example, the people in its capacity as a *public* that populates the Habermasian public sphere and in its capacity as a shifting aggregate of opinions that influences both executive action and the relations among the separated powers.

Concerning the second aspect of the definition, vesting the voters with pro-tempore full constituent power is an attack against *constitutional* liberal democracy.[20] Insofar as they worship majorities, but reject checks and balances, populist forces revive an

---

[17] Lindahl, *Authority* (n 15) 69.
[18] Claude Lefort, *Democracy and Political Theory* (Polity Press 1988) 88.
[19] For this enlarged conception of 'the people', see Pierre Rosanvallon, 'A Reflection on Populism', Books&ideas.net (2011), accessed at http://www.booksandideas.net/IMG/pdf/20111110_populism.pdf, p 7. Concerning the impact of the 'people of polls'—*la gente*, in Italian—on democratic governments' short-termism and on the balance among the separated powers, see Bruce Ackerman, *The Decline and Fall of the American Republic* (Harvard University Press 2010) 131–35.
[20] On the anti-liberal but not anti-democratic nature of populism, see Canovan, *The People* (n 5), as well as her 'Trust the People!' (n 6) 14–16.

ancient split between democracy and liberalism which many strands of democratic theory of the late twentieth century, not only political liberalism, had successfully sutured. Populism is *post-liberalism* premised on the idea that the electorate is endowed with *full constituent power*—that is, not just the power to amend the constitution along lines consistent with its original design and spirit (whether subject to, or independent of, the review of a judicial interpreter of the constitution) but also the power to entirely revise the constitution when the present one is deemed inadequate beyond amendability. Depending on the institutional specificities of a democratic regime, this aspect of populism takes the form either of parliamentary proposals for constitutional amendments supplemented, where and when possible, by confirmatory constitutional referendums (as in Italy in 2016 and Turkey in 2017) or of a pressing request that the pronouncements of constitutional courts be responsive to the orientation of the majority of the electorate.

Concerning the third defining feature, populist forces reject pluralism and embrace the idea of *presumptively justified intolerance*. Populism presupposes not only—like many non-populist conceptions of democracy, such as deliberative and participatory democracy, classical social-democratic, Christian-democratic, and socialist views, and many others—the existence of a common good or public interest that can be epistemically tracked, but also that 'there is only one proper common good to be discerned by the authentic people'.[21] Ironically, contemporary Italy offered until 2021 a tangible confutation of that stance: of the two major populist parties (the *Five Star Movement* and the *League*) that purported to represent the will of the people, one partook of the government coalition while the other was in opposition. Through these two parties 'the people', ecumenically, both ruled and opposed the government. Presumptively justified intolerance presupposes a rejection of the epistemic humility mandated by the burdens of judgment and explains another ubiquitous facet of the populist outlook: impatience with internal dissent. The leader reaches out directly to the rank and file,[22] in comparison with traditional parties where there is less collegiality in decision-making and a smaller number of intermediate organizational layers between the rank and file and the leader in chief—a feature shared in common with fascism in Italy and Spain.

3. Populism and Democracy

The latter observation leads us back to the relation of populism to democracy. Several political theorists find comfort in observing that twenty-first-century populists, even of the most nationalistic and white-suprematist kind, may attack important junctures of the liberal-democratic rule of law—the independence of the judiciary, freedom of the press and of association, freedom of movement—but never question the electoral

---

[21] Jan-Werner Müller, '"The People Must Be Extracted"' (n 11) 487. On the refusal, typical of populist forces and leaders, to accept self-limitation in the exercise of their majoritarian edge, see Urbinati, *Me the People* (n 4) 91.
[22] This aspect of populism is perspicuously highlighted by Nadia Urbinati under the heading of 'direct representation', see Urbinati, *Me the People* (n 4) 163–69.

mechanism, never threaten to suspend or postpone elections, and never fail to accept the results of elections, with the notable exception of former President Trump. That crucial divide, which separates today's populists from their dictatorial and totalitarian predecessors of the 1920s and 1930s, would then earn the colourful, vociferous, and at times disconcerting populist leaders of the twenty-first century the status of being internal to the complexities and tensions of the democratic tradition: 'populism pertains to the interpretation of democracy'.[23] Once again, the idea reemerges that populism would be anti-liberal, but not anti-democratic. This is not a nominalist quibble. At stake is the best way to conceptualize the outer boundaries of democracy in our times.

While it makes sense to locate the threshold between muscular, authoritarian, populist versions of democracy on one hand, and fascism proper on the other, at the conceptual juncture where intolerance enlists the coercive force of the law and of the state in order to suppress all opposition and to persecute resisters,[24] nevertheless there is something unhistorical and abstract in this way of distinguishing the two phenomena and accepting populism among the forms of democracy. A major epoch-marking watershed is overlooked. With the rise and affirmation of 'the democratic horizon' after 1989, democracy—in spite of its being obviously a contested term, to which many meanings can be attached—has become, for the majority of human beings, no longer one among several, but *the* form of political rule considered fully legitimate.[25] Evidence for this claim is the fact that only a handful of the 195 regimes of the world dare dispense with electoral legitimation,[26] even though elections are often unworthy of the name.[27] That all but a few rulers perceive convening elections as to their advantage means that the dividing line between elected and non-elected rulers no longer neatly separates democratic and non-democratic, authoritarian, or fascist regimes. At the same time, the fact that neither in China, where no national elections are held, nor in Russia, where they are, does the opposition have any chance of coming to power, testifies to the at best tenuous relation of democracy to elections. Consequently, it becomes questionable, in our times, to grant populism the credentials of being 'internal to democracy' merely because its leaders do not object to elections.[28]

---

[23] See ibid 71.
[24] 'Fascism is the state and the people merging. It is not merely parasitical on representative government, because it does not accept the idea that legitimacy springs freely from popular sovereignty and free and competitive elections. Fascism is tyranny, and its government is a dictatorship. Fascism in power is anti-democratic all the way through, not only in words but also de jure. It is not content with dwarfing the opposition through daily propaganda: it uses state power and violent repression to *silence* the opposition', ibid 21. On a similar wavelength, see the chapter 'A New Fascism or Far-Right?' in Roger Eatwell and Matthew Goodwin, *National Populism: The Revolt Against Democracy* (Pelican Books 2018) 60–62.
[25] Alessandro Ferrara, *The Democratic Horizon: Hyperpluralism and the Renewal of Political Liberalism* (Cambridge University Press 2014) (hereafter Ferrara, *Democratic Horizon*) 1–3.
[26] Qatar's first general elections ever, scheduled for 2013, were postponed to 2016, then again to 2019, and were finally held in October 2021. Brunei and Saudi Arabia have no general elections, and China has no national elections of the National People Congress. A few other countries have delayed elections.
[27] See Freedom House's Report *Freedom in the World 2021: Democracy Under Siege*, https://freedomhouse.org/report/freedom-world/2021/democracy-under-siege, accessed on 11 February 2022.
[28] A similar point is made by David Rasmussen when he describes populism as being 'parasitical on liberal democracy'. See David Rasmussen, 'Reflections on the nature of populism and the problem of stability' (2019) 9–10 Philosophy and Social Criticism, special issue on populism 1062. On the radical discontinuity of populism and democracy, and on the relation of populism to elections, see Leonardo Fiorespino, *Radical Democracy and Populism: A Thin Red Line?* (Springer 2022) 289–307. More generally, on the tenuous

Fascism, in the historical form in which it appeared, is pretty much gone as a viable option, in the same sense as no one in the twenty-first century can seriously claim that an absolute monarchy without a constitution, in the guise of the European monarchies of Louis XIV or Charles I Stuart, is the best form of government. This neglected but plausible observation further corroborates the thesis that the contrast of elective and non-elective forms of political rule can no longer serve the purpose, as it did a century ago, of sorting parties, movements, and polities that deserve democratic credentials from those that do not. The line between democratic and non-democratic forms of political rule, after the rise of the 'democratic horizon', must be drawn in an entirely new way: the relevant question no longer concerns whether elections are held, but *how* they are held and what sort of political and legal context surrounds the electoral arena.

Once that point is accepted, the evaluative scenario changes completely. The mix of features associated with populism—conflation of the people and the electorate, with or without an attendant ethnicization of 'the people', attribution of full constituent power to the electorate, presumptively justified intolerance and consequent polarization of the public sphere, attempts to curtail rights and reduce the independence of the judiciary, and intimidation of the press and of opponents—amounts to such a blatant violation of the idea, integral to any notion of a democratic society, of a just and stable society of free and equal citizens who refrain, when they happen to be a majority, from oppressing each other through the use of the force of law or political power, that it makes sense, far from absolving populism as an overzealous or exaggerated advocate of the popular-sovereignty component of democratic rule, to understand populism as the closest approximation to fascism from within the democratic horizon.

This redrawing of the line between democratic and non-democratic regimes now *within* the camp of election-based political rule enjoins us to rethink the democratic rule of law. The populist phenomenon directs our attention to the focal point at the centre of this book: the nature and limits of the constituent power of 'the people' and its relation to the amending power of its living segment, as well as to the separated constituted powers, in a well-ordered democratic regime. An implication of such reformulation may well be that many populist forces end up falling beyond the dividing line between democracy and non-democracy, in spite of their formal acceptance of elections as a legitimating procedure. As Kim Scheppele has aptly put it,

> if the authoritarians of the 20th century came cloaked in nefarious ideologies with which they whipped up support for action without limits, the autocrats of the 21st century come wrapped in democratic pretence, holding out the promise that they will provide precisely what their voters want and that they will give voters what they want by legal means. By grounding their legitimacy to rule in election victories and legal change, populists occupy the turf of democrats who can't quite figure out what is wrong with this picture.[29]

relation of democracy to elections, see also Samuel Issacharoff, *Fragile Democracies: Contested Power in the Era of Constitutional Courts* (Cambridge University Press 2015) 3–10.

[29] Kim L Scheppele, 'The Opportunism of Populists and the Defense of Constitutional Liberalism' (2019) 20 German Law Journal 330–31.

One of the aims of this book is to contribute to figuring out what is wrong with that picture, and to show that political liberalism embeds a notion of constituent power helpful in that respect. To anticipate: whilst they appear on stage 'wrapped in democratic pretence', as representatives of the will of the people, populist leaders in fact ask us to underwrite the nonsensical claim that players can legitimately change the rules of the game while they are playing and, by conflating the voters and the people, they hide the obvious fact that a majority of the voters still is a minority of the transgenerational people. Its legislating will can be binding only if it accords with the will of the larger people, reflected in the constitution.

4. The Populist Stream and Its Tributaries

If populism counts as 'the other of democracy' in convenient electoral disguise, two advantages of our definition can be highlighted. First, because all its three facets must be simultaneously present, the definition encompasses populism's extreme diversity: for example, such movements and parties as Salvini's *League* and Meloni's *Brothers of Italy*, Le Pen's *National Rally* in France, and Orbàn's *Fidesz* in Hungary, and at the opposite end of the spectrum, Maduro's *United Socialist Party* in Venezuela, the *Five Star Movement* in Italy, and *Podemos* in Spain. Second, the definition enables us to make sense of the extraordinary appeal of populist movements and leaders by sorting out those three components and allowing us to trace the *non-populist* sources that inspire these forces. The relation of the single components to the whole configuration of populism can be grasped by evoking the metaphorical imagery of a stream with three tributaries. Just as the flow rate of a major stream accrues from tributaries that may run through landscapes quite different from the final one, so traces of populism are observable in contexts and traditions which cannot by any means be classed as populist. The three prongs of our definition alert us to phenomena that by themselves would not be perceived as indicative of populism.

Traces of populism can then be found in historical contexts and among political, intellectual, and cultural traditions located topographically very far from populism proper, in institutions and political subjects which on the whole do remain separated from populism. It is an instructive exercise for a theory of populism to trace these sources, and to follow the course of the streams that originate from them and contribute as tributaries to the high-flow stream of today's populism. What we find in the landscapes traversed by the tributaries, before they finally flow into the populist stream, is an astonishing variety of institutional, academic, and media-related contexts. Our definition, then, alerts us to the relevance of phenomena that, considered in isolation, would risk going unnoticed.

a. The people and the electorate

Let me start with an example of what the conflation of the people and the electorate—the first prong of the definition—means. Italy is a parliamentary democracy: the prime minister (called the President of the Council of Ministers), not elected by the voters but appointed by the President of the Republic, must assemble a coalition of parties willing to share a programme and capable of obtaining a confidence vote in both houses of Parliament. Coalitions are unstable, and Italy is famous for having an average cabinet life expectancy of less than two years. When Prime Minister Conte, initially reputed to be a figurehead installed by Di Maio and Salvini, the leaders of the two 2018 election-winning populist parties, resigned in August 2019, he received from the President a mandate to verify, before possibly dissolving Parliament and calling for new elections, whether a different confidence-sustaining majority could be assembled under his leadership. He succeeded by replacing Salvini's *League*, responsible for having ignited the crisis in the first place, with the PD (Democratic Party), formerly in the opposition. The *Five Star Movement* hesitated but accepted the new alliance with the former opposition party, the required votes were gathered, and the new Conte cabinet was sworn in. At the same time, demonstrators in the streets of Rome, led by Salvini, were shouting 'you're stealing sovereignty!' at the new governmental coalition. The subtext was that in the preceding elections of 4 March 2018, 'the people' had given a mandate to the two populist parties to form a government reflective of its will, and now thanks to the manoeuvring of politicians and the propensity to compromise of the *Five Star Movement*, the *League* was banished to the opposition—all of this without electorally consulting again with 'the sovereign people'.

This episode exemplifies what the conflation of the people and the electorate means. In utter disregard of the procedure set by the Constitution, by no means violated by the change in the composition of the coalition supporting the second Conte cabinet, a populist force vented the resentment of its electoral constituency by claiming that those voters' will, combined with that of the *Five Star Movement*'s constituency, amounted to the 'will of the people'.[30] There is no shortage of similar examples from other political contexts. In Donald Trump's inaugural address, a central passage read: 'we are not merely transferring power from one administration to another or from one party to another, but we are transferring power from Washington, DC and giving it back to you, *the people*'. Similarly, among the leading slogans of Marine Le Pen's presidential campaign of 2017, we find 'Au nom du peuple' (in the name of the people).

These are examples of certified and fully fledged populism, so to speak. But the powerful appeal of these formulations is accrued—like the flow of a large river is accrued by the flow of its tributaries—by the capillary presence of this theme in institutional, political, and cultural venues that cannot be considered populist. One indicative example is offered by the US Supreme Court. On the occasion of the *Obergefall* case of 2015 on same-sex marriage, one year before the election of President Trump, in their dissenting opinion Justice Roberts, joined by Justices Scalia and Thomas, argued that 'five lawyers have closed the [democratic] debate and enacted their own vision of marriage as a matter of constitutional law. Stealing this issue from the people will for many cast a cloud over same-sex marriage, making a dramatic social change that much more difficult to accept'.[31] Calling the Court's opinion 'an act of will, not legal

---

[30] For an enlightening collection of studies on Italian populism, see Paul Blokker and Manuel Anselmi (eds), *Multiple Populisms: Italy as Democracy's Mirror* (Routledge 2020).
[31] *Obergefell v Hodges*, 576 US (2015), Roberts CJ, dissenting, 2.

judgment', and an act that abruptly 'invalidates the marriage laws of more than half the States', the dissenting Justices argued that the majority of the Court

> seizes for itself a question the Constitution leaves to the people, at a time when the people are engaged in a vibrant debate on that question. And it answers that question based not on neutral principles of constitutional law, but on its own understanding of what freedom is and must become.[32]

In another dissenting opinion, filed by Justice Thomas (with Scalia joining), one can read that

> Had the majority [of the Court] allowed the definition of marriage to be left to the political process—as the Constitution requires—the People could have considered the religious liberty implications of deviating from the traditional definition as part of their deliberative process. Instead, the majority's decision short-circuits that process, with potentially ruinous consequences for religious liberty.[33]

Scholars in the tradition of 'political constitutionalism', for example Jeremy Waldron,[34] offer further corroboration to the thesis that, by limiting or reversing the electorate's will, supreme or constitutional courts interfere with or occlude the will of the people. While substantively concurring with the Supreme Court's opinion in *Obergefell*, Waldron argues that caution ought to have been exercised by the Court, in order not to proceed 'too far in advance of changing public opinion'.[35] Caution is demanded not just in consideration of the possibility of coming up with 'the wrong answer' but also 'because even if the Court gets the outcome right there is a cost to democratic self-determination in the process involved'.[36]

I believe that the conceptual content of the alleged 'cost to democratic self-determination' is not convincingly specified by Waldron. When, after illustrating the momentous change ushered in by *Obergefell*, he adds 'this is a change for *the people* to make, not their judges',[37] he is simply *assuming*, in tune with today's populists without being one, that 'the people' is represented primarily by legislation. Similar considerations could be repeated about Richard Bellamy. He, along with Waldron, equates the constitution with the democratic process and 'the political rather than the legal

---

[32] ibid 3.

[33] *Obergefell v Hodges*, 576 US (2015), Thomas J, dissenting, 16.

[34] See Jeremy Waldron, *Law and Disagreement* (Oxford University Press 1999) and *The Dignity of Legislation* (Cambridge University Press 1999).

[35] Waldron, 'What a Dissenting Opinion Should Have Said in *Obergefell v Hodges*', 2016, http://papers.ssrn.com/sol3/papers.cfm?abstract_id=2844811, 9.

[36] ibid. The same line of thought undergirds the recently published opinion of the Supreme Court on abortion: 'it is time to heed the Constitution and return the issue of abortion to the people's elected representatives ... That is what the Constitution and the rule of law demand', *Dobbs et al v Jackson Women's Health Organization*, 6. As Justice Kavanaugh has added, the decision to overrule *Roe* v *Wade* 'properly returns the Court to a position of neutrality and restores the people's authority to address the issue of abortion through the processes of democratic self-government established by the Constitution', Kavanaugh, J., concurring, 3.

[37] ibid 18.

system'.[38] Their conflation of the rules of the democratic game and the playing of the game in the actual political arena is grist to the mill of those who claim that 'the constitution' is nothing more than the regularities and recurrences observable on the playing field of democratic politics, nothing more than what results from the electoral and parliamentary contest of the prevailing majority and the minorities. Political constitutionalism certainly cannot be considered equivalent to populism, but nonetheless it is a tributary of the populist stream insofar as it contributes to blur the distinction between (i) the will resulting from the diverse orientations of the present voters and (ii) the will imputable to the author of the (written or unwritten) constitution.

b. Full and unlimited constituent power

A second, impetuous tributary of the populist stream flows in the vicinity of the one surveyed above. Many of those who conflate the people and the electorate also tend to attribute full constituent power to the voters—an unconstrained prerogative to realign the rules of the political game with their prevailing political sentiment. Such unbound constituent power is meant here as a *descriptive* notion, designed to capture the second important feature common to all populist forces. From a *normative* perspective, it will be argued in Chapters 3 and 5 that such a view makes little sense, and a different one will be propounded according to which constituent power is constrained by the normativity of the 'most reasonable for us' traceable back to the later Rawls. For the present purpose, however, the constituent power attributed by populist parties, movements, and leaders to the voters as representatives of 'the people' will be descriptively taken as unconstrained. Two examples will illustrate this view.

A glimpse at the second tributary of populism can be observed in France in 1962. President de Gaulle, aware that once his personal charisma would no longer be available, a president elected by an electoral college would be at a disadvantage in confronting a prime minister who, although designated by the president, would obtain a confidence vote from a National Assembly elected directly by the voters,[39] planned to remedy this flaw by having the president also elected directly. Assisted by special circumstances, he chose an 'unconventional' solution. When in August he was the target of a failed assassination attempt in retaliation for his 'betrayal' in Algeria, he announced while parliament was in recess that 'he would *unilaterally proceed with a referendum on the popular-election amendment*'.[40] The referendum took place on 28 October 1962 in a climate in which the National Assembly toppled prime minister Pompidou with a no-confidence vote and 'censured the president for "violating the Constitution"'.[41] De Gaulle, in response, dissolved the National Assembly, called for new elections, and stepped up his campaign by 'equating his opponents in the

---

[38] Richard Bellamy, *Political Constitutionalism: A Republican Defence of the Constitutionality of Democracy* (Cambridge University Press 2007) 5.
[39] See Bruce Ackerman, *Revolutionary Constitutions: Charismatic Leadership and the Rule of Law* (Harvard University Press 2019) (hereafter Ackerman, *Revolutionary Constitutions*) 187–88.
[40] ibid 189.
[41] ibid 190.

democratically elected parliament to the seditious conspirators who had tried to kill him'.[42] His reform succeeded by 62 per cent to 38 per cent in the referendum, but today de Gaulle's conduct would certainly fall under the rubric of *populism*. The constitutionality of the referendum was then challenged by the President of the Senate. But the French Conseil Constitutionnel argued that the constitutionality of the referendum, even though de Gaulle had convened it in violation of the formal procedure, was ensured by the fact the people had voted and the Conseil could not review measures 'adopted by the people following a referendum, which constitutes the direct expression of national sovereignty'.[43] The Conseil apparently attributed a *self-validating nature* to a referendum, regardless of the conditions under which it has been convened.[44]

Over half a century later in 2017, in Turkey, the idea was echoed by the Minister of Justice Bekir Bozdag, commenting, on behalf of the government headed by Recep Tayyp Erdogan, on the legal case brought before the Council of State about the irregularities connected with a referendum, called in the wake of a failed coup in 2016, on an extensive reform of the Turkish constitution in the direction of presidentialism, by stating that 'no court can undo/change the decisions of the nation'.[45]

These two examples are indicative of an issue which still has unsolved political philosophical ramifications today. Constituent power is the power to start a new political order and, after the example of the eighteenth-century revolutions, usually its exercise takes the form of enacting a constitution on the part of 'the people'.

According to Hobbes's absolutist version of contract theory, the commonwealth is established by a human collectivity that is transformed, by the act of sealing a pact, from a multitude of unrelated individuals to a people composed of subjects of the same sovereign. After the creation of the commonwealth, in the Hobbesian scheme, the people becomes politically inert, entirely ruled by the sovereign power it has created. Constituted power rules over a constituent power that enters lethargy after having acted once. The absoluteness of the sovereign's rule is mitigated only by the proviso that it would cease in the case that the sovereign failed at discharging the function for which it has been created—securing life. In Hobbes's words, 'The Obligation of Subjects to the Sovereign, is understood to last as long, and no longer, than the power lasteth, by which he is able to protect them'.[46] However, acting on this proviso and reclaiming one's natural freedom takes the form of countless individual acts of seeking rescue—a massive yet non-political 'every man for himself'. When the state's enemies, external or internal, gain a final victory and the sovereign's capacity to protect the subjects wanes, 'then is the Common-wealth DISSOLVED, and every man at liberty to protect himself by such courses as his own discretion shall suggest unto him'.[47]

---

[42] ibid 191.

[43] ibid 192.

[44] The Conseil Constitutionnel has consistently adopted the doctrine that when a constitutional referendum takes place, there the French people exert sovereignty and thus their will cannot be overruled by a constituted power such as the judiciary. For an accurate reconstruction of this doctrine, see Richard Albert, Malkhaz Nakashidze, and Tarik Olcay, 'The Formalist Resistance to Unconstitutional Constitutional Amendments' (2019) 70 Hastings Law Journal 22.

[45] See https://archive.is/20170422164902/http://abcnews.go.com/International/wireStory/turkeys-justice-minister-contesting-referendum-moot-46952730, accessed on 4 February 2020.

[46] Thomas Hobbes, *Leviathan* (1651), edited and with an introduction by CB Macpherson (Penguin 1985) (hereafter Hobbes, *Leviathan*) Chapter 21, 272.

[47] ibid Chapter 29, 375.

With Locke's liberal version of the contract, for the first time the constituent power of the people does not evaporate after creating the commonwealth. The 'right of resisting', to be exercised whenever an 'alteration of the legislative' or any other equally threatening violation of the rule of law is committed by the constituted government, testifies to the enduring presence of constituent power in a latent, yet merely defensively vigilant and not transformative, modality.[48] The citizens, who have brought a commonwealth into being, remain entitled to pass judgment on the fidelity of their governmental officials to the original constitutional design and to rebel against actual deviations or even to act on the reasonable suspicion of such an intention. Such a prerogative authorizes them basically to restore the original design of their commonwealth, rather than changing its structure in a new direction.

Locke's framework—explicitly taken up by Rawls in the few paragraphs where he addresses constituent power—offers a conceptual foothold, so to speak, for identifying the ambiguity on which twenty-first-century populism thrives. All that we have to do, in order to pinpoint such ambiguity, is to imagine a time lapse of several generations between the commonwealth-instituting people and the rebelling people. Our contemporary problem then emerges, though it remains somehow barely visible, because the reigniting of constituent power for Locke has primarily the defensive function of avoiding 'the insolence of office', the abusive exercise of constituted authority over the people that created the commonwealth.

Imagine, however, that across a number of generations the authorities of a commonwealth have consistently displayed the same, hypothetically moderate, degree of abuse of power, yet only one, the nth generation of the people, rebels. Are these citizens overreacting to conduct that none of their predecessors found questionable or are they finally seeing through and standing up against abusive conduct that previous generations irresponsibly let go? If the latter, in what sense is their act of rebellion legitimate and imputable to the entire, transgenerational people of that country, as opposed to the specific set of individuals that belong to the rebellious generation? Under what conditions can the present generation retrospectively claim to be rebelling in the name of the entire people and not just in its own name? Under what conditions can the constituent power of the few the living generations—claim to be identical with, and representative of, the constituent power of *all* the generations of the people?

With Rousseau and Sieyès the problem from which one, perhaps the major, tributary to the populist stream originates becomes fully visible, though it remained unthematized by them. The people for Rousseau or the nation for Sieyès possesses a sovereignty which is indivisible, inalienable, and above all unbound by its own antecedent will. For Rousseau, popular sovereignty is exercised through the general will, which tracks the common good and proceeds to capture it in the form of 'general laws', arguably closer to constitutional provisions defining the basic structure than to ordinary statutes regulating limited areas or promoting policy goals. For

---

[48] John Locke, *Two Treatises of Government* (1690), with an introduction and notes by Peter Laslett (New American Library 1965), *Second Treatise*, Chapters 18–19, § 208, and generally §§ 199–243. For enlightening comments on Locke's indebtedness to the views of George Lawson, as expressed in *Politica Sacra et Civilis* (1657) (Cambridge University Press 1992), see Joel I Colón-Ríos, *Constituent Power and the Law* (Oxford University Press 2020)(hereafter Colón-Ríos, *Constituent Power*) 162–65.

him, 'laws properly speaking are no more than a society's conditions of association'.[49] Governments or constituted powers are supposed to act as delegates of the sovereign people, and in the case of ordinary legislation in larger states Rousseau even advocated the institution of the imperative mandate, binding on the elected representatives.[50] Rousseau's point is that constituted powers set a ubiquitous trend in motion: 'every government in the world, once it is in command of the public forces, sooner or later usurps sovereign authority'.[51] As a remedy, he envisaged 'periodical assemblies' of the people—constitutional conventions, which should be automatically convened at regular intervals and should mandatorily deliberate and vote on the persisting desirability (i) of 'the present form of government' and (ii) of leaving 'the administration of government in the hands of those to whom it is now entrusted'.[52]

For Sieyès, 'the nation exists prior to everything; it is the origin of everything. Its will is always legal. It is the law itself ...'.[53] As Rousseau also argued, the nation delegates the function of governing to a number of constituted powers, and through a constitution instructs such delegated powers to bring about what the nation's inalienable constituent power wishes. 'It would be ridiculous to suppose that the nation itself was bound by the formalities or the constitution to which it had subjected those it had mandated'.[54] The sovereignty of Sieyès's nation, just as Rousseau's 'people',[55] appears no less absolute than that of Hobbes's sovereign.

It is true that both Rousseau and Sieyès at times did acknowledge that constituent power is not altogether boundless. Rousseau, adverse to the notion of natural rights that would detract from the sovereignty of the people's will, did conceive of three *procedural* limitations to the exercise of the general will. *First*, the object of deliberation must be general and apply equally to all the citizens.[56] *Second*, the socio-economic inequality that inevitably persists even in a political community unified by the social contract must enable no one to purchase the consent of any other citizen and incline no one to sell her consent.[57] *Third*, in a move that turns Montesquieu's republic-sustaining

---

[49] Jean Jacques Rousseau, *The Social Contract* (1762), translated and with an introduction by C Betts (Oxford University Press 1994) (hereafter Rousseau, *Social Contract*), Book II, Chapter 6, 75. On the meaning of the term 'law' for Rousseau and the relation of proper laws to the constituent power of the people, see Colón-Ríos, *Constituent Power* (n 48) 35–40.

[50] Rousseau, 'Considerations on the Government of Poland and on its Proposed Reformation' (1782) (ISN ETH), 17, accessed at https://www.files.ethz.ch/isn/125482/5016_Rousseau_Considerations_on_the_Government_of_Poland.pdf on 16 September 2020. A few years later, Sieyès opposed the imperative mandate on the ground that its intrinsic rigidity would obstruct compromise and make lawmaking excessively difficult. See Emmanuel J Sieyès, 'Views of the Executive Means Available to the Representatives of France in 1789' in *Political Writings*, which includes the debate between Sieyès and Tom Paine in 1791. Edited, with an introduction and translation of 'What is the Third Estate?' by M Sonenscher (Hackett 2003) (hereafter Sieyès, *Political Writings*) 12.

[51] Rousseau, *Social Contract* (n 48) Book III, Ch 18, 133.

[52] ibid.

[53] Sieyès, 'What is the Third Estate?' (1789), in Sieyès, *Political Writings* (n 50) 136.

[54] ibid.

[55] Colón-Ríos emphasizes the different centrality of reference to the 'people' for Rousseau and to the 'nation' for Sieyès, in *Constituent Power* (n 48) 78–84.

[56] In the Chapter entitled 'The Limits of Sovereign Power', Rousseau makes the point that the general will must be general 'also in respect of its object', that is, 'it must issue from everyone in order that it should apply to everyone' and 'it loses its natural rightfulness when it is directed towards some specific, individual object', *Social Contract* (n 48) II, 4, 68.

[57] 'No citizen should be rich enough to be able to buy another, and none so poor that he has to sell himself', ibid II, 11, 118.

'virtue' into a necessary requisite of the general will, the deliberating citizens must prioritize the common good over factional advantage.[58] Sieyès conceived of the limits to constituent power in more *substantive* terms, and mentioned 'natural law' as the only normative frame antecedent to and binding on the nation, but the content of natural law was then summed up in the generic principle 'Do wrong to no man',[59] posited as the source 'of all patriotic laws'. The generic quality of Sieyès's overarching principle makes the nation's constituent power only *nominally* bound by natural law—in fact bound by natural law *as interpreted by the nation*.

It might *prima facie* seem preposterous to include the author of *The Social Contract* and the most articulate theorist of representative government in revolutionary France as part and parcel of a genealogy of twenty-first-century populism,[60] but once we overcome our disconcerted surprise, their thinking—especially when examined in conjunction with the real-life historical episodes recalled above—directs our attention to the relevant question. While both champion the view that all the citizens or 'members of a nation' are free and equal in their rights and obligations, we gather no sense, from Rousseau and Sieyès, that the *generations* of a people or nation whose existence may date back centuries and is open-ended in the future should *also* be equal in terms of rights and of their ability to shape the nation itself. We gather no sense of a distinction between (i) the constituent power of the people's generation that creates the polity—thereby turning an ethnic nation into a *demos*—on the basis of a constitutional project and (ii) the constituent power of the *subsequent* generations that do not start *ex nihilo*, but inevitably exercise their 'equally free' constituent power within an inherited context.

If we accept the assumption that all the generations of a people are 'free and equal', then each generation intuitively seems under the obligation—integral to 'sequential sovereignty'—to refrain from impairing the equal freedom of the generations not yet living or of the past ones that live in the present through their constitutional legacy.

---

[58] 'When a law is proposed in the assembly of the people, what they are asked is not precisely whether they accept or reject the proposal, but whether it is or is not in conformity with the general will, which is their will; everyone, by voting, gives his opinion on the question; and counting the votes makes the general will manifest. When an opinion contrary to mine prevails, therefore, it proves only that I had been mistaken, and that the general will was not what I had believed it to be', ibid IV, 2, 138. For a commentary on these three procedural constraints of the constituent power of the people, see Alessandro Ferrara, *Modernity and Authenticity: A Study of the Social and Ethical Thought of Jean-Jacques Rousseau* (SUNY Press 1993)55–58.

[59] Sieyès, 'What is the Third Estate?', in Sieyès, *Political Writings* (n 50) 70. For interesting discussions of Sieyès's constitutional theory, see Colón-Ríos, *Constituent Power* (n 48) 76–84; and Marco Goldoni 'At the Origins of Constitutional Review: Sieyes' Constitutional Jury and the Taming of Constituent Power' (2012) 32 Oxford Journal of Legal Studies 211, as well as his *La dottrina costituzionale di Sieyès* (Firenze University Press 2009). For an account of the influence of the interpretations of Sieyès offered by Schmitt, Arendt, and other twentieth-century theorists, see Lucia Rubinelli, *Constituent Power: A History* (Cambridge University Press 2020), 222–29.

[60] In fact, on the basis of an ingenious reconstruction of Rousseau's considerations on certain Roman institutions (the 'comitia', the 'tribunate', the 'dictatorship') in Book IV of *The Social Contract*, John P McCormick has built a powerful defence of the thesis that Rousseau was actually an 'anti-populist' theorist of constitutionalism. See his 'Rousseau's Rome and the Repudiation of Populist Republicanism' (2007) 10 Critical Review of International Social and Political Philosophy 3. See also Chiara Destri, 'Rousseau's (not so) oligarchic republicanism: Reflections on McCormick's *Rousseau's Rome and the Repudiation of Populist Republicanism*' (2016) 19 Critical Review of International Social and Political Philosophy 206. On the thesis that Rousseau's views prefigure some populist themes, see Andrew Arato, *The Adventures of Constituent Power: Beyond Revolutions* (Cambridge University Press 2017), 81, n 102.

Ironically, it will be for such an antinormative thinker as Carl Schmitt to point out that nominally the sovereignty of the British nation may be vested in the Westminster Parliament, but it is 'incorrect to claim' that—notwithstanding 'the so-called sovereignty of the English [sic] Parliament' and the ensuing possibility that 'a constitutional statute can be concluded by way of the simple legislative process'—a majority vote at Westminster could legitimately turn the United Kingdom into a Soviet Republic.[61]

Why not? The full answer to that question will have to await our discussion of constituent power in the light of political liberalism's implicit constitutional theory. For the purpose of highlighting the remote sources of populism, suffice it to underscore that from the very influential conceptions of popular sovereignty bequeathed to us by Rousseau and Sieyès no sense can be gathered in which single cohorts of the people would *not* be possessed of the full right to reshape entirely 'the present form of government' as they see fit. Nor could we conceptually extrapolate implicit limits. For any limitation to the prerogative to reshape 'the present form of government' would count as an undue curtailment of the nation's or the people's (serial) sovereignty. According to both Rousseau and Sieyès, just as for Hobbes,[62] any limitation over and beyond natural law or the procedural respect for equality would instantly turn a sovereign entity into a subordinate power subject to the *real* sovereign, namely the source and enforcer of said limitation.

c. Presumptively justified intolerance

The third tributary which swells the stream of populism is the assumption that there exists only one correct interpretation of the common good or general interest of the people, articulated by the leader and his inner circle, the other views being divisive or misleading projections of elite interests detrimental to the people's interests. As Jan-Werner Müller puts it,

> what populism necessarily has to deny is any kind of pluralism or social division: in the populist imagination there is *only* the people on one hand and, on the other hand, the illegitimate intruders into our politics.... And there is only one proper common good to be discerned by the authentic people. Hence, according to the populist *Weltanschauung*, there can be no such thing as a *legitimate opposition*—which, after all, is one of the key features of liberal democracy.[63]

Consequently, the populist way of running electoral campaigns often consists of a demonization of the opponent by attacking his or her moral integrity, as opposed to a mere questioning of his or her policies, as it is proper in an adversarial relation. Party

---

[61] Carl Schmitt, *Constitutional Theory* (1928). Translated and edited by J Seitzer, foreword by E Kennedy (Duke University Press 2008) (hereafter Schmitt, *Constitutional Theory*) 146.

[62] 'Whosoever thinking Sovereign Power too great, will seek to make it lesse; must subject himselfe, to the Power, that can limit it; that is to say, to a greater', Hobbes, *Leviathan* (n 48) Ch 20, 260. Nevertheless, 'Soveraigns are all subject to the Lawes of Nature, because such lawes be Divine, and cannot by any man, or Common-wealth, be abrogated', ibid Ch 29, 367.

[63] Müller, '"The People Must Be Extracted"' (n 11) 487.

pluralism, one of the pillars of a democratic polity, is thrown into question and at best is paid lip service to when populist forces reject mainstream parties as illegitimate representatives of elite interests alien to those of the people. Presumptively justified intolerance has other effects as well.

First, it favours the suppression of the intermediate layers between the rank and file and the populist leader: 'If there is only one common good and only one way to represent it faithfully ... then disagreement within the party that claims to be the sole legitimate representative of the common good obviously cannot be permissible'.[64]

Second, democracy in this illiberal vision ceases to be an arena where different platforms for policy are debated and eventually approved by the election of those who represent them. Insofar as the democratic process morphs into a public space where one political actor is blessed by electoral success because it supposedly represents the nation's vision of the common good, then the temptation arises to colonize state institutions: 'if only one party truly represents the people, why should the state not truly become the instrument of the people—via the method of filling state offices with ostensibly partisan actors?'.[65] Finally, the temptation arises of amending the constitution, changing the rules of the game in order to entrench the present victory in the uncertain future.

Political liberalism—joined, in this case, by Habermas's version of deliberative democracy—can be helpful not only for diagnosing the causes of the populist distortion of democracy but also for assessing the damage inflicted by populist forces to the democratic polity. Both Rawls and Habermas draw a distinction between (i) an institutional core of the polity (the 'public forum' for Rawls and 'strong publics' for Habermas)[66] where legislative, administrative, and judicial decisions binding for all are made and (ii) a less structured domain (the 'background culture' for Rawls, the 'public sphere' by Habermas) where deliberative exchanges take place and public opinion is formed. In this outer sphere less stringent criteria of propriety apply, although for both authors certain required dispositions must be presupposed here, in order not to disrupt the democratic process. For instance, the epistemic humility generated by the acceptance of the burdens of judgment, tolerance, and the virtue of civility must be assumed, for Rawls. For Habermas what qualifies a public space as a public sphere is a kind of disinterested interrogation, on the part of the participants, concerning the best answer to a given question. In contexts where populism prevails, these attitudes are the first to fade away.

Drawing on Rawls and Habermas, we can then distinguish two levels of the democratic backsliding induced by populism: *enfeebled* and *hollowed-out democracies*. In the case of enfeebled democracies, the populists' presumptively justified intolerance has only infected the outer circle, that is, the public sphere or background culture. The actors no longer relate to one another as fellow inhabitants of a 'space of reasons' who deliberate about what is best for them, about policies to be pursued, the way

---

[64] ibid 488.
[65] ibid 489.
[66] See Rawls, *PL* 220, and 'The Idea of Public Reason Revisited', ibid 443; Habermas, *Between Facts and Norms: Contributions to a Discourse Theory of Law and Democracy*, tr William Rehg (MIT Press 1996) 306–08, and 'Religion in the Public Sphere: Cognitive Presuppositions of the "Public Use of Reason" by Religious and Secular Citizens', in *Between Naturalism and Religion* (Polity Press 2008) 114–47.

institutions function, or any issue of common interest. They instead relate to one another as members of opposite fan clubs. They exchange insults and derogatory terms of address and hardly exchange anything that resembles a reason. When this happens, the public sphere degenerates into a mere *public space*,[67] similar to a stadium. Certainly not a private space, the stadium is a public space where publics only cheer their favourite teams and never cross their divides. Their communicative acts are only *expressive* and vent intolerance at each other.

One of the most poisonous fruits of the populist style of government is the polarization of society to such an extent that opposite camps clash no longer on policy, political values, or different views about the implications of rights but on each other's democratic legitimacy.[68] The charisma of populist leaders may wane over time, but their poisonous style lingers on and it is difficult for constituencies used to smearing their opponents as undignified enemies to ever backtrack into 'exchanging reasons' with them. Political adversaries can easily turn into enemies, but enemies rarely revert to being mutually recognizing adversaries. This is the single most severe damage inflicted to Italian democracy by the four Berlusconi governments between 1994 and 2011. Communism, long gone as a political movement of any substance, was still used as a term for delegitimizing the *Democratic Party*, eventually headed by Matteo Renzi, as an enemy of freedom. Polities where this degeneration affects primarily the public sphere, but the public forum somehow continues to function according to standards of propriety, civility, and reasonableness, can be described as *enfeebled democracies*.

Hollowed-out democracies, instead, are regimes in which *presumptively justified intolerance* has infected the public forum through the demise of civility, principled intolerance, factionalism, and the demonization of political adversaries as enemies. Usually, parliaments and elective presidential offices are affected first, because of their elective nature and direct contact, through the electoral campaign, with the moods and feelings of public opinion. But once parliaments are filled with elected supporters of populism, or once a populist candidate becomes president or prime minister—as the cases, among others, of Trump, Johnson, Bolsonaro, Maduro, Orbàn, and many other attest—it is a short step before they nominate populists in government posts, where this is possible. The last institution to be reached, on account of its mostly nonelective mode of recruitment, is the judiciary.

The effect of this process amounts to a deep change of style in the operation of the public forum. What Rosanvallon has called a 'democracy of interaction'—where the executive, but also the other branches, relate to the citizens 'by rendering account, providing explanations and involving associations and intermediary groups that are affected'—slowly shrinks to a 'democracy of authorization'.[69] One of the possible outcomes of the process is the affirmation of a practice that Ackerman has dubbed 'government by emergency': the post-liberal president or prime minister poses as the

---

[67] See Walter Privitera, *The Public Sphere and the Populist Challenge* (Mimesis 2017) 81–88.
[68] See Walter Privitera, 'La critica in sfere pubbliche populiste' (2012) 12 Quaderni di Teoria Sociale 5.
[69] Pierre Rosanvallon, 'A Reflection on Populism' in *Books and Ideas, Dossier: Democracy—Bridging the Representation Gap* (2011) p 2. Accessed at http://www.booksandideas.net/A-Reflection-on-Populism.html on 5 January 2017.

saviour of the national interest in some emergency in a language directed almost exclusively at the electorate and the public of polls.[70]

This tributary of the large populist stream also feeds from sources that we hardly associate with populism. Of course, many sources of intolerance can be found in the ideologies of the past two centuries, but they do not have democratic credentials and are not worth exploring in our context. More unsettling and worth mentioning is the fact that the phenomena denounced by Rosanvallon and Ackerman as 'democracy of authorization' and 'government by emergency' receive scholarly endorsement from authoritative academic quarters.

In their influential *The Executive Unbound: After the Madisonian Republic*, Eric Posner and Adrian Vermeule argue in favour of rescripting the separation of powers given the condition of contemporary societies immersed in a globalized economy and facing global challenges such as terrorism and climate change. The old ideal of balancing the Montesquieuian three powers with one another in terms of parity and equal influence should rather yield to what has already become a reality on the ground: the primacy of the executive, relative to the legislative and the judiciary. In *The Imperial Presidency*, Arthur Schlesinger reconstructed the historical process of the rise of the Presidency of the United States of America to a position of prominence relative to Congress and the Supreme Court during the twentieth century.[71] Posner and Vermeule argue that the executive branch not only is but *ought to* be 'unbound'[72] on account of its superior ability, relative to the legislative and the judicial branches, to keep abreast of events, master a comprehensive view of the situation, and envisage and carry out rapid response. For different reasons, related to their mode of operation and internal complexities, the other branches are less capable, especially in times of acceleration of all political and communicative processes, to react to economic, ecological, terroristic, and conflict-related contingencies with the same rapidity as the executive. They can only exercise a check on the action of the executive, but then inevitably also risk reducing the efficacy of the executive's response to the crisis of the day.

Thus, Posner and Vermeule conclude that a post-Madisonian republic should take stock of this basic fact of the political life of the twenty-first century and allow for the executive to be 'unbound'. Unbound does not mean unaccountable, they hasten to specify. The unbound executive of the post-Madisonian republic is still subject to a powerful check—an electoral one, at the end of its mandate. Presidents or prime ministers should be free from fetters, unfold their action as they see fit during their mandate, obtain tangible results, and then reach out directly to the electorate for confirmation at the next election. Accountability, in this case, ceases to be a matter of checks and balances and becomes a matter for electoral campaigning and voter mobilization. The post-Madisonian republic endorsed by the two distinguished jurists is just one of the tributaries that swell the flow of the populist impatience with the technicalities of Madisonian checks and balances. They understand the accountability

---

[70] See Bruce Ackerman, *The Decline and Fall of the American Republic* (Harvard University Press, 2010) 73–75.
[71] Arthur B Schlesinger, *The Imperial Presidency* (Houghton Mifflin 1973).
[72] See Eric A Posner and Adrian Vermeule, *The Executive Unbound: After the Madisonian Republic* (Oxford University Press 2011).

of the executive as a plebiscitary showdown between enthusiastic supporters of the action of government and defeatist, nostalgic, or corrupt defenders of views contrary to the best interests of the nation.

As even this cursory reconstruction confirms, the populist stream of the twenty-first century draws its imposing flow rate from tributaries that have traversed very extended territories and very different landscapes, and have their fountainheads in familiar areas of our political imaginary.

5. Is Left-Wing Populism Significantly Different?

On the surface, it might seem disconcerting to propose a definition of populism that embeds no distinction between right-wing, nationalist, exclusionary, nativist, white-suprematist, racist, anti-migrant, culturally conservative, homophobic populism on one hand and progressive, anti-elite, redistributionist, egalitarian, pro-welfare, anti-austerity, left-wing populism on the other. Indeed, it is a conceptual strategy that requires some words of justification. Although the two kinds of populism produced very different historical manifestations—as polarized as the totalitarian fascist or nazi outcomes of initially anti-liberal populism of the 1920s and the progressive versions that flourished in Latin America with Perón,[73] Chavez, Morales, and Correa, and recently also emerged in the global North (*Indignados, Occupy, Syriza, Podemos, Five Star Movement*)—nevertheless the three components of our definition highlight more commonality than difference. Our examples in the previous sections have mainly concerned right-wing populism, but the point about the convergence of the two kinds of populism can be illustrated by examining three influential views of left-wing populism articulated by Ernesto Laclau, Chantal Mouffe, and Nancy Fraser.[74]

We owe to Ernesto Laclau the daring proposition that 'populism is the royal road to understanding something about the ontological constitution of the political as such'.[75] That claim is vindicated by the most robust attempt available today to develop an understanding of 'the political' premised on the idea that it consists of the successful construction of 'a people' through a performatively efficacious discourse that links together a chain of equivalents. In this sense populism, for Laclau, is not a type of movement but rather 'a political logic'.[76] What type of 'political logic'? One that includes among its basic components a set of specific 'demands', really the building blocks for the construction of the people. Some political subject, leader, or party must accomplish a crucial symbolic task: certain 'isolated, heterogeneous demands' must be fused into a more general 'demand' via the articulation of a symbolic construct posited

---

[73] See Federico Finchelstein, *From Fascism to Populism in History* (University of California Press 2017); Carlos de la Torre, *Populist Seduction in Latin America* (Ohio State University Press 2010); Michael L Conniff (ed), *Populism in Latin America* (University of Alabama Press 2002); Manuel Anselmi, *Populism: An Introduction* (Routledge 2018)11–14; Camila Vergara, 'Populism as Plebeian Politics: Inequality, Domination, and Popular Empowerment' (2020) 28 The Journal of Political Philosophy 222.

[74] For a discussion that instead emphasizes the difference between left-wing and right-wing populism, see Mark Tushnet, 'Varieties of Populism' (2019) 20 German Law Journal 382.

[75] Ernesto Laclau, *On Populist Reason* (Verso 2005)(hereafter Laclau, *Populist Reason*) 67.

[76] ibid 117.

by the leader(s) and accepted by the constituents, who are meanwhile on their way to emerging as a 'people'.[77] This passage, Laclau specifies, 'does not follow from a mere analysis of the heterogeneous demands themselves—there is no logical, dialectical, or semiotic transition from one level to the other—something qualitatively new has to intervene'.[78] What enables that passage is the ability to successfully construct a chain of symbolic equivalences, 'a stable system of signification',[79] which Laclau—drawing on Saussure's idea of signification via arbitrary oppositions, and on the consequent positional value of meaning—understands as only loosely (if at all) anchored to the properties of the constituents. Indeed, the core signifier will be an 'empty signifier'.[80] As in all 'political-realist' approaches, in no way can Laclau's theory generate the claim that a certain equivalential chain of signifiers *deserves* to coalesce into a successful, that is, *hegemonic*, claim to 'peoplehood': the operation may work out (as in the case of Peron) or it may not (as in the case of Bossi's then secessionist *Northern League*),[81] and all the theory can do is to explain *ex post* why that has been the case.[82] The attainment of hegemony—a term derived from Gramsci—is the prize that all constructors of peoplehood aim at via their production of equivalential chains: 'There is no hegemony without constructing a popular identity out of a plurality of democratic demands'.[83]

The attainment of hegemony in society through the successful construction of a people is an intrinsically *antagonistic* process. Along with the people, the populist logic requires the construction of an 'antagonistic frontier': the enemy of the people is located on the other side. In Laclau's words,

> The identity of the enemy also depends increasingly on a process of political construction. I can be relatively certain about who the enemy is when, in limited struggles, I am fighting against the local council, those responsible for the health system, or the university authorities. But a popular struggle involves the equivalence between all those partial struggles, and in that case the global enemy to be identified becomes much less obvious.[84]

Such identity must be constructed by those who lay a claim to unifying the heterogeneity of the people. 'There is no unification of the protesting groups under the empty signifier of the people without identifying an enemy:

---

[77] ibid 110.
[78] ibid.
[79] ibid 74.
[80] 'Popular identity becomes increasingly full from an *extensional* point of view, for it represents an ever-larger chain of demands; but it becomes *intensionally* poorer, for it has to dispossess itself of particularistic contents in order to embrace social demands which are quite heterogeneous. That is: a popular identity functions as a tendentially empty signifier', ibid 96.
[81] 'The *League* did in fact have a "theory of the enemy"; its problem was that it was unable to identify that enemy in any precise way. Its members had the idea that, if a radical change was to take place, the social field had to be split into two confrontational camps, but they did not know on what basis that division would take place', ibid 188.
[82] In the same vein, Urbinati contends that Laclau's populist politics 'becomes essentially power seeking and power shaping: a phenomenon for which legitimacy consists simply in winning the political conflict and enjoying the consent of the audience', Urbinati, *Me the People* (n 4) 33.
[83] Laclau, *Populist Reason* (n 75) 95.
[84] ibid 86.

[P]opulism involves the division of the social scene into two camps. This division presupposes ... the presence of some privileged signifiers which condense in themselves the signification of a whole antagonistic camp (the 'regime', the 'oligarchy', the 'dominant groups', and so on, for the enemy; the 'people', the 'nation', the 'silent majority', and so on, for the oppressed underdog—these signifiers acquire this articulating role according, obviously, to a contextual history).[85]

Taking the Russian revolution as one exemplar of this process, and drawing on Althusser's analysis of it, Laclau claims that all the grievances and antagonisms present in Russian society coalesced around the demands for 'bread, peace, and land', but the injection of empty signifiers was decisive in creating the revolutionary amalgam. Thus 'empty terms' such as 'justice' and 'freedom' transmitted their own radicality to those demands 'which thus became the *names* of a universality that transcended their actual particular contents'.[86]

Laclau's political-realist account of populism as the form taken anytime and anywhere by 'the political' aims at providing a theory of radical, transformative democracy opposed to the enervated form of representative democracy typical of existing liberal democratic regimes. But in fact, as several commentators have pointed out, the paradigm is equally applicable to right-wing forms of mobilization. Indeed, being 'so malleable and groundless, populism is just as well suited to be a vehicle for rightist parties as for leftist ones'.[87]

Be that as it may, relevant for our argument is that Laclau's paradigm of populist politics can be intended as a radicalization of democracy beyond its representative form, yet perfectly fits all the three aspects of our definition. Laclau's 'people' has no historical depth: it is an empty signifier constructed by today's political entrepreneurs of radical transformation for the here and now. In the leader-produced chains of equivalences, the people may be associated with a future of emancipation from today's domination, but that merely functions as a rhetorical cement for merging the local requests into just one hegemony-worthy universalist 'claim'. The past generations' agency, before the empty signifier was created, is not on a par with the presently mobilized people. They are generations of individuals subjected to domination, the protagonists of occasional outburst of rebellion and resistance.

When eventually the potentially hegemonic empty signifier is made available, by a charismatic leader, and 'the people' mobilizes, Laclau understands the living (and struggling) segment of the people as manifestly endowed with full constituent power. Rescripting the rules of the political game anew, thoroughly reforming the constitution, or enacting an entirely new constitution are all within the purview of a populist subject that responds to no normativity beyond its own present will. A part of the whole posits itself as the whole and wields the constituent power that from a democratic perspective cannot but belong to the whole.

---

[85] ibid 87.
[86] ibid 97.
[87] See Urbinati, *Me the People* (n 4) 34. See also Perry Anderson, *The H-Word: The Periphery of Hegemony* (Verso 2017).

Finally, the mobilized people exercises presumptively justified intolerance vis-à-vis all those members of the total population, especially the formerly ruling elite, who do not belong in its ranks. Recall Lefort's felicitous phrase, to the effect that the people never really coincides with the population but must be extracted from it.[88] Laclau's radical democratic populism offers the converse view: the population (or at least parts of it) must be expelled from the people. In his words,

> the only possibility of having a true outside would be that the outside is not simply one more, neutral element but an *excluded* one, something that the totality expels from itself in order to constitute itself (to give a political example: it is through the demonization of a section of the population that a society reaches a sense of its own cohesion).[89]

The people, once it has coalesced around an empty signifier, posits itself not as a 'part *of* a whole', namely the population, but as 'a part that *is* the whole'. When this process is completed, argues Laclau, the relation of the part to the whole, in this case of the *plebs* to the *populus*, is turned on its head: populist politics 'becomes the locus of an ineradicable tension in which each term at once absorbs and expels the other'.[90] In full consonance with the third prong of our definition of populism, Laclau's successfully constructed people also cannot accommodate any legitimate opposition. In lieu of the allegedly moralistic ideal of a society of free and equal citizens who refrain, when they happened to be a majority, from forcing others to obey laws that reflect principles unacceptable to them, the radically leftist populism propounded by Laclau pivots around the notion that a part can self-appoint itself as the whole, and can morally expel the defeated elite or previous rulers as 'the other'. Radical left-wing populism, in the version offered by Laclau, fits our definition no less than nativist and nationalist populism does.

Chantal Mouffe, in tune with Laclau's perspective since their co-authored 1985 volume *Hegemony and Socialist Strategy*, and subsequently an agonistic critic of political liberalism and deliberative democracy,[91] has recently become one of the foremost advocates of left-wing populism among political theorists, advising movements like *Podemos* and leftist political figures. In her recent *For a Left Populism*, as already observed in Chapter 1, a kind of unconfessed crypto-liberalism emerges, centred on the distinction of destructive *antagonism* and democratic *agonism*. The latter of course presupposes that the clash of opposing constituencies be kept within limits that, in order to be effective, must be respected and consented to by *all* the parties: the ostensibly scorned neutral normativity integral to political liberalism has re-entered from the back door. When Mouffe describes the democratic arena as a 'battlefield on which hegemonic projects confront one another, with no possibility of a final reconciliation,'[92]

---

[88] See n 18, above.
[89] Laclau, *Populist Reason* (n 75) 70.
[90] ibid 225. On the exclusionary logic undergirding Laclau's view on the construction of the people, see Fiorespino, *Radical Democracy and Populism* (n 28) 199–206.
[91] See Ernesto Laclau and Chantal Mouffe, *Hegemony and Socialist Strategy* (Verso 1985), and Chantal Mouffe, *The Democratic Paradox* (Verso 2000) (hereafter Mouffe, *Democratic Paradox*).
[92] Chantal Mouffe, *For a Left Populism* (Verso 2018) 137.

she seems oblivious to the fact that 'reconciliation' must already somehow have occurred, at least at the level of the constitutional essentials, for antagonism to fade into the bland, merely adversarial agonism that she quite reasonably endorses.

Another pillar of Mouffe's left populism—her 'anti-essentialist approach according to which the "people" is not an empirical referent but a discursive political construction'[93] brought into existence via 'chains of equivalence'—also shows conspicuous conceptual cracks. How large is the people envisaged by left populists supposed to be? One soon discovers that, in spite of all the anti-essentialist and constructivist rhetoric, the people envisaged by Mouffe can be neither a metropolitan 'people' acting on a local, municipal scale nor a transnational people. The people that left populists ought to discursively construct via 'chains of equivalence' happens to be just the size of a nation, no differently to the nationalist, nativist, ethnic people that the right-wing populists strive to mobilize. The reader is left wondering why the scale of the people should mysteriously count as an exception to the rule that every feature of the people is the product of discursive construction.

Finally, according to Mouffe the goal of a left-populist project ought to be 'the construction of a collective subject apt to launch a political offensive in order to establish a *new hegemonic formation within the liberal democratic framework*',[94] a goal not too distant from the aim of winning fair elections that any Schumpeterian theorist could wholeheartedly endorse.

For the purpose of our argument, however, more important than the internal consistency of Mouffe's left populism is its perfect fit with the three features of the definition of populism outlined in Section 2. When she specifies the aim of left populism as 'the establishment of a new hegemonic order within the constitutional liberal-democratic framework' (including the division of power, universal suffrage, the multi-party system, and civil rights)[95] and with no 'radical break with pluralist liberal democracy',[96] it is clear that her 'people' is in fact nothing more than the electorate. At the same time, Mouffe's electorate, upgraded to people, must conceivably exercise constituent power if it is to sever the connection between capitalism and democracy and start 'challenging the capitalist relations of production'.[97] The third feature of populism—presumptively justified intolerance—in the case of Mouffe takes an attenuated form, due to her acceptance of the 'constitutional liberal-democratic framework', but it acquires a special nuance. In her words, left populism amounts to a special way of 'constructing the political', by way of 'establishing a political frontier that divides society into two camps, appealing to the mobilization of the "underdog" against "those in power"'.[98] Her view, as Urbinati has observed,

> makes democracy seem like wrestling, rather than a process by which oppositions can gain power. Antagonism is *one part* of the democratic movement; but change in

[93] ibid 96.
[94] ibid 122, my emphasis.
[95] ibid 78.
[96] ibid 73.
[97] ibid 79.
[98] Chantal Mouffe, 'The Populist Moment' DemocraciaAbierta 5 December 2016, https://www.opendemocracy.net/democraciaabierta/chantal-mouffe/populist-challenge.

government must be the other one. This means that antagonism is a *means*—it is *for* something—not a good or an end in itself.[99]

Nancy Fraser, one of the leading representatives of critical theory, understood by her as the articulation of a *Zeitdiagnose* that interprets, gives voice to, and enhances the prospect of social movements radically opposed to the injustices and inequality of capitalist society, has recently joined the company of 'progressive populists'. Coming from a perspective different to Laclau's and Mouffe's, she laments that the crossfire of left-liberalism and deconstructionism has 'effectively killed the left-Hegelian project, at least for a time',[100] keeps her version of radical democratic populism free from Schmittian overtones, and develops it in a sympathetic dialogue with Rawls's and Habermas's deliberative conception of democracy. Her criteria for 'distinguishing *emancipatory* from non-emancipatory claims' in the end comes down to nothing more than advocacy of the triad of 'non-domination, functional sustainability and democracy',[101] understood as 'generalizations of the first-order norms that participants use'.[102] Her progressive populism oscillates between the ambition to offer a comprehensive theory of capitalism's relation to gender, race, politics, and nature on one hand, and a moderate *socialist* alternative on the other, which makes it hard to distinguish Fraser's socialism from a political-liberal, liberal-socialist, or property-owning democratic regime with diffuse ownership of means of production, and with democratic participation and entrenched rights.

According to Fraser, the key to the realization of this programme is 'the construction of a counterhegemonic bloc around the project of *progressive populism*',[103] the 'left-wing project' associated with Sanders, Corbyn, Mélenchon, *Podemos*, and the early *Syriza*. The aim of progressive populism is to bring together, under an egalitarian banner, 'the whole working class and not just the fractions historically associated with manufacturing and construction ... but also those portions of the broader working class who perform domestic, agricultural, and service labor'.[104] Such a project could 'position the working class, understood expansively, as the leading force in an alliance that also includes substantial segments of youth, the middle class, and the professional-managerial stratum'.[105]

Assuming that generational and cultural gaps between the segments of the counterhegemonic bloc could be overcome, which is far from certain, why would the sensible project of 'joining a robustly egalitarian politics of distribution to a substantively inclusive, class-sensitive politics of recognition'[106] be best served by the qualification of being *populist* ? Why couldn't Fraser's project instead be qualified as a mix of

---

[99] Urbinati, *Me the People* (n 4) 145 (emphasis in original).
[100] Nancy Fraser and Rahel Jaeggi, *Capitalism: A Conversation in Critical Theory*. Edited by B Milstein (Polity Press 2018) (hereafter Fraser and Jaeggi, *Capitalism*) 7.
[101] ibid 178.
[102] ibid 179.
[103] ibid 216. See also Nancy Fraser, 'Against Progressive Neo-liberalism/A New Progressive Populism' Dissent Magazine, 28 January 2017, https://www.dissentmagazine.org/online_articles/nancy-fraser-against-progressive-neoliberalism-progressive-populism.
[104] Fraser and Jaeggi, *Capitalism* (n 100) 216–17.
[105] ibid 217.
[106] ibid 223.

progressive policymaking, full acceptance of the checks and balances, the separation of powers, and the distinction of constituent and constituted power, which together form the hallmark of constitutional democracy, thus the opposite of populism?

Furthermore, the word 'struggle' is ubiquitous throughout Fraser's case for 'progressive populism', and yet it remains unclear what it means that a social group 'struggles'. Is struggle the same if undertaken by exploited or expropriated groups? Do non-emancipatory struggles count as struggles? Are struggles within the frame of the rule of law or beyond it? Do struggles presuppose mobilization in a classical repertoire of forms of struggle (sit-ins, demonstrations, strikes, occupations, boycotts, etc) or do legal actions, for example class actions on behalf of oppressed groups of citizens, count as struggles? Does simply engaging in electoral campaigns or crowd-funding for a progressive candidate count as a struggle? Are struggles by definition extra-institutional collective action?

Fraser's progressive populism is certainly a political proposal less distant from political liberalism and democratic politics. Indeed, at times it simply appears as an alternative communication strategy for building a winning electoral coalition. Although no trace of presumptively justified intolerance can be found in it, the other two elements of populism are clearly present. No distinction is discernible, in her writings, between the electorate *qua* addressee of her call for a new 'counterhegemonic bloc' and the people as the subject entitled to 'edit' the constitutional project. They are implicitly and unreflectively conflated. Similarly, the counterhegemonic bloc which should revolve around the 'broader working class' and should include, in Fraser's view, 'substantial segments of youth, the middle class, and the professional-managerial stratum', appears endowed with constituent power, insofar as part of its agenda concerns the transformation of capitalist relations of production in a democratic socialist direction.

To sum up, a reconstruction of the work of three among the most distinguished proponents of progressive or left-wing populism shows that the three-pronged definition put forward in Section 2 indeed pinpoints core aspects of populism that are independent of the political orientation embraced by the relevant actors.

6. What the Definition Highlights and Some Questions It Leaves Open

The definition proposed calls attention to the fact that 'the people' evoked by right-wing and left-wing populists is really nothing other than the electorate. The three components of the definition—the reduction of the people to the electorate, the attribution of unconstrained constituent power to it, and presumptively justified intolerance—cut across the opposite political orientations of left and right populist movements, parties, and leaders.[107]

Furthermore, the three prongs of the definition contribute to explain the widespread appeal of populism as fuelled by populists' recourse to deep-seated tropes of

---

[107] Perhaps in the case of populism these orientations are not so opposite, given that in Italy the right-wing *League* and the self-described centre-left *Five Star Movement* have for more than a year been part of the same government coalition.

our political tradition: the omnipotence of the living segment of 'the people', serial sovereignty, the absolute and limitless nature of constituent power, pluralism as the product of ideology and as reflection of ill-conceived relativism, the state apparatus as being in the service of a 'hegemonic bloc', political confrontation as drawing the line between 'us' and 'them', and friends and foes. As tributaries that traverse variegated territories before flowing into the mainstream, so these diverse strands of our political tradition traverse areas of our cultures, societies, and political forms of association that can by no means be understood as populist.

Finally, my definition of populism helps to refine the agenda for revisiting and expanding the paradigm of political liberalism in a historical context different from the one to which Rawls responded in 1993. The following is among the questions made more pressing by the populist phenomenon: Can the classical binary of constituent and constituted power, respectively exercised by the people and the electorate and its representatives, exhaust the basic forms of power present in the polity? The living segment of the people coincides with the electorate, but it also partakes of the people, though not as coextensively as assumed by populists. If so, then the constitution, not owned but *co-owned* by the electorate, can be modified or amended by it, through the voters' representatives or in more direct forms, but not to the extreme point of repealing, replacing, or even altering its 'basic structure'. If so, then Rawls's 'five principles of constitutionalism' need to be supplemented with a reflection on the relation of this intermediate, lower-level constituent power to the constituted powers of the electorate and of the highest interpreter of the constitution on one hand, and to the full constituent power of the entire transgenerational people on the other.

Likewise, the binary, mentioned in the second principle of Rawls's constitutionalism, that opposes 'higher' and 'ordinary' law needs to be reexamined. Terms like 'landmark statute' and 'superstatute'[108] have been coined in order to designate statutes of such constitutional import that they reshape vast areas of social life with implications for rights (eg the Voting Rights Act, the Civil Rights Act, and the Fair Housing Act in the 1960s) and become the focus of a bi- or multi-partisan consensus that subtracts them from the ebb and flow of electoral politics. The status of constitutional amendments approved pursuant the formal provisions of a constitution should also be the object of reflection. Rawls's argument in favour of the structural entrenchment of constitutional essentials should be revisited, especially with regard to the assumption that the Supreme Court ought to be vested with the prerogative to review duly approved amendments.

In relation to Rawls's fourth principle, the 'fixing' and 'meliorative' modification of certain constitutional essentials—basic political rights and liberties—could take place in various ways, including judicial review and legislation. The matter intersects once again constituent and constituted power, the people and the electorate. Although it is a constituted power, a constitutional court—as it will be argued in Chapter 5—can be said to represent the people as author of the constitution, while legislative institutions represent the electorate. Thus, the question who is to fix, and update the fixing, of basic political rights and liberties in a 'living constitution' has to be addressed.

---

[108] William N Eskridge jr and John Ferejohn, 'Super-Statutes' (2001) 50 Duke Law Journal 1215 and Bruce Ackerman, *The Civil Rights Revolution* (Harvard University Press 2014) 34–35, 71–72.

The fifth principle of the constitutionalism propounded in *Political Liberalism* contains an ambiguity which will have to be cleared. When Rawls states that 'ultimate power', within a well-ordered liberal-democratic polity, should be held 'by the three branches in a duly specified relation with one another with each responsible to the people',[109] it is unclear what exactly 'the people' refers to. If we interpret the term as referring to the living segment of the people or the electorate, then the sense in which the 'least dangerous branch' is supposed to be responsible towards it becomes unclear. A constitutional court cannot respond to the voters' will in the same way as parliaments and presidents or prime ministers usually do, without thereby failing to represent 'the people' as author of the constitution. If instead we interpret the term as referring to the historical, transgenerational 'people', then we need to clarify the way in which in which legislatures and cabinets or administrations are responsible towards it.

These open questions supplement the ones raised in the 'Introduction', and await thorough discussion in the rest of this book.

---

[109] Rawls, *PL* 232.

3
Transcending an Ossified Binary
Political Liberalism on Constituent Power

> Constituent power is the generative principle of modern constitutional arrangements. It gives juristic expression to the forces that constantly irritate the formal constitution, thereby ensuring it is able to perform its political function.
>
> (Martin Loughlin, *The Idea of Public Law* 100)

> Sovereign are they in whom jurisdiction in the higher matters reposes.
>
> (Frank I Michelman, in A Ferrara and FI Michelman, *Legitimation by Constitution* 30)

John Rawls did not extensively address the notion of constituent power in his work. In the three main *loci* where he mentions it—the five principles of constitutionalism mentioned in *Political Liberalism*,[1] and briefly discussed at the end of Chapter 2[2]—Rawls approvingly recalls Locke's distinction of 'supream' or constituent and a constituted or ordinary power[3] and identifies the first kind of power as the superior 'power of the people to constitute the form of government'[4] and the second as the power 'of officers of government and the electorate'.[5] He leaves the meaning of these semantically rich terms—'the people', 'constituent power'—entirely implicit, as though the reader should have no doubt concerning their contours. The notion of 'the people' will be elucidated in the next chapter. The object of this chapter is to articulate the meaning of constituent power in a more detailed way, in order (i) to enable the paradigm of political liberalism to better respond to the populist challenge, and (ii) to realize its potential for offering an account of constitutional liberal democracy that overcomes the

---

[1] Rawls, *PL* 231–33. See also *Justice as Fairness: A Restatement*. Edited by Erin Kelly (Harvard University Press 2001) § 13.5 (hereafter Rawls, *Justice as Fairness*), and 'Reply to Habermas', in *PL* 406.
[2] See above Chapter 1, Section 1.a, and Chapter 2, Section 5.
[3] In the *Second Treatise of Government*, in the Chapter entitled 'Of the Subordination of Powers in the Commonwealth', Locke states that although in a 'constituted commonwealth' the legislative should be the 'supream power', nonetheless 'the Legislative being only a Fiduciary Power to act for certain ends, there remains still *in the People a Supream Power* to remove or *alter the Legislative, when they find* the *Legislative* act contrary to the trust reposed in them'. He then specifies that 'the *Community* may be said in this respect to be *always the Supream Power*, but not as considered under any Form of Government, because this Power of the People can never take place till the Government be dissolved', Locke, *Two Treatises of Government* (1690), with an introduction and notes by Peter Laslett (New American Library 1965), *Second Treatise*, Book II, § 149, 413 (hereafter Locke, *Second Treatise*).
[4] Rawls, *Justice as Fairness* (n 1) 46.
[5] Rawls, *PL* 231.

Sovereignty Across Generations. Alessandro Ferrara, Oxford University Press. © Alessandro Ferrara 2023.
DOI: 10.1093/oso/9780192871077.003.0004

binary opposition of Kelsen's formalist approach and Schmitt's organicist-existential view of the people.

Constituent power is a deeply contested concept at the centre of a clash between opposed paradigms of constitutionalism in the twentieth century—an extralegal notion of peripheral interest from a normativist Kelsenian perspective, an inescapable starting point of all constitution-making for Schmitt. His fleeting reference to Locke might mislead the reader of *Political Liberalism* into thinking that Rawls's constitutionalism has little to contribute to this debate. On the contrary, a political-liberal conception of constituent power can be developed by building on the key concepts of public reason, overlapping consensus, and the reasonable. I will outline this conception in dialogue between the two rival paradigms and will show how Rawls's notions allow us to break through their stalemate and to move beyond this threadbare binary.

In Section 1, after foregrounding areas of confluence, three points of divergence between Kelsen and Rawls are highlighted. In Section 2, after revisiting some aspects of Schmitt's constitutionalism in order to show its relevance for political liberalism, seven dissonances that set apart Rawls's and Schmitt's conceptions of 'the political' are detailed. Section 3 addresses the sense in which Rawls's constitutionalism cuts across the two rival paradigms of pure law and of the primacy of 'the political'. Against Kelsen, Rawls reaffirms the ineliminability of constituent power but, against Schmitt, rejects the idea that primary constituent power is unbound. Section 4 develops further Rawls's implicit theory of constituent power as responsive to, and thus assessable in terms of, a normativity *neither external nor entirely of its own making*: taking cue from Frank Michelman's seminal idea of constituent power as always acting 'under law', a Rawlsian 'liberal principle of legitimacy' for evaluating exercises of *constituent*, as opposed to constituted, power is propounded.

1. Rawls and Kelsen on Constitutionalism: Three Points of Discordance

It is useful to start our reflection on constituent power from Kelsen's debunking of this notion. Kelsen is not the only one, of course, to radically question constituent power. He is in the company of many liberal-democratic theorists, some of legal positivist inclination and others, most notably Ronald Dworkin, who are not.

For Kelsen, the people and its constituent power are postulates—in other words, fictions. The people, putatively exercising constituent power, 'is not, as is often naively imagined, a body or conglomeration as it were, of actual persons. Rather, it is merely a system of individual human acts regulated by the state legal order'.[6] The only coherent way of making sense of 'the people' is to understand its unity as 'the unity of the state's legal order'.[7] The law makes the people, for Kelsen, rather than the other way around. The *unity* of the state's legal order, in turn, consists of a hierarchy of norms as far as humanly possible consistent with one another. The constitution is the set of

---

[6] Hans Kelsen, *The Essence and Value of Democracy*. Edited by Nadia Urbinati and Carlo Invernizzi Accetti (Rowman & Littlefied 2013) 36 (hereafter Kelsen, *Essence*).
[7] ibid.

highest-ranking and *unity-securing* norms, from which all the other derive. In Kelsen's words, the constitution is

> a highest principle that determines the whole legal and political order, a principle that is decisive for the nature of the community constituted by that order. However one defines the concept of constitution, it always appears with the claim to encompass the foundation of the state, on which the rest of its order is constructed.[8]

Its validity does not rest on its being the product of constituent power, which is a political, not a legal concept for Kelsen. The validity or normative cogency of the constitution, like the validity of all legal norms, rests not on its content but on the norm's being duly authorized or produced according to a superordinate norm itself valid: 'The reason for the validity of a norm can only be the validity of another norm'.[9]

A formal system so conceived would seem destined to incur an infinite regress. That possibility is foreclosed by the postulation of a *Grundnorm* or 'basic norm' from which the constitution derives. This norm has a transcendental status: it must be presupposed as a condition of the possibility of the validity of a constitution, written or unwritten, and of the validity of all the lower-level norms comprised in a legal system. The basic norm 'is the common source for the validity of all norms that belong to the same order' and 'constitutes the unity in the multitude of norms by representing the reason for the validity of all norms that belong to this order'.[10]

The basic norm determines only the ultimate ground of all the other norms' validity, including the constitution, but not their *content*. Their substantive content may, in fact, vary according to the will of the different actors entrusted with generating those norms. In a theocratic society, for example, the basic norm for grounding the validity of the commands issued by the supreme religious leaders could mandate that obedience to the precepts of a sacred text, duly interpreted by a religious authority, should guide all social life. In a tribal society, the custom for the groom to pay a sum of money to the family for marrying one of the daughters may derive its validity from the customary norm that from time immemorial prescribes that every member of the tribe ought to respect the traditional mores.

The constituent power of a people that through its representatives in a constituent assembly produces a constitution does not have a different status. It may substantively differ from the other basic norms mentioned above, but from the point of view of the 'pure theory of law' it has the same status. It is a transcendental construction that accounts for the possibility of the unity of a legal system by having its legal norms putatively derive from lawmaking institutions that operate as constituted powers within the frame of a constitution directly willed by a sovereign people. In fact, as Kelsen

---

[8] Hans Kelsen, 'The Nature and Development of Constitutional Adjudication' (1929) in Lars Vinx (ed), *The Guardian of the Constitution: Hans Kelsen and Carl Schmitt on the Limits of Constitutional Law*. Translation, introduction, and notes by L Vinx (Cambridge University Press 2015) 28.

[9] Hans Kelsen, *Pure Theory of Law*, translation from the 2nd (revised and enlarged) German edition by M Knight (University of California Press, 1967) § 34, a, 193 (hereafter Kelsen, *Pure Theory*).

[10] ibid. § 34, a, 195. For two enlightening discussions of the basic norm, see Joseph Raz, 'Kelsen's Theory of the Basic Law' in *The Authority of Law: Essays on Law and Morality* (Oxford University Press 1979), 122–39, and Johan van der Walt, *The Concept of Liberal Democratic Law* (Routledge 2020) 198–204.

argues, it is not the will of the community or of the people that creates the basic norm, but rather it 'is the basic norm of the normative order that constitutes the community',[11] be it a tribe, a theocratic society, or a liberal-democratic polity premised on popular sovereignty. As Johan van der Walt suggests,

> Kelsen went so far as to insist that the existence of a people as a *people* depends on their ability to retrospectively maintain law that turns them into a people. His legal constructivism was deconstruction par excellence. It left no scope for romanticist or metaphysical conceptions of peoples as living presences and living causes of law.[12]

As we shall see, while Kelsen's breaking away from 'romanticist or metaphysical' views of the people certainly marks a significant convergence with political liberalism, one problem with his position is the priority of constituted power over all constituent moment, in fact the reduction of constituent power—to use a Biblical image—to a rib of constituted power. The positivist moment, within Kelsen's paradigm of 'pure law', lies in the fact that the self-referential normativity of law becomes, in the absence of all law-independent normative standards, parasitical on the *factual* existence of valid law. The *fact* of legally existing becomes the only ground of the normative validity of law, as though the rules of a game were retrospective projections of what the players do on the ground. However, Kelsen's paradigm should now be considered from the perspective of political liberalism.

Kelsen is not quoted in *Political Liberalism*, but for the purpose of outlining the meaning of constituent power from a Rawlsian perspective we need to elaborate a political liberal response to the challenge raised by Kelsen's paradigm of pure law and his rejection of constituent power as anything other than a construction of the mind. There are general and important points of convergence between Rawls and Kelsen on the nature of democracy. In different vocabularies both endorse the view that 'Tolerance, minority rights, freedom of speech, and freedom of thought, so characteristic of democracy, have no place within a political system based on the belief in absolute values',[13] and that 'the zeal to embody the whole truth in politics is incompatible with an idea of public reason that belongs with democratic citizenship'.[14] Democracy can only flourish when 'penultimate' truths, articulated by public reason, are exchanged in the public forum and ultimate ones are explored, cultivated, exchanged, and contested in the background culture through non-public forms of reason.

Furthermore, Kelsen would certainly endorse the opening question of *Political Liberalism*—'how is it possible for there to exist over time a just and stable society of free and equal citizens, who remain profoundly divided by reasonable religious, philosophical and moral doctrines?'[15]—as also undergirding his own quest for a legal order that by embodying certainty of the law, publicity, and unity can enable free and equal citizens who embrace divergent conceptions of the good to live together without

---

[11] Kelsen, *Pure Theory* (n 9) § 34, b, 197.
[12] Johan van der Walt, *The Horizontal Effect Revolution and the Question of Sovereignty* (De Gruyter 2014) 320 (hereafter van der Walt, *Horizontal Effect*).
[13] Hans Kelsen, 'Foundations of Democracy' (1955) 66 *Ethics* 38–39.
[14] Rawls, 'The Idea of Public Reason Revisited', in *PL* 442.
[15] Rawls, *PL* 4.

oppression. In spite of this significant common ground, an adherent of political liberalism would find three aspects of Kelsen's paradigm problematic.

a. Political realism in normative disguise

The *first* aspect is the implicit political-realist thrust that, somehow paradoxically, undergirds a paradigm that presents itself as the emblem of 'normativism'. Although at first sight Kelsen's claim that *only a higher norm*, all the way up to the basic norm, can make a norm valid seems to affirm the normative nature of 'pure law', in fact the validation of downstream norms takes place not by virtue of the *substantive aspects* of the superordinate norm, as in truly normative paradigms (eg the natural law tradition), but by virtue of the superordinate norm's mere existence and inclusion in the legal system. As he puts it, 'by "validity" we mean the specific existence of norms. To say that a norm is valid is to say that we assume its existence'.[16] If the mere fact of the legal existence of a norm coincides with its validity, if legal facts *are* norms, then it follows that 'invalid law' is a conceptual impossibility—a conceptual move that introduces a political-realist bias in Kelsen's theory.[17]

An example will illustrate the point. In Section 6.4 of Lecture VI, Rawls discusses the hypothetical case of a constitutional amendment, approved in complete respect of the formal provisions of Article V of the Constitution of the United States, that substantively repeals the First Amendment and establishes one religion as the religion of the state. According to Rawls, the Supreme Court should reject that formally impeccable amendment as 'invalid' in that it 'contradicts the constitutional tradition of the oldest democratic regime in the world'.[18] That move amounts to structurally entrenching the non-establishment clause of the First Amendment as unamendable.

The justification offered by Rawls turns on the distinction of two kinds of amendments that have occurred in the constitutional history of the United States: (i) amendments whose aim is 'to adjust basic constitutional values to changing political and social circumstances, or to incorporate into the constitution a broader and more inclusive understanding of those values',[19] and (ii) amendments of functional value, whose aim is 'to adapt basic institutions in order to remove weaknesses that come to light in subsequent constitutional practice'.[20] The first kind of amendments—including the three related to the Civil War and the Nineteenth Amendment granting the right to vote to women—were all meant to bring 'the Constitution more in line

---

[16] Hans Kelsen, *General Theory of Law and State* (1949). With a new introduction by AJTreviño (Transaction 2006) I, C, a, 30 (hereafter Kelsen, *General Theory*). For an enlightening discussion of this point, see Luigi Ferrajoli, *La logica del diritto: Dieci aporie nell'opera di Hans Kelsen* (Laterza 2016), 66–75.

[17] As Kelsen puts it, 'the usual saying that an "unconstitutional statute" is invalid, is a meaningless statement, since an invalid statute is no statute at all', Kelsen, *General Theory* (n 16) Section XI, H, b, 155. Wherever a written constitution is in place, a statute that violates one of the constitutional provisions is 'no statute at all'; it cannot both have 'force of law' and be invalid at the same time. Kelsen's theory binds him to reject the notion that formally impeccable amendments and statutes may be substantively unconstitutional: they never were law in the first place.

[18] Rawls, *PL* 239.

[19] ibid.

[20] ibid.

with its original promise'.[21] That fact makes a right to religious freedom 'entrenched in the sense of being *validated by long historical practice*', which renders its hypothetical repeal or curtailment, even if in accordance with formal procedures, a 'constitutional breakdown, or revolution in the proper sense, and not a valid amendment of the constitution'.[22] Rawls then concludes that the successful practice of the ideas and principles embedded in the Constitution, two centuries after its initial enactment, places 'restrictions on what can *now* count as an amendment, *whatever was true at the beginning*'.[23]

Kelsen's paradigm can certainly accommodate the entrenchment of single constitutional norms by explicit clauses[24]—for example the 'republican form' of the state declared unamendable by Article 139 of the Constitution of Italy and by Article 89 of the Constitution of France. However, the idea of law formally not in violation of law—in Rawls's example, an amendment passed in conformity with Article V over constitutional norms not declared unamendable—and yet invalid, void, undeserving of the status of law is unconceivable within the Kelsen's paradigm. Nor, in spite of Kelsen's advocacy of judicial review,[25] can Rawls's idea of constitutional adjudication as the exercise of public reason by the Supreme Court find any equivalent within Kelsen's perspective.[26]

It might be objected that a more charitable interpretation could deny that Kelsen's basic norm can be reduced to mere compliance with formal procedures (eg for amending the constitution) and could allow, or even prescribe, that the will of the amending power, vested in the voters or their representatives, counts as valid only when it respects the rights consubstantial with democracy. According to this interpretation, Rawls's point about implicit entrenchment could then be accommodated within the paradigm of pure law, by presupposing a 'liberal-democratic basic norm' that prescribes 'never to contradict or subvert the rights-respecting tradition of the oldest democratic regime in the world', or, in other words, that 'legal norms are valid insofar as they are properly enacted and in harmony with a constitution that emanates not from *any* momentary democratic will, but from the will of the people as respectful of certain fundamental rights, one of which is religious freedom and non-establishment

---

[21] ibid 238–39.
[22] ibid 239 (emphasis added).
[23] ibid (emphasis added). On the difficulties inherent in Rawls's formulation and on alternative justifications of structural entrenchment, see Alessandro Ferrara, 'Ferrajoli's Argument for Constitutional Democracy and Structural Entrenchment' (2011) 17 Res Publica 377–83.
[24] See Hans Kelsen, 'Derogation' in Ralph A Newman (ed), *Essays in Jurisprudence in Honor of Roscoe Pound* (American Society for Legal History 1962) 343–44. On Kelsen's views on democracy and *explicit* entrenchment, see Lars Vinx, *Kelsen's Pure Theory of Law: Legality and Legitimacy* (Oxford University Press 2007) (hereafter Vinx, *Legality and Legitimacy*) 124–34. On Kelsen and explicit unamendability, see Yaniv Roznai, *Unconstitutional Constitutional Amendments: The Limits of Amendment Powers* (Oxford University Press 2017) 135–36.
[25] See Hans Kelsen, 'The Nature and Development of Constitutional Adjudication' (n 8). For an interesting discussion of Kelsen on this point, see José Juan Moreso, 'Kelsen on Justifying Judicial Review' in G Ramirez, *Ecos de Kelsen: Vidas, obras y controversias* (Editorial Universidad Externado de Colombia 2012) 354–78.
[26] On the incompatibility of Rawls's view of the Supreme Court as exemplar of public reason and the function attributed to it by Kelsen, see Vinx, *Legality and Legitimacy* (n 24) 165.

of religion'. Under this rendition of the basic norm, if an amendment were passed that violated that fundamental right, it would be invalid.[27]

Let us accept, for the sake of the argument, this interpretation of the basic norm. All that is needed, in order to highlight the problem raised by it, is to shift our attention to the Second Amendment of the Constitution of the United States, which establishes 'the right to keep and bear arms'. Is this Amendment to be considered 'implicitly entrenched' too?[28] If hypothetically a majority of the electorate coalesced and lasted long enough to propose and ratify a Twenty-Eighth Amendment that curtailed the right to keep and bear arms by qualifying it, hedging it, introducing gun control in the constitution, or in any other way, should the Supreme Court invalidate a formally impeccable Twenty-Eighth Amendment because, to use Rawls's words, such new Amendment 'contradicts the constitutional tradition of the oldest democratic regime in the world'? Or would we rather say that the electorate has formed a new opinion on the matter and has joined the rest of the democracies counted by Freedom House in not finding a right to keep and bear arms so fundamental after all? One could imagine a Schmittian argument to the effect that the right to keep and bear arms is a fundamental existential decision of the American people, made under the historical conditions of the Revolution, and as such can never be renounced without altering the political identity of the American people. However, a Kelsenian argument for the unamendability, with reference to the Constitution of the United States, of the right to keep and bear arms, is hard to imagine. And a more general Kelsenian argument in favour of the right to keep and bear arms as a universal presupposition of democracy, that nonetheless has become positive constitutional law in only one country in the world, is even harder to imagine. Thus, the substantive and more charitable interpretation of the basic norm leaves us with an entrenched First Amendment and an unentrenched Second Amendment, up for majorities to change. In terms of provenance from the will of the people, the two provisions have exactly the same status, so how can we account for their different susceptibility to being amended? That difference obviously depends on their substantive content and not on their diverse provenance from some higher law, in this case from the basic norm. Nothing can be more un-Kelsenian than the idea that two norms with equal formal credentials, in our case two Amendments equally issuing from the 'will of the people', have different degrees of cogency (one being unamendable, the other being amendable) depending on their substance—as if some of the Ten Commandments had different degrees of bindingness, to the eyes of a believer.[29] In the end, the charitable interpretation of Kelsen's basic norm undermines the central point of the paradigm—that is, the formality and objectivity of law's validity as depending solely on another law—and is not tenable.

---

[27] I am indebted to Johan van der Walt, Frank Michelman, and Joel Colón-Ríos for having brought different versions of this objection to my attention. They would not necessarily agree with my response to it.
[28] The amendability of the Second Amendment will be addressed more extensively in Chapter 7, Section 3.d, in the context of a discussion of the proper limits of amending power.
[29] Herman Heller concurs in stating that 'to Kelsen, all positive law rules are equivalent. For the pure theory of law, a distinction between nullity and an appeal "from the weight of the violated norm" is obviously "completely and totally unjuristic" as a value judgment', in *Sovereignty: A Contribution to the Theory of Public and International Law* (1927). Edited and introduced by David Dyzenhaus (Oxford University Press 2019) 131 (heretofore Heller, *Sovereignty*).

If that is the case, then an irreducible difference separates Kelsen's and Rawls's constitutional theories. Its inherent legal-positivist thrust deprives Kelsen's paradigm of any normative benchmark for criticizing the substance of the constitution or of its subsequent amendments, as long as they respect the basic norm and effectively regulate the law-making, judicial, and administrative process of a polity. In Kelsen's revealing words, 'in presupposing the basic norm referring to a specific constitution, the contents of this constitution and of the national legal order created according to it is irrelevant—*it may be a just or unjust order*'.[30] For Rawls too, the constitution is designed to regulate legislation, government, and adjudication, but its normative cogency rests on more demanding credentials than mere conformity with a basic norm, and effectiveness: a constitution is binding because its essential elements are assumed to reflect a political conception of justice which in turn can both (i) be freestandingly outlined and (ii) become the object of a sufficiently deep, broad, and specific overlapping or at least 'constitutional' consensus.[31]

b. Law and 'the reasonable'

A *second* discordance between political liberalism and Kelsen's pure theory of law concerns the *motivation* or *disposition* that citizens are expected to develop vis-à-vis the constitution and the law in general. The Kelsenian view of the existence of a norm as coextensive with its validity blurs the distinction—central for political liberalism— between (i) citizens' endorsing the constitutional essentials because they reflect a political conception of justice equally accessible from their diverse, comprehensive conceptions of the good, and (ii) citizens' endorsing the constitutional essentials solely out of fear for the foreseeable consequences of lack of agreement or of the breakdown of a fragile consensus. From the perspective of political liberalism, the pure theory of law blurs the distinction between ultimately *justice-based* and primarily *prudence-based* reasons for citizens' abiding by the law, including higher law. Consequently, an endemic instability, imported from the modus-vivendi mode, in which cost–benefit considerations about compliance with the law prevail, will affect the law's capacity to integrate the polity and regulate effectively its institutions over time.

Kelsen's understanding of the state as a legal order, in other words, allows for a pragmatic and instrumental attitude to shape the citizen's relation to the institutions and

---

[30] Kelsen, *Pure Theory* (n 9) § 34d, 201 (emphasis added). Further evidence of Kelsen's political realism comes from his discussion of the role of *efficacy* in establishing the legitimacy of law: 'Suppose that a group of individuals attempt to seize power by force, in order to remove the legitimate government in a hitherto monarchic State, and to introduce a republican form of government. If they succeed, if the old order ceases and the new order begins to be efficacious, because the individuals whose behavior the new order regulates actually behave, by and large, in conformity with the new order, then this order is considered as a valid order. It is now according to this new order that the actual behavior of individuals is interpreted as legal or illegal. But this means that a new basic norm is presupposed.... If the revolutionaries fail, if the order they have tried to establish remains inefficacious, then, on the other hand, their undertaking is interpreted, not as a legal, norm-creating act, as the establishment of a constitution, but as an illegal act, as the crime of treason, and this according to the old monarchic constitution and its specific basic norm', Kelsen, *General Theory* (n 16) 118.

[31] On the distinct features of constitutional and overlapping consensus, see Rawls, *PL* 164–67.

also blurs the crucial political-liberal distinction of 'stability' and 'stability for the right reasons'.[32] From a Rawlsian point of view, the possibility is thereby undermined of making sense of constitutional orders, in the plural, as owing their different potential for stability to their citizens' diverse attitudes—reflecting primarily either *rational* or *reasonable* considerations—towards their central institutions. Writing about democratic legislation, Kelsen argues that

> if the specifically dialectical process within parliament has a deeper meaning, then surely it is that the opposition of the thesis and antithesis of political interests somehow results in a synthesis. Here, however, this can only refer to a compromise, and not—as those who confuse parliamentarism's reality with its ideology allege—a 'higher' absolute truth or an absolute value standing above group interests.[33]

While orientation to compromise certainly has its proper place in party politics within parliament, in the quoted passage there is no indication that what Ackerman calls 'constitutional politics'[34]—popular mobilization, activism, parliamentary activities, and formal proposals for amendment—should embed attitudes and dispositions any different from those that undergird *ordinary* politics. The Kelsenian idea of democratic politics, supposedly resting on compromise- or modus-vivendi-type orientations and rightly rejecting ideological crusading, misses the phenomenon identified by political liberalism—in a vocabulary convergent, but partially different from Ackerman's—as reasonable disagreement about matters of principle or rights. What about the space of contestation where public reason, rather than bargaining and negotiation, has its place? Kelsenian citizens, parties, or leaders relate to matters of constitutional significance in the same way as they approach routine policymaking. For whenever we step beyond the realm of negotiation between interests, there we seem to necessarily enter, according to Kelsen, the infamous realm of absolute truths or values.

The groundbreaking quality of Rawls's normative version of Ackerman's 'democratic dualism' consists of showing that *tertium datur*: in a liberal-democratic polity there may indeed be matters of political contestation that do stand above group interests—for example, the extension and implication of rights, the proper interpretation of the separation of powers, the implications of certain political values expressed in the constitution—without unleashing a polarized confrontation of absolutized rival truths. These matters form the domain where strategic, rational-choice-driven compromise ends and public reason, along with its standard of reasonability and the related dispositions, becomes operative. From a Rawlsian perspective, the problem with Kelsen's paradigm of 'pure law' is the assumption that *all* law-making, including constitutional law-making, 'ultimately turns on compromise and not on truth',[35] as though reference to truth as such, and not just to *controversial* or *contested* truths, were the problem. For Rawls, on the contrary, *shared* truth claims and *shared* normative claims are not only

---

[32] See Rawls, 'The Idea of Public Reason Revisited', *PL* 459. For an intepretation of Kelsen that allows for a greater role of the reasonable, see David Ingram, 'The Role of Recognition in Kelsen's Account of Legal Obligation and Political Duty' (2022) 51(3) OZP—Austrian Journal of Political Science, 52.
[33] Kelsen, *Essence* (n 6) 70.
[34] See Bruce Ackerman, *We the People*. Vol 1, *Foundations* (Harvard University Press 1991) 266–69.
[35] Van der Walt, *Horizontal Effect* (n 12) 322.

unproblematic, but they constitute the building blocks of public reason, the reason of democratic citizens. Truth-related deliberation poses no threat to democratic civility if and only if no party oversteps the boundaries of public reason, invoking or actually wielding legal coercion in order to back up and enforce *contested* truth claims.

To sum up: while Kelsen's idea that 'the law makes the people' embeds a constructivist perspective certainly in tune with the 'political constructivism' integral to political liberalism, that idea presupposes a dubious priority of constituted power over constituent power. Law becomes the creation of constituted, ordinary powers for the sake of buttressing the legitimacy of pro-tempore reigning agreements about law-making. Constituent power is dissolved, and with it also the line that separates conceptually the players on the ground and the rule-makers. Furthermore, because such constituted powers as legislative bodies are the locus of a strategic orientation towards compromise for the sake of mutual advantage and stability, the primacy of constituted power à la Kelsen also imports the prevailing of a 'rational' over a 'reasonable' perspective within the field of constitution-making and constitutional politics.

c. The groundlessness of the basic norm

The two preceding observations lead to a *third* point of friction between political liberalism and Kelsen's paradigm. The reduction of constituent power to a fictional projection, generated by the ordinary law-making process' bootstrapping itself into existence, makes the legal order respond to a finality that 'results from' this process. This finality can be reconstructed as a singular transcendental presupposition—each legal order having *its own* basic norm—but cannot be imputed to the intentional agency of any collective actor. The conceptual cost thereby incurred by Kelsen's paradigm stands out if we focus on the level that modern political philosophy has identified as the 'pact', the 'covenant', the 'social contract' putatively underwritten in order to establish a 'commonwealth'. Government—oligarchic, monocratic/monarchic, or democratic, with its principles and institutional specifications—logically comes *after* a decision to create a commonwealth, state, or polity has been made or, in Kelsen's terms, has been successfully presupposed to have taken place.

However, if one focuses on the *antecedent* decision, one can distinguish diverse forms, rationales, and justifications that such a decision to found a polity can assume. One need only pause to reflect on the difference that separates Hobbes's, Locke's, and Rousseau's versions of the contract: we may want to give birth to a polity (i) in order to protect our chances for survival by surrendering most of our previous freedom to a *legibus solutus* sovereign, (ii) in order to protect our natural rights to life, freedom, and property by reducing some of our freedom and agreeing to obey rulers who remain accountable to us, or (iii) in order to obtain all of the above while remaining as free as before the contract. Enter Kelsen. That fundamental choice, supposedly antecedent to the making of all law, including constitutional law, is virtually *no one's choice*.[36] Therefore, it also has *no rationale*. The choice between one or other alternative

---

[36] On this point, see also Hans Lindahl, 'Constituent Power and the Constitution' in David Dyzenhaus and Malcolm Thorburn, *Philosophical Dimensions of Constitutional Law* (Oxford University Press 2016) 149.

becomes the happenstance retrospective projection of the prevailing forces in the law-making battlefield located in the constitutional-assembly or constitution-making body. The outcome of the confrontation among political forces contesting in the arena of constitutional law-making will determine something of crucial importance for the profile of the polity we inhabit—namely *which specific basic norm it is then sensible for us to reconstruct*. Such confrontation, however, is no contest of *reasons* in favour of one or another set of constitutional essentials. Kelsen cannot but dismiss such a contest of substantive reasons as futile truth-tracking by educated armies that clash in daylight. From his viewpoint there can only be mutual-advantage-oriented compromise, where *balance* rather than reasonability is the lodestar.

These conceptual costs generated by Kelsen's paradigm of pure law make a political liberal hesitate before subscribing to it and look for an alternative conception that instead fully admits of constituent power.

2. Schmitt's Existential Constitutionalism and Its Relevance for Political Liberalism

Nothing could be further removed from the notion that the law makes the people and the unity of the people rests on 'the unity of the state's legal order'[37] than Carl Schmitt's constitutional theory. The aim of this section is not to offer one more reconstruction of the Schmitt–Kelsen debate of the 1920s and 1930s, on which an enormous literature has developed, but to recall aspects of it relevant for grasping the specifics of Rawls's notion of constituent power and for highlighting its inherent potential for transcending that polarity.

a. The state *is* a constitution

Schmitt starts from the assumption that a law can neither establish nor 'suspend itself'.[38] Some political actor must establish or suspend it. The same holds for a constitution. It does not conveniently self-establish itself only to then retrospectively call into existence its founding people. Constitution-making presupposes the political agency of a subject. In Schmitt's words, 'a constitution is valid because it derives from a constitution-making capacity (power or authority) and is established by the will of this constitution-making power'. Such political will must then be 'existentially present' and needs no authorization: 'its power or authority lies in its being' and it creates the state and its constitution with one and the same stroke.[39] In a lapidary, concise paragraph Schmitt tells us that

---

[37] Kelsen, *Essence* (n 6) 36.
[38] Carl Schmitt, *Political Theology: Four Chapters on the Concept of Sovereignty* (1922). Translated by George Schwab, foreword by Tracy B Strong (University of Chicago Press 2005) 14 (hereafter Schmitt, *Political Theology*). The same idea is expressed in Schmitt, *Constitutional Theory* (1928). Translated and edited by J Seitzer, foreword by E Kennedy (Duke University Press, 2008) 64 (hereafter Schmitt, *Constitutional Theory*).
[39] Schmitt, *Constitutional Theory* (n 38) 64. This idea of an intrinsic connection of the constitution-making power with a sovereign will undergirds also Hermann Heller's view of sovereignty: 'sovereignty

The state does not *have* a constitution, which forms itself and functions 'according to' a state will. The state *is* constitution, in other words, an actually present condition, a *status* of unity and order. The state would cease to exist if this constitution, more specifically, this unity and order, ceased to exist. The constitution is its 'soul,' its concrete life, and its individual existence.[40]

In turn, the state-which-*is*-a-constitution comes into being as a result of a unifying gesture that can be imputed to a sovereign actor. Most importantly, that unifying gesture 'presupposes the concept of the political'.[41] Turning on its head a common but misleading understanding of things 'political' as related to the state, Schmitt grounds the state on 'the political'. The political is the drawing of a line between friends and enemies, in a public sense, by way of positing a core of defining values and commitments. Those who wholeheartedly endorse them and, if needed, are willing to sacrifice even their lives for their defence are the 'friends'. Those who reject them are 'enemies'. The political, in this dramatic collective-existential sense, manifests itself at exceptional times, when the survival of a form of life is at stake. During 'normal times', instead, the political recedes from glaring visibility like embers from the incandescent founding moment, while the scene may well be dominated by the noisy skirmishes of parliamentary factions that contend over distributive or other ordinary matters.

Schmitt's famous opening phrase of 'On the problem of sovereignty'—'Sovereign is he who decides on the exception'[42]—means that after the initial instituting moment of a legal order, 'the political' will appear at the moment when a salient figure, whatever its institutional embodiment, will offer a binding judgment concerning whether 'normality' and, concomitantly, the current norms obtain or, on the contrary, an exceptional predicament has arisen, which calls for norms to be suspended and action against the 'enemies' be undertaken, in order to ensure the ongoing existence of the people. The figure of 'the sovereign' is then best understood as having a dual personification: as the initial holder of constitution-making power effecting a regime change or initiating one, and as the 'executive lord of the exception' when a regime is in place.[43] We cannot address here the many questions raised by the concept of enmity, the purported existential and 'non-moral' sense of the distinction,[44] and the ontological

---

describes the characteristic of the aboslute independence of a unit of will from other effective universal decision-making units; ... the respective unit of will is the highest universal decision-making unit in this particular order of rule' Heller, *Sovereignty* (n 29) 124.

[40] ibid 60.
[41] Carl Schmitt, The Concept of the Political (1932). Expanded Edition. Translated and with an introduction by George Schwab, with and introduction by Tracy B Strong and with notes by Leo Strauss (University of Chicago Press 1996) 19 (hereafter Schmitt, *Concept of the Political*). For a reconstruction of Schmitt's own sense of the importance of his 'upending' the received wisdom about the political and the state, championed by Georg Jellinek in his *Allgemeine Staatslehre* and by Max Weber, see Benjamin A Schupmann, *Carl Schmitt's State and Constitutional Theory: A Critical Analysis* (Oxford University Press 2017) 69–76 (hereafter Schupmann, *Carl Schmitt*).
[42] Schmitt, *Political Theology* (n 38) 5.
[43] On this point, see Andrew Arato, *Adventures of Constituent Power: Beyond Revolutions* (Cambridge University Press 2017) 26.
[44] Schmitt, *Concept of the Political* (n 41) 49. For an enlightening discussion of the difficulties inherent in Schmitt's friend/enemy distinction and in his conception of the political, see Richard Bernstein, 'The Aporias of Carl Schmitt' (2011) 18 Constellations 402 (hereafter Bernstein, 'Aporias of Carl Schmitt').

commitments therein contained, because we need to zoom in on Schmitt's constitutional theory.

Schmitt's thesis, quoted above, that the state does not properly *have* a constitution, but *is* a constitution, combines four distinct meanings of the term—which in turn include diverse sub-versions. The main notions contrasted in the first chapter of *Constitutional Theory* are the *absolute*, the *relative*, the *positive*, and the *ideal* constitutions. The absolute constitution captures the whole of the state in its distinctiveness, including both its 'political unity' and its 'social order'.[45] Thus it is much more than a set of legal norms; it is a 'form of forms' which makes of a certain country that particular state—France, Italy, Spain. The absolute constitution is said to be 'the soul' of polity in the sense of providing the moment of continuity and distinctiveness throughout historical change. Schmitt illustrates the idea through the image of a choir:

> The song or musical piece of a choir remains the same if the people singing or performing change or if the place where they perform changes. The unity and order resides in the song and in the score, just as the unity and order of the state resides in its constitution.[46]

The constitution is the score that ideally gets played out in the political life of a given polity.

The *relative* constitution, instead, reflects the legal-positivist approach, exemplified by Kelsen, that understands the constitution as a collection of constitutional provisions, assembled in a legal document called 'the Constitution'. In this case, 'the concept of *the* constitution is lost in the concept of individual constitutional *law*'.[47] The problem with equating the constitution with the sum total of the legal provisions included in the document called 'the Constitution' is, according to Schmitt, that all sense fades away of the different contribution that various provisions and sections offer to the 'unity of the state'. Fundamental rights on one hand, and matters that should be best regulated through statutes on the other, come to acquire the misleadingly equal status of 'constitutional provisions': for example,

> The clause of Art 1, 1 of the Weimar Constitution reading 'The German Reich is a republic', and that of Art 129 stating that 'civil servants are secure in their personal effects', are both 'basic norms', 'law of laws', etc. However, it is self-evident that in such instances of formalization, these individual provisions in no way retain a fundamental character. On the contrary, the genuinely fundamental provisions are relegated to the level of constitutional law detail.[48]

Furthermore, understanding the constitution as a *relative* constitution results in its demotion to the status of a statute writ large. A supermajority may be required for

---

[45] Schmitt, *Constitutional Theory* (n 38) 59.
[46] ibid 60.
[47] ibid 71.
[48] ibid 67–68.

amending it, but that fact merely confirms that the constitution so understood is only *degrees apart* from regular statutory law.

The third notion of the constitution distinguished by Schmitt is the 'positive' one, a term that covers the semantic spectrum of the 'material constitution',[49] namely, the 'constitution' as the outcome of a decision:

> the essence of the constitution is not contained in a statute or in a norm. Prior to the establishment of any norm, there is a fundamental *political decision by the bearer of the constitution-making power*. In a democracy, more specifically, this is a decision by the people; in a genuine monarchy, it is a decision by the monarch.[50]

A decision of this sort, often expressed in a Preamble (eg 'We the People of the United States, in order to form a more perfect Union ...'), establishes the *form* of political association that the legal consociates want to adopt. That form is best understood as *entrenched*, even if only implicitly, and the parts of the constitution that outline its contours are taken as having special qualities that set them apart from the other constitutional provisions:

> That 'the constitution' can be changed should not be taken to mean that the fundamental political decisions that constitute the substance of the constitution can be eliminated at any time by parliament and be replaced through some other decision. The German Reich cannot be transformed into an absolute monarchy or into a Soviet republic through a two-thirds majority decision of the Reichstag.[51]

It is interesting to compare the *absolute* and the *positive* constitutions. The positive constitution, by virtue of combining a specific form of political association with the situated, historically embodied constituent will of a given people, brings to expression the specific identity-defining commitments made by *this people at this specific point in history*. For example, the Constitution enacted at Weimar in 1919 included 181 constitutional provisions, but only five fundamental, identity-defining commitments. These were that the new German polity be (i) a democracy, (ii) a republic and no longer a monarchy, (iii) a federal state; (iv) a parliamentary democracy, and (v) a *Rechtsstaat* protective of fundamental rights. We will come back to the importance of these identity-defining commitments as unamendable, structurally entrenched aspects of the constitution.[52]

---

[49] On this point, see Joel I Colón-Ríos, *Constituent Power and the Law* (Oxford University Press 2020)203.
[50] Schmitt, *Constitutional Theory* (n 38) 77.
[51] ibid 79.
[52] See ibid 77–78. The status of these commitments is peculiar and often linguistically marked in the various observable 'positive constitutions'. As Schmitt points out, 'Clauses like "the German people provided itself this constitution," "state authority derives from the people," or "the German Reich is a republic" are not statutes at all and, consequently, are also not constitutional laws. They are not even framework laws or fundamental principles. As such, however, they are not something minor or not worthy of notice. They are *more* than statutes and sets of norms. They are, specifically, the concrete political decisions providing the German people's form of political existence and thus constitute the fundamental prerequisite for all subsequent norms, even those involving constitutional laws', ibid 78. The same could be said for the first three articles of the Italian Constitution: Article 1: 'Italy is a democratic Republic founded on labour. Sovereignty belongs to the people and is exercised by the people in the forms and within the limits of the Constitution';

Finally, the notion of the *ideal* constitution designates a 'polemical' version of this concept. Because it is an eminently political endeavour, often premised on the firm will to mark an irreversible transition from an oppressive, unjust, disastrous past— that is, the 'never again' premise often resounding in democratic constitution-making after totalitarian dictatorships—constitution-making is a confrontational activity in which opposing parties struggle for establishing *their* constitution. The 'ideal' constitution is the one reputed to reflect most closely what Rawls would call a comprehensive doctrine or conception of the good.

The analytical picture of the varieties of notions of constitution is not complete, however, without mentioning Schmitt's fine-grained distinction of several sub-varieties of the 'absolute constitution'. The absolute constitution comes in two main versions, each further differentiated in three more specific components that will be mentioned concomitantly with the elucidation of either version. We can consider the absolute constitution (i) as a *situated exemplar*, that is, a legal order embodied in a historical collectivity, or (ii) as a *normative system*, that is, an integrated and hierarchical system of norms.

If we understand the absolute constitution as a *situated exemplar*,[53] then we are considering not so much 'a system or a series of legal norms or principles' but 'the German Reich, France, or England, in its *concrete political existence*'.[54] We can then make better sense of Schmitt's claim that a state does not have a constitution, but *is* a constitution, and that the constitution is its 'soul', the internal principle that makes France or the German Reich the state it is. There are many democratic regimes in the world, but each is unique—'is' more than 'has' a unique 'absolute constitution'. Another facet of this situated version of the absolute constitution concerns the type of regime included in it: a state may be a monarchy, a constitutional monarchy, or a (presidential, semi-presidential, or parliamentary) democracy.[55] A third facet of the situated version of the absolute constitution concerns the dynamic process that has led to its existence. From this angle, we consider not so much the state 'as it is', but 'as it has come into existence' or has been 'integrated'.[56] Some states emerged through *revolution*, others through *elite compromise*, others from *dynastic alliances* and inheritance, others

---

Article 2: 'The Republic recognizes and guarantees the inviolable rights of the person, both as an individual and in the social groups where human personality is expressed. The Republic expects that the fundamental duties of political, economic, and social solidarity be fulfilled'; and Article 3: 'All citizens have equal social dignity and are equal before the law, without distinction of sex, race, language, religion, political opinion, personal and social conditions. It is the duty of the Republic to remove those obstacles of an economic or social nature which constrain the freedom and equality of citizens, thereby impeding the full development of the human person and the effective participation of all workers in the political, economic, and social organization of the country'. These articles are not 'programmatic' or 'declaratory', nor have the specific quality of provisions, but express the basic commitments to which the entire Constitution responds and as such should be unamendable. They should mark the limits of amendment power.

[53] Interpreters of Schmitt here offer a variety of terms for designating the *situated* type of absolute constitution: Martin Loughlin speaks of an 'existential' concept of the constitution and Benjamin Schupmann of a 'concrete' sense of the constitution. See Martin Loughlin, *Foundations of Public Law* (Oxford University Press 2010) 211, and Schupmann, *Carl Schmitt* (n 41) 141.
[54] Schmitt, *Constitutional Theory* (n 38) 59–60 (emphasis added).
[55] See ibid 60.
[56] See ibid 61.

through *struggles for independence*. These vicissitudes inevitably leave their unique mark on polities that in other respects may share the same kind of regime.

On the other hand, we may consider the absolute constitution from a more *normative* angle. The constitution is then a 'fundamental legal regulation', a 'unified, closed *system* of higher and ultimate *norms*'. When so considered, a constitution 'is not an actual existing condition': it is 'a mere command'.[57] Then this constitutional order derives its cogency from *substantive* considerations, for instance from its justice-tracking capacity. This normative view of the constitution, decontextualized and in some respects idealized, should not be confused, Schmitt hastens to point out, with Kelsen's positivistic view of the normativity of the constitution. In a caustic passage, Schmitt interposes an unbridgeable abyss between his 'absolute constitution *qua* normative system' and Kelsen's view, applicable to the constitution as well, that 'only *positive* norms are valid':

> Norms are not valid because they *should* properly be valid. They are valid, rather, without regard to qualities like reasonableness, justice, etc, only, therefore, because they are *positive* norms. The imperative abruptly ends here, and the normative element breaks down. In its place appears the tautology of a raw factualness: something is valid when it is valid and because it is valid. That is 'positivism'.[58]

Schmitt's normative version of the absolute constitution also has additional facets. First, being a 'norm of norms', it 'denotes a unity and totality'.[59] Second, as a 'command', the constitution draws its normative cogency not from a presupposed 'basic norm', but from being the object of the will of a political subject possessed of constituent power: 'the Weimar Constitution is valid because the German people "gave itself this constitution"'.[60] Third, in the heyday of the revolutionary Enlightenment, and to a much lesser extent in the times when Schmitt was writing, the absolute constitution in its normative version epitomizes the aspiration to a complete positive codification of political and social life. A trace of this rationalistic dream still survived in Max Weber's understanding of the rule of law as the rational calculability of the legal consequences of every social action.

b. Why Schmitt's constitutionalism is relevant for political liberalism: three points of interest

Three aspects of Schmitt's constitutionalism stand out as directly relevant for the constitutional theory implicit in political liberalism: (i) the differentiation of two levels of constituent power; (ii) the distinction of constitution- or regime-making on one hand, and the 'social contract' on the other; (iii) the identification of the 'guardian of the constitution'.

---

[57] ibid 62.
[58] ibid 64.
[59] ibid 62.
[60] ibid 65.

In *Constitutional Theory*, Schmitt not only distinguishes 'constituent' and 'constituted' power, but also differentiates the concept of constituent power into (i) the first-order constituent power to create a new political and legal order or enact a new constitution and (ii) the subordinate, second-order constituent power to amend the constitution. As Schmitt specifies,

> constitution '*making*' and constitutional '*change*' (more accurately, revision of individual constitutional provisions) are *qualitatively* different, because in the first instance the word 'constitution' denotes the constitution as complete, total decision, while in the other instance it denotes only the individual constitutional *law*.[61]

The holder of first-order constituent power—be it God, the monarch, or the people—may, directly or through a delegate (eg prophets, a cabinet of advisors, a constitutional assembly, or a convention), enact a new constitution, which may include provisions for the valid and legal amendment of some of its articles, as time and circumstances may require. These subsequent amendments are then to be put in place by a different institutional actor, a constituted power such as a legislative assembly or the electorate (through a referendum), that for the occasion exercise a derivative, secondary, or amending constituent power for the purpose of ameliorating the constitution.

For Schmitt, this second-order constituent power may legitimately amend single constitutional provisions, not the whole of the constitution or its grounding idea, and certainly not the 'absolute constitution' or the 'positive constitution'. To opine otherwise would amount to equating the constitution-making power of the people with the constituted power vested in the institutional actors involved in the legally regulated amending process, such as the two Houses of the UK Parliament or the electorate.[62] The point is corroborated by examples tinged with irony, one of which we encountered in Chapter 2. The doctrine of parliamentary supremacy vests in the Westminster Parliament a nominal constituent power, but it would be ludicrous to think that a majority of 51 per cent, or even larger, of the votes on the Westminster floor could legitimately abolish the monarchy and turn the United Kingdom into to a Soviet-style Republic.[63] That is the same idea expressed by the Supreme Court of India with its theory of the 'basic structure',[64] and by Rawls when he argues that an amendment that re-established religion, and implicitly repealed of First Amendment, would have to be rejected by the Supreme Court as invalid in spite of the hypothetically formal correctness of its approval.[65]

A *second* aspect of Schmitt's constitutional theory relevant for political liberalism is a distinction internal to fully fledged or primary constituent power. The act of framing a constitution is not an initial political Big Bang. The act of uniting a human collectivity

---

[61] ibid 80 (emphasis in original).
[62] See ibid 74. For a discussion of Schmitt's view of the limits of secondary or amending constituent power, in comparative perspective, see Andrew Arato, 'Multi-Track Constitutionalism Beyond Carl Schmitt' (2011) 18 Constellations 324 (hereafter Arato, 'Multi-Track Constitutionalism').
[63] Schmitt, *Constitutional Theory* (n 38) 79.
[64] See *Kesavananda Bharati Sripadagalvaru v State of Kerala* ((1973) 4 SCC 225), § 620 and *Minerva Mills Ltd v Union of India*, 1980 AIR 1789.
[65] See the discussion above in Section 2.b.

through a social contract, covenant, or pact is prior to constitution-making: 'a constitutional agreement does not *establish* the political unity. It presupposes this unity'.[66] Schmitt elaborates on this idea of a distinction between the pact or contract that establishes the state or polity on one hand, and the 'constitutional contract' or agreement that establishes what Rousseau calls 'les lois politiques' on the other. In Schmitt's words,

> the constructions of a social, societal, or state contract ... serve first to found the political unity of the people in general. The social contract, consequently, is already presupposed in the theory of the constitution-making power of the people when one considers its construction necessary at all. *The social contract is not at all identical to the constitution in a positive sense.*[67]

It is not clear how the 'social contract' moment relates to the constituent power of the people: to this point we will return in the next Chapter. Schmitt then moves on to outline the contours of constituent power and the modern bearer of it, that is, the people. In general, constituent power is free existential self-assertion, and as such 'unbound': 'the constitution-making power is the political will, whose power or authority is capable of making the concrete, comprehensive decision over the type and form of its own political existence'.[68] It is holistic: through its decision constituent power 'defines the existence of the political unity in toto'.[69] Furthermore, constituent power, as with the Hobbesian sovereign, is the source of all normativity and responds to none. Recalling Sieyès's theory, Schmitt identifies the modern subject of constituent power with the people or the 'nation': the nation

> denotes, specifically, the people as a unity capable of political action, with the consciousness of its political distinctiveness and with the will to political existence, while the people not existing as a nation is somehow only something that belongs together ethnically or culturally, but it is not necessarily a bonding of men existing *politically*. The theory of the people's constitution-making power presupposes the conscious willing of political existence .... The conscious decision for a particular type and form of this existence, the act through which the people gives itself a constitution, presupposes the state, whose type and form is being determined.[70]

Noteworthy is the transition, presupposed but left unelucidated by Schmitt, from 'the people not existing as a nation' yet, and therefore *not* possessed of constituent power, to the self-constituting nation that inscribes its political will in the unity, and

---

[66] Schmitt, *Constitutional Theory* (n 38) 113. A parallel view is offered by Rawls in his 'four-stage sequence', which opens up with the original position and the parties selecting, on behalf of the future citizens, the principles of justice on which the future constitution will be based. See John Rawls, *A Theory of Justice* (1971). Revised edition (Harvard University Press 1999) § 31, 195–201 (hereafter Rawls, *Theory*). Subsequent references to the four-stage sequence can be found in Rawls, 'Reply to Habermas', in *PL* 397, 403, and 406 (where it is discussed in relation to 'the constituent will of the people') and in *Justice as Fairness* (n 1) 173–74.
[67] Schmitt, *Constitutional Theory* (n 38) 112 (emphasis added).
[68] ibid 125.
[69] ibid.
[70] ibid, 127–28.

also in the single provisions, of the constitution. That transition seems to fall beyond the bounds of his doctrine of constituent power and to remain in need of clarification. We will return to this point in Chapter 4, when addressing the formation of a 'commitment to share joint commitments' as the conceptual watershed between a people as *ethnos* and one that has constituted itself as a *demos*. Constituent power appears self-evidently unbound to Schmitt perhaps as an effect of this unaccounted transition, a blind spot of his conception of the subject of constituent power.

Third, Schmitt addresses the problem of the 'guardian of the constitution', namely the institution invested with the mandate to oversee that the constitution not be exposed to erosion due to the tendency of institutions and constituted powers to follow their own logic and self-interest. In a polemical exchange with Kelsen, who defended judicial review, Schmitt argues that the defender of the constitution should be the President of the Weimar republic. His rejection of Kelsen's innovative plea for judicial review—an institutional practice which in Europe became widely accepted only after the Second World War—rests on the Montesquieuian thesis that judges must solely and strictly apply laws that they receive from the legislative power. Judicial independence, as based on this view of the separation of powers, bars judges from creating 'new law' by way of adjudicating.

Consequently, at a superficial glance it may seem that Schmitt could consider the function of preserving the constitution from the erosion coming, among other things, from the legislative activity of parliament as best served by an independent judicial institution—a court composed of non-elected, tenured, neutral judges. In fact, however, the independence-affirming subjection of the judge to statutory law cannot be easily replicated in constitutional matters, due to their complexity, their touching on matters of principle, and the politicization of the issues at stake.[71] Then, Schmitt continues, the advocates of judicial review are ostensibly pleading for a Montesquieuian judge who merely applies the law, but given the inapplicability of this ideal to *constitutional* adjudication, at closer scrutiny they are really implicitly advocating that the preservation of the constitution be entrusted to an 'independent and neutral authority'.[72] Furthermore, in the context of twentieth-century mass-democracy, constitutional controversies are *politicized*, and a judicial body entrusted with reviewing statutory law would not confront the decrees of royal ministers, as in the nineteenth century, but the majority of an elected parliament. For these reasons,

> the concentration of all constitutional disputes in a single court of justice, formed of professional civil servants who cannot be removed, and who are independent on that ground, would create a second chamber whose members would be professional civil servants. No amount of judicial procedure could veil the fact that such a *Staatsgerichtshof* or constitutional court would be a highly *political* authority endowed with a competence of constitutional legislation. From a democratic point of view, it will hardly be possible to transfer such powers to an *aristocracy of the robe*.[73]

---

[71] See Carl Schmitt, 'The Guardian of the Constitution' (1931), in Vinx, *The Guardian of the Constitution* (n 8) 165 and 171 (hereafter Schmitt, 'The Guardian of the Constitution'). For interesting commentaries, see Schupmann, *Carl Schmitt* (n 41) 166–71, and Vinx, *Legality and Legitimacy* (n 24) 149–50.

[72] Schmitt, 'The Guardian of the Constitution' (n 71) 165.

[73] ibid 168 (emphasis added).

If judicial review enters a tension with the democratic principle, Schmitt concludes, the question 'Who will preserve the constitution?' must be answered by pointing to another institution: the directly elected President of the German Reich. In a parliamentary republic in which the Chancellor runs the government, the President is the head of the State, embodies its unity and continuity, is endowed with the necessary authority, and satisfies a number of indispensable requisites:

> Both the relatively static and permanent aspects of the presidency (election for seven years, difficulty of recall, independence from changing parliamentary majorities) as well as the character of the president's competences ... have the purpose of creating an authority that is party-politically neutral, by virtue of its immediate connection with the whole of the state, an authority that is the appointed preserver and guardian of a situation that conforms to the constitution and of the constitutional functioning of the highest institutions of the Reich, and that is equipped, in the case of necessity, with effective competences for the active protection of the constitution.[74]

Interesting for our discussion of constituent power within a revisited political liberalism is Schmitt's argument in favour of the democratic credentials which would better qualify the President of the Reich, relative to a court, for the function of preserving the constitution. In Schmitt's words,

> The view that the president of the Reich is the guardian of the constitution, moreover, alone conforms to the democratic principle on which the constitution is based. The president of the Reich *is elected by the whole German people*, and his political competences as against the legislative institutions (in particular the dissolution of the Reichstag and the initiation of a popular referendum) are, in substance, *nothing but an 'appeal to the people'*. By making the president of the Reich the focal point of a system of plebiscitary institutions and competences that are party-politically neutral, the current constitution of the Reich aims, precisely on the basis of democratic principles, to form a counterweight against the pluralism of social and economic power-groups and to preserve the *unity of the people as a political whole*.[75]

It is worth observing that the non-judicial path outlined by Schmitt for preserving the integrity of the constitution blurs the line between the people and the electorate—a non-incidental factor in the legitimation of Hitler's claim, two years thereafter, to represent the will of the German people. The closing sentence of Schmitt's essay corroborates this fateful conflation of the people as a pluri-generational subject possessed of constituent power, and the living segment of it, endowed with subordinate amending power. Schmitt's constitutionalism identifies the constitution as the product of the will of the entire people as a historical and 'existential' unit, but entrusts its preservation to a President who represents only a temporal portion of that political subject:

---

[74] ibid.
[75] ibid 172 (emphasis added).

The Weimar Constitution ... presupposes the whole German people as a unity that is immediately capable of action, and not merely by virtue of the mediation of the organizations of different social groups, a unity that is capable of expressing its will, and that is supposed to come together across the pluralistic divisions, in the decisive moment, and make itself prevail. The constitution, in particular, seeks to give to the authority of the president of the Reich the opportunity to connect itself immediately with this *unified political will of the German people* and to act, on that basis, as the guardian and the preserver of the constitutional unity and wholeness of the German people.[76]

c. Schmittian themes in political liberalism?

Let me bring political liberalism back into the picture. A number of scholars have tried to distil the teachings of Schmitt's constitutionalism that can bear a relevance for democratic theory, in spite of the fiercely anti-liberal inclination of the author. Some have claimed that Schmitt's critique of liberalism leaves room for enlisting some of his insight for defending democracy,[77] but other commentators—Ellen Kennedy, Mariano Croce and Andrea Salvatore, Benjamin Schupmann and David Dyzenhaus—have also pointed to the presence of Schmittian themes in the political thought of the later Rawls.

Before addressing these authors' interpretations, let me single out the first and perhaps foremost among these themes: namely, Rawls's rejection of the aspiration to a purely formal procedural approach to justice and legitimacy, and his acknowledgment that values, ethical substance, ideas of the good, are ineliminable from the normative picture. The later Rawls has taken distance from the strongly *procedural* understanding of normativity[78] that runs from Kant to Kelsen to Habermas. *Political Liberalism* includes an entire chapter—Lecture V, on 'The Priority of the Right and Ideas of the Good'—in which the details are spelled out of several 'ideas of the good' at the centre of the liberal polity. These substantive ideas include: goodness as rationality,[79] primary goods,[80] the polity-specific 'political values' and certain general 'political virtues' (fair social cooperation, reasonableness, toleration, civility, and the sense of fairness),[81] and the good of a well-ordered political society.[82] A terminological clarification may be necessary on the procedural–substantive polarity. As the term is used here, 'procedural' is synonymous with 'formal' or 'content-independent'. Truly 'procedural' in this sense are Kant's categorical imperative, Habermas's principles 'U' and

---

[76] ibid 172–73.
[77] See Renato Cristi, 'Carl Schmitt on Sovereignty and Constituent Power' in David Dyzenhaus (ed), *Law as Politics: Carl Schmitt's Critique of Liberalism*. With a preface by R Beiner (Duke University Press 1998) 179–95 (hereafter Dyzenhaus, *Law as Politics*); Chantal Mouffe, *The Return of the Political* (Verso 1993), especially Chapters 7 and 8, and 'Carl Schmitt and the Paradox of Liberal Democracy', in Dyzenhaus (ed), *Law as Politics*, 159–75 (hereafter Mouffe, 'Carl Schmitt').
[78] See Rawls, *PL* 191–95.
[79] *PL* 176–78.
[80] *PL* 178–81.
[81] *PL* 194.
[82] *PL* 201–04.

'D', and Bentham's utilitarian moral principle of the 'greater happiness for the largest number'. Primary goods and the other four 'ideas of the good', from this perspective, are pretty enmeshed with substance: catalogues of liberties and rights legitimately may vary from one democratic polity to another; powers and prerogatives of office again may vary significantly, even within similar types of democratic polities (eg a French President can dissolve Parliament and call for elections, the President of the United States cannot dissolve Congress); the social bases of self-respect are subject to ample variation; and the democratic virtues (toleration, reasonability, civility, etc) as *virtues* are by definition substantive and not procedural. On the other hand, one may call primary goods 'procedural' in a different and looser sense: namely, as shared normative benchmarks useful for bridging, or narrowing down, political divides.

The choice of the first, more restrictive, meaning of 'procedural' aims at emphasizing the twofold significance of what Rawls achieves in Lecture V. First, contrary to the Kant–Kelsen–Habermas line of thinking, he shows that the justness of a liberal-democratic society need not be seen as resting on a 'purely procedural' or 'formal' decision procedure but may accommodate aspects of 'the good', indeed *five* ideas of the good. Second, Rawls's vision of the 'just and stable society of free and equal citizens' is thereby shielded against the critiques of formalism articulated by Hegel and Schmitt. Schmitt's point about the ineliminability of the all-too-substantive 'political' has traction only against the formal/procedural models à la Kelsen and Habermas, but leaves Rawls's notion of the just and stable society unscathed, precisely thanks to Rawls's inclusion of more 'substantive' (though still 'procedural' in a looser sense) normative aspects.[83]

Over and beyond these shared notions of the good, political values, and virtues, the notion of overlapping consensus introduces a more substantive conception of the integration of a liberal-democratic society. It has also been argued that Rawls's criticism of modus-vivendi-type patterns of political integration, relative to the overlapping consensus pattern, dovetails with Schmitt's rejection of Kelsen-type compromise, and for similar reasons, namely its intrinsic instability in comparison to non-prudential forms of political association.[84]

Dyzenhaus and Schupmann emphasize a certain militant aspect of Rawls's liberalism. Schupmann traces this motif back to *A Theory of Justice*, in a passage in which Rawls states that 'justice does not require that men must stand idly by while others destroy the basis of their existence'.[85] Dyzenhaus traces other *loci* in Political Liberalism where Rawls addresses the need to 'contain' constituencies that endorse unreasonable comprehensive conceptions inconsistent with the constitutional essentials.[86] He claims that Rawls is brought to that conclusion by an implicitly Schmittian move. Because in the public forum public reason, the standard of reasonability, and the political values supposedly prevail (though not exclusively, after Rawls's introducing the *proviso*),[87] then the unreasonable comprehensive views embraced by certain constituencies will

---

[83] I am grateful to Frank Michelman for having prompted me to clarify the sense in which the term 'procedural' is here used. For an interesting Kantian view of justice along not entirely formalistic lines, see Rainer Forst, *The Right to Justification* (Columbia University Press 2012), 117–18.
[84] See Mouffe, 'Carl Schmitt' (n 77) 169.
[85] Rawls, *Theory* (n 66) 192.
[86] See Rawls, *PL* 64, and Dyzenhaus, 'Introduction', in Dyzenhaus (ed), *Law as Politics* (n 77) 15.
[87] See Rawls, 'Introduction to the Paperback Edition', *PL* xlix–l.

end up marginalized in what Dyzenhaus calls 'the social' (presumably an equivalent of Rawls's 'background culture'). These excluded groups may then endeavour to reclaim some control over politics and regain access to the public forum: at that point they could legitimately be contained insofar as they would threaten the core values of the liberal polity. In the end, for Dyzenhaus and Schupmann the later Rawls comes to endorse a view not so distant from a domesticated Schmittian view of the political. This argument recurs in various forms in the writings of the other authors mentioned above and is worth considering in more detail.

The just and stable society envisaged by political liberalism is traversed by a deep rift. On one hand, there are constituencies that endorse comprehensive conceptions very diverse but not *so* diverse as to prevent them from converging on a modular political conception of justice (hopefully, but not necessarily, 'justice as fairness') thick enough for sustaining constitutional essentials shared from diverse angles by all these citizens. The overlapping consensus on that political conception of justice, on certain political values, ideas of the good, and ultimately on a robust core of constitutional essentials, allows for the 'stability for the right reasons' of the just and stable liberal-democratic polity. On the other hand, and this is the Schmittian flipside of political liberalism emphasized by these commentators, there is an 'inner periphery' of the well-ordered society, populated by citizens who embrace unreasonable or partially unreasonable conceptions, are not party to that overlapping consensus, are protected by rights they have not concurred in shaping, are the object of policies resting on principles they do not endorse, and are not even owed 'political justification'.[88] Upon discovering that the constitutional regime in place, blessed by an overlapping consensus that fails to include them, works against the persistence over time and potential subsequent affirmation of their privately held conceptions, these unreasonable citizens may seek redress through political action, and are to meet 'containment' as a response.

Two passages, often quoted by these authors, are footnote 19 of Lecture II of *Political Liberalism*, where the persisting of 'doctrines that reject one or more democratic freedoms' is called by Rawls 'a permanent fact of life', that sets for the well-ordered liberal-democratic polity 'the practical task of containing them—*like war and disease*—so that they do not overturn political justice',[89] and a like sounding passage of the 'Introduction', in which the existence of 'unreasonable and irrational, and even mad, comprehensive doctrines' is described as a definite possibility that calls for their containment so that 'they do not undermine the unity and justice of society'.[90]

In the rendition put forward by the advocates of the convergence argument, these passages cast a different light on the adjective 'political', as used by Rawls in *Political Liberalism*. Over and beyond the original meaning of 'non comprehensive' or 'non metaphysical', now the adjective comes to designate something close to the Schmittian 'political'—a wholeheartedly shared, non-procedural but all-substantive endorsement

---

[88] See Jonathan Quong, *Liberalism Without Perfection* (Oxford University Press 2011) 290–314 (hereafter Quong, *Liberalism Without Perfection*).
[89] Rawls, *PL* 64.
[90] ibid xvi–xvii. This footnote and the passage of the 'Introduction' to *Political Liberalism* are the *pièces de résistance* of the Rawls–Schmitt commentaries found in Dyzenhaus, 'Introduction' in Dyzenhaus, *Law as Politics* (n 77) 15; Ellen Kennedy, *Constitutional Failure: Carl Schmitt in Weimar* (Duke University Press 2004) 3–4; Mariano Croce and Andrea Salvatore, *The Legal Theory of Carl Schmitt* (Routledge 2013) 169–70.

of certain values taken as constitutive of the identity of the liberal-democratic polity, and the resolute rejection and marginalization of those who fail to endorse them. Rawls at some point, before and after the publication of *Political Liberalism*, even used the term 'the political'.[91] This line of interpretation of political liberalism raises the question: Is the later Rawls covering with a liberal-democratic veneer Schmitt's notion that the state is premised on 'the political'? In the next section, I argue that seven difficulties of this convergency thesis suggest a negative answer to that question.

d. Seven dissonances between Rawls and Schmitt on the nature of 'the political'

Several important differences distinguish Rawls's and Schmitt's understandings of the political and tend to be overlooked by interpreters keen on lending democratic credentials to Schmitt's theory. These differences should make us wary of interpreting the relation of the reasonable comprehensive conceptions coalescing around a political conception of justice to the unreasonable doctrines as a restatement of Schmitt's thesis of the dependency of the state on the political.

First, let us recall that for Schmitt constitution-making is the product of a constitution-making power that needs no authorization and by establishing a form of government or regime unifies the polity—which has already come together by virtue of a contract, pact, or covenant—around a political order responsive to some substantive values. This unification process occurs against the background of a shared conception of politics, the state, and government, which is comprehensive and enjoins the consociates to partake of some 'cultural artefact' (a philosophical doctrine, a popular ideology, a politicized religious message) purportedly enclosing 'the whole truth'. Schmitt's view of the state and the constitution as tightly integrated is premised on a larger view of society as unified by *one* unitary political will and *one* cluster of values that reach throughout the entire social body to all regions of social life.[92] The

---

[91] See John Rawls, 'The Domain of the Political and Overlapping Consensus' (1989) in Derek Matravers and Jonathan Pike (eds), *Debates in Contemporary Political Philosophy: An Anthology* (Routledge 2003) 160–81 (hereafter Rawls, 'Domain of the Political'). See also 'The Idea of Public Reason Revisited', in *PL* 458.

[92] This view reflects mainly Schmitt's position in the early 1920s. In the early 1930s he came to acknowledge accommodating pluralism as one of the functions of the state, linked with the overarching one of preventing the eruption of 'political' conflict: 'Even the absolutist prince of the seventeenth and eighteenth centuries was forced to respect divine and natural law and ensure the widest respect for traditional institutions and vested rights. State unity was always a unity from social pluralities. At various times and in various countries it was very different but always complex and, in a certain sense, intrinsically pluralist'. The homogeneous unity created by the sovereign decision generated various forms of political unity, one of which was argued by Schmitt to rest on *consensus* and to possibly give rise to a 'state ethics of pluralism, the ethical meaning of which is apparently to ethically accept only *unity through consensus*', Carl Schmitt, 'State Ethics and the Pluralist State' (1930), in Arthur J Jacobson and Bernhard Schlink (eds), *In Weimar: A Jurisprudence of Crisis* (University of California Press 2000), 306. Thanks are due to Mariano Croce and Andrea Salvatore for having brought this essay to my attention. See their enlightening reflections on Schmitt's institutionalist turn in *Carl Schmitt's Institutional Theory* (Cambridge University Press 2022), especially 84–105. However, even taking into account this more 'institutionalist' version of Schmitt's thought, the tension with political liberalism persists. For both Schmitt and Rawls one of the functions of state institutions is to keep conflict at bay and avoid the threat of dangerous ideological confrontation. For Schmitt, however, given that pluralism carries an inherent risk of degenerating into all-out enmity, the more legally mediated homogeneity it is possible to obtain, the better (and complete cultural integration remains an ideal). For Rawls, instead, given

existential texture of the inaugural unifying gesture, attested by the whole theory of the exception as response to the threat of annihilation, merges the institutional, legal, historical, cultural, and social aspects of the polity in what basically amounts to *one* life form and its attendant political-institutional ordering. Ideally, the constitution reflects what Montesquieu called 'esprit générale d'une nation'.

Rawls's overlapping consensus, instead, although marked off from the non-concurring unreasonable doctrines, has two features that find no correspondence in Schmitt's view: (i) it is far from comprehensive, but limited to the narrower range consisting of the basic structure, the political conception of justice, the fundamental rights and basic liberties, plus whatever 'constitutional essentials' exceed the previous enumeration; (ii) it is *internally pluralized in a non-trivial sense*, insofar as the core of consensual matters represents the area of overlap of a constellation of broader, comprehensive, often rival, conceptions that are endorsed by different constituencies and motivate them—as lamented by Habermas[93]—to endorse the consensual core for quite diverse reasons.

The litmus test of the difference between the Schmittian and the Rawlsian versions of a legitimating consensus underlying a democratic regime lies in the fact that the Rawlsian citizen, who operates within the bounds of public reason, would never grasp her concurrence to the overlapping consensus and her effort to enlarge it as motivated by a relentless effort to win the rest of the citizens 'to the whole truth',[94] whereas to a member of the Schmittian people the constitution and the institutions of the state would appear as crucial instruments for the purpose of affirming a comprehensive form of life.

Second, both perspectives eschew proceduralism and revolve around some prima facie similar version of 'the political' as line-drawing, the demarcating of friends from enemies of the polity, reasonable from unreasonable citizens and political forces. Rawls, however, never tires of emphasizing that for him the political is 'a special domain with specific distinctive features'.[95] It includes the basic structure of society, the exercise of political power by the state's institutions and authorities, and also 'the power of equal citizens as a collective body'. The political so conceived is distinct 'from the associational, which is voluntary in ways that the political is not; it is also distinct from the personal and the familial, which are affectional domains, which again the political is not'.[96] This list is not exhaustive. As Rawls specifies, there might by other areas of society that are 'nonpolitical'.

On the contrary, Schmitt never tires of stressing that the political may be *ubiquitous*. Any controversy, in *any* realm of institutional or social life, could become the vehicle and focus of a 'political' opposition of friends and enemies.[97] Elections, but

---

that pluralism results from the unimpeded exercise of human reason, the desirable level of homogeneity only concerns the basic structure, a political conception of justice, fundamental rights, basic liberties, and their balancing.

[93] See Jürgen Habermas, '"Reasonable" versus "True," or the Morality of Worldviews' in *The Inclusion of the Other* (MIT Press 1998) 86.
[94] Rawls, 'The Idea of Public Reason', in *PL* 442.
[95] Rawls, 'The Domain of the Political' (n 91) 160; *PL* 137.
[96] Rawls, 'The Domain of the Political' (n 91) 167; *PL* 137.
[97] See Schmitt, *Concept of the Political* (n 41) 26–27.

also scientific debates or juridical and constitutional controversies, not to mention religious disputes or distributive issues, or even the ordinary functioning of institutions, could become 'politicized': there simply is no area of social life which is shielded from 'the political'. Strictly speaking, there is no *domain of the political*, for Schmitt, because *any* area of social life could become 'political'.

Third, Rawls's constitutional and overlapping consensus, even if taken as instantiations of the political in liberal clothes, have an intrinsic dynamic that Schmitt's political lacks entirely. Once a constitutional consensus on procedures and rights supersedes an initial modus vivendi,

> political groups must enter the public forum of political discussion and appeal to other groups who do not share their comprehensive doctrine. This fact makes it rational for them to move out of the narrow circle of their own views and to develop political conceptions in terms of which they can explain and justify their preferred policies to a wider public so as to put together a majority. As they do this, they are led to formulate political conceptions of justice.... These conceptions provide the common currency of discussion and a deeper basis for explaining the meaning and implications of the principles and policies each group endorses.[98]

The political as understood by Schmitt, instead, exhibits a kind of static divisiveness. Of course, the line between friends and enemies may shift at any time, but it shifts as an effect of the happenstance modification of the sovereign will that commands constituent power, not as the likely, though by no means necessary, outcome of a dynamic intrinsic to the political. Furthermore, in addition to an intrinsic tendency of constitutional and overlapping consensus to expand, Rawls mentions the effect of political-philosophical reflection. The first task of that reflection, in his opinion, is to reduce divisions, enlarge the basis of consensus, and render 'the domain of the political' more inclusive. In his words, the first of four roles of political philosophy

> is to focus on deeply disputed questions and to see whether, despite appearances, some underlying basis of philosophical and moral agreement can be uncovered. Or if such a basis of agreement cannot be found, perhaps the divergence of philosophical and moral opinion at the root of divisive political differences can at least be narrowed so that social cooperation on a footing of mutual respect among citizens can still be maintained.[99]

Fourth, there is a tendency, among those who compare Rawls and Schmitt on the political, to understand *reasonableness* as a *liberal* standard for public reason and as a *liberal* virtue: consequently, the 'unreasonable', who fall on the other side of the line demarcating 'the political' and deserve nothing but containment, are identified as the *non-liberal* or *illiberal*. That is an inaccurate interpretation that needs to be corrected. It fosters, if left unexamined, the idea that Rawls might be smuggling in 'comprehensive'

---

[98] Rawls, *PL* 165.
[99] Rawls, *Justice as Fairness* (n 1) 2.

liberal values and standards under the pretence of neutrality.[100] I doubt one could find in *Political Liberalism* passages that suggest that reasonability, as a standard of public reason, or public reason itself, or the political virtue of reasonableness are the exclusive precinct of liberals. To be reasonable means (i) to accept the burdens of judgment and (ii) to be willing to cooperate with others on terms that *all*, not just liberals, can accept on a basis of reciprocity.[101] It is hard to imagine why people who endorse comprehensive non-liberal conceptions, religious or secular, would be barred from qualifying from reasonableness so defined. Furthermore, if epistemic humility and the disposition to cooperate on the basis of reciprocity were strictly and exclusively liberal dispositions, one would wonder why Rawls felt the need to take distance from the comprehensive liberalisms of the past (Kant, Mill, Constant, or his own comprehensive position in *A Theory of Justice*) and outline a *political* liberalism.

Fifth, containment may not be the first choice concerning how the plurality of constituencies that partake of overlapping consensus should relate to the unreasonable supporters of conceptions averse to that consensus. There exists a range of possible alternatives on this crucial point of political liberalism. At one extreme, closer to the Schmittian 'exclusivist' notion of the political, we find Jonathan Quong's proposal to sharpen the line and even fortify it. He suggests expanding the realm where recourse to public reason is mandatory: that realm should cover 'all our political decisions and deliberations' and not just the discussion over constitutional essentials and matters of basic justice.[102] Furthermore, he suggests that political justification is not bound to address the premises of the unreasonable.

Finally, he advocates a 'containment' of unreasonable doctrines by way of adopting policies 'whose primary intention is to undermine or restrict the spread of ideas that reject the fundamental political values, that is, (i) that political society should be a fair system of social for mutual benefit, (ii) that citizens are free and equal, and (iii) the fact of reasonable pluralism'.[103] At the other end of the spectrum, at maximum distance from the Schmittian 'exclusive' view of the political, one finds a number of interesting attempts to reshuffle the rigid binary of reasonableness and unreasonableness and envisage 'degrees of reasonableness' as well as a sort of duty to help the partially unreasonable to become fully reasonable. Let me mention Erin Kelly's and Lionel McPherson's argument, based on reasonableness as linked with the burdens of judgment, for tolerating at least some of the unreasonable;[104] Andrew March's conjectural argument for engaging an ideal-typical Muslim believer in a dialogue on reconciling the duties of faith and the duties of political liberal citizenship;[105] and Benedetta Giovanola's and Roberta Sala's groundbreaking insertion of two intermediate categories between reasonable and unreasonable citizens, that is, the 'partially reasonable' and the

---

[100] See Dyzenhaus, *Law as Politics* (n 77) 16. For the same point articulated from the converse perspective, that is, contrasting Schmitt's full grasp of 'the political' with Rawls's lack thereof, see Chantal Mouffe, *The Democratic Paradox* (Verso 2000) 31–32.

[101] See Rawls, *PL* 50.

[102] See Quong, *Liberalism Without Perfection* (n 88) 11.

[103] ibid 299.

[104] Erin Kelly and Lionel McPherson, 'On Tolerating the Unreasonable' (2001) 9 Journal of Political Philosophy 38–55.

[105] Andrew March, *Islam and Liberal Citizenship: The Search for an Overlapping Consensus* (Oxford University Press 2009).

'non-reasonable'.[106] I have myself suggested softening the binary of reasonableness and unreasonableness and understanding Rawls's 'just and stable' well-ordered society as a *multivariate* democratic polity in which political justification is addressed to *all*, not just to the reasonable citizens, and in which the inclusion of the 'partially reasonable' is made possible by allowing prudential considerations for endorsing the political values and the overlapping consensus.[107] This variety of positions attests the diversity of possible interpretations of Rawls's thesis on the 'containing' of the unreasonable doctrines and their supporters. Such variety of interpretations then inevitably detracts from the soundness of the convergence thesis concerning Rawls and Schmitt on 'the political'.

Sixth, the commentators who emphasize said convergence tend to gloss over a discrepancy as palpably glaring before anyone's eyes as Poe's purloined letter. Schmitt's political-realist perspective and existential pathos turn the political into an entirely *subjective* matter. For him,

> the friend and enemy concepts are to be understood in their concrete and existential sense, not as metaphors or symbols, not mixed and weakened by economic, moral, and other conceptions, least of all in a private-individualistic sense as a psychological expression of private emotions and tendencies. They are neither normative nor pure spiritual antitheses.[108]

Earlier in the twentieth century, Émile Durkheim intimated that the opposition of the sacred and the profane cannot be connected with any external, objective content— the sense of the sacred, especially in totemic religions, being attachable to anything— but is to be understood in purely relational terms. The sacred can only be identified through the repulsion that the idea of its admixture with the profane arouses. Much in the same way, for Schmitt there is no external vantage point, let alone criterion, that can determine *who* can turn into a public enemy. The absolutely subjective quality of this choice—a quality connected with its being the ultimate expression of unbound *sovereignty*—is emphasized repeatedly:

> only the actual participants can correctly recognize, understand, and judge the concrete situation and settle the extreme case of conflict. Each participant is in a position to judge whether the adversary intends to negate his opponent's way of life and therefore must be repulsed or fought in order to preserve one's own form of existence.[109]

Consequently, the only key to assessing a given sovereign act of separating these 'friends' from those 'enemies' is its actual success (i) in rallying a people around a given representation of the line separating it from its public enemy and (ii) in mobilizing political energy in defending that line.[110] There is no normative foothold, in the

---

[106] Benedetta Giovanola and Roberta Sala, 'The Reasons of the Unreasonable: Is Political Liberalism Still An Option?' (2022) 48(9) Philosophy & Social Criticism, 1226–1246.
[107] Alessandro Ferrara, *The Democratic Horizon: Hyperpluralism and the Renewal of Political Liberalism* (Cambridge University Press 2014) 105–08.
[108] Schmitt, *The Concept of the Political* (n 41) 27–28.
[109] ibid 27.
[110] On the internal difficulties of filtering away the normative dimension from the existential one, as if the life jeopardized by the enemy was just the 'bare life' and not a normatively articulated construct, see

Schmittian paradigm, for raising the question whether a certain enmity *should* be declared in existence or another denied any real import.

On the contrary, Rawls goes to great lengths to keep his understanding of a political conception of justice, susceptible to coalescing an overlapping consensus around its principles, distinct from the subjective, preference-aggregative 'idea of consensus used in everyday politics'. He reminds us that a normative understanding of the overlapping consensus on a political conception of justice—a consensus allegedly functioning as an equivalent of 'the political' for distinguishing who is and who is not an addressee of political justification—works in a way completely different from a political compromise driven by the composition of subjective preferences:

> We do not look to the comprehensive doctrines that in fact exist and then draw up a political conception that strikes some kind of balance of forces between them. To illustrate: in specifying a list of primary goods, say, we can proceed in two ways. One is to look at the various comprehensive doctrines actually found in society and specify an index of such goods so as to be near to those doctrines' center of gravity, so to speak: that is, so as to find a kind of average of what those who affirmed those views would need by way of institutional claims and protections and all-purpose means.... This is not how justice as fairness proceeds; to do so would make it political in the wrong way. Rather, it elaborates a political conception as a *freestanding* view working from the fundamental idea of society as a fair system of cooperation and its companion ideas. The *hope* is that this idea, with its index of primary goods arrived at from within, can be the focus of a reasonable overlapping consensus.[111]

'Stability for the right reasons'[112] is the concept that functions as a foil, for the later Rawls, against a political-realist understanding of overlapping consensus as a liberal equivalent of Schmitt's notion of the political, designed to produce integration via drawing the line between friends and enemies. The Rawlsian 'political', that is, the overlapping consensus on a political conception of justice, may fail to materialize—and in this respect shares the radical contingency of Schmitt's political—but cannot be produced at will or 'believed to exist'. It presupposes a freestanding view of justice that constitutes at the same time the normative benchmark for assessing its quality.

Seventh, for Schmitt the sovereign will that draws the line between friends and enemies is as unbound as any act of constituent power. That will creates the fundamental bipartition of the political universe without being itself subject to any non-political standard, and the moment of the exception, of impending chaos that would make any law inapplicable, makes the nature of this sovereign will all the clearer. After the founding of a state which *is* a constitution, and the settling in of ordinary law and politics, the 'exception reveals most clearly the essence of the

---

Bernstein, 'The Aporias of Carl Schmitt' (n 44) 415–17. Enlightening reflections can also be found in his article with regard to the problematic, unclear relation of individual and public enmity (see ibid 410–11), and on Schmitt's implicit commitment to a metaphysical negative anthropology in tension with the programmatic autonomy of politics (see ibid 411–13).

[111] Rawls, *PL* 39–40 (emphasis added). See also 'Introduction to the Paperback Edition', *PL* xlv–xlvi.
[112] See n 32, supra.

state's authority. The decision parts here from the legal norm, and (to formulate it paradoxically) authority proves that *to produce law it need not be based on law*.'[113] The founding and the exception are the moments when the power to decide—which Locke did capture, contrary to Schmitt's opinion, under the 'prerogative', but without linking it with 'the political'[114]—operates in its purest form. Thus 'the political' comes somehow 'before' the law, even before the higher law consubstantial with the creation of the state: the state presupposes the political, not the other way around.

Nothing could be further removed from Rawls's understanding of the 'domain of the political' and its relation to the law. It is not accidental that the few occurrences of the term 'constituent power' in his work are associated with the name of John Locke.[115] In contrast with Rousseau, Sieyès, and Schmitt, Locke found no difficulty in reconciling constituent power and natural law. While for Sieyès the nation is *nominally* 'under natural law', but in practice under natural law 'as interpreted by the nation'—who could challenge, and from what podium, the interpretation of natural law offered by the nation through its representatives?—for Locke natural law comes down to specific natural rights (Jefferson's 'inalienable rights') that offer a point of leverage for challenging positive law and a secure anchoring for the right of rebellion. Locke's natural law is much more than just a general normative backdrop, summed up in the principle 'Do wrong to no man':[116] it is a source of active inspiration for a vigilant citizenry and can become an active element of real political struggle and even insurgency on the part of the citizenry against their rulers. Locke's constituent power could *never* create a commonwealth disrespectful of the natural rights to life, liberty, and property. Such an error would instantly render it preferable, for the subjects on whose consent the legitimacy of the commonwealth and of its attendant form of government depends, to remain in the state of nature.

Political liberalism, of course, has no place for natural rights, or any other foundationalist notion, within its conceptual framework. But neither has it a place for the absolute sovereignty vested in a constituent power that grounds the political, the state, and its constitution in a world as devoid of all normativity as the Hobbesian state of nature. While Schmitt discusses constituent power in all of its manifestations, Rawls is interested only in the conditions of the possibility *of a liberal-democratic just and stable society*. Thus, the normativity to which constituent power responds is the normativity grounded in a political conception of justice provisionally articulated, for the time being, in a freestanding way, in the hope that an overlapping consensus will later materialize. Far from being 'above' the law, for Rawls constituent power, as we will see in the following sections, is metaphorically 'under' a law of sorts.

---

[113] Schmitt, *Political Theology* (n 38) 13 (emphasis added).
[114] 'Prerogative is nothing but the Power of doing publick good without a Rule', Locke, *Second Treatise* (n 1) § 165, 425. Schmitt questionably argues that the idea of the exception 'was something incommensurable' with Locke's theory of the constitutional state. See Schmitt, *Political Theology* (n 38) 13.
[115] For his view of 'Supream Power', see Locke, *Second Treatise* (n 3) Ch XIII, § 149.
[116] See Chapter 2, n 59.

3. Transcending the Kelsen–Schmitt Binary: Constituent Power within Rawls's Constitutionalism

As recalled in the opening sentence of this chapter, in vain would one scan Rawls's opus in search for an explicit theory of constituent power. However, from various passages that speak to the theme it is possible to reconstruct a coherent, albeit implicit, Rawlsian view that breaks new ground and cuts across the Kelsen-versus-Schmitt binary into which the discourse of constituent power has found itself locked.[117]

Rawls unreservedly sides with Schmitt in affirming the non-fictional, not merely retroactively or 'constructed', existence of constituent power as the power of a subject—the people, in democratic theory—to 'establish a new regime',[118] to bring into being 'a framework to regulate ordinary power', and to articulate in a constitution its political ideal 'to govern itself in a certain way'.[119] He also shares with Schmitt the idea that such power persists, after the founding of a new regime, in a form subordinate but still outranking the constituted (and duly separated) powers of government and the electorate. That secondary form of constituent power belongs to the living segment of 'the people', which can exert it either through specific institutions invested with the power to propose and enact amendments to the original constitution, or through direct consultation in referendums. Rawls and Schmitt further agree on the limits to which such secondary constituent power is subject: although it can modify even important aspects of the original constitution, it cannot alter its basic design, core values, and commitments.[120]

They diverge, however, on the nature of the limits to amending power and on the proper way to identify them. For Schmitt, unalterable (regardless of whether such unamendability is codified in some 'eternity clause' or is implicit) is the political-existential decision resulting in a state form or institutional order to which the constitution is integral. For Rawls, the limit is coextensive with a broader set of constitutional essentials, fundamental rights, and basic liberties. His example, in fact, of structural entrenchment of the constitution against an unconstitutional constitutional amendment concerns the right to religious freedom.

How to identify then the unamendable content of a constitution? Schmitt has been criticized for variously identifying it as 'the constitution *as a whole*, as a *total* decision, as the *essence* of the constitution or its *spirit* or its *identity*, and even its identity *and*

---

[117] For an innovative and germane way of articulating what he calls 'the paradox of constituent power'— 'neither the people nor the constitution is primordial'—see Hans Lindahl, *Authority and the Globalisation of Inclusion and Exclusion* (Cambridge University Press 2018), 402–03. Drawing on Heller (n 29) William Scheuerman also highlights how Kelsen and Schmitt perspectives, apparently so fiercely opposed, in fact share a common positivist foundation: 'Schmitt answers Kelsen's legal theory of the *will-less norm* with an alternative theory of the *norm-less will*. In slightly different terms, Kelsen's pure theory of law becomes Schmitt's "pure theory of the will"'. William Scheuerman, *The End of Law: Carl Schmitt in the Twenty-First Century* (2nd edn, Rowman & Littlefield 2020) 84–85.
[118] Rawls, *PL* 231.
[119] ibid 231–32.
[120] On the convergence of Rawls and Schmitt on this point, see also Joel I Colón-Ríos, *Weak Constitutionalism: Democratic Legitimacy and the Question of Constituent Power* (Routledge 2012) 127–32 (hereafter Colón-Ríos, *Weak Constitutionalism*).

continuity'.[121] However, he does offer a distinction between (i) 'constitutional laws', that is, provisions that acquire that status by virtue of their being included in the constitution, but are dispensable without detracting from the uniqueness of the constitutions, and (ii) other provisions, formally undistinguishable from the former, but non-dispensable and non-amendable insofar as they reflect some identity-defining commitments on the part of the bearer of constituent power. In the case of the Weimar Constitution these decisions, to repeat, concerned the democratic, republican, federal, parliamentary, and right-protecting nature of the new German Reich.[122]

Rawls, instead, offers a kind of murkier argument in this respect. As already recalled in Section 1.a, he justifies the structural entrenchment of fundamental rights in terms of their '*being validated by long historical practice*' and their having hitherto been only *expanded*, as part of an intergenerational endeavour to bring 'the Constitution more in line with its original promise'. Ultimately, it is then the *factual* element of the 'successful practice of [the Constitution's] ideas and principles over two centuries' that now imposes 'restrictions on what can count as an amendment, whatever was true at the beginning'.[123] This formulation has one normative core—bringing the constitution more in line with its initial promise, as opposed to derailing it—to which additional layers of meaning are added: an implicit notion of the expansion and not reduction of rights, and the factual reference to the successful practice of the constitution's 'ideas and principle' for a 200-year period. The first aspect evokes a philosophy of history, which sits uneasily with the spirit of political liberalism.[124] The second fits only the American context that undergirds Rawls's reflection, but raises difficulties when generalized beyond the French or the British cases: are newly or recently enacted constitutions defenceless against being disfigured by rights-curtailing amendments due to the lack of a long enough 'successful practice'?

Furthermore, Rawls parts ways with Schmitt's constitutionalism in several additional respects, for example the idea that the 'guardian of the constitution' could be a figure like a head of state, such as the President of the Weimar Republic, and not a constitutional court. Rawls is at one with Kelsen in maintaining that there are no alternatives to a strong and final form of judicial review of congressional legislation but—as implied by his defence of the structural entrenchment of fundamental rights—Rawls would, in contrast to Kelsen, also extend judicial review to amendment proposals that respect amendment-regulating provisions.[125]

In relation to Kelsen's theory of 'pure law', Rawls certainly endorses the downplaying of all reference to contentious truths in the arena of rival democratic claims for

---

[121] Arato, 'Multi-Track Constitutionalism' (n 62) 331.

[122] See Schmitt, *Constitutional Theory* (n 38) 77–78. For useful commentaries, see Colón-Ríos, *Weak Constitutionalism* (n 120) 129; and Schupmann, *Carl Schmitt* (n 41) 145–46.

[123] Rawls, *PL* 239. Along similar lines, Frank Michelman points to the 'idea of an upward path of clarification of a founding American idea of basic liberty, the arc or telos of which is at least occasionally accessible to glimpse by at least some in our midst', Frank I Michelman, 'Human Rights and Constitutional Rights: A Proceduralizing Function for Substantive Constitutional Law?' in Silja Voneky and Gerald Neuman (eds), *Human Rights, Democracy, and Legitimacy in a World of Disorder* (Cambridge University Press 2018) 92.

[124] For a discussion of the tension imported within political liberalism by the philosophy of history presupposed by Rawls's argument, see Alessandro Ferrara, *Justice and Judgment: The Rise and the Prospect of the Judgment Model in Contemporary Political Philosophy* (Sage 1999)155–56, and below, Chapter 7.

[125] See Rawls, *PL* 238–39.

legitimacy, but not to the point of banning or treating with suspicion 'political' truth claims shared across the factional divides of a democratic society. For political liberalism, truth and claims to justice, in contrast to how they appear in the paradigm of 'pure law', are not simply vehicles of conflict and divisiveness. They are also symbolic resources that allow for convergence and agreement to transcend the realm of bargaining and compromise and to benefit from the stability-enhancing force of morally motivated consent. Justice matters, though in a special sense: in lieu of a 'basic norm' retrospectively reconstructed, for Rawls the higher-order legitimacy of the legitimacy-buttressing constitution rests on the constitution's reflecting a 'political conception of justice' that can be grounded in a freestanding way.

In consonance with Schmitt, Rawls considers prudential and instrumental considerations, as reflected in compromises, an unacceptably weak basis for the integration of a constitutional order. Substantive ethical convergence, the buttressing of the rule of law with the normativity of moral judgement—in other words, consent on the basis of rightness, as opposed to convenience—is indispensable. But one major difference separates Schmitt and Rawls beyond this point of commonality and leads political liberalism again to converge with Kelsen. While for Schmitt the ethical substance reflected in the law ideally should be as all-encompassing as Hegel's *Sittlichkeit*, uniquely holistic as a *Lebensform* or the 'esprit general d'une nation', or as existentially indispensable as *Volksgeist*—if deprived of it, 'we the people' would turn into something other than we are—for Rawls that ethical substance is qualified by three distinctive aspects. First, the entrenched 'ethical substance' of the liberal-democratic polity is limited to the special 'domain of the political' as including the basic structure, fundamental rights, and the basic liberties. Second, it may or may not individuate the polity as unique: the 'domain of the political' is not required to be 'original', and in given countries may, due to historical circumstances, just reproduce the standard list of rights found in *any* other liberal-democratic polity. Third, the entrenched aspects of the constitution should leave ample room for pluralism in important areas of human concern and not just in secondary aspects of the moral culture.

Finally, Rawls's constitutionalism takes distance from the diverse, yet concurring political-realist and legal-positivist bent of Kelsen and Schmitt. Both Kelsen's 'normative' legal system crowned and enabled by the basic norm, and Schmitt's existential-political decision to unify a multitude into a people living in accordance with a 'positive constitution', raise a claim to internal acceptance by participants and external recognition by observers on the basis of nothing more than their mere existence. Neither can be meaningfully argued to be *deserving* or *undeserving* of compliant recognition, for lack of a normative foothold on which such merits could rest.

For Rawls, instead, the original position—though no longer attributed the foundational role it played in *A Theory of Justice*, but now downgraded to a 'device of representation'[126]—nonetheless exerts the normative function, for which no equivalent exists in Kelsen's and Schmitt's paradigms, of free-standingly elucidating, in tandem with the methodological guidance offered by reflective equilibrium, the reasons why rational and reasonable citizens could place their hopes for the coalescing of an overlapping

---

[126] Rawls, *PL* 27.

consensus on justice as fairness, the *most reasonable* political conception of justice that 'we' can use as normative backdrop for elaborating constitutional principles.[127]

We are then back to Rawls's non-accidental choice of Locke as classical reference for developing his view of constituent power. For Rawls, as for Locke, constituent power does have a referent in the real political world but is not unbound. Its work of political creation does not proceed *ex nihilo*. It rests on 'something', some ethical substance which is *already there*—the sediment of a 'primitive normative accumulation' as it were, in the guise of a customary, tradition-based, implicit normativity that constituent power 'makes explicit'. The positive legal normativity of the constitution may then either reflect or fail to reflect that 'something'—and Rawls here parts ways with the comprehensive, natural-law framework undergirding Locke's notion of constituent power—in a way that remains to be elucidated, in the next section.

4. The Liberal Principle of Constitutional Legitimacy

What sort of normativity is constituent power responding to, then, within *Political Liberalism*? We are treading an unexplored territory, for all we have is the supposition that the attractiveness of Locke's concept of constituent power lies in its being not unbound. It is hard to imagine, consistently with the *Two Treatises of Government*, that a people could use its 'supream power' in order, for example, to create a commonwealth not respectful of property rights. Natural rights, opposed by Rousseau precisely on account of their detracting from the sovereignty of the people's general will, are a clear instance of the kind of normativity that cannot be what Rawls in *Political Liberalism* had in mind. Our question is then: What other form of normativity could bind constituent power?

Less clear is that such normativity cannot be that of 'justice as fairness' taken as the outcome of the original position as elucidated in *A Theory of Justice*. That interpretation is precluded by footnote 7 to Lecture II of *Political Liberalism*. After explaining that 'justice as fairness does not try to derive the reasonable from the rational',[128] Rawls in the footnote adds the following:

> Here I correct a remark in *Theory*, p 16, where it is said that the theory of justice is a part of the theory of rational decision. From what we have just said, this is simply incorrect. What should have been said is that the account of the parties, and of their reasoning uses the theory of rational decision, though only in an intuitive way. This theory is itself part of a political conception of justice, one that tries to give an account of reasonable principles of justice. There is no thought of deriving those principles from the concept of rationality as the sole normative concept.[129]

---

[127] In his new 'Introduction to the Paperback Edition' of *Political Liberalism* and then in 'The Idea of Public Reason Revisited', Rawls has modified this normative picture, by acknowledging the possibility that in lieu of one most reasonable political conception of justice, a family of reasonable liberal political conceptions of justice may coexist as focal points of the overlapping consensus and of the liberal principle of legitimacy. See 'Introduction to the Paperback Edition' of *Political Liberalism* xlvi–xlvii and 450–51. The implications of this new picture will be addressed below in Section 4.b, n 152.

[128] Rawls, *PL* 52.

[129] ibid 53.

Then the footnote ends with the perhaps over-optimistic statement 'I believe that the text of *Theory* as a whole supports this interpretation'.[130] Be that as it may, what we gather from this key passage, buried in a footnote, is not that justice as fairness *as such* cannot provide the normative anchoring that we are seeking, but that it cannot provide it in the decontextualized, foundationalist way that rational choice theory offers. 'The reasonable', we are told, must also be figured in among the normative sources of a proper theory of justice. The reasonable, however, brings the burdens of judgment in its train. How can then a product of 'the reasonable' play the function of normative touchstone that orients constituent power? We have to take a short detour through the elaborate answer that an eminent constitutional theorist has offered from the perspective of political liberalism.

a. Constituent power as 'always under law'

In his seminal paper 'Always Under Law?', Frank Michelman has addressed our question. He starts out with an operation of mental clean-up:

> We commonly take the idea of the sovereignty of the people to imply that the collective will of the governed ... strictly *constitutes* the highest law of the state. Popular *sovereignty*, in other words, we commonly take to imply that the people acting to resolve their country's higher law cannot then themselves be acting under the sign of law. The people's sovereign act of higher lawmaking law must itself, as sovereign, be above and beyond all law. That, I say, is how we usually *think* we think about popular sovereignty. The always-under-law thesis, however, contradicts this ordinarily unreflective take on how participants in constitutional democracy think about the provenance of higher law.[131]

Then we are reminded, in a train of thought that might be relevant for interpreting the later Rawls's perspective, that 'the law that even the highest politics is under is itself a politically immanent creation, not a deliverance of transcendent, trans-political reason'.[132] Thus, what makes 'our scheme of government', our 'basic political arrangements' justified?[133]

Michelman enumerates some metatheoretical characteristics requested of the answer to that question. A proper 'constitutional-democratic' answer should include the demand for 'government under law'—that is, the demand for '*consistent* regulation, by some *public and unified* set of *durable, antecedently binding* principle of justice and right, of *all* determinations, interpretations and resolutions of a political society's operative scheme of constitutional essentials'.[134] A proper 'constitutional-democratic' answer should also be contextual:

---

[130] ibid.
[131] Frank I Michelman, 'Always under Law?' (1995) 12 Constitutional Commentary 231 (hereafter Michelman, 'Always under Law?').
[132] ibid.
[133] ibid 233.
[134] ibid 237 (emphasis in original).

constitutional-democratic political justification must, then, concretely consist in establishment of *a* set of reasons why this people (these people)—in their conditions as they make them out given their ways of understanding self, freedom, society, and value—can rationally see they have for submitting to the actual scheme in force over them.[135]

Furthermore, from a *democratic* standpoint we must also require that these reasons be reasons *of the same people* who supposedly are *self*-governing, a twist of the question that evokes again the issue of instability:

> the reasons a people have or consider themselves to have for submitting to a scheme of government may not be fixed once and for all. It seems *likelier that these would be changeable over time*, in ways that would call for corresponding change in the operative scheme of constitutional essentials.[136]

What reasons might we then have for saying that the people, switching now to the singular, as holder of constituent power, does want to have *trans-temporal consistency* in its higher law-making? The reasons recalled above and pointing to requisites of consistency, publicity, antecedence, unity, and durability, cannot apply automatically one step up, so to speak, to the holder of a sovereign constituent power. 'Additional reasons' are needed and, according to Michelman, they exist. Resorting to the figure of political identity, he contends that these additional reasons 'arise from the conceptual need to confer an identity on "the People" that is continuous across an event of higher lawmaking, leaving them the same People after as they were before the event. Without such a conferral of continuous identity, we cannot affirm popular sovereignty.'[137] If we did not presuppose this 'continuous identity', Michelman continues, we would incur conceptual difficulties. For example, a people exercises constituent power and enacts a constitution, which includes, among other things, provisions for constitutional change (Article V, in the case of the United States) designed for registering important changes of orientation that over time may arise in the people. But then, apparently,

> there is a dimension of political freedom that we both attribute to the chartering People (represented by the authors and ratifiers of Article V) and deny to the People as thus chartered—that is, the freedom to decide upon procedures of higher lawmaking. The charterers ('We the People of the Unites States') seem to stand, then, on a different plane of authority from the chartered ('our posterity') as *creators to creatures*.[138]

The idea of *self-sameness*, of sharing in one common political identity, prevents that undesirable outcome and allows us to continue to think—as required by a common definition of democracy—that the people who make higher law are the same as the

---

[135] ibid.
[136] ibid 239 (emphasis added).
[137] ibid 239–40.
[138] ibid 240 (emphasis added).

people whose life will be regulated by that law. That self-sameness is ensured by the sharing across time of a 'political identity' which 'not only continues through the process of enactment undissolved and self-identical', but also—this being an unnecessary corollary to which we will return in Chapter 4—'pre-exists the process'.[139]

These strategic moves urged by Michelman authorize us to narrow down the initial question, which now takes the following form: What factor(s) may confer '*political* identities on empirical human aggregates, identities of the sort that allows us to check for the sameness of the identities of the People who lay down constitutional law and the People to whom it is laid down'?[140] Is there an 'identity-fixing factor'?

Michelman argues that this factor may reside in a population's sense 'of its members as, in their higher lawmaking acts, commonly and constantly inspired by and aspiring to some distinct *regulative idea of political justice and right*, but an idea that itself has sprung from the politics of the self-same self-governing People'.[141]

We are back to the notion that some idea of justice or political right ('droit politique'), thick enough to allow for the construction of an institutional order, a rule of law, a state should be of guidance for constituent power. But at the same time, Michelman points out, we have not yet escaped a paradoxical situation. We seem to be cornered in the alternative either (i) to give up on the ideal of a 'prior legal authorization for every lawmaking stage', that is, of 'government under law', and thus relapse into Sieyès's and Schmitt's idea of an unbound constituent power that merely *posits* an idea of political right, or (ii) to give up the democratic requirement of popular sovereignty understood as the 'prior democratic authorization for every institutionalization of democracy', including the framing of a constitution. In this latter case, the subject of constituent power at some point must be thought to recognize the normative cogency of an idea of right and, consequently, to cut down to size its own self-representation of sovereignty.

How does Michelman respond to this paradoxical predicament? He outlines *two* distinct paths out of it. The *first path* keeps closer to the project of political liberalism and to Rawls's recasting of the ultimate normative credentials of justice as fairness as its being the conception of justice *most reasonable for us*. This Rawlsian path anticipates Michelman's suggested rejection of a need for 'a democratic warrant for setting the project off on its first iteration'[142] and the concomitant claim that, in spite of its unwarranted beginnings and lack of safeguard from embedded injustice or bias, the present liberal-democratic constitutional arrangements can be understood as the most justice-tending arrangements known to, and reasonable for, us. We will then take refuge in a kind of 'political', not 'comprehensive' understanding of truth and political rightness, and will then confidently endorse 'fundamental-law resolutions that we can see to be in some material degree deviant from justice, while seeing also that those resolutions are ensconced in a nest of historical events of politics that we judge to be reasonably defensible as justice-tending and justice-seeking'.[143]

---

[139] ibid 241.
[140] ibid 241.
[141] ibid.
[142] Alessandro Ferrara and Frank I Michelman, *Legitimation by Constitution: A Dialogue on Political Liberalism* (Oxford University Press 2021) 28.
[143] ibid 28–29.

The *second path* is more ambitious. It leads back to the original version of Michelman's 'always under law' thesis, now recast as 'sovereignty as jurisdiction'. The idea is that the practice of amending the existent constitution counts as evidence that the highest law can itself be judged inadequate or in need for correction—like the rules of a game may be in need of correction—and the act of judgment involved in amending the constitution can be understood as an interpretation of the community's *'ultimate law* or *proto-law'* of which the occasionally enacted, amended, and interpreted constitution relates as an application.[144]

In other words, the practice of amending presupposes that the existing constitution is an ameliorable interpretation of a normative core reflected in its specific provisions. Thus, whether it is a court on behalf of 'the people' or the electorate through a referendum that assesses the acceptability of a proposed constitutional alteration, this judgment can be construed as an *act of application of a preexistent higher law*. A 'jurisdictional' reservation of this judgment for the people, Michelman concludes, might then be seen as reconciling the always-under-law thesis, that is, that the constitution tries itself to track and reflect a normativity superordinate to it, and the assumption of popular *sovereignty*. Schmitt's famous dictum 'Sovereign is who decides the exception' can then be ingeniously recast along constitutional-democratic lines as: 'sovereign are they in whom jurisdiction in the higher matters reposes'.[145]

b. The 'most reasonable' as the normativity constituent power is under

However, Michelman's second path generates two problems that call for further consideration. The first, addressed in the final two chapters of this book, concerns the outline and justification of a division of labour between a highest court, entrusted with the interpretation of the constitution on behalf of 'the people', and the living segment of the people in whom ultimately 'jurisdiction in the higher matters reposes'.

The second problem, to be addressed here, concerns the fact that even if we reserve for the living segment of the people, through some institutional procedure, the judgment as to whether the existing constitution or the proposed amended version counts as a better application of a 'preexistent higher law', 'ultimate law', or 'proto-law', still our move does not efface the interrogation as to (i) the exact nature of the superordinate normativity cogent both for the existent constitution and for the amended version under scrutiny and (ii) the relation of this superordinate normativity to the constituent power of the democratic subject.

Michelman's claims that this superordinate normativity amounts to 'some distinct regulative idea of political justice and right, but an idea that itself has sprung from the politics of the self-same self-governing People'.[146] This claim clarifies a *genealogical*

---

[144] See ibid 29.
[145] ibid 30. A germane idea is put forward by Karl Loewenstein: 'Sovereign is who, among the different powers, decides about the reform of the constitution' ('soberano es aquel entre los detentadores del poder que decide sobre la reforma constitucional'), see *Teoría de la Constitución* (Ariel Editorial 1965) 172. Thanks are due to Joel Colón-Ríos for having pointed out this convergence to me.
[146] Michelman, 'Always Under Law?' (n 131) 241.

aspect of the solution—that is, in order to be legitimate higher law must spring from the holder of constituent power—which is only a necessary, not yet a sufficient condition for the legitimacy of a constitution. The *sufficient* condition for the legitimacy of the constitution seems to be that, over and beyond originating from the people, the constitution responds to 'some distinct regulative idea of political justice and right'. The necessary condition is genealogical, but the sufficient condition needs substantive articulation: *which* idea of political justice and right should guide the people's higher lawmaking? The answer can neither be that *any* idea of political justice and right would do, as long as it is *believed* to be cogent by the people, because that would lead us back to Schmitt, nor be that the people *discovers* such idea in a normative universe 'outside the cave', or via transcendental deduction. In the closing paragraphs of this section, I will offer an answer of my own that combines Rawls's notion of the 'most reasonable' with the idea of exemplarity, the situatedness of the people, and the method of reflective equilibrium.

This consideration leads us back to Michelman's 'first path' and back to Rawls. What law can the democratic sovereign possibly be under that leaves it undiminished as a sovereign? I see a solution in the unpacking of 'the most reasonable for us'. That normative something is pinned down by Rawls as the special subdomain of the things normative—a constitution, an ordering of the basic liberties, a format for the basic structure and, to be sure, the 'political conception of justice' to which constituent power is responsive—that are 'most reasonable for us'. That phrase occurs at two key points within the work of Rawls after *A Theory of Justice*,[147] in both cases as the ultimate normative credential for justice as fairness.

Elsewhere I have reconstructed the normativity of the 'most reasonable' as connected with the normativity of the exemplary.[148] Suffice it here to recall that the only hint offered by Rawls as to what makes something reasonable 'most reasonable' somehow relates to central aspects of who we are. Justice as fairness acquires the qualification of most reasonable for us 'given our history and the traditions embedded in our public life'.[149] Another important element is added to the picture when Rawls, in a passage of the 'Introduction to the Paperback Edition' of *Political Liberalism*, for the first time envisages a well-ordered liberal society to possibly be home not just to a reasonable pluralism of comprehensive doctrines, but also to a 'family of reasonable liberal political conceptions of justice', some of which may be not only different but even 'incompatible'.[150]

We may even imagine liberal-democratic societies in which political conceptions of justice other than justice as fairness may be deemed 'most reasonable'. The crucial point, however, is that a distinction persist between a political conception of justice's quality of being 'most reasonable' and its being 'just reasonable'. An interpretation of the later Rawls's paradigm as entailing either the jettisoning of the 'most reasonable/

---

[147] John Rawls, 'Kantian Constructivism in Moral Theory' (1980) 88 Journal of Philosophy 519, and *PL* 28 (hereafter Rawls, 'Kantian Constructivism').
[148] See Alessandro Ferrara, *The Force of the Example: Explorations in the Paradigm of Judgment* (Columbia University Press 2008), 69–79. On exemplary normativity more generally, 16–61.
[149] Rawls, 'Kantian Constructivism' (n 147) 519.
[150] Rawls, 'Introduction', *PL* xlvi–xlvii.

just reasonable' distinction or the demoting of the conception of justice reflected in the constitution as 'just reasonable' would generate three negative consequences.

First, an 'invisible circle' would divide the free and equal citizens partaking of the overlapping consensus: *inside* the circle we would find the lucky ones who happen to embrace the conception of justice reflected in certain constitutional essentials as 'most reasonable', *outside* the less fortunate who live under constitutional essentials that reflect a conception of justice for them 'at least reasonable' but way short of 'most reasonable'.

Second, would legal coercion exercised in harmony with constitutional essentials backed up by a political conception of justice 'merely reasonable' for me/us be less legitimate than coercion exercised in harmony with constitutional essentials backed up by the political conception of justice 'most reasonable for me/us'? If we answer positively, then the legitimacy of coercion comes to depend on the happenstance alignment of my opinion and the prevailing one concerning the reasonability of the constitution-backing political conception of justice. If we answer negatively, considering legitimacy unaffected by the 'at least' or 'most' reasonable status of the constitution-backing conception of justice, then deliberation about conceptions of justice becomes a futile exercise, a matter for the background culture alone.

Third, should the standard of the 'most reasonable' be replaced by that of being 'at least reasonable', then the family of political conceptions of justice reflected in the public forum may come to include both deontological conceptions (eg justice as fairness, a Dworkinian view of justice, a Habermasian discursive version of Kant's generalization test, etc) and consequentialist views (all kinds of utilitarianism, Neo-Aristotelian eudaimonism, Marxist-type ethics of historical progress, etc). As the response to the COVID-19 pandemic shows, prevailingly consequentialist moral cultures may incline lawmakers and the public to endorse policies (eg the pursuit of 'herd immunity') to which deontological moral cultures react with moral shock. Views of justice rooted in these two moral outlooks, though reasonable, may just be too polarized for citizens endorsing one not to feel oppressed by policies endorsed by majorities that endorse the other.

Although textual evidence is not entirely univocal,[151] on the whole it seems safe to assume that justice as fairness is believed by Rawls to deserve being considered the 'most reasonable', on account of a threefold rationale. It best satisfies, relative to its competitors (we can imagine here 'political' versions of utilitarianism, discursive deliberative democracy, republicanism, etc) three conditions: (i) a specification of certain rights, liberties, and opportunities; (ii) a special priority for these freedoms; (iii) measures assuring all citizens, whatever their social position, adequate all-purpose means to make intelligent and effective use of their liberties and opportunities.[152]

On this basis, it is safe to conclude that the potential of justice as fairness to normatively orient constituent power in enacting certain constitutional essentials rests not

---

[151] Some passages suggest that Rawls might have envisaged the possibility that legitimacy could rest the constitution's conformity with an 'at least reasonable' conception of justice (*PL* lviii); other passages suggest that he believed that *A Theory of Justice* and *Political Liberalism* both aimed at presenting 'a candidate [political conception of justice, ie justice as fairness] for the most reasonable' (ibid lx).

[152] See Rawls, 'Introduction', *PL* xlvi–xlvii.

on an *objective* quality, as though its principles were 'discovered' outside Plato's cave, but on the judgment, direct or indirect, that the subject of constituent power forms upon due reflection—standing sideways at the entrance of the cave, so to speak. The reformulation of Plato's allegory of the cave suggested earlier can now bear its fruits.

Recall that in Chapter 1, Section 1.c the meaning of the 'most reasonable' was reconstructed with reference to a *non-epistocratic* reformulation of Plato's allegory of the cave, according to which not just one, but a group of philosophers ascended to the world outside the cave. Assuming that the burdens of judgment had resulted in their having partially overlapping but also partially diverging accounts of the outside world, we can imagine that the philosophers would agree, at the entrance of the cave while on their way back to rule its population, never to enlist legal coercion in support of contentious parts of their accounts, but only in support of the overlapping parts. The normative status of that ban mirrors precisely what Rawls would call *the most reasonable principle of conduct for ruling the cave* that the philosophers could reach through their common public reason. The location where that agreement is reached, sideways at the entrance of the cave, symbolizes that the 'most reasonable' somehow partakes not just of one, but of two worlds—namely, that of the finite, imperfect, factual nature of the subject of justice on one hand, and the perfect, ideal, purely normative quality of justice on the other—and combines them in the best mix 'for one singular case'.

One predecessor of this exemplary, uniqueness-affirming normativity is Rousseau's account of the legislator's function. The 'legislator-assisted' constituent power of the citizens, according to Rousseau, should not aim at adopting 'laws that are good in themselves',[153] but rather at selecting laws fit for the people eventually subject to them. Although the object of the legislator's advice to the citizens concerns their use of constituent power to establish 'laws' related to the institutions and functioning of the state (the equivalent of Rawls's basic structure), Rousseau's implicit normative intimation for constituent power is unequivocal: 'Do not author (constitutional) laws that you're not fit to be respectful of'. This does not mean that the selection of the basic structure is unprincipled, prudential, or a projection of the constituent subject's preferences. The intimation rather means that constituent power *ought to* balance principle optimality—for Rousseau, being guided by the overall point of the social contract,[154] for Rawls being guided by the two principles of justice as fairness—with the historical experiences and the political culture(s) available to the people on its way to being 'constituted'. Rawls, furthermore, offers 'reflective equilibrium' as a methodological resource for making sense of *when* that balance is achieved.

We are finally in a position to answer our question about the normativity that binds constituent power. The 'law' or normativity that constituent power is under, for Rawls, emanates from justice as fairness not *qua* outcome of a decontextualized thought experiment—the original position as presented in *Theory*—but as the most reasonable political conception of justice for us, where 'most reasonable' means that among all

---

[153] Jean Jacques Rousseau, *The Social Contract* (1762), translated and with an introduction C Betts (Oxford University Press 1994) Book II, Chapter 8, 46.

[154] Namely, to 'find a form of association which may defend and protect with the whole force of the community the person and property of every associate, and by means of which each, coalescing with all, may nevertheless obey only himself, and remain as free as before', ibid Book I, Chapter 6, 17–18.

the available 'merely reasonable' liberal conceptions of justice, it is the one that, in the judgment of the subject of constituent power, realizes the best fit—as tested through reflective equilibrium—between its core principles and the historical and political-cultural features salient for the *intended* constituted people. In other words, justice as fairness is the one political conception of justice, among several possible, that *in the domain of the political* promises to realize 'the most of justice' that we deem 'realizable' at the historical juncture at which we are located.

The normativity that constituent power is under is then neither derived from transcendental models, nor resting on the local normativity of existing cultures and traditions. It is the normativity of a judgment concerning the best fit of *one* of the 'merely reasonable' political conceptions of justice or political right with who we are historically, politically, and culturally. It is neither a purely speculative normativity of moral justification, nor a hermeneutics of self-understanding, but the normativity of the reflective judgment that brings the two into optimal equilibrium.

c. The liberal principle of constitutional legitimacy

It might be useful, at this point, to condense our reconstruction of Rawls's view of constituent power in the form of a principle. Rawls's groundbreaking liberal principle of legitimacy is mainly geared to the legitimacy of exercises of 'constituted power', though in 'The Idea of Public Reason Revisited' the principle is explicitly said to be applicable both to the 'constitutional structure itself' and to 'the laws enacted in accordance with that structure'.[155] Be that as it may, Rawls's acknowledgment of the existence and operation of the constituent power of the people raises the question, not explicitly addressed in *Political Liberalism*, of the legitimacy of an *act of constitution-making* or an exercise of primary constituent power. The answer that *im*plicitly undergirds *Political Liberalism* can be made explicit in the form of the following 'Liberal principle of constitutional legitimacy':

> **Liberal principle of constitutional legitimacy**
> *Constituent power is justifiably exercised when it is exercised in accordance with a political conception of justice most reasonable for its free and equal holders.*

The above principle received elucidation from the preceding discussion and no further clarification of its terms is needed. Rather, it is worth mentioning, in closing, the normative gap that it calls for us to bridge. To reconstruct the normative notion of legitimacy by which the framing and enacting of constitutions are assessed is perhaps the first and foremost, but not the one and only, step towards developing the view of constituent power that lies buried within the paradigm of political liberalism. Considered in combination, Rawls's liberal principle of legitimacy and the principle of 'constitutional legitimacy' delimit an extended normative continuum, at one end of which we find the fine-grained plethora of legislative, administrative, judicial acts

---

[155] Rawls, 'The Idea of Public Reason Revisited', *PL* 447.

of various import, that incessantly fill the public forum of a liberal-democratic society and are assessed for legitimacy, and at the opposite end of which we find 'the constitutional essentials'—namely, fundamentals of the structure of government and the political process (the powers of the legislature, executive, and the judiciary and their separate jurisdiction; the scope of majority rule), as well as equal basic rights and liberties (ie the right to vote and participate in politics, liberty of conscience, and freedom of thought, of association, and of speech, and the protections of the rule of law)[156]—that function as standards for orienting our judgment.

Between those two extremes an intermediate area extends that includes non-essential (and thus non-entrenched) aspects of the constitution, such as new separated powers to be created, partial transformations of the form of government (eg changing term limits, changing the rules for appointment to certain offices, modifying the lines of separation among existing powers, changing the electoral law, instituting or abolishing electoral colleges), the codification of new rights, the 'landmark statutes' and 'judicial super-precedents and landmark cases' of constitutional significance that often replace the role of amendments,[157] and of course, constitutional amendments of a varied nature.

In this vast area, the power being exercised falls in between the constituted, separated ordinary powers and the primary constituent power to create a new regime or enact a new constitution. It is a power vested both in constituted powers and in the living segment of 'the people'. The legislative houses invested with the power of proposing an amendment, the supreme or constitutional courts that check on the constitutionality of proposed or even approved amendments, the electorate convened to vote in referendums—all of these are instantiations of this 'amending power', the legitimacy of whose acts calls for a specific principle of legitimation. The legitimacy of exercises of this secondary constituent power cannot be equated with mere conformity with the constitutional essentials, using Rawls's liberal principle of legitimation as a framework, for the simple reason that at stake is precisely the transformation of a single constitutional provision in a democracy-enhancing direction. At the same time, it is hard to imagine that specific constitutional provisions or even a given constitutional essential under consideration possess enough generality and normative texture for their legitimacy to be assessed directly in terms of the political conception of justice undergirding the whole of the constitution.

This normative gap needs to be bridged by a distinct and additional principle of legitimacy, consistent with the paradigm of political liberalism and especially designed for such intermediate range of political acts at the crossroads of constituted and

---

[156] See Rawls, *PL* 227.
[157] See Bruce Ackerman, *We the People*, Vol. 3, *The Civil Rights Revolution* (Harvard University Press 2014) 45–47. As examples of landmark statutes he cites the *Civil Rights Act* (1964), the *Voting Rights Act* (1965), and the *Fair Housing Act* (1968). Exemplary judicial cases of the same period include *Brown v Board of Education* (1954), desegregating schools; *Loving v Virginia* (1967), invalidating statutes that prohibited interracial marriage. The exemplary judicial case having greatest constitutional significance is perhaps *Marbury v Madison* (1803), establishing judicial review, as such not included in the text of the Constitution of the United States.

constituent power, of the transgenerational people and its living segment. This will be the topic of Chapter 7.

A more urgent task awaits completion. After constituent power, its subject and bearer—'the people'—needs to be put under closer scrutiny, from the angle of political liberalism. This will be the topic of next chapter.

4
Political Liberalism and 'the People'

> The fact that nations are socially constructed does not suggest that they are less real or are to be regarded with suspicion. Some people focus on the fact that they are 'imagined' communities to suggest that they may have no basis in 'reality.' Here it is important to distinguish between 'imagined' communities and 'imaginary' ones.
>
> (Margaret Moore, *The Ethics of Nationalism* 13)

Constituent power needs a subject capable of exercising it. As we learn from Schmitt, neither a law nor a constitution can self-institute itself: they must be enacted by someone. What characteristics must this subject have? The question is far from otiose. We live in times when disembedded financial markets of global reach affect the destiny of local regimes, democratic and non-democratic, and to some extent even shape the profiles of these regimes: their power may well be 'absolute', not in the sense of standing above law but in the sense of being capable of obtaining complacent laws, but we certainly do not call it 'constituent'. Markets are mere aggregations of convergent individual preferences, their power[1] lacking the focused intentionality, even just the imputed intentionality, of an exercise of constituent power.

Constituent power, instead, needs a sovereign actor endowed with singular intentionality. In a democratic context, its object is the setting in place of stable, regulatory *terms of cooperation* among free and equal consociates, in the form of a written or unwritten constitution. The subject possessed of it is by definition 'the people', as many constitutions declare. Some begin with a reference to 'the people' in the first-person plural, usually consigned to a preamble, and thus claim authorship on behalf of 'the people' for the ensuing articles of the constitution: 'We the People' is the opening phrase of the Constitution of the United States of America, but also of fifty-two other constitutions.[2]

Other constitutions refer to 'the people' in the third person and explicitly connect it with sovereignty. The second clause of Article 1 of the Constitution of Italy

---

[1] See Alessandro Ferrara, 'The Absolute Power of Disembedded Financial Markets' in Albena Azmanova and Mihaela Mihai (eds), *Reclaiming Democracy: Judgment, Responsibility and the Right to Politics* (Routledge 2015) 110.

[2] See the Constitutions of Afghanistan, Albania, Angola, Bangladesh, Belarus, Bhutan, Cambodia, Cameroon, Chile, Côte d'Ivoire, Cuba, Equatorial Guinea, Eritrea, Fiji, Gambia, Ghana, Iceland, India, Iraq, Ireland, Japan, Kazakhstan, Kenia, Kiribati, Korea (Republic of), Kosovo, Kyrgyzstan, Liberia, Marshall Islands, Micronesia, Mongolia, Namibia, Nauru, Nepal, Nigeria, Pakistan, Palau, Papua New Guinea, Rwanda, Samoa, Seychelles, Solomon Islands, South Africa, Suriname, Swaziland, Tajikistan, Tanzania, Turkmenistan, Uganda, Vanuatu, Zambia, Zimbabwe.

reads: 'Sovereignty belongs to the people and is exercised by the people in the forms and within the limits of the Constitution'. The second clause of Article 20 of the Constitution of Germany states that 'All state authority is derived from the people. It shall be exercised by the people through elections and other votes and through specific legislative, executive and judicial bodies'. Article 3 of the Constitution of France reads: 'National sovereignty shall vest in the people, who shall exercise it through their representatives and by means of referendum'. Article 1 of the Constitution of Spain states: 'National sovereignty belongs to the Spanish people, from whom all state powers emanate'. Article 3 of the Constitution of Portugal reads: 'Sovereignty shall be single and indivisible and shall lie with the people, who shall exercise it in the forms provided for in this Constitution'. Furthermore, the notions of the 'sovereignty of the people', 'people's sovereignty' or 'popular sovereignty', or sovereignty residing in the people are mentioned in the constitutions of ninety other countries.[3]

Could all these countries, in their fundamental law, refer to an entity that has the same status as 'the present King of France' or 'phlogiston'?[4] Should we hesitate to embrace that hypothesis, if only for the charity principle applied to half the constitutional texts operative in the world, we are then left with the question: what exactly is a people?

Remarkably, the urgency of this question is not matched by a corresponding degree of attention within modern and contemporary political philosophy. The founding figures of classical contract theory—Hobbes, Locke, Rousseau—understood the legitimacy of political regimes as resting (along absolutist, liberal, or democratic lines) on the consent of 'the people'—the aggregate of individuals who contribute to create these regimes. But they shared a blind spot: they never questioned the legitimacy of the bestower of legitimacy, namely the people. This 'bestower of legitimacy' is posited as a historical given: it exists; it is there. Being the source of legitimacy, its legitimacy is beyond question.[5]

Leading contemporary political philosophers reproduce a similar schema and the same blind spot: in *A Theory of Justice*, *Political Liberalism*, and *The Law of Peoples* Rawls assumes that somehow a people *already* exists—and chooses, as the case may be, the principles of justice that will be reflected in its future constitution, constitutional essentials that respond to a political conception of justice, or the principles that

---

[3] One or more of these expressions occur in the constitutions of Albania, Algeria, Andorra, Angola, Argentina, Azerbaijan, Belarus, Benin, Bolivia, Brazil, Bulgaria, Burkina Faso, Cape Verde, Central African Republic, Chad, Chile, Colombia, Comoros, Congo (Democratic Republic of the), Congo (Republic of the), Costa Rica, Côte d'Ivoire, Cuba, Djibouti, Dominican Republic, Ecuador, Egypt, El Salvador, Equatorial Guinea, Eritrea, Ethiopia, Gabon, Gambia, Ghana, Greece, Guatemala, Guinea, Guyana, Haiti, Honduras, Indonesia, Kenya, Korea (Republic of), Kosovo, Kuwait, Kyrgyzstan, Lebanon, Lithuania, Macedonia, Madagascar, Mali, Mauritania, Mexico, Micronesia, Moldova, Montenegro, Morocco, Mozambique, Namibia, Nepal, Nicaragua, Niger, Nigeria, Paraguay, Peru, Philippines, Romania, Russian Federation, Rwanda, Senegal, Serbia, Sierra Leone, South Sudan, Sri Lanka, Sudan, Suriname, Taiwan, Tajikistan, Tanzania, Timor-Leste, Togo, Tunisia, Turkey, Turkmenistan, Uganda, Ukraine, Uruguay, Vanuatu, Venezuela, Zimbabwe.

[4] This expression was made into an iconic focus of debate within twentieth-century philosophy of language. See Bertrand Russell, 'On Denoting' (1905) 14 Mind 479 and Peter F Strawson, 'On Referring' (1950) 59 Mind 320. For the discarding of the phlogiston theory of combustion, see James B Conant (ed), *The Overthrow of Phlogiston Theory: The Chemical Revolution of 1775–1789* (Harvard University Press 1964).

[5] This point is brilliantly brought out by Sofia Näsström in her 'The Legitimacy of the People' (2007) 35 Political Theory 624 (hereafter Näsström, 'Legitimacy of the People').

will orient its relations with other already-constituted peoples. We are never told how a people comes into existence as a people. Habermas candidly concedes that the idea of a people voluntarily creating itself via constitution-making is a natural-law fiction. In the real world, 'who in each instance acquires the power to define the disputed borders of a state is settled by historical contingencies, usually by the quasi-natural outcome of violent conflicts, wars, and civil wars'.[6]

Trying to make the best with their conceptual framework, classical and contemporary political philosophers have given up on questioning the legitimacy of the coalescing of 'the people' or of the constituting of constituent power. Even imagining a vote on who should be included in a newly forming people, the boundaries of the constituency allowed to vote on membership would be arbitrary, unless they were in turn determined by a vote, generating an infinite regress. Hence the prevailing opinion maintains that if it is impossible to assess the legitimacy of the coming together of a people, then such process must fall beyond the scope of any normative theory of legitimacy and must be understood as mere historical contingency.[7] It is an unfortunate lacuna of contemporary liberal-democratic theory that this *idolum fori* persists, according to which the formation of a people is understood either as a historical contingency immune from all judgment about its legitimacy or as a retrospective projection, transcendentally 'necessitated' by an accepted constitution.

1. A Self-Constituting People? Lindahl's Paradox of Constituent Power

One notable exception to this theoretical standstill is represented by Hans Lindahl's reflections on the 'paradox of constituent power' and the process of self-constitution of the people. My understanding of 'the people' as ineliminable subject of constituent power is indebted to his seminal idea, which I will develop along somewhat different lines, of drawing on analytical theories of 'self-constitution' in order to make sense of the coming into being of 'the people'.

As Lindahl has observed in relation to the Constitution of Germany, it is noteworthy that the term 'people' in the cases cited is preceded by the definite article 'the':

> The definite article is anything but innocent because the emergence of what is deemed a common territory and a common history goes hand in hand with the more or less forceful marginalization and/or subordination of all other collectives that have populated what today is called Germany. Accordingly, the representation of *this* people is

---

[6] Jürgen Habermas, *The Inclusion of the Other* (MIT Press 1998) 141.
[7] On this point, see Näsström, 'The Legitimacy of the People' (n 5). In her latest book *The Spirit of Democracy: Corruption, Disintegration, Renewal* (Oxford University Press 2021) 33–57 (hereafter Näsström, *Spirit of Democracy*), Näsström expands this point into a thought-provoking critique of the paradoxes generated by conceiving of 'the people' as the bearer of sovereignty (or, in her terms, by falling into 'Rousseau's trap') and argues that those paradoxes can be avoided by replacing the notion of a self-constituting sovereign people with that of a 'spirit of democracy' premised on emancipation. The political conception of a people outlined below, the theory of self-constitution built on it, and the distinction of *ethnos* and *demos* are designed to offer a different solution to the Rousseauian 'conceptual trap' that she exposes.

always also the de-presentation of *that* people, as a result of which those who are included are never simply part of 'the' people. They can raise demands for the recognition of an identity/difference that are, to a lesser or greater extent, unorderable for the collective: the other in *ourselves* who is other than us. In this, Germany is no different to any other state.[8]

Arguing against a view of the cogency of a constitution premised on its reflecting a normativity antecedently cognizable on some transcendental basis, and not on the process that brought it into existence,[9] Lindahl rightly maintains that a constitution cannot be disconnected from constituent power because it is always

> [t]he constitution *of* a collective, large or small; but ... there can be no collective absent a representational act that seizes the initiative to affirm that there is a collective and what it is that joins together its members as a unity. There is no constitution without the individuation of a manifold of individuals into a specific collective.... Who posits a constitution does so in the name not merely of a numerical set of individuals but rather of these individuals as a *whole*.[10]

Superficially, Lindahl's thesis might sound like a manifesto for the organic unity of the people, but in fact he stresses time and again with great emphasis that the same gesture of inclusion and self-definition on which constitution-making rests 'introduces non-identity into collective identity'. That 'non-identity' can take the form of residues of population not included in 'the people' or of different normative substance that demands constitutionalization in addition or as a partial alternative to the actual constitution.[11]

---

[8] Hans Lindahl, *Authority and the Globalisation of Inclusion and Exclusion* (Cambridge University Press 2018) (hereafter Lindahl, *Authority*) 396.

[9] The polemical foil is provided here by Mattias Kumm, 'The Best of Times and the Worst of Times: Between Constitutional Triumphalism and Nostalgia' in P Dobner and M Laughlin (eds), *The Twilight of Constitutionalism?* (Oxford University Press 2010) 208.

[10] Lindahl, *Authority* (n 8) 399.

[11] After the enactment of a constitution (and the creation of constituted powers), Lindahl understands constituent power to emerge as manifestation of 'non-identity' in the form of *a-legality*, see ibid 400. On the concept of 'a-legality', see Lindahl, *Authority* (n 8) 195–99, 307–10; Hans Lindahl, *Fault Lines of Globalization: Legal Order and the Politics of A-Legality* (Oxford University Press 2013) 1; and Hans Lindahl, 'Inside and Outside Global Law' *Julius Stone Address* (2019) 41(1) Sydney Law Review 17. For an insightful appraisal, see Ferdinando Menga, 'Contextualizing Hans Lindahl's Legal-Philosophical *Oeuvre*' (2019) 21(3) Etica & Politica/Ethics & Politics 363, as well as his 'Political Conflicts and the Transformation of Legal Orders: Phenomenological Insights on Democratic Contingency and Transgression' (2019) 5 The Italian Law Journal 549. On the retroaction of constituted on constituent power, see also Ferdinando Menga, *Potere costituente e rappresentanza democratica: Per una fenomenogia dello spazio istituzionale* (Editoriale Scientifica 2009) 88–89, and his *Ausdruck, Mitwelt, Ordnung: Zur Ursprünglichkeit einer Dimension des Politischen im Anschluss an die Philosophie des frühen Heidegger* (Fink 2018). For a critical discussion of Lindahl's notion of 'a-legality', see Alessandro Ferrara, 'A Crypto-Liberalism of Collective Self-Restraint? On H Lindahl's *Authority and the Globalization of Inclusion and Exclusion*' in (2019) 21/3 Etica & Politica/Ethics & Politics 371, and Lindahl's rejoinder, published as 'A-Legality, Representation, Constituent Power: Reply to Critics' (2019) 21/3 Etica & Politica/Ethics & Politics, XXI 418–39. The nexus of a-legality and constituent power is further elaborated in Alessandro Ferrara, 'Further Thoughts on A-Legality, Exemplarity and Constituent Power: Responding to Hans Lindahl' (2020) 22/2 Etica & Politica/Ethics & Politics 461, and Hans Lindahl 'Representation Redux: A Rejoinder to Alessandro Ferrara' (2020) 22/2 Etica & Politica/Ethics & Politics 475.

Constituent power for Lindahl has a paradoxical structure, which sheds light on the subject that exercises it. The paradox is the following:

> Whoever seizes the initiative to speak of a putative we*, projecting a representation of collective unity—a constitution—that enables a manifold of individuals to identify themselves as a group that would engage in joint action, is the constituent power of a legal order. Yet this initial act of identification and empowerment only works as a constituent act if its addressees retroactively identify and recognize themselves as the group that authorized the constitution by exercising the practical possibilities it makes available to them, i.e. if the *group* is the constituent power. Hence, an act only succeeds—never fully, only provisionally—as the exercise of constituent power if, in hindsight, it appears to have been the act of a constituted power: a representation of who we* already are. *Strictly speaking, neither the people nor the constitution is primordial.*[12]

In this sense, Lindahl's reflections on constituent power are helpful for completing the project of transcending the Kelsen/Schmitt dichotomy, after reconstructing Rawls's view of constituent power. If neither the people nor the constitution are 'primordial', what *is* primordial?

According to Lindahl, primordial is the self-constitution of the subject of constituent power. This subject accepts representing itself 'as this or that political unity'—thereby raising an epistemic claim, in principle open to competing representations by an observer—and eventually understands itself along the lines then included in 'the Constitution'. In other words, constitution-making begins by first calling into being the subject of constituent power, by way of representing the collectivity whose life will be regulated by the constitution *as* a certain kind of collectivity. There is an element of *narrativity* in this operation, which Lindahl brings out eloquently:

> The exercise of constituent power is never only the *legal* articulation of what a group is deemed to hold in common and to which its members owe allegiance. Revisiting earlier ideas on the subject, the exercise of constituent power is also, and essentially, a *narrative* achievement that embeds the constitution in a broader story about the collective's emergence into the world, explaining why the existence of *this* collective is important and why it must assert what it stands for in the face of adversity ... the meaning of our history is to become who we* really are. *No constituent power without the power of narrative representation.*[13]

At this point, Lindahl retrieves the previous thread of non-identity and otherness. Whoever simply vests constituent power in the people, and not also in its 'other', falls

---

[12] Lindahl, *Authority* (n 8) 402 (emphasis added). The term 'we*' is used by Lindahl to convey the idea of a group whose members 'acting together ... take up a first-person plural perspective'. For a clarification, see Lindahl, ibid, 48–49. What we always observe is not 'the constitution *of* a political unity *through* a legal order' but rather 'the constitution of a legal order *by* a political unity', Lindahl, 'Constituent Power and Reflexive Identity: Towards an Ontology of Collective Selfhood' in Martin Loughlin and Neil Walker (eds), *The Paradox of Constitutionalism* (Oxford University Press 2007) 22.

[13] Lindahl, *Authority* (n 8) 404 (emphasis added).

'prey to political Cartesianism'.[14] The reason is that 'the unification required for the individuation of a collective into "the" people is paired to fragmentation or pluralization, whereby those who are included are never only part of "the" people'.[15] Once the constitutional order is established, 'the other *in ourselves* who is other than us' can always press demands that expose the partiality of the unification gesture that set the constitution in place. Such constituent power 'is exercised by the people's *other*, not by "the" people as individuated by the extant constitution'.[16] In conclusion, 'a political way of being is never simply "our" way of being, in the sense of what we* are in and of ourselves. It begins *elsewhere*, in the other (in ourselves) who challenges *us*, and in so doing co-determines that and what we* are as a collective'.[17]

Lindahl's account works egregiously for post-colonial contexts and for settler societies in their relation to formerly colonized or aboriginal groups, but is not as easily applicable to constituent power exercised across regime change when totalitarian, authoritarian, or otherwise oppressive regimes are being overturned or simply left behind. When constituent power brings into being the Italian Republic, then the people's other is fascism, for Germany it is nazism, for democratic Spain Francoism, for South Africa the regime of apartheid, and so on. In all these cases, and in post-communist Eastern Europe, it seems problematic to posit that constituent power is co-exercised by 'the people's *other*', vividly present in the memory of the citizens and perhaps still latent in some niches of the newly formed polity.

However, we do not necessarily need to follow Lindahl's views about non-identity. Undeterred by the charge of political Cartesianism, we can take our cue from Lindahl's locating the key to transcending the Kelsen–Schmitt binary in the act of *self-constitution*, mediated by narrativity, that enables both constitution-making and the coming into being of the people qua constitution-maker. We need to spell out what is involved in this crucial juncture.

That elucidation requires that we take a closer look at the collectivity that self-constitutes into a people by way of representing itself *as* a certain collectivity. For that purpose, we need (i) to make some preliminary stipulations; (ii) to elucidate and dispel the ambiguity of the term 'the people'; (iii) to reformulate a famous riddle, about 'the people', proposed by Rousseau; (iv) to further detail the notion of 'self-constitution'; and (v) finally to put it to use in order to solve Rousseau's riddle.

2. A Political Conception of the People

Consistently with the paradigm of political liberalism, we need to start from a 'political conception of the people',[18] homologous with Rawls's 'political conception of the

---

[14] ibid 408.
[15] ibid 407.
[16] ibid.
[17] ibid 408.
[18] I'm very much indebted to Frank Michelman for having coined the felicitous phrase 'a political conception of the people'. Michelman develops his view in the context of debating the applicability of 'legitimation by constitution' to the transnational context, thus mainly envisaging a people as a collective subject relating to other peoples within a scheme of fair cooperation. My focus here is on a political conception of the people as bearer of domestic constituent power. In both cases alike, 'a *political* conception of a constituent—person

person'. We need to conceive of a people in the most general terms, with minimal assumptions concerning its inclinations, propensities, social-psychological characteristics, culture, and historical context.

a. The two political capacities of a people

For that purpose, such political conception of a people starts with defining 'the people' in general as a special kind of 'human grouping', endowed with 'two political capacities'. A people is a human grouping capable (i) of collective *political* action, at least in the minimal sense that some political collective action can be justifiedly imputed to it, and (ii) of self-regulating its political action through adopting, implicitly or explicitly, certain *constitutive* rules.

A people acts and reacts differently to a market or a social system. Even if it is not a macro-individual in the guise in which Leviathan is usually portrayed on the front cover of Hobbes's eponymous work, even if the formation of its political will proceeds not face to face but through anonymous, media-based paths, including the casting of ballots, as Habermas has intimated in his theory of the public sphere, a people can *act politically* in the sense of publicly choosing, in law-regulated ways, one policy over another, thus prioritizing one collective end over another in a decision-making process that binds, or at least significantly affects, every member.[19]

When we attribute to a market, or to a social system, positive or negative reactions to circumstances, we are really using those terms as a shorthand for what millions of individuals, independently but convergingly, do. When instead we attribute to *a people* positive or negative reactions to possible options, we imagine that some sort of interindividual exchange of reasons—however minimal, anonymous, or impersonal—does take place, a minimal consultation according to some mechanism that in the end, if only via simple majority rule or acclamation, selects one or other option as *imputable to the whole collectivity*. While the philosophies of difference discussed in Chapter 1 are driven to nonsensical implications by their denying that collectivities may have unity of purpose—for example, it becomes impossible for them to demarcate a single political collectivity from humanity at large or from random groupings that exercise no agency—our 'political conception of a people' must assume that each of the peoples whose constitution was cited above is capable of enough shared intentionality to author it.[20] Then, in order to exercise *constituent* power a people must possess not

---

or people as the case may be' is understood by Michelman and myself as a '*motivating* conception but still one that can count in its context as non-perfectionist': Alessandro Ferrara and Frank I Michelman, *Legitimation by Constitution: Dialogues on Political Liberalism* (Oxford University Press 2021) 154 (hereafter Ferrara and Michelman, *Legitimation by Constitution*).

[19] I am drawing here on my definition of politics as 'the activity of promoting, with outcomes purportedly binding or at least influential for all, the priority of certain relevant ends over others not simultaneously pursuable, or of promoting new ends', Alessandro Ferrara, *The Democratic Horizon: Hyperpluralism and the Renewal of Political Liberalism* (Cambridge University Press 2014) 30.

[20] For a germane analysis of law, rather than politics, in terms of coordinated collective action, see Lindahl, *Authority* (n 8) 46–62. On the distinction of the 'communal' and the 'statistical' notion of collective will, see also Ronald Dworkin, *Freedom's Law: The Moral Reading of the American Constitution* (Harvard University Press 1996) 19–26.

only a capacity to act politically but also the capacity to shape its own political conduct and the political conduct of certain institutional segments of the polity (the separated powers) in terms of self-consciously chosen, not just statistically habitual, patterns.

The second political capacity that must be assumed for a people to conceivably exercise constituent power and to act politically is the ability to envisage, adopt, and enforce constitutive rules that define proper political actions. Constituent power presupposes constitutive rules that regulate the practice of politics. Consequently, the assumption that constitutive rules, no less than other kinds of norms, do not self-institute, leads us to attribute to the people the capacity to establish rules or norms that shape the practice of politics in a certain polity.[21] The adverbs 'implicitly or explicitly' allow the definition to cover instances in which the constitutive rules of politics in a polity are collected in a document known as 'the Constitution' as well as cases in which such rules regulate politics 'implicitly'. Even the most rudimentary conception of democratic politics—say, a problem of common concern is singled out; alternative solutions are proposed, debated and voted; and the one solution voted by the majority or by a plurality is implemented—rests on implicit constitutive rules that define, more or less precisely, how a problem can be put on the agenda, who can propose solutions, what counts as a valid vote, and several other aspects.[22]

However, a 'political conception of a people' just limited to the specification of these two political capacities—that, no less than the two moral powers of the person, partake respectively of the spheres of 'the rational' and 'the reasonable'[23]—would remain still too general for our purposes and would fail to dispel an ambiguity inherent in the very term 'people', so widely adopted in the constitutions of many countries. This ambiguity can be illustrated by paraphrasing a famous passage of *The Social Contract*. One could say, in Rousseau's footsteps: A people can give itself a constitution. Then a people is a people before it gives itself a constitution.[24] And when has it become a people? By virtue of which act? When is a group of individuals entitled to call itself 'a people'? Who determines which people constitute a people?

Let me call this complex of questions 'Rousseau's riddle'. No theory of constituent power, let alone a *political-liberal* theory of constituent power, can be viable unless it addresses this riddle and offers a plausible solution. As anticipated above, in order to fill this lacuna we must clarify the ambiguity inherent in the notion of 'the people' (subsection b), distinguish the two notions therein conflated and on their basis reformulate Rousseau's riddle (c), then briefly outline the idea of 'self-constitution' (d), and finally highlight the solution to Rousseau's riddle in the light of the above political conception of a people (e).

---

[21] For the term 'constitutive rule' (as opposed to 'regulative rule'), see Chapter 2, n 14.

[22] Along similar lines, Michelman writes: 'A "people" is being politically conceived here as an executant, not of its moral powers, exactly, but of its constitution. A people's convergence on its constitution stands in place of a citizen's deployment of the moral powers, as the expression of the people's motivational individuality *qua* people', Ferrara and Michelman, *Legitimation by Constitution* (n 18) 156.

[23] Thanks are due to Matteo Bianchin for a conversation that prompted me to emphasize this point.

[24] The original passage read: 'A people, says Grotius, can give itself to a king. According to Grotius, then, a people is a people before it gives itself to a king', Jean-Jacques Rousseau, *The Social Contract* (1762), translated and with an introduction by C Betts (Oxford University Press 1994) Book I, Chapter 5, 53–54 (hereafter Rousseau, *Social Contract*). My calling this conundrum 'Rousseau's riddle' reflects an optimistic hope that it can be solved, differently from Näsström's pessimistic defining it as a 'trap' in her *Spirit of Democracy* (n 7).

b. Dispelling the conceptual ambiguity of 'the people'

We political liberals are stuck with 'the people', not with the people. Political philosophy can clarify the terms that are used but cannot wish them away. 'People' is a terribly ambiguous term in English, French (*peuple*), Italian (*popolo*), Spanish (*pueblo*), and Portuguese (*povo*). However, the reason that makes it appear ludicrous to dismiss the people as an inexistent referent like 'the present king of France'—namely, the fact so many constitutions include reference to it—makes it unlikely that a philosophical argument can rid our political discourse of this term. 'The people' is here to stay, as long as democracy lives on, and the best we can hope for is to dispel its inherent ambiguity by casting light on it.

Derived from the Latin *populus*, the people has often signified the whole of the citizenry, though not necessarily the population, of a given territory, but also just the lower ranks of the citizenry in opposition to the ruling or just social elite. It was so in republican Rome, where the '*populus* as crowd in the forum' would then, when it convened (via representatives of its tribes) to pass laws in the *comitia*, be transfigured into the *populus Romanus*, understood as the whole political community.[25] Yet *populus* was also the plebeian part of the *populus*, 'inferior to patricians but privileged by comparison with slaves', that in the mixed republican government was courted by patricians of one orientation against those of another.[26]

In the long medieval era, the *populus Romanus* of the dismembered empire became juxtaposed to Christendom and to the *respublica Christiana* with its *populus Dei*.[27] Then, with Machiavelli, the term 'popolo' came to reacquire the double meaning of the republican citizenry, active and capable of self-legislation, and of the plebeian commoners whom the prince should in any event be wary of alienating. But due to the particularity of the English language, as Canovan notes, the term people 'could appear also as an incoherent, but appealing amalgam of the *national* people with its proud inheritance of law and *individual* people, equal souls before God'.[28]

It was later, with the burgeoning of the 'Westphalian' system of sovereign states, that the people came to designate one collectivity among others, similarly organized in a state, or the people became synonymous with the 'nation'. Yet at the time of the Glorious Revolution, the idea of the people as sovereign and bearer of constituent power was far from established. When in the mid-1680s discontent broke out at the prospect of a Catholic and authoritarian monarch, James II Stuart, even greater repulsion was expressed by conservative circles at the idea of the 'sovereignty of the rabble': as Canovan sums up,

---

[25] See Margaret Canovan, *The People* (Polity Press 2005) 12 (hereafter Canovan, *The People*). For an interesting comparison with China, see also Hans Beck and Griet Vankeerberghen, 'The Many Faces of "the People" in the Ancient World' in Hans Beck and Griet Vankeerberghen (eds), *Rulers and Ruled in Ancient Greece, Rome and China* (Cambridge University Press 2021) 1–21.
[26] Canovan, *The People* (n 25) 12–13.
[27] ibid 13.
[28] ibid 19.

worries about how far down society 'the people' might extend troubled many of those who eventually found themselves supporting the 1688 Revolution, encouraging them to accept the fiction that James had 'abdicated' rather than to understand their rebellion in terms of the strong theory of popular authority put forward by John Locke.[29]

Only with the American and the French revolutions did the idea of the people as the holder of sovereignty and constituent power arise, to complement the other meanings of the people as citizenry populating a polity; as the less privileged within the polity; or as the bearer of a tradition, a 'national character', and later a 'culture'. It was in the time span from the Declaration of Independence to the ratification of the Constitution drafted in Philadelphia that these semantic threads came to configure a new amalgam, to which the paradigm of political liberalism is heir. As Canovan aptly points out,

> The Roman Imperial legacy of the *sovereign people* in reserve was reunited with the Roman Republican legacy of *popular government*, including a political role for the *common people*. The *people as nation* claimed their right to self-rule as a special, distinct collectivity—but did so in terms that linked nation, republic and sovereignty to *people in general*, the bearers of universal natural rights. Last but not least, the Revolution established a resonant and enduring *myth of the sovereign people* in action.[30]

At the same time, monarchy as the standard form of rule was replaced with a democratic process, within which 'the people' also became the common people, in a gradual expansion of the suffrage that culminated in the enfranchising of all citizens of age—a development that gives rise to the tension, at the thematic centre of this book, between 'the people' as author of the constitution and bearer of primary constituent power, and the living segment of it, configured as the 'electorate' in the regular democratic process and as the holder of a secondary amending power.

Suggestive though this reconstruction by Canovan might be, it has one drawback of special significance for the purpose of solving Rousseau's riddle. It generates the impression that these diverse meanings of the term 'people' stratified one onto the other in the course of time and somehow coexisted side by side for the benefit of political leaders, parties, and movements that ground their fortunes on emphasizing one or the other. In so operating, Canovan's reconstruction dilutes a crucial polarity, inherent in all the modern derivations of 'populus'—a polarity that might prima facie appear as just another semantic nuance but instead, because of the confusion it generates, would by itself justify jettisoning the term 'people' from a discussion of constituent power, were it not for its impressive fortune in the language of modern constitutions. Just like the term 'nation'—which had greater diffusion in the Neo-Latin linguistic areas (whereas in the German-speaking world a similar role is played by the term *Volk* and in the Russian and Slavic one by the term *Narod*)—'the people' unduly conflates two concepts that need to be differentiated, for our purposes, and are best designated by two Greek terms: *ethnos* and *demos*.

---

[29] ibid 24.
[30] ibid 27.

Both terms denote aggregates of individuals or human groupings. In the case of an *ethnos*, individuals are related on the basis of *non-political* characteristics: for instance, but not exclusively, the use of a language, patterns of conduct, lifestyles, shared codes of politeness and civility, dietary habits, historical memories, and clusters of shared preferences in broad areas of life. About 7,000 distinct idioms are documented to exist.[31] Some are spoken by no more than a few hundred persons, and about 3,000 of them are expected to undergo extinction during the twenty-first century. Considering only languages spoken by thousands of speakers, about 700 to 800 languages can be counted and to each of them corresponds *at least* one *ethnos*—strong and widespread languages such as English, Spanish, and Arabic being obviously spoken by more than one *ethnos*.

A *demos* is instead an *ethnos* about which it can defensibly be stated, by members and by external observers, that at a certain juncture it has taken the form of a body politic or of a political order, and that thereafter its members have been living according to commonly adopted constitutive rules for political action and within commonly accepted structures of authority, democratic or non-democratic. Both the conflation of *demos* and *nation*—the ultimate legacy of Jacobinism and the seed of all sorts of nationalism—and the conflation of *ethnos* and *nation* have to be avoided. It is between 1748, when Montesquieu introduced the term 'spirit of a nation',[32] and a few decades later, when Herder theorized the existence of a 'national character',[33] that an *ethnos* came unreflectively to be attributed a sort of naturally 'national' magnitude. In the ancient world, in the Middle Ages, as well as in early and contemporary modernity many *ethnoi* have existed on a more local scale: the so-called *nationes* of Roman antiquity, city-states as *demoi* premised on a subnational scale, and now the 'aboriginal nations' of today's multiethnic democratic states.

On the scale of the Anthropocene, merging, assimilation, and conquest have brought the world's *ethnoi* to coalesce in ever broader and more inclusive *demoi*: it has been calculated that 5,000 years ago about 600,000 human settlements existed, each with its own distinct structure of authority and customary 'constitution'.[34] Today the officially recognized *demoi* are 195 sovereign states, within which only a few hundred *ethnoi* exist.

To sum up: the ambiguous term 'people' cannot be jettisoned but at least we should be aware that it refers to two quite distinct forms of human sociation. After outlining the two political capacities of a people—(i) to act politically and (ii) to establish (and modify) the constitutive rules that define its political practice—a 'political conception

---

[31] See Gary F Simons and Charles D Fennig (eds) *Ethnologue: Languages of the World*, twenty-first edition (SIL International 2018). Online version: http://www.ethnologue.com, accessed on 11 November 2018.

[32] Montesquieu, *The Spirit of the Laws* (1748). Edited by Anne M Cohler, Basia Carolyn Miller, and Harold Samuel Stone (Cambridge University Press 1989) Book 19, Chapter 5, 325–26.

[33] On the idea of '*national character*', Herder suggested that 'just as entire nations have one language in common, so they also share favorite paths of the imagination, certain turns and objects of thought: in short, one *genius* that expresses itself, irrespective of any particular difference, in the best-loved works of each nation's spirit and heart', Johan G Herder, *Another Philosophy of History and Selected Political Writings*. Translated, edited, and with notes by Ioannis D Evrigenis and Daniel Pellerin (Hackett 2004) 119.

[34] Alexander Wendt, 'Why a World State is Democratically Necessary?' transcript of a presentation given by Alexander Wendt at Hiram College, 2 July 2015, accessed at http://wgresearch.org/why-a-world-state-is-democratically-necessary/, 17 March 2018, p 2.

of the people' should then specify the relation between these two forms of human sociation. Each *demos* originates in an *ethnos*: as in an iceberg, it constitutes the politically visible tip of it. There simply cannot exist a *demos* as an abstract creation without ethnical roots, which is not to say that a demos must emerge from just one *ethnos*, as in most nationalistic narratives. All *demoi* in the world, except perhaps North Korea, are multiethnic.[35] On the other hand, while all *demoi* are also *ethnoi*, not every *ethnos* gives rise to a *demos*. For historical reasons of various kinds, including domination by stronger political subjects, lack of material or cultural resources, inadequate leadership, geographical dispersion, and many other adverse contingencies, many *ethnoi* never come to transform themselves into *demoi*. Finally, in today's world we observe supranational structures of authority and institutional orders that operate without one single *demos* (and *a fortiori* without an *ethnos*) but on the basis of a plurality thereof. The EU lacks a unitary *demos* and even more a unitary *ethnos*, though it regulates the life of half a billion individuals who are citizens of a plurality of *demoi*.

Finally, after substituting the polarity of *demos* and *ethnos* for the misleading accretion of meanings that coalesce under the heading of 'the people', a political conception of the people can help us reformulate Rousseau's riddle in a way that makes it solvable.

c. Rousseau's riddle reformulated: *ethnos* and *demos*

Written constitutions are a recent phenomenon. Neither Hobbes nor Locke had ever seen a proper constitution, but only their forerunners—the Magna Carta (1215), Cromwell's Instrument of Government (1653), and the Bill of Rights (1689). Rousseau outlined only the Constitution for Corsica, in 1768. While in the late eighteenth century constitutions were the exception, in the nineteenth and to an even greater extent in the twentieth century, written constitutions became the paradigmatic political act through which a *demos*, not an *ethnos*, came into being.[36] By no means a necessary condition, as the case of UK attests, a population's endorsement of a constitution has become a sufficient condition for transforming an *ethnos*, or a collection thereof, into a *demos*. An *ethnos* becomes a *demos*—it takes on a *political* identity—through the act of ratifying or accepting a constitution.

Then Rousseau's intimation—'it would be as well, before we examine the act by which a people elects a king, to examine the act by which a people is a people'[37]— can be rephrased in the following way: Before examining the act by which a people 'elects a king' or, more generally, adopts a scheme of government, it would be proper to examine the act by which an *ethnos* turns into a *demos*. That is the transitional moment

---

[35] See Will Kymlicka, *Multicultural Citizenship: A Liberal Theory of Minority Rights* (Oxford University Press 1995)196. Over the last twenty-five years, migration has turned Iceland and South Korea (two societies mentioned by Kymlicka as examples of ethnically homogenous societies) into multiethnic societies, leaving North Korea as the only standing exemplar of monoethnic polity.

[36] Of all the states formed after the French Revolution, 85 per cent enacted a constitution within their first two years of life, and 95 per cent within the first five years. Including all the states that have meanwhile been terminated, and those which adopted more than one constitution during their existence, about 900 written constitutions exist. Tom Ginsburg, *Written Constitutions Around the World* (2015) Insights on Law & Society 15.

[37] Rousseau, *Social Contract* (n 24) Book I, Chapter 5, 54.

on which we need to focus. For starters, our reformulation casts a different light on the neglect of the legitimacy of people-formation by classical and contemporary normative theorists. The formation of an *ethnos* is a factual process, best explained from an anthropological, sociological, or historical point of view. To argue about the legitimacy of the coming into being of an *ethnos* makes no more sense than to debate the legitimacy of the formation of Mount Everest or of the riverbed of the Danube. Only the transformation of an *ethnos* into a *demos* can be sensibly assessed as legitimate or not, insofar as it amounts to a voluntary action of sorts, either retrospectively imputed to a collective subject (Kelsen) or posited as a preliminary step towards establishing a social compact (Schmitt). The challenge for a political-liberal theory of constituent power consists of spelling out what exactly pre-exists the transformative event and the nature of the transformation undergone by this pre-existing entity.

There are many facets to this challenge and for my present purposes I can only take up one. It concerns the setting of the boundaries of an *ethnos*, which have some (though not exclusive) influence on the boundaries of the future *demos*. Assuming, for the purposes of its argument, a society entered by sedentary citizens at birth and exited at death, political liberalism takes the boundaries of the polity as a fact, ignoring the exercise of power and the issues of legitimacy connected with them. What justifies the fact that existing *demoi* (eg the Italian, French, South Korean, Bolivian, Tunisian) comprise exactly the *ethnoi* that (voluntarily or to various extents forcedly) concurred in their formation? Can the South-Korean population raise a valid claim to have been excluded from being part of the Italian *ethnos* that eventually gave rise to an Italian *demos*? Can the Southern French population living in Nice or the Croatian population of Rijeka (which were respectively part of the Kingdom of Sardinia or of unified Italy at some point in history) raise a claim to that effect? For our limited purpose of clarifying how constituent power operates, we cannot but refer to the factual formation of a self-conscious sense of commonality, of an undetermined yet detectable gradient of strength, which assigns to individuals located in Southern France, Croatia, and South Korea different probabilities of feeling part of a proto-Italian ethnical formation. This is not to say that such self-conscious sense of commonality is all there is to an *ethnos*. It is only an *initial* stage, past which the self-transformation into a *demos* retroacts and co-determines the self-perception of the now transformed *ethnos*, which then also becomes susceptible to assessment in terms of legitimacy. Below, in Section 3.c an example of this process will be offered, and the famous comment offered by Italian author and politician Massimo d'Azeglio upon the political unification of Italy in 1861 will be recalled. At the moment that an Italian *demos* came into being, he noted that 'Italians'—meaning a nation—were still to be made: the creature retroacts on the creator.

Be that as it may, one facet of the transformation of an *ethnos* into a *demos* that we are in a position to clarify, in response to Rousseau's riddle, concerns how a human grouping within which a sense of commonality, however vague, has come—for whatever reasons left for future inquiry to determine—to be self-consciously recognized and thematized can ever morph into a *demos* of free and equal citizens living under self-given (higher) laws. At this juncture, contemporary theories of self-constitution can be of help.

Long before it would become the core of analytical theories of subjectification or subject-formation, which will be briefly discussed in the next section, the basic idea of the paradigm of self-constitution was formulated in 1580 by Montaigne, when in his autobiographical *Essays* he wrote a groundbreaking and concise sentence: 'I have made this book to no greater extent than this book has made me'.[38] Subjectivity emerges from reflection rather than the other way around.

We need to go back to the paradoxical structure of constituent power. According to Lindahl, constituent power takes place by seizing the initiative, putting forward a tentative representation—often couched as a *narrative*—of who a targeted, intended, future 'we' *is* and *is about*.[39] If this 'call', which may be rejected or ignored (in which case the proponent subject, individual or collective, so to speak 'makes a fool of itself'), will be accepted and a coordinated structure of action along the suggested pattern will congeal, if a constituted power will stabilize, only then will such 'act' or 'call' retroactively, 'in hindsight',[40] be attributed the quality of an act of constituent power. In that sense, constituent power 'presupposes that which it creates'.[41] But Lindahl wants to avoid the idea that 'there is a meaning that is already there, given prior to and independently of its representation, such that (constitutional) interpretation is nothing more than ex-plicating the im-plicit'.[42]

And yet, Lindahl continues, 'constituent power can only originate a collective if it succeeds in presenting itself as a constituted power that represents the original community, the community we already are, *prior to the representational act*'.[43] In other words, 'the foundation of a novel legal order can only come about as its *re* foundation, as the continuation, albeit in a legal guise, of an *extant collective*'.[44] How can that be possible? How can the act of constitution-making both address an 'extant collective' and yet not be reduced to 'ex-plicating the im-plicit'?

The answer is not altogether clear. Presumably, the closure brought about by constituent power never quite exhausts the collectivity that it aims to constitute as a 'we' but leaves unaccounted non-identical aspects that stand for 'the other in us' and burst the explication operation as always partial and in need of completion, thereby paving the way to further exercises of constituent power. In other words, the representation moment embedded in the making explicit, by the *demos*-constituting power, of something implicit in the *ethnos*, always to some extent amounts to a *mis-representation*. Furthermore, a paradox of representation, according to Lindahl, is always present in the process of collective awareness-building or 'self-recognition' described above. As he puts it,

---

[38] 'Je n'ay pas plus faict mon livre que mon livre m'a faict', Montaigne, *Essais* (Garnier-Flammarion 1969) Livre 2, 326.
[39] See Lindahl, *Authority* (n 8) 404.
[40] ibid 402.
[41] Hans Lindahl, 'Constituent Power and the Constitution' in David Dyzenhaus and Malcolm Thorburn, *Philosophical Dimensions of Constitutional Law* (Oxford University Press 2016) 148.
[42] ibid 152 n 15.
[43] ibid 150 (emphasis added).
[44] ibid (emphasis added).

On one hand, an identity is posited as given when the members of a collective recognise themselves as a group capable of acting in certain ways in response to a challenge to its existence. On the other, collective self-recognition is the creation of a group-identity, *in response to a challenge*.[45]

Lindahl's thesis is a sound one, but a different way exists of avoiding that a political-liberal theory of constituent power be trapped into the Sisyphus-like task of tracing the non-identical in a-legality only to then be cornered between either failing to encompass it or assimilating it, in either case detracting from the non-oppressive quality of the polity. This alternative strategy (outlined in subsection e) consists of differentiating the ambiguous term 'the people' into *ethnos* and *demos*. Constituent power then starts from something already existing, *ethnos*, but not at all identical to the final author of the constitution. Constituent power is only *elicited*, not exercised by the summoner of it—a revolutionary or transformative movement, party, leader, in the role of Rousseau's legislator. It is exercised when a collectivity *accepts* (in a diversity of legally regulated ways) a constitution, whereupon the transition is completed from the 'unconstituted' *ethnos* to the constituted *demos*.

More details need to be added to this preliminary step. Is an *ethnos* to a *demos* like an essence to its manifestations? This was a basic theme of the historical school of German jurisprudence, starting from Savigny.[46] A *Volksgeist* consists of ethical substance, mores, the diffuse normativity of a *Sittlichkeit*, that under favourable historical circumstances find their way to their formalization as constitutional provisions that regulate the life of the *demos*. A liberal-democratic echo of this view can be found in Dewey's 'Fragment on Democracy', where he states that democracy 'is a personal way of life', an ethos in other words, and that 'instead of thinking of our dispositions and habits as accommodated to certain [democratic] institutions we have to learn to think of the latter as expressions, projections and extensions of habitually dominant personal attitudes'.[47] A solution to Rousseau's riddle conceived along these lines—that is, a people becomes a people or, in our terms, an *ethnos self-constitutes* itself as a *demos* when it adopts a constitution as reflective as possible of its identity as an *ethnos*—would lend itself to being negatively cast as essentialist and epistemic originalism, in sofar as the exercise of constituent power would then be evaluated in terms of 'ethnical fidelity'. Incommensurably more sophisticated than this form of originalism, Lindahl's solution to the paradox of constituent power nonetheless continues to be affected by an infinitesimal, almost imperceptible reflection of this representational anchoring of normativity: because constituent power offers a tentative representation of who a targeted, intended, future 'we' is and *is about*, then *who we are tends to overshadow who we want to be*.

---

[45] See Lindahl, *Authority* (n 8) 323 (emphasis added).
[46] Friedrich K von Savigny, *The Vocation of Our Age for Legislation and Jurisprudence*. Translated by A Hayward (Lawbook Exchange 2002).
[47] John Dewey, 'Creative Democracy—The Task Before Us' in J Dewey, *The Later Works: 1925–1953. Volume 14: 1939–1941. Essays, reviews and Miscellany*. Edited by Jo Ann Boydston, with an introduction by RW Sleeper (Southern Illinois University Press 1988) 226.

d. Excursus on self-constitution

At this point, a closer look at self-constitution is in order. Four centuries after Montaigne, theories of self-constitution elaborated by Korsgaard, Frankfurt, and Larmore have developed his insight along 'practical' rather than cognitive lines.[48] Although their focus is generally on *individual* self-constitution, their teachings apply to collective self-constitution too. Korsgaard offers an individual equivalent of Rousseau's riddle: 'How can you constitute yourself, create yourself, unless you are already there?'[49] The answer lies in a *practical* turn. Self-constitution should not be conceived, in other words, as a state achieved once and for all and whence action then follows, but as 'action itself'. Subjects constitute themselves through the actions they perform, and through making their actions respond to what they *reflectively endorse* in the light of reasons rooted in principle.

Underlying this philosophical programme is the idea that a person's (or a collective subject's) capacity 'to act for a reason' requires not just that the person have a capacity for 'reflectively endorsing' her own first-order desires—for 'taking them up' on the basis of a certain representation of her own self or on the basis of a description under which she values herself[50]—but also requires a capacity to *act under principles* capable of conferring unity to the subject.[51] For Korsgaard, identity functions as a *normative* source of selectivity with regard to first-order desires, so that the obligation dimension of Luther's 'I can do no other' remains dependent on at least some reasons that are somehow 'agent neutral.' It is this neutrality that distinguishes Luther's stance from the arbitrariness of a hypothetical 'I don't *want* to do any other' stance, equivalent to a view of constituent power as unbound. Agent neutrality, in turn, is construed by Korsgaard in terms of two gradients of universality corresponding to two layers of the actor's identity: namely, the individuated 'practical identity' of the particular actor and the 'moral identity' shared by all moral actors. The normative dimension of 'practical identity' consists in the fact that to take up a certain reason to act means to raise the claim that anyone would have to do the same *if analogously situated*. Korsgaard's programme is to combine the view that ultimately, as suggested by Luther's saying, 'normativity derives from our self-conception'[52] with the idea that such self-conception must respond to an irrecusable imperative if we want to preserve our unity as subjects.

Also Paul Ricoeur and Charles Larmore anchor authentic individual conduct to the *practical*, as opposed to the *cognitive*, relation that we establish with our self. From

---

[48] See Charles Larmore, *Les pratiques du moi* (PUF 2004) (hereafter Larmore, *Pratiques*); Christine Korsgaard, *The Sources of Normativity* (Cambridge University Press 1996) (hereafter Korsgaard, *Sources*) and *Self-Constitution* (Oxford University Press 2009) (hereafter Korsgaard, *Self-Constitution*); Harry Frankfurt, *The Importance of What We Care About: Philosophical Essays* (1988) (Cambridge University Press 2007). For a discussion of how Rousseau's implicit theory of the authenticity of the self can correct some shortcomings of these theories of self-constitution, see Alessandro Ferrara, *Rousseau and Critical Theory* (Brill 2017) 34–45.
[49] Korsgaard, *Self-Constitution* (n 48) 20.
[50] Korsgaard, *Sources* (n 48) 101.
[51] See ibid 232.
[52] ibid 249.

their perspectives, the authentic quality of an action depends on our *commitments*[53] and not on our beliefs about who we are: authenticity for an individual, and the exercise of sovereignty for the collective, cannot consist of 'becoming what one is' or what one 'represents oneself as being', for two reasons. First, such imperative would amount to a tyranny of the existent, inflected in the first-person singular or plural. Second, subjectivity so conceived misses the fact that by committing itself to something the self is not hostage to its own past, but rather orients itself to the future and to becoming something which it still is not. The fulfilment of the self does not consist in coincidence with something represented as actual, but rather in 'coinciding with its own essential non-coincidence'.[54]

Furthermore, for Larmore anchoring individual or collective self-constitution primarily to self-*knowledge* and self-*representation* entangles us with the problematic 'authority of the first person'. If I say 'I believe that it's raining,' no one can question my believing so. In this immunity of the first person to error a tradition stemming from Descartes has seen the foundations of sound knowledge. Larmore, however, highlights the paradoxical implications of assuming that the self has a privileged cognitive access to its own mental states. What kind of knowledge could it be? It can neither be knowledge gained through observation, as the knowledge that mediates our relation to the external world, nor inferential knowledge of a logical form. We are then left with assuming a kind of 'auto-telepathy' with our mental states based on our somehow 'owning' them,[55] a mysterious faculty variously captured by Ryle's claim that we are always 'better informed' about ourselves than about anybody else,[56] by Anscombe's suggestion that some cognitions stem neither from observation nor from logical inference,[57] by the notion of 'self-intimation' (Shoemaker),[58] or by a 'non-cognitive kind of knowledge' (Tugendhat).[59]

To avoid these difficulties, Larmore argues that the authority of the first person is best understood along *non cognitive lines*. The self, in other words, is constituted not by self-*description*—as still suggested by equating constituent power with describing the people 'as' something—but by *committing* itself to being a certain kind of self through *avowals* or declarations.[60] The problem of justifying the special authority of the first-person (singular or plural) does not disappear altogether. Whatever the scope and significance of these *avowals*—whether I say 'I love oysters' at a dinner party or collectively we declare to ordain a constitution 'in Order to form a more perfect Union, establish Justice, insure domestic Tranquility, provide for the common defence, promote the general Welfare, and secure the Blessings of Liberty to ourselves and our Posterity'—the attribution of motives must yield to the authority of the 'first-person'-utterer of the sentence. However, if we assume the priority of the *practical* over the

---

[53] This term is used here as a common denominator standing for what Korsgaard calls 'reflexive endorsement', Larmore calls 'engagement', Ricoeur calls 'attestation', and Frankfurt calls 'wholehearted identification'.
[54] Larmore, *Pratiques* (n 48) 10. That formulation is close to what Lindahl understands as self-constitution.
[55] ibid 153.
[56] See Gilbert Ryle, *The Concept of the Mind* (Harper & Row 1949) 179.
[57] See GEM Anscombe, *Intention* (Blackwell 1957), §§ 28–32.
[58] See Sidney Shoemaker, *The First-Person Perspective* (Cambridge University Press 1996).
[59] See Ernst Tugendhat, *Selbstbewusstsein und Selbstbestimmung* (Suhrkamp 1979), 132–33.
[60] Larmore, *Pratiques* (n 48) 156.

cognitive relation of the subject to itself, the authority of the first person no longer rests on the dubious assumption that 'no one better than me can know' whether I adore oysters or we care for justice, security, welfare, and liberty but, rather, on the claim that no one can be in a better position than me or us to *take up those commitments*.

Larmore in the end severs all connection between our *avowals* and the supposition of their conveying 'self-knowledge'. Drawing on Ricoeur's notion of 'attestation',[61] Larmore understands assertions about our beliefs or intentions as 'stances' or 'indications' about how we plan to act in the future. Even making a statement becomes like promising to act in accordance with my declared belief—something which *only I* am entitled to promise, not insofar as I'm the one who knows best about my true intentions, but insofar as I'm the only owner of my agency. My promise *creates*, as opposed to *describes*, my commitment to act in a certain way, for example to act in a way appropriate for someone who says 'I love you' to someone else. Such commitments share with promises the quality of not being susceptible to being 'false', at least in the sense descriptions can be false. They can be untruthful, 'inauthentic' as it were, but 'inauthentic' in a future-oriented sense—like a promise that remains unfulfilled. This theme will surface again, below, in Section 3.a—'Regime change and constitutional authenticity'.

Returning now to the transition from *ethnos* to *demos*, the theories of self-constitution help us to grasp such transition in the following terms: an agent, as the catalyst of the transition (a single charismatic leader, a movement, or a party), ventures into offering to an *ethnos* (or a plurality thereof), or to an already constituted *demos* on the verge of possible regime-change, not a cognitive rendition of who they *are* and who *is* included, but a new set of normative commitments concerning the terms of their association henceforth. These new commitments are drawn not from an ideal playbook, but from a notion of 'political right' that the (singular or plural) catalytic agent—standing 'sideways at the entrance of Plato's cave', equally aware of their addressees as they are and the ideal citizens they could be—understands as most reasonable for the collective to embrace.

The relation between articulating such proposal for 'political self-constitution' and its acceptance by the collective as a basis for exercising its constituent power is not a relation of necessity but, as Rawls put it in relation to justice as fairness and the overlapping consensus, one of 'hope'. Evidence of acceptance is the stabilization of powers constituted along those, and no other, normative lines. But the 'accepting collectivity' is not merely a retrospective projection. It is a *real referent* that makes the difference between a successful and an aborted exercise of constituent power. When in the 1990s the Italian *Northern League*, as it was then called, tried to call for the secession of the Italian regions north of the Po river and for the creation of a new *demos* of the Po Valley, that proposal—enriched with folkloric and picturesque ritual offerings to pagan Northern divinities—fell flat on the indifference of all but a few devotees. It failed to call into existence any *demos*.

---

[61] Paul Ricoeur, *Oneself as Another* (University of Chicago Press 1992) 21–23.

e. Rousseau's riddle solved: the commitment to share commitments

How does the conceptual splitting of the people into *ethnos* and *demos*, and our *excursus* through theories of self-constitution, help to solve Rousseau's riddle? Shouldn't a collectivity, as in the standard version of the riddle, *already exist* in order to commit itself to certain terms of cooperation? Not really. The distinction of *ethnos* and *demos* allows us to claim (i) that the people does not exist *in the same way* before and after the exercise of constitution-making power and yet (ii) that the former incarnation of the people, qua *ethnos*, is no mere fiction or projection. An *ethnos* has an empirically attestable existence *qua* finite set of human beings that share certain non-political characteristics, diverse from those descriptive of other groupings. Existing as an *ethnos* is not the same as existing as a *demos*, therefore it is false that a *demos* must 'already exist' in order to make commitments like electing a king. An ethnic collectivity *becomes* a *demos*, or a previously existing *demos* transforms itself into a new one, *through* that act, as Lindahl has rightly put it.

However, not every *ethnos* is prepared and willing to make such commitments, or perhaps no catalyst agents are available to stimulate that transition through a proposal. Between the two modes of existence of a people—as *ethnos* and as *demos*—lies a *necessary but not sufficient condition* for the possible activation of constituent power. Drawing on Arendt's famous 'right to have rights',[62] let me call the necessary but not sufficient condition that functions as a bridge or link between *ethnos* and *demos* a 'commitment to share joint commitments'. That condition is empirical; no normativity can oblige us to make commitments together any more than legal norms can command love to arise. Here we meet the one residue of *Willkür* or arbitrary volition antecedent to the formation of constituent power. The 'commitment to share joint commitments' is a condition of the possibility of constituent power. It is only a preparatory step, akin to what Arendt identifies as the power of mutual promising: the force that keeps human individuals together 'is the force of mutual promise or contract'. Sovereignty is generated at that moment, in the form of a 'limited independence from the incalculability of the future' or 'of a body of people bound and kept together, not by an identical will which somehow magically inspires them all, but by an agreed purpose for which alone the promises are valid and binding'. At that juncture of collective commitment-making, the condition is set for a human group to fulfil that uniquely human potential for *natality* or 'beginning something new'.[63]

Only after that still generic disposition to share commitments or reciprocal promises is formed and diffused within a population, according to processes that partly result from enabling conditions (territorial contiguity, mutual linguistic and cultural understanding, shared orientations) and partly originate from conscious effort (settling in certain areas, kindling dialogue and interaction, teaching a common language, cultivating a shared memory) can a proposal be addressed to that ethnic

---

[62] Hannah Arendt, *The Origins of Totalitarianism* (1950). New edition with added prefaces (Harcourt 1976) 296–97.
[63] Hannah Arendt, *The Human Condition: A Study of the Central Dilemmas Facing Modern Man* (1958) (Doubleday Anchor 1959) 220–22.

agglomerate in order to formalize the population's generic willingness to 'commit to joint commitments' into a *specific* proposal for a script of constitutional significance, to then be adopted, on the basis of its being *the most reasonable for* the subjects of constituent power.

In this transition, 'we the people-as-*ethnos*' (or as the pre-regime-change *demos*) transform ourselves, in the literal sense that some aspects of who we are migrate into the new *demos* that we are going to be, but other aspects are shed away and new ones are embraced. There is no priority, in this process, of who we are over who we commit ourselves to being, as in essentialist models of popular sovereignty and constituent power. On the contrary, there is a priority of '*who we most reasonably may want to be*' as future *demos*, over who we *are* as an *ethnos*. The process that constitutes us as a *demos* also transforms *who we are as an ethnos*, while keeping a foothold in that life form: the new *demos* is a transformation *of us*.

Returning to Montaigne, in lieu of the self-image we adopt, it is the specific *commitments* we make, after having formed a *commitment to enter joint commitments*, that makes us, no less than we make them.

3. Four Manifestations of Constituent Power

The solution outlined above to Rousseau's riddle—based on distinguishing two ways of being a people and on the idea of 'political self-constitution'—can help us make sense of how a human grouping called 'the people' could perform collective acts that, on one hand, presuppose its existence, such as selecting a form of government or 'electing a king', and, on the other hand, mark its political birth. That solution, however, applies mainly to the ideal case envisaged by contract theorists: the transition from a variously conceived absence of political incorporation (the state of nature) to a new associated life, in a polity where relations among the members of the people are regulated by law. Nowhere can that hypothesized initial situation be observed today. We must then inflect our purely analytical solution to Rousseau's riddle into four more specific modes, which correspond to the diverse ways in which constituent power is actually exercised on the ground.

First, historical occurrences of constituent power rarely transform an *ethnos* into a *demos*, but manifest themselves more often as transformations of an *already constituted demos* into a new one. Regime change is the name for this common manifestation of constituent power. *Second*, at other times constituent power transforms a subsection or a portion of an existing *demos* into a new one, often by claiming its own ethnic diversity as the ground for seceding from the larger, already constituted *demos*. *Third*, at other times—sometimes explored by classical contract theorists under the headings of 'the death of Leviathan', the 'dissolution of society', and 'the death of the body politic'[64]—we observe the inverse transformation of a *demos* into an *ethnos*,

---

[64] See Thomas Hobbes, *Leviathan* (1651), edited and with an introduction by CB Macpherson (Penguin 1985) Chapter 29, 363–76; John Locke, *Two Treatises of Government* (1690), with an introduction and notes by Peter Laslett (New American Library 1965), *Second Treatise*, 19, § 211, 454–55; Rousseau, *Social Contract* (n 24) Book III, Chapter 11, 121–22.

either by the rare (and mostly unintentional) collapse of the extant form of associated way of life or, more frequently, by inclusion into a larger *demos*. Finally, in a fourth case constituent power simply transforms the terms of association in a more limited and partial way, leading neither to a new *demos* nor to a new regime, but simply to an amended constitution. This special case, and the normativity that it responds to, will be the object of Chapter 7. These are all manifestations of constituent power that have independent dynamics worth briefly highlighting in the light of our political conception of the people.

a. Regime change and constitutional authenticity

Regime change in an already constituted *demos* can occur in many different ways: a coup d'état, external occupation, unilateral constitution-giving on the part of a far-sighted monarch, dynastic inheritance by a different royal house, and, of course, democratic replacement of a non-democratic previous regime. Focusing on the latter case, Bruce Ackerman has recently offered one of the most groundbreaking theoretical statements, constructed on a comparative basis, of how so-called revolutionary constitutions, the epitome of the people's constituent power in action and by definition born out of a regime change, arise and consolidate. Comparing the successful cases of India, South Africa, France, Italy, Poland, Israel, and Iran, Ackerman shows that the 'revolutionary', as opposed to the 'establishmentarian' or 'elitist', pathway to constitution-making typically manifests a four-stage sequence of: (i) regime change under the guidance of charismatic democratic leadership; (ii) a race against time to constitutionalize revolutionary charisma of either a personal or institutional kind;[65] (iii) succession crises; (iv) the intervention of previously less decisive constitutional courts through judicial review.[66] Alongside a path-breaking historical reconstruction of intra-regime constitutional change in the history of the United States, across 'constitutional moments' (the Founding, the Reconstruction, the New Deal, and the Civil Rights era) all marked by the occurrence of various kinds of 'unconventional adaptation',[67] Ackerman offers an account of seven instances of the use of constituent power for regime change.

---

[65] See Bruce Ackerman, *Revolutionary Constitutions: Charismatic Leadership and the Rule of Law* (Harvard University Press 2019) 4 (hereafter Ackerman, *Revolutionary Constitutions*); on the contrast of leadership charisma and organizational charisma, see ibid 35–36.

[66] See ibid 8–9; for enlightening commentaries, see Roberto Gargarella, pointing to an insufficiently developed 'theory of history' and a less than satisfactory account of the transition from each stage to the next (Gargarella, 'Bruce Ackerman's Theory of History' in the edited volume Richard Albert (ed), *Revolutionary Constitutionalism: Law, Legitimacy, Power* (Hart 2020) 62–65; Stephen Gardbaum and Tom Ginsburg, pointing to anomalies concerning the lack of charismatic leadership to be later constitutionalized (Gardbaum, 'Uncharismatic Revolutionary Constitutionalism', ibid 146–48; Ginsburg 'Charismatic Fictions and Constitutional Politics', ibid 120–22; Andrew Arato, pointing to the overlooking of the influence of the international context on the local evolution of the four-stage sequence (Arato, 'Revolution on a Human Scale: Liberal Values, Populist Theory?', ibid 108–11.

[67] On the constitutional moments in the history of the United States, see Bruce Ackerman, *We the People.* Volume 1, *Foundations* (Harvard University Press 1991); We the People. Volume 2, *Transformations* (Harvard University Press 1998); and *We the People.* Volume 3, *The Civil Rights Revolution* (Harvard University Press 2014). For Ackerman's view of 'unconventional adaptation' see *Transformations* 9–12 and *Revolutionary Constitutions* (n 65) 34. On distinguishing a variety of kinds and degrees of unconventional

The kinds of regime changes involved are different: India and Israel are cases of establishing a first democratic regime after colonial rule or a mere non-state territorial status, in both cases at the instigation, but not under the control, of the colonial or protecting power. South Africa's case amounts to a successful transformation of an exclusionary regime founded on apartheid into an inclusive constitutional democracy. France and Italy are successful cases of regime change after the collapse of the collaborationist Vichy regime and fascism, with France then following up on a major transformation from parliamentary to presidential democracy. Poland is a case of a post-communist regime change in the wake of 1989 and Iran of the revolutionary toppling of an authoritarian secularist regime.

Of interest to us are the first two stages in Ackerman's sequential pattern. We can observe different actors who are the catalysts, or 'summoners' of constituent power: one party representing the Indian or the South African *demos* (the Nehru-led *Congress Party* in India and the Mandela-led *African National Congress* in South Africa), or a plurality of Catholic, Communist, and Socialist, as well as liberal-democratic, parties (with the above-the-fray charismatic leader de Gaulle in France, and a plurality of prominent leaders such as De Gasperi, Togliatti, and Nenni in Italy, none of whom were in a position to lead the constitution-making process solo), one hegemonic, initially union-based, movement with a charismatic leader (*Solidarity* and Walesa) in Poland, one of several parties (*Mapai*, but also *Herut*) but with the outstandingly charismatic leader David Ben-Gurion in Israel, and a revolutionary movement inspired by Ayatollah Khomeini and led by five representatives of him in Iran. These catalysts of the constituent process called on constituencies that ranged from very established *demoi*—as the French, Italian, and Polish ones at one extreme—to weaker *demoi* that existed under colonial rule (India), or in the context of a settler society (South Africa) or within a Protectorate (Jews in Palestine).

Ackerman's point is that while transformative political movements, parties, and leaders are often present, they only rarely succeed in 'constitutionalizing charisma' or, in another vocabulary, in having their call for a new self-constituting moment responded to by their addressee—a necessary condition in order for the distinction between an authoritarian coup and a moment of democratic self-definition to make sense. There is always a 'race against time'[68] underway before the window of historical opportunity closes—a race for consolidating the transformation of self-definition on the part of the *demos* in the form of a new constitution marking the beginning of a new regime. At that decisive juncture, the reciprocal relation of all the ingredients of political liberal constituent power become visible: the activating of constituent power at the catalyst's summoning, the coalescing of a new communal commitment, the situated normativity that such exercise of constituent power responds to, and the

---

adaptation, see Alessandro Ferrara, 'Unconventional Adaptation and the Authenticity of the Constitution' in Richard Albert (ed), *Revolutionary Constitutionalism: Law, Legitimacy, Power* (Hart 2020), 157–68 (hereafter Ferrara, 'Unconventional Adaptation').

[68] As the case of Poland teaches, regime-changers 'should recognize that they are running a race against time at the Founding. If they fail to constitutionalize the high-energy politics of commitment during the first few years of their ascendancy, the resulting alienation can cast a dark shadow on their country's political development for a long time to come', Ackerman, *Revolutionary Constitutions* (n 65) 281. On the implications of the 'race against time' for the cases of Burma and Israel, see ibid 282–323.

non-cognitive and thus non-essentialist but primarily *practical* nature of the new commitment, often couched in negative terms: 'Never again!'.

The case of Italy exemplifies the interaction of all these elements in the process of 'political self-constitution'. The present Constitution of Italy was enacted on 1 January 1948. The Italian people was not invented then, of course. Long in existence as an *ethnos*, which Machiavelli yearned would turn into a national *demos*, possibly at the hands of Cesare Borgia, in the footsteps of the Spanish and the French monarchies, the Italian people was brought into existence as a national, unified *demos* on 17 March 1861 by King Victor Emmanuel II of Savoy. The constitutional framework, within which the Proclamation of the Kingdom (by a regular act of parliament)[69] took place, preexisted unification. It was an *octroyée* constitution 'conceded' by King Charles Albert of Savoy in 1848 to his subjects that established liberal rights but was so flexible as to be able to accommodate fascism without formal suspension or repeal. That liberal but not democratic constitution, which secured a constitutional monarchy for the newly founded Italian *demos*, formally lasted until 1948.

For Italians, the 1948 Constitution marks a new beginning and a radical break with the Fascist regime hosted within the framework of the Statuto Albertino. It was drafted by an elected Constitutional Assembly, in representation of the constituent power of the Italian people that, after the formal resignation of the Mussolini government in 1943, had risen up, with different degrees of determination in different parts of the country, against the Nazi former allies turned occupants and against the remnants of the fascist regime. It was drafted by representatives of all the major political cultures of Italy, and within its provisions traces of the Catholic, Marxist, and liberal political cultures of the country can be found.

The Constitution broke new ground. The first 12 of its 139 Articles, grouped under the heading 'General Principles', include some of the commitments that members of the *demos* perceive as distinctive of the Italian republic. For example, generations of Italians, across political cleavages, have always identified as distinctively their own the qualification of Italy, in Article 1, as a democratic republic 'founded on labour' (*fondata sul lavoro*). That peculiar expression was coined by Amintore Fanfani, Christian democrat framer and future leader, as a compromise between the 'republic of workers', advocated by Togliatti, and the absence of any specific qualifier, advocated by liberal groups. The clause has come to be understood not in a restrictive way, as though 'work' or 'being a worker' designated an extra-requisite, beyond citizenship, for participating as free and equal in the life of the republic, but as gesturing to the full inclusion and participation of citizens from all classes. Giuseppe Saragat, Constituent Assembly member and President between 1964 and 1971, famously commented that Article 1 calls attention to the priority of labour over property. Property being a sediment of labour, as Locke suggested, in order for property to exist, and require protection, there must be labour. The expression 'founded on labour', Fanfani maintained, implicitly denies that the republic might be premised on privilege, hereditary lineage, or someone else's toil. It also implies that citizens have a duty to contribute to the country's flourishing and that the well-being of the national community presupposes

---

[69] Law of 17 March 1861, n 476, enacted by the Parliament of the Kingdom of Sardinia.

that everyone be in a position to offer her best contribution to the 'common prosperity'. 'Founded on labour', Fanfani concludes, counts as a basic commitment of the Italian Constitution.[70]

With Article 2, the constituent power of the *demos* 'recognizes' that the rights of the person are not its own creation, but can only be 'guaranteed' by the Republic. It is also explicitly acknowledged that these rights are the possession of the person as an individual and as a member of intermediate 'social formations', a formulation close to Rawls's 'social unions'. This formulation has far-reaching implications: for example, insofar as these rights are not created by the *demos*, 'they are *inviolable*: nobody can be stripped of his or her rights, the state has no power to repeal them and even constitutional amendments that infringe upon the core of those individual rights are considered unconstitutional'.[71] In the same article it is stated that the relation of the citizens to the *demos* as a whole is not confined to rights only, but includes also the duties of 'political, economic and social solidarity'.

> Article 2 of the Italian Constitution
> The Republic recognizes and guarantees the inviolable rights of the person, both as an individual and in the social groups where human personality is expressed. The Republic expects that the fundamental duties of political, economic and social solidarity be fulfilled.

In Article 3, other crucial self-constituting commitments can be observed. The first clause is a standard equality provision, not dissimilar from analogous provisions found in many constitutions and autonomously adopted by the framers. The second clause, however, is perceived as perhaps the most important locus of the 'authenticity' of the Italian Constitution.

> Article 3 of the Italian Constitution
> All citizens shall have equal social dignity and shall be equal before the law, without distinction of gender, race, language, religion, political opinion, personal and social conditions.
> It shall be the duty of the Republic to remove those obstacles of an economic or social nature which constrain the freedom and equality of citizens, thereby impeding the full development of the human person and the effective participation of all workers in the political, economic and social organization of the country.

The second clause, in which the liberal value of equality is combined with the republic's concern for the flourishing of 'the person', is perceived as so authentically distinctive of the Italian political identity that even after two decades of Berlusconian neoliberal

---

[70] Italian Chamber of Deputies, *Digitalized Record of the Constituent Assembly*. Session of 22 March 1947, afternoon, accessed on 24 June 2018 at http://legislature.camera.it/frameset.asp?content=%2Faltre%5Fsezionism%2F304%2F8964%2Fdocumentotesto%2Easp%3F.

[71] This comment also owes its authority from being the interpretation of Article 2 put forward by the former Chief Justice of the Constitutional Court of Italy and Minister of Justice, Prof Marta Cartabia. See Marta Cartabia, 'The Italian Constitution as a Revolutionary Agreement' in Albert (ed), *Revolutionary Constitutionalism* (n 67) 318 (hereafter Cartabia, 'Italian Constitution').

FOUR MANIFESTATIONS OF CONSTITUENT POWER 161

individualism, followed by populism, no one has ever dared to publicly question it. That clause states that the *flourishing* of each citizen—not just her equality before the law—is such a paramount constitutional value that it is incumbent on 'the Republic' to remove the (mostly socio-economic) obstacles that by limiting their freedom and equality end up also limiting the citizens' potential for flourishing. The second part of the second clause, which reflects the views of the Communists and the Socialists, is equally unique, but perceived as dated and not pervaded by the same aura of authenticity.

Article 3 was meant to detail what being 'founded on labour' implied for the new Republic. The framers had a clear preoccupation that the principle of equality of the 1789 French Revolution could idle inoperative, reduced to a merely *formal* 'equality before the law' or 'equal protection of the laws' (in its pre-*Brown* version), unless the powerful socio-economic impediments to the inclusion of workers within the democratic life of the country were removed. Lelio Basso, a socialist Assembly member and co-author of Article 3, connected Articles 3 and 1 in the following way:

> We do not wish to have a republic of abstract individuals, a republic of citizens who only share a legal bond, we strive to create a republic, a State in which each participates proactively through his work, in the life of all.[72]

Aldo Moro, future Christian democrat leader kidnapped and assassinated by the Red Brigades in 1978, summed up the point of Article 3 as a

> commitment, on the part of the newly formed Italian State, to solve as best as possible ... the problem of integrating ever more closely within the social, economic and political life of the country those working classes that, for a number of reasons, had been longer excluded from the State and from the economic and social life.[73]

These elucidations, coming from such diverse quarters, signal that Articles 1, 2, and 3 exert not just a normative, regulatory function but constitute the *expressive pivot* on which the authenticity of the Italian Constitution revolves. I would also add Article 11, whose first clause reads 'Italy rejects war as an instrument of aggression against the freedom of other peoples and as a means for the settlement of international disputes'. While the second clause plainly confirms Italy's willingness to cede as much sovereignty as needed for the functioning of proper international organizations that may secure 'peace and justice among the nations', the first clause is much more emphatic in its principled rejection of war in all cases when international disputes cannot be settled.

All of these are joint commitments, binding for any partisan political actor who then represents sectors of the electorate, rather than *descriptions* of what the *demos does* or has customarily been doing before constitutional codification. It would be

---

[72] Italian Chamber of Deputies, *Digitalized Record of the Constituent Assembly*. Session of 6 March 1947 at 1824, accessed 25 June 2018, at http://legislature.camera.it/frameset.asp?content=%2Faltre%5Fsezionism%2F304%2F8964%2Fdocumentotesto%2Easp%3F.
[73] ibid.

inaccurate to imagine that a pre-existing Italian *demos* used to ground interaction among its members 'on labour' and then, after a change of regime, in 1948, decided to register this descriptive facet of what the Italian *demos* 'is about' in a charter (approved with 453 votes for and 62 against) that declares the Italian republican life to be founded 'on labour'. Rather, a constitutional assembly, invested with constituent power through a democratic election, drafted a new constitutional charter premised, among other principles, on a communal *commitment* to the priority of labour over property.

Following Montaigne, through the commitments they embed—for example, to recognize the priority of labour over property, to recognize the inviolable rights of the person but also 'to remove those obstacles of an economic or social nature which constrain the freedom and equality of citizens, thereby impeding the full development of the human person',[74] or to reject war[75]—constitutions make a *demos*, no less than a *demos* makes a constitution. The regime change that, through the agency of its democratically elected constituent assembly, the Italian *demos* was effecting in 1946–48 leaves no doubt as to the future-oriented and not 'essence-reflecting' nature of those provisions: the past was the Statuto Albertino, which accommodated laissez-faire liberalism and then fascism, and contained no commitment to labour and no mention of a 'recognition' of 'inviolable rights' (though civil and political rights were attributed to 'free and equal subjects' (*regnicoli*) or duties of solidarity. Furthermore, the Statuto Albertino allowed for a Westphalian understanding of war as an instrument of politics (which eventually led to colonial wars and to the disastrous belligerent adventurism of Mussolini). Nor can it be claimed that these constitutional elements were part of an extra-legal social praxis of the Italian *demos*. They were aspirational, future-oriented commitments that could only be made by the collective author of new, post-regime-change terms of cooperation. These constitutional essentials serve an *expressive* function, which is of fundamental importance: they allow the members of the newly reformed *demos* to perceive the constitution as unique and distinctive of their *political* identity.[76]

This constitution-making process was embedded in the constant flow of intra-*demos* partisan politics. It has been maintained that these largely aspirational commitments served a compensatory function for a *demos* united more by rejection of the fascist past (a rejection that was the common denominator of communist, socialist, Christian-democrat, and laissez-faire liberal political parties) than by a shared vision of the future, and with Christian-democrat and laissez-faire liberal forces willing to concede to the left-wing parties some programmatic radicalism in exchange for a renunciation of its political implementation.[77] While there is much truth in this

---

[74] Article 3, Constitution of Italy.
[75] Article 11, Constitution of Italy.
[76] On the expressive moment of higher law making, see Cass R Sunstein, 'On the Expressive Function of Law' (1996) 144 University of Pennsylvania Law Review 5 2021; Mark Tushnet, *Weak Courts, Strong Rights: Judicial Review and Social Welfare Rights in Comparative Constitutional Law* (Princeton University Press 2008), 12–14: Richard Albert, 'The Expressive Function of Constitutional Amendment Rules' (2013) 59 McGill University Law Journal 226. On an alternative, non-expressive view of the constitution as legitimate insofar as based on the normativity of reason, see Alon Harel and Adam Shinar, 'Two Concepts of Constitutional Legitimacy. Global Constitutionalism' (2022 Forthcoming), Hebrew University of Jerusalem Legal Research Paper No. 22-13, Available at SSRN: https://ssrn.com/abstract=4122333.
[77] On this point see Piero Calamandrei, *La Costituzione e le leggi per attuarla* (1955) (Giuffrè, 2000) 7–8, quoted and commented upon in Cartabia, 'The Italian Constitution' (n 71) 313, 319. As Cartabia writes, 'In

description, it is equally hard to dispute that these commitments jointly form the core of what might be called 'the authenticity of the Italian Constitution'.[78]

At over a dozen *loci* within Ackerman's *Revolutionary Constitutions* reference is made to the perceived 'authenticity' of a constitution or the perceived lack of authenticity in the relation of the *demos* to its own constitution.[79] Those formulas raise the question what the authenticity of a constitution might possibly mean, beyond the obvious, baseline meaning of its being the product of the unconstrained autonomous will of its author. To answer that question, we can now put to use the 'political conception of the people' and the notion of 'political self-constitution' outlined above, in Section 2. The authenticity of a constitution, as illustrated by the Italian case, is best understood not as an essentialist coincidence between constitution and *ethnic Volksgeist*—a coincidence which, if it could ever be realized, would detract from the freedom of the democratic sovereign and make 'the people' hostage to its history—but as the *exemplary uniqueness* or *distinctiveness* of the commitments that its author has come to posit as irrecusable, identity-defining.

Those commitments did not exist prior to the drafting the Italian Constitution of 1948. In that sense, the Constitution has made the Italian contemporary *demos* no less than the *demos*, through its Constitutional Assembly, has made the Constitution. And yet there exists a collective actor—the Italian *demos*—that elected that Constitution-drafting body and several decades later, shaped also by those commitments along with other historical vicissitudes, perceives them as non-negotiable ingredients of its political identity. The point of the democratic authorship of the laws is really the setting up of constitutive rules, for the political practice of a polity, which include—over and beyond many other stipulations of functional and regulatory interest—a number of commitments that form the focal point of a possibly unique and *authentic* project of communal political life.

A *demos* may pre-exist those constitutionalized commitments *as a partly different demos*—indeed, some author of those commitments must exist, because they cannot self-produce—but it then becomes *the present demos that it is* by virtue of first making them, and then sustaining them, avoiding letting them evaporate through *desuetude*.[80]

b. *Demos* and secession

The classical transition, envisaged by contract theorists, from an unincorporated *ethnos* to a chartered *demos*, has become nearly impossible to observe, because at this historical juncture we live in a world where no lawless lands exist, but only lands where law, though existing, fails to establish its rule. Thus, the only cases of an *ethnos* turning itself into *a new demos*, and *creating* rather than changing a regime, are those

---

the Italian case, the Constitution, rather than translating the chief tenets of a political revolution into higher legal principles, provides a legal framework that leaves room for a revolution yet to come. The question of whether this promise was later maintained is another matter', ibid 314.

[78] See Ferrara, 'Unconventional Adaptation' (n 67) 173–74.
[79] See Ackerman, *Revolutionary Constitutions* (n 65) 18–21, 116, 166, 170, 227, 261, 275, 281, 282, 370.
[80] On constitutional change by mere desuetude, see Richard Albert, 'Constitutional Amendment by Constitutional Desuetude' (2014) 62 American Journal of Comparative Law 641.

that originate from *secession*. In this second mode of exercising constituent power, an *ethnos* included within a larger *demos* secedes and self-constitutes itself as a new *demos*. What normativity binds this second manifestation of constituent power? Can any portion of a *demos* declare itself to be an *ethnos* that wishes to self-constitute itself as a new *demos*?

In our post-Westphalian world, we can start from certain recognized sources of global constitutionalism: the Charter of the United Nations explicitly mentions 'the principle of equal rights and self-determination of peoples',[81] and both the International Covenant on Civil and Political Rights (1966) and the International Covenant on Economic, Social and Cultural Rights (1966) expand on that notion. In both documents, their respective Articles 1, section 1, provide that 'All peoples have the right to self-determination. By virtue of that right *they freely determine their political status* and freely pursue their economic, social and cultural development'. These formulations do not answer our question. Taken literally, they seem to suggest that *any ethnos* has a right to decide at *any time* to claim the status of a *demos* and to ground an independent legal order. Nothing could be more misleading. Minorities blessed with the privilege of being concentrated in naturally richer or in more developed areas by seceding could worsen the overall prosperity of the *demos* of which they are still part. Fundamentalist minorities could secede in order to create illiberal states that oppress their own internal minorities and threaten regional security. No right can be absolute and self-determination is no exception. If so, how such right ought to be balanced against other rights is an open question, not to be addressed here. Relevant for our argument is the fact that, in a global context in which no lawless lands exist, the normative question 'when can an *ethnos* legitimately self-constitute itself into a *demos* exercising constituent power?' should be reformulated as: 'Under what conditions is it legitimate for an *ethnos* to *secede* from a preexisting *demos* in order to constitute a new *demos*'?

The answer to this question fills the lacuna in classical and contemporary normative political philosophy concerning the 'legitimacy of the bestower of legitimacy', the people. The self-constitution of a new *demos* out of a previously embedded *ethnos* can be subjected to a judgment about its legitimacy, if we can rely on a normative theory of secession. In this regard, theoretical options are broad and diverse, but finally come down to the ramifications of two alternative paradigms.

The first paradigm—call it the 'intrinsic right' paradigm of secession—assumes that the peoples referred to by Article 1, s 1 of the two Covenants are to be understood either as *ethnoi* embedded in larger *demoi* (otherwise it would be pointless to attribute them a right to self-determination that they, democratically or not democratically, *already exercise* in their political life) or, in a more general, sense, as the majority of the citizens living in a certain area of a recognized state, regardless of their ethnical or multi-ethnic affiliations. These constituents are at any time entitled to determine, through their unimpeded will, whether they prefer to remain embedded in the larger *demos* or form a new independent one.

---

[81] Article 1, section 2 includes among the purposes of the United Nations: 'To develop friendly relations among nations based on respect for *the principle of equal rights and self-determination of peoples*, and to take other appropriate measures to strengthen universal peace'.

The second paradigm—call it the 'derivative right' paradigm of secession—builds on three problematic implications of the first one and reconceives the right to self-determination as a reparative right triggered by a documented and grave wrongdoing suffered by the secessionist *ethnos* or group. These problematic implications are: (i) the non-obvious link of free self-determination with territorial sovereignty, considering that secession of a territory inflicts on possible dissenters the loss of their favourite national membership or, alternatively, the burden of relocation; (ii) the destabilizing effect of a possible leveraging use of such a right; and (iii) the possible infliction of loss of material and non-material resources onto the remainder *demos*.

Both these paradigms have strengths and weaknesses, and although their opposition cannot ultimately be transcended, a political conception of the people premised on political liberalism can significantly reduce their distance, by offering a philosophically non-partisan understanding of the disembedding of a previously embedded ethnos. For that purpose, it is worth briefly outlining the respective difficulties inherent in the two paradigms.

The 'intrinsic right' paradigm of secession gives rise to three problems, which only partially coincide with the three implications mentioned above. *First*, the nature of the subject of self-determination is to be spelled out. Avishai Margalit and Joseph Raz have most outspokenly identified that subject as an *ethnos*, in their terminology an 'encompassing group' defined by six characteristics: (i) a pervasive, identity-sustaining, and tradition-generating though differentiated culture, (ii) that via socialization affects the personality of most of the group members; (iii) mutual recognition of membership by all group participants, and (iv) the importance of such recognition of membership for their members' self-identification; (v) membership being defined through belonging and not achievement; and (vi) large membership that exceeds mere face-to-face interaction.[82] Different human groupings—for example voluntarily assembled groups, like utopian-minded fellow citizens organized in movements, sects, parties—for Raz and Margalit lack enough potential for stability. Other voices within the same paradigm have objected to the unjustified reductiveness and conservative bias inherent in requiring what amounts to 'national status' for legitimately seceding, and have instead attributed that right to *any* local collectivity, even if created on a voluntaristic and not ascriptive basis: 'any group of individuals within a defined territory which desires to govern itself more independently enjoys a prima facie right to self-determination',[83] provided that they can sustain themselves viably.[84] Although

---

[82] See Avishai Margalit and Joseph Raz, 'National Self-Determination' (1990) 87 The Journal of Philosophy, 443–47. For a critical appraisal of their view as potentially offering an incentive for multiethnic states to undercut, via assimilationist policies, the existing 'encompassing groups', see Allen Buchanan, 'Theories of Secession' (1997) 26(1) Philosophy & Public Affairs 55 (hereafter Buchanan, 'Theories of Secession').

[83] Daniel Philpott, 'In Defense of Self-Determination', in (1995) 105 Ethics 353–85.

[84] Thus, a certain minimal group size is to be imagined: 'to be independent, there are certain functions which any state must perform: maintain its roads and utilities, educate its children, preserve minimal domestic order, and provide basic public goods. I do not include economic or military self-sufficiency, for, if these were requirements, a group's self-determination could easily be blackmailed by a neighboring state, not to mention that it would disqualify numerous states in the world for the sovereignty they presently enjoy. A state only has to meet basic public needs, which would be difficult to expect from a neighborhood or family", ibid 366. Along similar lines, see Harry Beran, *The Consent Theory of Political Obligation* (Croom

this second version of the paradigm apparently avoids the essentialist nuance connected with the Margalit–Raz approach, it incurs the cost of severing the link between the holistic, life-form-shaping quality of creating a polity and its subject: defective integrative cross-generational capacity and therefore instability may result from it. Finally, a political conception of a people should be consistent with Rawls's assumption that society, in our case the new society under construction, does not have the special ends that associations—even large social movements unified around one or a cluster of comprehensive views—possess. For that purpose, the 'generic-subject' variant of the 'intrinsic-right' paradigm of secession is less apt to being included in a political conception of the people, though certainly settler societies like the United States, Australia, South Africa, Canada, and Latin American countries all testify to the possibility that human groupings may develop ethnic ties that were only loosely present at the early stages of the formation of those societies.

Second, the assertion of a right to secession may generate political unrest and violence, and the 'intrinsic-right' paradigm is burdened—to a much greater extent than the rival one—by the need to specify the extent to which the holder of the right to secede is entitled to the use of force in the assertion of that right. We might have a sound grievance or claim against another government or state, but in our post-Westphalian world this does not entitle us to wage war. There are cases in which the parties come to a rapid and peaceful agreement concerning the secession initiated by one group, as attested by the secession of Slovakia from former Czechoslovakia in 1993 or, earlier in 1905 of Norway from Sweden. Even easier are those exceptional cases in which secession is regulated by constitutional provisions: the Constitution of Ethiopia stipulates that 'every Nation, Nationality and People in Ethiopia has an unconditional right to self-determination, including the right to secession' (Article 39(1)),[85] subject to five conditions (approval by two-thirds of the Legislative Council of the seceding unit, a federal-level confirmative referendum held within three years of such approval, a majority vote in such referendum, followed by a transfer of powers, and repartition of assets in accordance with the law). The partition of ex-Yugoslavia brings immediately to mind the opposite case: while the secession of Slovenia was relatively smooth, an internecine war accompanied the secession of Croatia, Bosnia-Herzegovina, Macedonia,

---

Helm 1987) 42, and Lea Brilmayer, 'Secession and Self-Determination: A Territorial Interpretation' (1991) 16 Yale Journal of International Law 177–202 (hereafter Brilmayer, 'Secession and Self-Determination').

[85] In fact, seventy-two constitutions explicitly reaffirm the indivisibility of the state, thus preempting all possibilities of a legally regulated secession. Cass Sunstein has forcefully denied that a well-constructed constitution can admit of secession: 'the existence of occasionally powerful moral claims supplies insufficient reason for constitutional recognition of the right to secede', 'Constitutionalism and Secession' (1991) 58(2) University of Chicago Law Review 633–70 at 670. Wayne Norman, instead, plausibly points out that such aversion is rather the fruit of the nationalist climate of constitution-making in the nineteenth century: 'If different nationalities were to decide voluntarily to form states these days they would almost certainly demand clear rules for exit; the way parties do even for international trade deals such as NAFTA'. Furthermore, Norman continues, if constitutions drafted today started having provisions for secession, then 'we would almost certainly think of the morality of secession much as we now think of the morality of electoral systems or amending formulas', Wayne Norman, 'Ethics of secession as the regulation of secessionist politics' in Margaret Moore (ed), *National Self-Determination and Secession* (Oxford University Press 2003) 55 (hereafter Norman, 'Ethics of Secession').

and Kosovo causing a bloodshed that lasted intermittently between 1991 and 1999. Whereas the exercise of constituent power in the first two cases is unproblematic, when the remainder of the *demos*, beyond the secession-seekers, fiercely opposes secession, 'intrinsic-right' theories incur difficulties in justifying the use of force on the part of the secessionist *ethnos* or group, in the absence of valid grievances about being the victim of rights violations, deportation, genocidal policies, and de-culturation, and the introduction of these circumstances narrows the gap with 'derivative-right' theories.

A *third* problematic area for the 'intrinsic right' paradigm concerns the relation of the subject of constituent power to physical territory and resources. Both land and assets are by definition owned by the whole *demos* from which the human grouping in question—whether as 'encompassing group', *ethnos*, or generic collectivity of like-minded citizens—wishes to politically depart. How can the assumed right to secede or to self-determination translate into a right to appropriate land and other assets? One contribution to this discussion of legitimate secession comes from the distinction between the constituent power of the people, the constituted power of the voters, and the amending power of the voters acting as living segment of 'the people'. The seceding subset of the present electorate appropriates, by constituting a separate state unit, land and material resources that had from the beginning belonged to the whole people. If the generations of a people are to be considered free and equal, it is not obvious how the will of the presently living generations can legitimately curtail the territorial and asset basis of the future generations of the people. I vividly recall the personal conversation with a colleague based in Belgrade unsettled at being forced to reconfigure his sense of national belonging from a medium-size country, with its own recognized international profile as leader of the so-called non-aligned countries, to a pretty much isolated small homeland perceiving itself as under siege.

The 'derivative right' paradigm of secession is immune from these challenges because it posits that the right to break up a political union is 'remedial' or aimed at rectifying a predicament in which the seceding group 'suffers what are uncontroversially regarded as injustices and has no reasonable prospect of relief short of secession'.[86] Then the question turns on the kind of injustices that can justify secession and impose on the remainder of the *demos* a duty of non-interference. Allen Buchanan deserves to be credited for one of the best and most complete answers, according to which the justifications of secession can be projected on a gradient of cogency. At the bottom of the normative scale are the justifications of secession based on consensus and self-determination, typical of the 'intrinsic right' paradigm.[87] They are not completely inert or unsound, but these justifications are binding only in those rare cases of bilateral consensus, when the rest of the *demos* agrees that it is best for the secessionists to secede. At an intermediate layer of the normative scale, justifications based on self-protection and on the safeguarding of the cultural heritage appear stronger. In Buchanan's words,

---

[86] Buchanan, 'Theories of secession' (n 82) 44. Along similar lines, see Norman, 'Ethics of Secession' (n 85) 44, and Brilmayer, 'Secession and Self-Determination' (n 84).

[87] See Allen Buchanan, *Secession: The Morality of Political Divorce from Fort Sumter to Lithuania and Quebec* (Westview Press 1991) 74.

Among the types of state-perpetrated injustices that can justify secession are not only the violations of basic individual civil and political rights that orthodox liberal political philosophy recognizes as legitimate grounds for revolution but also the injustice of discriminatory redistribution, the state's exploitation of one group to benefit others. Under certain highly circumscribed and extreme conditions, reasons other than the grievance of state-perpetrated injustice can justify secession. These include the need to preserve a group's culture and the necessity of a group's defending itself against threats to the literal survival of its members by third-party aggressors when the group's own state is not protecting it.[88]

The protection of ethnic culture, however, does not by itself justify secession, according to Buchanan, unless five stringent conditions are met. *First*, the threat to cultural survival must exceed the risks that '*all* cultures face' in a global world. *Second*, no other solutions for cultural protection short of secession (eg the granting of minority rights and federal arrangements) must be available or adequate. *Third*, the culture of the secessionists 'must meet minimal standards of moral decency'. *Fourth*, secession must not be likely to result in the building of 'an illiberal state' (ie the new state must respect individual human rights and guarantee free expatriation). *Fifth*, neither the remaining state 'nor any third party has a valid claim to the seceding territory', in which case only overriding reasons of 'self-defense against threats to the literal survival of the members of the group can justify secession'.[89]

Finally, according to Buchanan the normatively strongest grounds for secession are reparation of historical dispossession of land and systematic distributive injustice against the secessionists on the part of the state from which exit is sought. 'No taxation without representation' was one of the strongest grounds for the secession of the American colonies from the United Kingdom, and reappropriation of land unjustly taken from the secessionist population is best exemplified by the case of the Baltic republics' secession from the Soviet Union in 1991:

> Secessionist movements in the Baltic states enjoy the strongest and clearest justifications: The most obvious ground for severing from the Soviet Union in each of these cases is that of rectificatory justice. Latvia, Estonia, and Lithuania were all sovereign states at the time of Soviet conquest, and each had as clear a title to territorial sovereignty as one is likely to find, none apparently being guilty of having unjustly taken their territories from identifiable groups that could still be said to have a legitimate claim on it.[90]

The 'derivative right' paradigm is also not exempt from normative challenges. The first is the tension between the conservative, pro-status-quo bias inherent in the paradigm, and the openness of a democratic polity that is shaped by the public autonomy of free and equal citizens. The point of friction lies in the idea that our having inherited a political world composed of 195 polities imposes a strong duty, superordinate even with

---

[88] ibid 152–53.
[89] ibid 153.
[90] ibid 158–59.

respect to the constituent power of the world's *demoi*, not to alter such configuration in any way, unless in response to grave violations of human rights. The idea that the political autonomy of citizens and constituent power of collective subjects can only be reactive, and that before legitimately self-activating it needs to offer evidence of having suffered severe wrongdoing, is deeply counterintuitive. Kai Nielsen has poignantly highlighted this difficulty, by drawing an analogy with divorce, considered as 'individual secession' from the antecedent unity of marriage:

> the right of secession should be treated like the right to a no-fault divorce. We should have no-fault secession as well as no-fault divorce. No prior or imminent injustice need be shown in either case.... If Mary wishes to split with Michael she should have the right to do so provided there is a fair settlement of their mutual properties, adequate provision and care of any children they may have is insured, and the like. Similarly if Quebec wishes to split with Canada it should have the right to do so provided a fair settlement of mutual assets and debts is made and the like. Just as Mary does not have to prove that Michael has been a bastard or anything like that for her to be able to divorce so Quebec should not have to prove that grave injustices have resulted from Quebec's union with Canada or, if you will, the rest of Canada, to justify secession.... No party need be at fault to justify divorce. It is enough that Mary no longer wishes to live with Michael. Similarly it is enough that Quebec wishes to leave Canada (if that is what Quebec wishes) to justify secession. Quebec does not have to show that it has been harmed by Canada.[91]

This suggestive analogy pinpoints an apparent difficulty with the 'derivative right' paradigm: the derivative view of secession seems to uneasily combine a deontological core with a consequentialist outer shell. Intuitively, the normative ground of the right to secede is deontological and rooted in the undeniable equal right of all 'peoples' to start a new polity according to the constitutive rules they autonomously set for themselves, but Buchanan's 'derivative right' paradigm subordinates the reach of this deontological principle to the consequentialist assessment of its impact onto the world of existing international relations.

At closer scrutiny, however, the polarity between these two paradigms for making sense of the use of constituent power in a world entirely composed of sovereign states can be best understood on the basis of the political-liberal normative ideas of the rational and the reasonable. In a way, within the framework of political liberalism the exercise of constituent power on the part of a collective subject needs, no less than the autonomy of the citizens, to partake of *both* dimensions.

On one hand, the undeniable equal right of all 'peoples' to start a new polity according to constitutive rules autonomously set by themselves for themselves seems homologous to the person's capacity to form and revise a conception of the good. On the other hand, the subordination of the exercise of this right to the consequentialist assessment of its impact onto the world of existing international relations corresponds to the embedment of the person in a larger scheme of fair social cooperation—a

---

[91] Kai Nielsen, 'Secession: the Case of Quebec' (1993) 10(1) Journal of Applied Philosophy 29–43 at 35.

scheme not to be torn asunder in the pursuit of one's unilaterally posited conception of the good. As in *Political Liberalism*, the reasonable tracks justice, that is, the sense of the limits to be duly observed in the pursuit of one's own rationally posited conception of the good. And that vision of the good, for the person and the secession-seeking *ethnos* alike, shows the point, that is, provides the motivation for political action.

c. Turning a *demos* into an *ethnos*

It would be misleading to imagine that the alteration of an existing *demos* through regime change and the transformation of an *ethnos* into a newly constituted *demos* exhaust the manifestations of constituent power. These phenomena gather scholarly attention because of the political impact they usually exert, but they are by no means the most frequent. Over five millennia humanity has travelled the distance from an estimated 600,000 human settlements that simultaneously existed, each with a form of political authority and interacting as a political unit with other political units,[92] to today's world of 195 incorporated and chartered *demoi*. The most frequent manifestation of constituent power is certainly not the formation of new Leviathans but their demise and their merger into larger units.

The end or death of the body politic is a 'genre' with few variations within classical contract theory: addressed by Hobbes, Locke and Rousseau, the dissolution of the social compact is basically linked with military defeat by external powers and, more rarely, with a conscious decision on the part of the citizens. Here, however, I will address a different and much more frequent manifestation of constituent power: the *voluntary* dissolving of a previously existing *demos*, possessed of the two political capacities, into a larger *demos* within which it then comes to count as an ethnic niche of the population.

In the decade prior to its unification, the population of Italy was still an *ethnos*, as it had been for several centuries: Italy was 'a geographical expression', as Austrian Chancellor Metternich famously quipped at the Congress of Vienna. In the 1850s, Italy remained divided in a number of distinct *demoi*: the Kingdom of Sardinia and Piedmont, the Kingdom of Lombardy–Venetia (under the Austrian Crown), the Duchy of Parma and Piacenza, the Duchy of Modena and Reggio, the Grand-Duchy of Tuscany, the State of the Church, the Kingdom of the Two Sicilies. Some of these political units were annexed to the Kingdom of Sardinia and Piedmont through military pressure: parts the Kingdom of Lombardy–Venetia in 1859, the Kingdom of the Two Sicilies by the Garibaldi-led insurgency in 1860, the Papal State through military occupation. However, referenda were also held. The principal among these were in 1859 for the population of the Duchy of Parma and Piacenza and in 1860 the population of the Duchy of Moderna and Reggio and of the Romagna Provinces of the State of the Church, the Granduchy of Tuscany, the Neapolitan and the Sicilian provinces of the Kingdom of the Two Sicilies, the Provinces of Umbria and Marche, and the State of the Church all overwhelmingly voted to join the Kingdom of Sardinia and Piedmont with

---

[92] See n 34, above.

the understanding that the resulting *demos* would be transformed, albeit by the will of King Victor Emanuel II and not by democratic self-determination, into a unified Kingdom of Italy.[93]

'Risorgimento'—national resurgence—was the name given to the broad movement, not just political, but also social, cultural, and literary, that began in the aftermath of the Congress of Vienna. It was influenced by Romantic themes and fuelled the growth of a consciousness of the Italian nation that provided the background for the strictly political thrust of the local elites and professional classes aspiring to the unification of the separate states into one modern nation state. Risorgimento was largely aspirational, had its own fervent spokesman in Mazzini, and embedded republican ideas of self-government and constituent power, but then, in the end, in the crucial years 1858–61, had to yield to the realities of power politics. After the restoration of the old rulers in the subnational kingdoms and principalities in the wake of the Congress of Vienna, friction between the Austrian Empire and France for influence and domination of Italian politics made it evident that only traditional diplomacy and statecraft in the hands of Camillo Benso, Count of Cavour and prime minister of the Kingdom of Sardinia and Piedmont, could deliver significant results.

Unification eventually came into being, but the mode of its realization led to feelings of a dimidiated Risorgimento, yet to be completed, in a way not dissimilar from the feeling, experienced by the most radical sectors of the left, that the Constitution of 1948 represented a half-victory and a promise yet to be fulfilled. Referring precisely to this sobering and somehow frustrating predicament, a widely cited and duly famous saying, attributed to Massimo d'Azeglio, former prime minister of the Kingdom of Sardinia, novelist and painter—'We have made Italy. Now we must make Italians'— captures exactly, unbeknownst to its author and most of his later interpreters, the gist of the self-constitution of a new *demos*. A condition of the possibility of nation-building, 'making Italians', through education, politics, national parties, unions, and of course external wars in the nineteenth and early twentieth centuries, was that the pre-existing *demoi* of Italy-as-a-geographical-expression more or less voluntarily relinquished their constituent power and accepted rethinking of themselves as a plurality of ethnic segments of the new Italian *demos*.

Another exemplary manifestation of constituent power in the service of transforming a *demos* into an ethnic segment of a larger *demos* occurred in 1990 with the reunification of Germany. Again, we can distinguish the plane of prudent statecraft in the public forum of constituted powers and the exercise of constituent power. When in November 1989 popular protest against the socialist regimes of Central and Eastern Europe culminated in the Fall of the Berlin Wall, the government of the German Democratic Republic, led by Erich Honecker, found itself in no position to stem the tide of individuals and families who would abandon the country, initially via the partially opened border with Hungary. Helmut Kohl, Chancellor of what was then the Federal Republic of Germany, by late November seized the initiative, in a favourable international constellation marked by the reforming policies of Mikhail Gorbachev,

---

[93] See Derek Beales and Eugenio F Biagini, *The Risorgimento and the Unification of Italy* (Routledge 2002). See also Denis Mack Smith, *Victor Emanuel, Cavour, and the Risorgimento* (Oxford University Press 1971).

172   POLITICAL LIBERALISM AND 'THE PEOPLE'

and in a famous address to the Bundestag outlined the contours of a possible reunification of the two German States:

> State organization in Germany has almost always meant a confederation or a federation. We can certainly draw on these historical experiences. No one knows today what a reunified Germany will ultimately look like. That unity will come, however, when the people in Germany want it—of this, I am certain.[94]

He later delivered a game-changing speech in front of a huge crowd at the ruins of the Frauenkirche in Dresden, on 19 December 1989. Calling the prospect of reunification a 'bright future not oblivious of the darkness of the past', Kohl addressed the crowd as 'liebe Landsleute!' (*fellow countrymen*) as though unity was already achieved, and called for full awareness of the context in which reunification would take place, a context that should remain mindful of the reasons why a *reunification* of a divided Germany was on the agenda.[95]

The ensuing elections of 18 March 1990 in the GDR sanctioned the demise of the ruling party and the rise of the *Christian Democratic Union*, propelled to a prominent position by its platform calling for rapid reunification. This electoral outcome paved the way to the 'Treaty Establishing a Monetary, Economic and Social Union between the German Democratic Republic and the Federal Republic of Germany', signed in May and becoming effective in July 1990. The key aspect of the Treaty was to allow the Western Deutsche Mark to have currency in the still formally surviving GDR, whose local currency had plummeted once the economy had been opened up. Furthermore, subsidies to the welfare state and social policies of the GDR started flowing in from the solid economy of the Federal Republic.

At this point the crucial choice was made, on the part of the Kohl cabinet. The merger of the two *demoi* would amount not to the creation of a new German state, marked by dual regime change and possibly by a new *Verfassung* or even a thoroughly overhauled *Grundgesetz*. Rather, the merger would find a normative foothold in Article 23 of the extant *Grundgesetz* of the Federal Republic of Germany. Article 23 provided that new territories inhabited by German-speaking populations—in all effects, *ethnically* German territories—could spontaneously decide to join the Federal Republic as new *Länder* and be integrated in it under the *Grundgesetz*. On that basis, a 'Unification Treaty' was signed on 31 August 1990 and approved, by a vote held with the required supermajorities, in the legislative assemblies of both countries. The 'Unification Treaty', set to be in force as of 3 October 1990, would sanction the accession of the

---

[94] Helmut Kohl, 'Zehn-Punkte-Programm zur Überwindung der Teilung Deutschlands und Europas' ['Ten-Point Programme for Overcoming the Division of Germany and Europe'] (28 November 1989) in Volker Gransow and Konrad Jarausch (eds), *Die Deutsche Vereinigung: Dokumente zu Bürgerbewegung, Annäherung und Beitritt* (Verlag Wissenschaft und Politik1991) 103.

[95] 'Dear friends, in a few days, on 1 January 1990, the ninetieth year begins, the last decade of this century. It is a century that has seen, especially in Europe and also with us in Germany, much distress, much misery, much death, much sorrow—a century, that placed a special responsibility on us Germans—in the face of the evil that happened', see the detailed and insightful analysis of Kohl's speech (based on the German text available at *Deutsches Bundesarchiv*) by Imogen Morley, available at https://imogenmorley.wordpress.com/2017/07/24/anatomy-of-a-speech-dresden-19th-december-1989-chancellor-helmut-kohl/, accessed on 2 June 2020.

former German Democratic Republic to what was now a unified Germany, in the form of the five new additional *Länder* of Brandenburg, Mecklenburg-Vorpommern, Saxony, Saxony-Anhalt, and Thuringia. The merger of two *demoi* took the legal form of the integration of one into the other, with distinct territorial and administrative segmentation.

At the same time, a merger of two *demoi* is not merely a legal process. In this case, in 1990 neither of the two pre-existing *demoi* could understand itself as reflected in an institutional framework that was an unalloyed projection of its will. They were not exactly on the same footing: the accession of the former German Democratic Republic had been an accession to a *Grundgesetz* already in place. Nevertheless, the resulting new German *demos* cannot be regarded as exactly the same as the previously existent ones. This certainly holds for the acceding former Easter German *demos*, which finds itself now as an ethnic segment of a larger nation integrated within a Western system of international alliances, in a domestic market economy and directly in the global economy. However, identity change also holds for the *demos* on the receiving side, which finds itself in the position of being the majoritarian ethnic segment of the unified *demos*, with the responsibility of somehow leading the project of integration without tarnishing it with assimilationist tones.

Constituent power is almost imperceptible here: all along we just observe constituted powers—cabinets, parliaments, and electoral bodies—at work in a constitutional process that, as Ackerman has emphasized in relation to 'elite constitutionalism', recoils from all emphasis on the power of the people, in spite of occasional rallying cries animating the street demonstrations in former German Democratic Republic. Yet, the process of self-constitution is fully at work. The accession via treaty, the amendment of the German *Grundgesetz* in order to accommodate the five new East-German *Länder* and bring to a final close the process of 'reunification', and the exclusion of further accession of formerly German-ruled territories in Poland, Lithuania, and even Russia (Kaliningrad, the birthplace of Immanuel Kant under the former Prussian name of Königsberg) in the future[96] can all be said to have altered the constitutive commitments of the German *demos* precisely by recognition of a sort of 'mission accomplished' statement and renunciation of further claims. At the same time, the two converging *demoi* found themselves in the position respectively of a majority and a minority with distinct cultural, social, and historical ethnic features. To this day, in the height of the populist surge, that distinctiveness still appears to have political significance.

Many other examples could be adduced of the formation of the modern nation states, by drawing on the history of Spain, the United Kingdom before unification, of Canada, and other countries. Most novel, however, is a process of regional aggregation, observable in the European Union and to a lesser extent in other contexts (eg ASEAN,[97]

---

[96] Such renunciation to further eastward expansion of the German borders was stipulated with the *Treaty on the Final Settlement with Respect to Germany*, signed in Moscow on 12 September 1990, with the four victorious powers of the Second World War. The signing of this treaty was a precondition for then proceeding to the formal reunification of Germany and the international recognition of the expanded state.

[97] The Association of Southeast Asian Nations, founded in 1967, includes Indonesia, Malaysia, Philippines, Singapore, Thailand, Brunei Darussalam, Vietnam, Laos, Myanmar, and Cambodia.

SAARC,[98] the African Union,[99] and USAN[100]). In a polity located somewhere beyond a confederation but not fully federal, the *demoi* that undergird the member states are of course less sovereign than *demoi* that remain outside the Union or have left it after Brexit, but certainly cannot be thought to have reduced themselves to mere ethnical segments of a larger, and still not fully existent, *demos*. It's too early to say whether this uncertain status—more than an *ethnos*, less than a fully fledged *demos*—that characterizes the peoples of the member states will become an entirely new manifestation of what we understand by the term people—neither *ethnos* nor *demos*, as it were—or whether at some point a 'closer Union' will effectively reduce the French, Spanish, Italian, German, and the other peoples of the member states to the status of *ethnoi*.

d. Reigniting the radical democratic embers: the self-correcting *demos*

The constitution is an ongoing project. Constituent power never enters complete hibernation, as in the Hobbesian model or as Habermas accused the political liberal paradigm of presupposing. Reading Rawls through Kelsenian lenses dismissive of constituent power, Habermas wrote, in a passage of his historical exchange with Rawls:

> From the perspective of the theory of justice, the act of founding the democratic constitution cannot be repeated under the institutional conditions of an already constituted just society, and the process of realizing the system of basic rights cannot be assured on an ongoing basis. It is not possible for citizens to experience this process as open and incomplete, as the shifting historical circumstances nonetheless demand. *They cannot reignite the radical democratic embers of the original position in the civic life of their society, for from their perspective all of the* essential *discourses of legitimation have already taken place within the theory; and they find the results of the theory already sedimented in the constitution.*[101]

A political liberal would reply with a smirking 'Why not?' and would put forward two plausible theses: (i) 'any actual society is more or less unjust', and (ii) 'no

---

[98] The South Asian Association for Regional Cooperation, founded in 1985, includes Afghanistan, Bangladesh, Bhutan, India, Maldives, Nepal, Pakistan, and Sri Lanka.

[99] The African Union was founded in Addis Ababa, in 2001, and includes Algeria, Angola, Benin, Botswana, Burkina Faso, Burundi, Cameroon, Cape Verde, Central African Republic, Chad, Comoros, Congo, Democratic Republic of the Congo, Côte d'Ivoire, Djibouti, Egypt, Equatorial Guinea, Eritrea, Ethiopia, Gabon, Gambia, Ghana, Guinea Bissau, Guinea, Kenya, Lesotho, Liberia, Libya, Madagascar, Malawi, Mali, Mauritania, Mauritius, Mozambique, Namibia, Niger, Nigeria, Rwanda, Saharawi Arab Democratic Republic, São Tomé and Príncipe, Senegal, Seychelles, Sierra Leone, Somalia, South Africa, Sudan, Swaziland, Tanzania, Togo, Tunisia, Uganda, Zambia, and Zimbabwe.

[100] The Union of South American Nations, founded in 2008, includes Argentina, Bolivia, Brazil, Chile, Colombia, Ecuador, Guyana, Paraguay, Peru, Suriname, Uruguay, Venezuela, and Mexico and Panama as observers.

[101] Jürgen Habermas, 'Reconciliation through the Public Use of Reason: Remarks on John Rawls's Political Liberalism' (1995) 92/3 Journal of Philosophy 128 (emphasis added) (hereafter Habermas, 'Reconciliation').

(human) theory could possibly anticipate all the requisite considerations bearing on these problems under existing circumstances, nor could the needed reforms have already been foreseen for improving present arrangements'.[102] If so, then 'the ideal of a just constitution is always something to be worked toward'.[103] Public reason then is not, as claimed by Habermas, a form of discourse in the exclusive service of the 'preservation of political stability' within already-set guidelines,[104] but a form of discourse that allows citizens to articulate their sense of persisting constitutional shortcomings, of the urgency of regulating new matters, redefining significant essentials (eg the meaning of 'equal protection of the laws'), and making new commitments (eg to the protection of the environment against climate change). Rawls likens Habermas's point to Jefferson's suggestion, in the footsteps of Rousseau, that a constitutional convention be convened every nineteen years in order to re-examine and re-enact the constitution anew.[105] Only then will each generation of citizens be offered the possibility of fully expressing its political autonomy without submitting to the past generations' will and wit. However, the notion of an unjust disparity inherent in autonomously endorsing a constitution or amending it, as opposed to framing it anew, is qualified by Rawls as an 'entirely misplaced' view that 'cannot sensibly be entertained'.[106]

Contingency is the reason why this is so. Whether a generation of citizens is able to frame, amend, or simply reflectively endorse a constitution depends on contingencies of a society's history not at its, or anyone's disposal: 'that the founders of 1787–91 could be the founders was not determined solely by them but by the course of history up until that time'.[107] Whatever role the contingency of history assigns to one temporal segment of a *demos*, the embers of the founding, of the constitution-making era, can always be reignited by new historical contexts, by contestation, or by the inner unfolding of normative ideas combined with the need to make the rule of law consistent. Thus, the exercise of constituent power certainly peaks at historical junctures when regime change, or secession, or merger of one or more *demoi* (and the corresponding ethnicization of previous *demoi*) occurs. But constituent power is also operative at historical times when no such peak of political creativity is under way and yet politics somehow exceeds the bounds of what Ackerman calls the routine of 'ordinary politics'.

At times when, pursuant to the diverse provisions for amendment included in each constitution, political contestation in the public forum and in the background culture revolves around proposals for constitutional amendments, a fourth manifestation of constituent power can be observed: a *demos* engages in an *exercise of self-correction of its own commitments* that exceeds the limits of ordinary constituted political legislation but falls short of regime change. Public reason—oriented by its standards of

---

[102] Rawls, 'Reply to Habermas', in *PL* 400–01.
[103] ibid 401.
[104] Habermas, 'Reconciliation' (n 101) 128.
[105] See Thomas Jefferson, *The Portable Thomas Jefferson*. Edited and with and introduction by Merril D Peterson (Penguin 1979) 449. This idea, at the core of the 'serial' conception of popular sovereignty, will be discussed more at length below in Chapter 5, Section 3.c.
[106] Rawls, 'Reply to Habermas', *PL* 408, n 45.
[107] ibid 403.

reasonability and of the 'most reasonable'—is the medium within which such self-correction unfolds. However, this aspect of the exercise of constituent power, located at the crossroads of the normativity that constrains constitution-making, the constitutional provisions for amendment, and the political will of the electorate, requires a discussion of its own. That discussion will be the object of Chapter 7.

5
Sequential Sovereignty
On Representing 'the People' and the Electorate

> Political questions are not likely to be as arbitrary as the choice between two foods; nor are they likely to be questions of knowledge to which an expert can supply the one correct answer.
> (Hanna Pitkin, *The Concept of Representation* 212)

In the previous chapters, it has been argued that while 'the people' only exists as a construction, though not as a fictional notion, and spans all the generations of citizens from the inception of the democratic polity to those of the future, the *electorate* is embodied in the totality of the living and enfranchised citizens.

It has been assumed that representative institutions—parliaments, legislatures, congresses, diets, dumas, etc—represent the electorate to various degrees of proportionality, ranging from minimal (in first-past-the-post electoral systems) to medium (in mixed electoral systems of various kinds) to maximal (in purely proportional electoral systems). Also the officials vested with executive power can be argued to represent the electorate, either directly (as in the case of elected presidents, regardless of whether elected by the voters or through the mediation of an electoral college) or indirectly (as in the case of prime ministers, who remain accountable to confidence-confirming parliamentary majorities).

It has been argued that the function of representing the people *qua* author of the constitution has historically been assigned to constitutional or supreme courts, as highest interpreters of the constitution, though in principle that function could conceivably be attributed to elective institutions separate from the ordinary legislature and entrusted with monitoring the alignment of ordinary and higher law, with reviewing the ongoing adequacy of constitutional provisions in the light of a changing historical context, and with setting forth proposals to be then assessed through the formal mechanisms for amendment.

It is now time to address a question that has thus far remained buried in the background. Does the verb 'to represent' as it occurs in both phrases—representing the people, representing the electorate—convey the same meaning? Is the representing of the people, by whichever institution is entrusted with this function, the same as the representing of the electorate by whoever performs this function?

In order to outline an answer, a closer look at the concept of representation is needed. The pioneering account by Hanna Pitkin, and especially her discussion of representation as 'standing for' somebody, provides a useful starting point. Then more recent contributions on representation, which build on and modify Pitkin's paradigm, will be examined and in the final section our question will be answered in the light of these models.

1. Understanding Political Representation: Pitkin's Paradigm

The first step towards answering our question consists of unpacking different forms of political representation. No better place from which to start a reconstruction of the vocabulary of representation can be imagined than Hanna Pitkin's groundbreaking study *The Concept of Representation*, but then we will examine subsequent developments in political theory—mainly the so-called constructivist turn, the representative claim, the intrusion of 'anticipatory representation', and the specific dimensions of the 'trustee/delegate polarity'.

Pitkin's theory of representation is particularly fit for answering our question because it neatly builds on distinctions that single out, and then highlight, the agential aspects of representation and the implicit standards that allow us to assess the activity of representing. She famously begins by reconstructing four notions of representation. While all of them have some significance for politics, only two are more directly related to our question and one—*substantive* representation, itself subdivided in two modalities—bears a crucial relevance. The broad spectrum of the term 'representation' and 'to represent' in English—similar to the French *représentation* and *représenter* and the Spanish *representación* and *representar*—in other languages is covered by different terms: for example, in German by the verbs *darstellen* and *vertreten*, and the corresponding nouns *Darstellung* and *Vertretung*. In Italian, that semantic distinction is captured by the two nouns *rappresentazione* and *rappresentanza*, but only one verb exists: *rappresentare*.

Although the two *darstellen*-type instances of representation discussed by Pitkin may be relevant to politics, the sense in which we ask if the meaning of 'representing' is the same in the case of the people and the electorate is primarily linked with the two *vertreten*-related versions of the concept of representation, and to one of them in particular. For this reason, I take the liberty of altering the order of Pitkin's sequential illustration of the four senses of 'representation', gradually zeroing in on the one of direct interest for our question.

a. Descriptive representation and its limitations

Let me then start from *descriptive* representation (the second type in Pitkin's classification). In this case, the representative element 'stands for' the represented one because analogically it closely resembles or mirrors it in some relevant and crucial respect. Of course, this relation of representation is of broader than political significance: it is the way in which a photo and the photographed subject, a portrait and the portrayed person, a map and a given territory, a sample and the surveyed population are related. In each of these pairs, the former represents the latter element in the sense of *darstellen*. Descriptive representation, however, also has a distinctly political meaning, as when we say for example that the composition of a parliament ideally 'should be an exact portrait, in miniature, of the people at large'.[1] Many defences of proportional representation evoke this idea of legislative institutions as a mirror of the larger society, of representation as 'accurate reflection'. Of political significance in this broader view of descriptive representation is also the debate concerning whether the mirroring of society exhausts the function of legislative institutions. If the answer is negative, then it can be argued that conclusiveness of the decisional process, as well as the effectiveness of policy implementation over time, may depend on institutional qualities that stand in tension with 'accuracy of representation' and speak in favour of more aggregative kinds of electoral mechanisms: for example, 'first past the post' electoral procedures, or special seat-multipliers attributable to prevailing pluralities, or mechanisms of indirect representation such as the Electoral College in the United States.

Furthermore, if *accuracy of reflection* is what representation is understood to be primarily about, then the representativeness of representative institutions could be better served by non-electoral mechanisms, such as sortition or random sampling combined with a certain selective design. This idea of representation has recently re-emerged in the form of an interest for mini-publics,[2] in the wake of interest in deliberative polling. Fishkin's idea of using sampling techniques to monitor not just instant and unreflective opinions on subjects that the respondent may know little about but also the transformation of initial opinions in the course of debate under close to ideal conditions of nonpartisan information,[3] has proven fertile. Moving beyond a mere deliberative or consultative role,[4] mini-publics have been envisaged as entitled to make policy decisions that are binding.[5] Another interesting proposal in this area is a combination of sortition and election, combined with a new kind of functional bicameralism that revives the Athenian distinction of a body of proponents of policies and a restricted body of representatives, drawn by lottery, who approves or rejects the proposals received from the other house.[6] Over and beyond the disappearance of electoral campaigns and the related contest of articulate orientations, the main problem with sortition is that the parameters to be figured in the sampling model are potentially infinite. No one would care that the sampled or sortitioned legislature mirror the

---

[1] John Adams, 'Letter to John Penn', quoted in Pitkin, *The Concept of Representation* (University of California Press 1967) 61 (hereafter Pitkin, *Representation*).

[2] For an enlightening discussion of the implications and limits of the use of mini-publics as 'shortcuts' to the realization of deliberative democracy, see Cristina Lafont, *Democracy Without Shortcuts: A Participatory Conception of Deliberative Democracy* (Oxford University Press 2020) 109–34.

[3] See James S Fishkin, *The Voice of the People: Public Opinion and Democracy* (Yale University Press 1997), *When the People Speak* (Oxford University Press 2009), *Democracy: When the People are Thinking* (Oxford University Press 2018). For an attempt to transpose the scheme of deliberative polling to the larger population, see Bruce Ackerman and James S Fishkin, *Deliberation Day* (Yale University Press 2004).

[4] Over and beyond Fishkin and Ackerman, along similar lines see also Christopher F Zurn, *Deliberative Democracy and the Institutions of Judicial Review* (Cambridge University Press 2007) (hereafter Zurn, *Deliberative Democracy*).

[5] See David Van Reybrouck, *Against Elections: The Case for Democracy* (Random House 2016) and Hubertus Buchstein, 'Reviving Randomness for Political Rationality: Elements of a Theory of Aleatory Democracy' (2010) 17 Constellations 435.

[6] See Keith Sutherland and Alex Kovner, 'Isegoria and Isonomia: Election by Lot and the Democratic Diarchy', paper read at the Association for Political Thought Conference, Exeter, 2020.

larger population in relation to eye colour, weight, height, favourite hobbies, sports practiced, musical tastes, colour preference, or preference for Coca Cola versus Pepsi. We would care about the drawn legislature to mirror perhaps age, gender, education, class, income, geographical distribution, profession, and religious affiliation. This circumstance raises normative difficulties that need to be addressed. Either, to paraphrase Carl Schmitt, 'the sovereign is who designs the sample', or we should have a democratic deliberation concerning how to design the sample, but then again the constituency allowed to vote on that point will have somehow to be constituted according to some (not undisputable) criterion, and an infinite regress would be inevitable.

Descriptive representation, in other words, is always descriptive of the represented not in an absolute sense, but from *one or a number of* points of view selected as relevant from a potentially infinite set of possible points of view.[7] In spite of these conceptual difficulties, the *descriptive* approach to representation continues to exert appeal in radical versions of democratic theory as well as in the standard justification of representative government. As far as the first are concerned, the idea is that representative democracy is a second best to direct democracy:[8] if the impediment to every person's directly taking part in political decisions that affect her rights or interests is the sheer size of the polity and the impossibility of convening the entire *demos* in one place, then the next best thing is to have representatives to deliberate and decide *in lieu of* the citizens. For that purpose, the composition of the assembly ought to be as similar to that of the citizenry, so that their decisions can be defensibly portrayed as equivalent to the decisions that the citizens themselves would make. As Pitkin points out, that justification of representative democracy predates the radical versions of today, which often include the corollary that only representatives similar along gender, racial, generational, or ethnic lines can represent the respective constituencies.[9] At the Philadelphia Convention of 1787 it was argued that 'Representation is made necessary only because it is impossible for the people to act collectively', and that observation was meant to support the idea that the legislative assembly should be reflective of the nation.[10] Finally, the crucial limitation of the descriptive approach to political representation lies in its inability to generate a significant benchmark for assessing the quality of the *representing*. This approach only tells us that the more a representative resembles the represented then the higher her 'representativeness' is. However, representatives more closely resembling their constituents might prove disastrous and representatives who do not resemble their constituents might prove more effective: from the perspective of descriptive representation, no benchmark can be derived for assessing what the representative *does*, as opposed to what he or she *is*.

---

[7] See Pitkin, *Representation* (n 1) 88–89.
[8] ibid 84–85.
[9] For contemporary defence of descriptive representation as conducive to redressing domination of discriminated constituencies, see Iris M Young, *Justice and the Politics of Difference* (Princeton University Press 1990) (hereafter Young, *Politics of Difference*) and *Inclusion and* Democracy (Oxford University Press 2000) (hereafter Young, *Inclusion and Democracy*); Jane Mansbridge, 'Should Blacks Represent Blacks and Women Represent Women? A Contingent "Yes"' (2003) 61 The Journal of Politics 628.
[10] Max Farrand (ed), *The Records of the Federal Convention of 1787* (Yale University Press 1927) I, 132.

b. Symbolic representation

Symbolic representation (the third type in Pitkin's classification) is also a kind of relation in which the representative element 'stands for' the represented element, but the regularity and force of its 'standing for' rests on *convention* rather than on analogic resemblance as in the previous case. Indeed, such 'standing for' is as arbitrary a relation as, in Saussure's theory of linguistic signification, 'chien' in French and 'cane' in Italian can equally 'stand for' the animal known in English as a *dog*. Thus, the fact that a green, white, and red flag 'stands for' Italy rests not on any analogic similarity between that mix of colours and Italian-ness (unless one draws a superficial analogy with an iconic pizza with mozzarella, tomato sauce, and basil leaves) but only on the convention known as Article 12 of the Italian Constitution: 'The flag of the Republic is the Italian tricolor: green, white and red, in three vertical bands of equal size'. As Pitkin writes,

> Early Christian artists used the fish as a symbol of Christ, especially for secret reference, on the basis of an acrostic on the Greek word ιχθύς. The fish was a symbol of Christ, but not a representation of him. The artist who painted a fish was not representing (showing) Christ as a fish; he was making no allegations about Christ's appearance. Unlike representations, symbols are not likenesses of their referents, and do not resemble them. They make no allegations about what they symbolize, but rather suggest or express it.[11]

Interestingly, the process of representing symbolically bears no relation with representing as descriptive representation. We may represent Jesus Christ *as* a tall man: we do not represent him *as* a fish but rather *by* a fish. Ordinary language registers this fact lexically. As Pitkin observes,

> That is why there is no such concept in our language as 'mis-symbolizing' to correspond to 'misrepresenting'. Nor are they accurate and inaccurate symbols. Accuracy of correspondence is not an issue in symbolic representation, even when there is some connection, some correspondence of (hidden) characteristics between symbol and referent.[12]

The arbitrary nature of symbols prevents all normative assessment of the quality of symbolic representation. 'Symbolic representation' can only be assessed in terms of recognition of the symbol by those who are its ideal addressees. The relation of symbolic representation may be successful on the basis of mere *visual recognition* of the meaning, as when I correctly interpret a road sign, or it may require some measure of *emotional identification*, as when I come in contact with my country's flag or national anthem.

Under this rubric fall the totalitarian fascist representation and what Urbinati has called direct representation.[13] In both cases, a charismatic leader becomes a symbol

---
[11] Pitkin, *Representation* (n 1) 394.
[12] ibid 99.
[13] See Chapter 2, n 22.

of a movement and at the same time of all the followers, but in the case of fascism and Nazism we can observe a kind of peculiar inversion. 'What matters is always the alignment of wills between the rule and the ruled; representation *is* that alignment, no matter how it is brought about'.[14] The inversion applies to the direction of representation. The charismatic fascist leader projects a political will which is echoed by his followers, rather than reflecting the opinion and feelings of the constituency: 'if there is representation, it is inverse representation, proceeding downwards from the leader. The party represents the leader: the people, so far as it takes its color from the party, equally represents and reflects the direction of the leader'.[15]

Although occasionally they have appeared in various historical circumstances, neither descriptive nor symbolic representation can adequately capture the democratic nature of the relation of a people or an electorate to their representatives. Symbolic representation is inadequate on account of its conventional or potentially authoritarian Caesaristic nature: representatives possessed of any quality and its opposite can and may come to represent a people or an electorate. Furthermore, symbolic representation is difficult to reconcile with a normative perspective. It works or it fails to work: but we do not have a foothold for claiming that it *should* work. A similar drawback affects descriptive representation: we can assess the degree of resemblance, reflection, or mirroring of the represented in the representative but we are left without a conceptual foothold for evaluating what the representative *does*. The criterion of 'the more similar, the more representative' forces us, once again, to comparatively assess a variety of representatives on the basis of what they *are* and not on the basis of their intentional action. Instead, for the purpose of grasping the similarity or difference of representing the people or the voters, we need to turn to Pitkin's other two models for grasping *political* representation, each of which is in turn characterized by a polarity.

c. Two kinds of formalistic representation

'Formalistic representation' focuses on what makes a representative a *real* representative of the represented individual or collective. The answer to the question 'What distinguishes a true from a bogus representative?' comes in two versions. The *first* version, championed by Hobbes, pivots around a theory of *authorization*: a true representative is a *duly authorized* representative. Another version, championed by less prominent authors and reconstructed by Pitkin by bringing together the accounts of various political scientists, answers the question in terms of *accountability*: a representative is someone 'who is to be held to account, who will have to answer to another for what he does'.[16] Both views ultimately share the same blind spot as descriptive and symbolic representation in Pitkin's eyes.

Hobbes's view of representation, discussed in Chapter 16 of *Leviathan*, is in line with the overarching aim of ensuring stability:

---

[14] Pitkin, *Representation* (n 1) 108.
[15] Ernest Barker, *Reflections on Government* (1942), 377, quoted in Pitkin, *Representation* (n 1) 109.
[16] Pitkin, *Representation* (n 1) 55.

> A Multitude of men, are made *One* Person, when they are by one man, or one Person, Represented; so that it be done with the consent of every one of that Multitude in particular. For it is the *Unity* of the Representer, not the *Unity* of the Represented, that maketh the Person *One*. And it is the Representer that beareth the Person, and but one Person: And *Unity*, cannot otherwise be understood in Multitude.[17]

In *political* relations the authority of the representative rests on the mandate of the principal, called by Hobbes 'the Author', because he is the real 'owner' or subject of imputation of the action of the representative. In society at large, the authorization of the representative need not be given by the represented, as the case may be with insane people or minors, or even 'inanimate Things',[18] but it may be given by guardians, curators, owners. The point, however, is that the principal or 'Author' remains the 'owner' of his own and his representative's actions, while the words and actions of an 'Artificial person' or 'Actor' or representative are considered to belong to someone else.[19] Thus when many severally authorize an 'artificial person', the absolute sovereign, to act in their name, they cannot 'disown' the actions of their representative.

Pitkin points to a tension in Hobbes's theory but overlooks another weak point. The Hobbesian sovereign has duties to his subjects—to ensure their survival and security—but these duties, elementary though they are, cannot be collectively claimed.[20] When grossly disattended, this fact can only allow *individual* 'principals' or 'Authors' to defect. Typical of the Hobbesian sovereign is also a complete *unaccountability* to his principals: the relation of representation cannot be undone, qualified, or subjected to any condition, and the sovereign/representative cannot be accused of misrepresenting his principals now turned into his 'subjects'. Hobbes's theory still contains a liberal-democratic kernel in the message that a sovereign appointed by the inhabitants of the state of nature, now turned into legal consociates, is much preferable to a sovereign imposing himself from above, so to speak, onto his subjects. Yet the tension lies in the unjustified asymmetry between the agent and the action: prior to the artificial creation of the sovereign/representative, each one is owner of his or her actions, free to reverse the course of any action and undo it. Equally free is the sovereign relative to the laws that express his will: he can repeal them at any time when his will changes. However, the consociates turned into subjects cannot undo the act, performed when still in the full and unimpeded freedom of the state of nature, by which they created the representative. They turn into hostages of their own representative.

In a moderate, liberal form, the authorization view of representation is recast by Weber in the twentieth century in terms of imputation: in certain cases, most frequently but not exclusively in traditional forms of social organization, 'certain kinds of action of *each* participant may be imputed to *all* others, in which case we speak of "mutually responsible members" (*Solidaritätsgenossen*); or the action of certain

---

[17] Thomas Hobbes, *Leviathan* (1651), edited and with an introduction by CB Macpherson (Penguin 1985) 220.
[18] 'A Church, an Hospital, a Bridge, may be Personated by a Rector, Master or Overseer', ibid 219.
[19] See ibid 217–18.
[20] Pitkin, *Representation* (n 1) 33.

members (the "representatives") may be attributed to the others (the "represented").[21] In the legal theory developed by Gierke and Jellinek, akin to Weber's, the representative is like an 'organ' of the group that she represents.

The flaw of this 'authorization' view of representation consists, once again, in its preventing a normative assessment of good or poor *representing*. Representation, Pitkin argues, becomes a 'black box' brought into being by authorization. The only parameter for evaluating the relation is whether the representative has acted *within* or *beyond* the limits set by the principal. As Pitkin puts it, 'there is no such thing as representing well or badly; either he [the representative] represents or he does not'.[22]

The *second* version of a formalistic approach to representation focuses not on the conditions under which a representative agent is authorized by its principal, but on the opposite vector, namely the need for a representative to account for her actions to the principal. Pitkin observes that this specific view lacks a prominent theorist of the calibre of Hobbes, but nonetheless appeals to the intuitions of many. For example, while for an 'authorization' theorist to be a duly authorized representative means to be free to act as one sees fit, for an 'accountability' theorist such as Carl J Friedrich, the opposite holds: 'if A represents B, he is presumed to be responsible *to* B, that is to say, he is answerable to B for what he says and does'.[23] However, this view is affected by the same blind spot as the authorization view:

> Where the one group defines a representative as someone who has been elected (authorized), the other defines him as someone who will be subject to election (held to account). Where the one sees representation as initiated in a certain way, the other sees it as terminated in a certain way. Neither can tell us what goes on *during* representation, how a representative ought to act and what he is expected to do, how to tell whether he has represented well or badly. Such questions do not even make sense in terms of the formalistic definitions like the authorization and accountability views.[24]

In order to grasp representational agency as it relates to the people and the electorate, these two formalistic views are closer to target than the descriptive and symbolic ones, but still they do only allow for a yes/no answer to the qualification of the representative, and do not offer a conceptual foothold for assessing the adequacy of the representing performed by the representative. If our point of interest is adequacy in representing the people, we need to examine what Pitkin terms *substantive* representation.

d. Substantive representation

Substantive, as opposed to formalistic, representation consists not of 'standing for' someone else, either by appointment, through analogic resemblance, or via a symbolic

---

[21] Max Weber, *Economy and Society*, edited by G Roth and C Wittich (University of California Press 1978), 46–47.
[22] Pitkin, *Representation* (n 1) 39.
[23] Carl J Friedrich, *Constitutional Government and Democracy* (Little, Brown & Co 1941) 263, quoted in Pitkin, *Representation* (n 1) 55.
[24] Pitkin, *Representation* (n 1) 58.

relation, but of 'acting for' someone else. In acting for someone else the quality of the activity of *representing* can become the object of evaluation. We need then to reconstruct the normative standard which undergirds such evaluation.

Pitkin groups the most frequent terms, by which this variety of representation is ordinarily designated, within four clusters that tend to highlight one specific dimension of 'acting for'. 'Actor', 'factor', and 'agent' emphasize the element of *action, even limited to one instance*; 'trustee' or 'guardian' and 'procurator' emphasize the element of acting *in the interest of* the represented; then 'deputy', 'attorney', 'vicar', 'lieutenant' emphasize the idea of acting in another's place *on a continuous basis*; and terms like 'ambassador' or 'delegate' emphasize the notion of acting *on someone else's explicit instructions*.

Among these dimensions, defining which is preferable between two is crucial for our purpose: 'trustee' or 'delegate'? Should the representative be allowed independence of judgment or be given a strict mandate? As Pitkin sums up the alternative: 'Should (must) a representative do what its constituents want, and be bound by mandates or instructions from them; or should (must) he be free to act as seems best to him in pursuit of their welfare?'[25] She understands the question as concerning the *intrinsic* quality of the representing, independently of its appreciation by the represented constituency: a good representative may fail to be re-elected because its constituency is entrapped in false beliefs about her conduct, or a very inadequate one may be re-elected only because he hires an outstanding campaign manager. Representation in that respect functions like legitimacy: from a normative point of view neither can be conflated with the empirical belief of the concerned subjects.[26]

One of the interesting aspects of Pitkin's reflections on substantive representation is that she deems the 'mandate-independence controversy' unsolvable in abstract terms. In her words:

> There is no universal, safe principle to guide one in that dilemma. Neither 'follow their wishes' nor 'ignore their wishes' will do; the decision must depend on why they disagree, and in a practical case that means his judgment on why they disagree. But the standard by which he will be judged as a representative is whether he has promoted the objective interests of those he represents.[27]

In other words, we can say that good representing resembles a Goldilocks dilemma, an activity which necessarily oscillates between two extremes that dissolve representation completely: a representative who always and consistently acts contrary to his constituents' orientation appears as an unresponsive oligarch; a representative who follows all the oscillations of his constituents' opinions is perceived as just their tool. However, the Goldilocks criterion allows conceptual leeway for differently nuanced versions of the notion of substantive representation. Typically, the difference will depend: (i) on whether the *object* of representation is reputed to be 'unattached interests', 'attached interests', or concrete people; (ii) on the assumed 'relative intelligence and ability of rulers and ruled'; (iii) on the relative weight attributed to national or local

---

[25] ibid 145.
[26] See ibid 165.
[27] ibid 166.

prosperity; (iv) on the assumed opinion concerning the role and importance of parties; and, finally, (v) on metatheoretical assumptions about human nature, society, and politics.[28]

Pitkin reconstructs two significant examples of balancing the two principles of representation: on one hand, Burke's 'trusteeship'-oriented notion of representation, motivated by his understanding of representation as directed at representing 'unattached interests' and, on the other hand, Madison's comparatively more 'delegation'-oriented notion of representation, motivated by his understanding of representation as directed at representing 'people who have attached interests'.

e. The trustee version of substantive representation

The trustee version is best summed up by Edmund Burke in his eloquent and famous saying,

> Parliament is not a congress of ambassadors from different and hostile interests, which interests each must maintain, as an agent and advocate, against other agents and advocates; but Parliament is a deliberative assembly of one nation, with one interest, that of the whole—where not local prejudices ought to guide, but the general good, resulting from the general reason of the whole. You choose a member, indeed; but when you have chosen him he is not a member of Bristol, but he is a member of Parliament.[29]

The rationale for this position lies in the strong epistocratic premises of Burke. Politics, statesmanship, the art of government is not a matter of will. It is a matter of getting the right answers to the political dilemmas of the day. Just as in science it would make no sense for the more knowledgeable to defer to the majoritarian judgment of the less knowledgeable, so in national politics the correct balancing for Burke consists of allowing for elections, on the basis of a limited franchise, to identify the elite who will then be entrusted with attending the common interest of the nation in total freedom of judgment. 'Virtual representation' is the extreme form of trusteeship: even those constituencies that do not elect representatives in Parliament are *virtually* represented, according to Burke, if members of Parliament duly deliberate for the good of the whole nation.

Virtual representation, however, rests on the idea that *interests* are what is to be represented. On that basis Burke rejects the idea that the real grievances and interests of the American colonies or of the Irish Catholics are being virtually represented. In fact, none of the representatives elected to Westminster by other constituencies shares or even accepts the interests of the Irish Catholics and the American colonists, and thus the crux of the matter is that their interests, not their populations, go unrepresented. We should not let ourselves misled by the terminology and the historical context of Burke. The idea he is suggesting is very much present in our time under the

---

[28] See ibid 166–67.
[29] Edmund Burke, 'Speech to the electors of Bristol' (1774), quoted in Pitkin, Representation (n 1) 171.

heading of 'discursive representation': a carefully assembled, non-elective 'Chamber of Discourses' could be envisaged to supplement regular legislative assemblies, and entrusted with the task of representing not individuals or groups, but 'discourses' present in the public sphere on a number of relevant issues.[30] Thus, according to Pitkin, Burke does accept the idea of extending the franchise as a matter of prudent inclusion of unrepresented *interests*, not a matter of 'abstract' rights. This view of representation rests, as Pitkin points out, on a strong epistemic understanding of interests. Interest is

> very much as we see today scientific fact: it is completely independent of wishes or opinion, of whether we like it or not; it is just so. This means, on the one hand, that an intelligent, honest representative can find it; and, on the other hand, that his constituents eventually will accept it.... Long-range disagreement between representative and constituents can occur only if the representative is corrupt or incompetent.[31]

Time is a fundamental factor. It sets deliberation apart from rash opinion. Thus, the test of time becomes actually a convergence test. While in the short run the opinion of the uncultivated and undeliberative constituents should never prevail or even influence the representative's conduct in Parliament, in the long run a persisting gap between parliament and the electorate 'is inconsistent with true representation. A Parliament cannot indefinitely stand in the people's way and still be considered representative.'[32]

However, alongside a reflection of the due representation of interests, Burke articulates a distinct notion of the representation of the *feelings of persons*. Interestingly, while opinions are unworthy of representation, on account of their volatility, feelings have a different status. Feelings are not reflections of reality—inaccurate as opinions or accurate as scientific theses—but expressive articulations of experiences of suffering, pain, and humiliation on which the person is the ultimate authority: hence, for Burke 'it becomes important for the people's feelings to be transmitted accurately to the government'.[33] Feelings are reliable indicators of possible interests. Thus, perceiving and making sense of these feelings can help the representative to piece together the interests of the people, like a doctor uses the symptoms or feelings of pain as an indicator that can guide him to locate the exact illness to be cured.

For Burke, then, the House of Commons must be 'the express image of the *feelings of the nation*.'[34] Instead of mirroring the proportional distribution of *opinion* in the population, it should reflect its prevailing *feelings* and most heartfelt grievances. 'Good representing' then is an admixture of knowing the interests and grasping the feelings of the constituents—a 'communion of interest and sympathy in feelings and desires'.[35] Its object is the discerning of the good of the nation, through deliberation and the balancing of conflicting interests. The feelings of the population are the indicators of where to look at in order to retrieve as yet overlooked interests. The national common

---

[30] See John Dryzek and Simon Niemeyer, 'Discursive Representation' (2008) 102(4) American Political Science Review 481 (hereafter Dryzek and Niemeyer, 'Discursive Representation').
[31] Pitkin, *Representation* (n 1) 180.
[32] ibid 181–82.
[33] ibid 184.
[34] Burke, quoted in ibid 184.
[35] Burke, quoted in ibid 184.

interest cannot emerge from sacrificing partial or local interests, for Burke, but from their deliberative mediation. Representing starts then from feelings and proceeds to interests.

Finally, Burke's idea of representing as deliberating about the general interest of the people takes the form of a consensual mediation. As Pitkin reconstructs his view,

> Voting, the counting of noses in Parliament, is of no importance; what is required is the fact that all arguments be accurately and wisely set forth. This is why, also, a group's having legitimate grievances is evidence that it is not being represented. If its interest has even a single competent member in Parliament, it will be looked after, because it is not his vote but his arguments that matter.[36]

f. The delegate version of substantive representation

When we move to a *liberal* understanding of representation, epitomized by Madison, representation becomes a *right*, and is understood as representation *of the individual citizen*, not of the aggregate interests of a locality. Interests are now cast under the negative light of being the basis of factions, the natural enemy of the general interest of the nation. As Pitkin points out, in this new picture interests are no longer 'clearly defined, broad, objective groupings that compose the nation; no longer do people or places "belong to" or "partake of" an interest'.[37] Interests are entirely subjectivized as individual preferences and inclinations. They play the same role as Burke's 'opinions': they are unstable and almost impossible to reconcile into a coherent picture. They are also more fragmented. It is not just 'commercial', 'manufacturing', or 'landed' interests that play a role, but also a host of more specific ones, linked with identifiable single groups, such as religious denominations, localities, and group ties and loyalties. And, crucially, they are no longer 'unattached'. They lack any basis independent of individual belief and preference. For Burke, interests are somehow objective. For Madison 'a man's interest is what he thinks it is, just as his opinion is what he thinks'.[38]

Interests so conceived coalesce in factions and factions prioritize their interest over the general one. They are the main enemy of a well-ordered republic. Madison's remedy is the dispersion of these particular interests through the breadth of representation and through territorial extension, which by itself will lead to differentiation and mutual exclusion or neutralization of rival interests. Because 'enlightened statesmen will not always be at the helm',[39] the Burkean remedy to the plurality of interests—namely, deliberation on the part of representatives reputed as superior in discernment and cultivation than their constituents—will not apply. Madison envisages, instead,

---

[36] ibid 188. Again, a similar idea reemerges in the research paradigm of 'discursive representation'.
[37] ibid 191.
[38] ibid 192.
[39] *Federalist Papers*, n 10 (Madison), with an introduction, table of contents, and index of ideas by C Rossiter (Penguin 1961) 80.

a republic extended enough so that local interests, even when represented by leaders that project them onto the national scene, will be neutralized by the plurality of other competing interests.

For Madison, as for Burke, time becomes an important factor. The projection of a multiplicity of these interests on the national stage will impress a completely different tempo to their articulation, relative to the tumultuous and vociferous leaders and communities that push local interests. Locally impetuous streams of protest and interest will meet the calm waters of national legislation and will not be able to upset them: stalemate ensuing from reciprocal vetoes and the dilution of time inherent in national legislative process will temper the momentum of factional interests.

The difference in perspective is correctly traced by Pitkin to the diversity of underlying metatheoretical assumptions. While Burke endows his representative with the capacity to see through the opinion of the constituents and grasp their real interests better than they themselves do, 'Madison's representative does not know his constituents' interests better than they do themselves; if anything, he is in this respect roughly their equal.'[40] Burke consequently entrusts the balancing of conflicting interests to the wisdom of men, while Madison instead mistrusts that solution and relies on 'check and balances', that is, on institutional design.

The utilitarian tradition has produced a variant of Madison's argument about the large extension of the republic as an antidote to factionalism. Internal diversity within each faction matters too. In *Considerations on Representative Government*, John Stuart Mill describes classes of citizens along lines close to Madison's factions and considers desirable that their number and divisions neutralize their factionality. However, even a reduced number of classes or factions need not exert a degenerative impact on the republic, if each of them is not entirely homogeneous but contains some moderate members who share the particular faction-defining interest, *but do not prioritize it over the general interest*. Then this internal minority, composed of members who care for 'the good of the whole', 'joining with the whole of the other [class/faction], would turn the scale against any demands of their own majority which were not such as ought to prevail.'[41]

One aspect of Mill's view of representation needs further exploration: how to reconcile the notion that some subsection of a class and some representatives orient themselves to the common good and prioritize it over particular interests, and in so doing make their 'real' interests prevail over the short-term, misguided, 'apparent' interests, with the assumption of the subjective quality of interests, supposedly coextensive with what each individual deems in her interest? The desirable prevailing of the 'real' interests over the 'apparent' ones is the reason why constituents should defer to their representatives' more enlightened judgment. But is this conclusion consistent with the premise—shared by Mill and Madison—that each individual is the best judge of her own interests?

Pitkin's suggestion is to recast Mill's point, following Ayer's interpretation, as the claim that individuals are *not likely* to know their true or best interest, because tracking

---

[40] Pitkin, *Representation* (n 1) 197.
[41] John Stuart Mill, *Considerations on Representative Government* (1861) (Floating Press 2009)158.

it requires that the particular be figured in the general interest, but they remain the irreplaceable arbiters of whether the realization of their interest is for them a cause of pain or of pleasure. This formulation combines the ontological priority of individual judgment and the possibility of the epistemic superiority of the expert or representative. As Pitkin sums up Ayer's point, 'only the wearer can tell if the shoe pinches. But this does not mean that the wearer knows in advance which shoe will pinch him; in fact, it is much more likely that a shoe specialist will know this better than he'.[42] In conclusion, Pitkin argues, the great achievement of liberalism is to allow us to have it both ways. In her words:

> Representation makes it possible for each to participate in government as the final judge of whether his particular shoe pinches; yet it allows the rulers to use their wisdom and information to further people's true interests, where direct action would be misguided by short-range, hasty decisions. And, at the same time, representation makes it to the interest of the ruler to act in the interest of the subjects—not to give in to their passing whims, but to act in their true interest. For if he gives in to their passing whims, they will not really be pleased; the shoe that looked so attractive in the store will turn out to pinch. Only if he uses his wisdom to promote their true, long-range interests will they be truly pleased, and support him at the polls.[43]

Pitkin's thesis that the more subjectivist our understanding of interest, the more our concept of representation leans toward the 'delegate' end of the spectrum, receives further corroboration from Rousseau's theory of the impossibility of representation. As he puts it,

> Sovereignty cannot be represented, for the same reason that it cannot be transferred; it consists essentially in the general will, and the will cannot be represented; it is itself or it is something else; there is no other possibility. The people's deputies are not its representatives, therefore, nor can they be, but are only its agents; they cannot make definitive decisions. Any law that the people in person has not ratified is void; it is not a law.[44]

This approach nullifies the possibility of representation in terms other than delegation: less than total delegation amounts to total alienation of the principal's will. As in the authorization model championed by Hobbes, the representative can only be duly authorized, but no standards can help us assess her performance at representing, which is another way of saying that the representative can freely act as she pleases without forfeiting her status of authorized representative.

---

[42] Pitkin, *Representation* (n 1) 204.
[43] ibid 205.
[44] Jean Jacques Rousseau, *The Social Contract* (1762), translated and with an introduction C Betts (Oxford University Press 1994) 127 (hereafter Rousseau, *Social Contract*).

g. Political representation, reasonable pluralism, and public reason

Finally, we can sum up the Goldilocks view of political representation in the following terms. Political representation disappears into technical expertise if the alternatives from which to choose are so deeply embedded in a field of expert knowledge as to lie totally beyond the grasp of democratic constituencies. In this case, political representation fades into the performance of an expert making decisions for a patient or a client, much in the same way as a parent or a guardian chooses for a minor. Real representation remains possible, in such a case, only in relation to the setting of alternative parameters. Pitkin's account at this juncture tends to reflect the climate of confidence in science typical of the age and to concede a bit too cavalierly that certain questions may be entirely of a technical nature. The difficulty becomes evident if we take the example of the thresholds of air pollution in urban settings, for the purpose of limiting the circulation of carbon-dioxide-emitting vehicles. The level of acceptable pollution can technically be correlated with the number of circulating vehicles of diverse kinds and the related necessity for restrictive measures, but the definition of 'acceptable pollution' cannot be reduced to a technical question. For example, given a statistically average rate of deaths due to respiratory and cancer-related diseases, the determination of what deviation from the standard is acceptable is not a technical question at all, but an ethical and political one on which experts have no privileged access.

After correcting that bias, however, Pitkin's point remains valid: the more technical and epistemically dense an alternative is, the more representation approximates the trustee model. For example, insofar as the mandate of the governor of a central bank can be understood to represent the interests of the national public in the realm of monetary policy, it certainly belongs in the trustee model. Past a critical point, however, representation mutates into expert advice.

At the other extreme, the more the alternatives are a matter of sheer subjective preference, like dishes on a menu or the choice of colouring of surfaces, the more representation entails an obligation to consult with the constituents and inevitably moves towards reflecting their point of view and preferences. 'At the extreme, again, substantive acting for others becomes impossible'[45] and we end up with purely 'ambassadorial' understandings of representation: the representative becomes a messenger of the principal.

The same Goldilocks dilemma applies to the epistemic and moral relation of the representative to the principal or constituent. The differential of knowledge, moral standing, and capacity for judgment must lie within an optimal range at the two extremes of which, again, representation disappears: 'a true expert taking care of a helpless child is no representative, and a man who merely consults and reflects without acting is not representing in the sense of substantively acting for others'.[46]

Thus, as the chapter epigraph suggests, 'Political questions are not likely to be as arbitrary as the choice between two foods; nor are they likely to be questions of knowledge to which an expert can supply the one correct answer'.[47] What, then, are they

---

[45] Pitkin, *Representation* (n 1) 210.
[46] ibid 211.
[47] ibid 212.

like? If they are choices that relate to deep commitments shared by the constituents and the representative, how can commitments be the object of representation? From a Weberian perspective, commitments relate to values and value choices are ultimately impervious to cogent reasons and remain a matter for Frankfurt's 'wholehearted identification' or existential choice.

Pitkin's argument on representation belongs on a philosophical horizon where Rawls's reasonable pluralism, not to mention the normativity of what is 'most reasonable for us', are absent. As she argues,

> What becomes of terms like 'interest' and 'justifiable' if there can be lifelong, profound disagreement among men as to what their interest is—disagreement that remains despite deliberation and justification and argument? To the extent that this is so, the possibility of a substantive acting for others breaks down, and that view of the concept becomes irrelevant to politics. To the extent that this happens in practical political life, *we seem then to fall back on descriptive representation; we choose a representative who shares our values and commitments and prevent the irresoluble conflict.* Failing that, we can retreat to symbolic representation; we can let ourselves be influenced by emotional ties in spite of our doubts about whether our interests are being served. Or, failing even that, we can cling to our formal and institutional representative arrangements even when they seem devoid of substantive content. We can continue to obey, although we feel abused, or continue to remove a series of accountable representatives from office, although none of them serves our interest.[48]

In the last chapter of her book, Pitkin moves on to address some problems that affect representation in the context of present-day liberal democracies. One word of comment is in order on pluralism. Pitkin addresses the problem from within an old Weberian, existentialized version of the 'warring gods': as a democratic citizen I cannot but choose a representative who worships my favourite god and thus descriptive representation creeps back in. When we reconsider the matter from the angle of political liberalism, the picture changes: reasonable pluralism does not prevent public reason from operating. We can thus envisage, on one hand, representatives who are partisans and share a comprehensive conception of the common good with their constituents and, on the other, representatives who appeal to their constituents by virtue of their superior ability to operate in the public forum through public reason and to embody virtues of tolerance, reasonability, and civility. The idea of public reason frees us from the pressure to fall back on descriptive representation in the face of irreducible pluralism.

The problem of representing large constituencies in electoral districts is addressed by Pitkin as a matter of reconciling the local interests and the national interest. The national interest, however, is a construction of the mind, no less than 'the people', which is incumbent on representatives to generate. Again, a Goldilocks dilemma must be solved:

---

[48] ibid 213 (emphasis added).

The initial-interest-claim of a locality or group can be and often is opposed to the initial-interest-claim of the nation. But the nation also has an interest in the welfare of the parties and members, and they have in interest in its welfare. So, in theory, for each case there should exist an ideal final-objective-interest settlement (whether or not we can find it or agree on it), giving just the right weight to all considerations. A minor benefit to the whole nation purchased at the price of severe hardships to a part may not be justified. A minor benefit to a part purchased at the price of serious damage to the nation probably is not justified.... Politics entails the reconciliation of conflicting claims, each usually with some justice of its side; the harmony of final-objective-interests must be *created*.[49]

This insight by Pitkin constitutes a bridge to the next section, on developments of the concept of representation after Pitkin.

2. Rethinking Representation after Pitkin

The subsequent fifty years of reflection on representation, after Pitkin's account, have brought three main new elements into the picture: Mansbridge's reshuffling of Pitkinian categories, Saward's constructivist turn, and Rehfeld's distinction of three separate dimensions within the mandate–independence binary. These innovative approaches have a specific significance for our problem of understanding the difference between representing the electorate and representing the people.

a. Mansbridge's fourfold typology of representation

In 'Rethinking Representation',[50] Jane Mansbridge reshaped Pitkin's typology of concepts of representation, by replacing her categories with four new notions: *promissory*, *anticipatory*, *gyroscopic*, and *surrogate* representation. Descriptive and symbolic representation now disappear as specific types. Gyroscopic representation, however, bears a strong resemblance to Burke's trustee polarity in substantive representation, as Mansbridge herself concedes, though they are not identical.[51] A gyroscopic representative embeds the wide degree of discretion of a Burkean trustee but allows for goal-oriented discretion: the voter may choose as representative someone 'who will always vote for a particular policy, such as lower taxes, that the voter may desire for purely self-interested reasons'.[52] *Surrogate* representation, occurring 'when

---

[49] ibid 218.
[50] Jane Mansbridge, 'Rethinking Representation' 97(4) American Political Science Review 515 (hereafter Mansbridge, 'Rethinking Representation').
[51] Jane Mansbridge, 'The Fallacy of Tightening the Reins' Keynote Address to the Austrian Political Science Association, Vienna, 10 December 2004, 9–10. See also Mansbridge's more recent concept of 'recursive representation', which casts the representative as an *interlocutor* of the constituent, in Jane Mansbridge 'Recursive Representation' in D Castiglione and J Pollak, *Creating Political Presence: The New Politics of Democratic Representation* (University of Chicago Press 2019) 298.
[52] ibid 9.

legislators represent constituents outside their district'[53] is an update of Burke's 'virtual representation'. And *promissory* representation is largely a reconstruction of the ideal of electoral representation in contemporary democracies: a constituent votes for a representative who 'pledges' or 'promises' to do her best for the advancement, in future legislative activity, of values and related policies favoured by the constituent. Mansbridge's promissory representation is a revisiting of the delegate model, softened by assuming that the substance of the promise could be broad, value-related, and complex enough to require the exercise of judgment in order to be carried out.[54] The one truly groundbreaking contribution brought by Mansbridge to the debate on representation and the mandate/independence polarity is the notion of *anticipatory* representation, 'in which the representative tries to please future voters'.[55]

Much more than a mere shift in temporality is entailed by anticipatory representation, which has become more and more descriptive of a fluid situation in contemporary parliamentary and presidential democracies, when political parties experience a profound crisis of legitimacy, of recruitment and fidelity of their voters, and when new charismatic and populist parties emerge.

As Mansbridge points out, 'the shift in temporal emphasis in anticipatory representation brings unexpected normative changes in its wake'.[56] In promissory representation, regardless of whether the promise issues from a trustee-type or a delegate-type representative, the relation of the representative to her principal has a *normative* nature: the representative *ought* to keep the promise by which she got elected. Instead, the elected representative who seeks to woo the vote of future constituents is *prudently* seeking to intercept their preferences—acting as a firm trying to acquire new clients. There is no accountability involved or any practical obligation, just strategic calculation. Mansbridge acknowledges the shift brought into being by this new form of representation, but glosses over its six implications.

First, the whole point of the climaxing structure of Pitkin's book consists in the fact that in the end *substantive* representation (whether in the delegate or trustee versions) allows for what the previous concepts of representation had no place for, namely an evaluation of the quality of the *representing*. That possibility still survives in promissory representation but disappears in anticipatory representation: a firm that fails to attract new customers simply misses them; a politician who fails to attract new voters is *not* representing them in any sense of the word. The quality of an inexistent practice cannot be evaluated. We can only assess the quality of the representing once a new promissory-type relation has been formed. A further corollary is that the more anticipatory representation acquires preponderance, the less significant the evaluation of the quality of representation becomes. We're left with a mere assessment of the representative's success or failure in gaining new constituents.

---

[53] Mansbridge, 'Rethinking Representation' (n 50) 515.
[54] For a discussion of promissory representation as an extension of the 'delegate' model, see Andrew Rehfeld, 'Representation Rethought: on Trustees, Delegates, and Gyroscopes in the Study of Political Representation and Democracy' (2009) 103(2) The American Political Science Review 220 (hereafter Rehfeld, 'Representation Rethought').
[55] Mansbridge, 'Rethinking Representation' (n 50) 517.
[56] ibid 518.

Second, Mansbridge's two forms of representation exhibit a zero-sum dynamic. If we exclude the competition for new voters, every additional constituent anticipatorily won over by a given representative, is a constituent subtracted from some other representative who previously had a promissory relation to that constituent.

Third, among the positive implications of anticipatory representation Mansbridge includes the fact that it 'forces normative theory to become systemic',[57] that is, to move from focusing on the quality of promise-keeping to focusing on the overall quality of the mutual communication of representatives and constituents. An anticipatory representative could just try to guess the preferences of possible new constituents and try to initiate mutual communication with them. But presumably the quality of this communication, conducive in turn to the strategic success of anticipatory representation, 'depends much more on the functioning of the entire representative process—including political parties, political challengers, the media, interest groups, hearings, opinion surveys, and all other processes of communication'.[58] Consequently, according to Mansbridge, the expansion of anticipatory representation indirectly involves an incentive for the relevant actors to invest in improving the quality of the public sphere. It remains unclear, however, why the same reasoning would not apply to promissory representation: constituents would also benefit from the same aspects of the public sphere in their monitoring the fulfilment of the promises they accepted and in their looking out for alternative representatives. Dubious as its special applicability to anticipatory representation might be, this incentive placed by anticipatory representation on multidimensional, multichannel, and coercion-free communication might also stimulate other less desirable effects, never considered by Mansbridge.

Fourth, among these undesirable effects we could probably count the representative's advantage in keeping the most flexible and nondescript profile, a profile good 'for all seasons' and capable of appealing to a multiplicity of diverse possible addressees. That flexibility and ambiguity would maximize appeal and opportunity, while a consistent and focused legislative action and a high-profile identity could turn into a competitive disadvantage for a representative.

Fifth, anticipatory representation fosters indifference concerning whose votes are wooed. This fact therefore puts an incentive on representatives' seeking the votes of the groups most credulous and easy to manipulate: those votes cost less effort to be obtained. Easy targets of manipulative openings then become over-targeted, and constituencies that are more reflective, informed, or simply traditional may, on the contrary, suffer a relative communicative neglect on account of the amount of effort it takes to intercept their votes. A reflection on this collateral, mostly negative, effect of anticipatory representation is needed but absent from Mansbridge's text.

Sixth and finally, anticipatory representation can only be successful insofar as a promissory relation of representation fails or gets derailed by the attractiveness of a new, untested, anticipatory relation. Then an overall effect of deteriorating trust can be expected—and trust is a fundamental public good that sustains the possibility of democratic life—as a consequence of the diffusion of anticipatory representation. As a constituent of a promissory relation of representation, in fact, I must take into account

---

[57] ibid.
[58] ibid 519.

the fact that my representative will balance the cost of keeping his promise to me with the benefit of gaining new and possibly larger support among other constituencies.

b. Saward's 'representative claim'

Michael Saward's reconsideration of representation brings another important element of novelty into the picture. In his influential *The Representative Claim*, criticizing Pitkin for focusing her analysis primarily on the representative rather than on 'the represented'[59] and acknowledging that Mansbridge goes some way towards shifting emphasis from the dyad principal–representative to a more systemic focus on social flows of communication and on less formal aspects of representation,[60] Saward mentions seven distinct areas in which the theory of political representation is in need of re-examination and his new 'constructivist' paradigm, which reconfigures representation as a *claim*, has something distinctive to offer.

First, while present accounts have tended to depict representation as 'a thing' which exists and awaits definition, it is more urgent to focus on what representation *does*. *Second*, while Pitkin's and other accounts have by and large approached representation as a unilinear relation, an approach more open to its multiple dimensions is needed. *Third*, the predominantly normative thrust of past and present approaches to representation ought to give way to a more descriptive and phenomenological one. *Fourth*, while past and present approaches have privileged the definition and classification of representative roles (trustees, delegates, surrogates, stewards, etc), a more fine-grained grasp is needed of the more elementary aspects of representation undergirding those roles. *Fifth*, whilst past and present theories have focused too closely on *electoral* representation, urgently needed is an investigation of other, more informal kinds of representation. *Sixth*, their focus on electoral representation has by and large led theories of representation to limit their investigation to representation within the nation state, but new concepts are needed for analysing representation within structures of transnational or supranational governance. *Seventh*, while so far theories of representation have shied away from engaging new forms of representative claims, we need an approach capable of accounting for newly emerging, and rapidly expanding, 'non-parliamentary representative claims, cross-border claims, the environmental agenda and therefore claims about the representation of (for example) non-human animals'.[61]

All of these programmatic points come together in Saward's new paradigm cantered on the 'representative claim'. Rather than just a relation between a principal and a representative over representing an interest of the principal, a representative claim occurs when 'a *maker* of representations ("M") puts forward a *subject* ("S") which stands for an *object* ("O") that is related to a *referent* ("R") and is offered to an *audience* ("A")'.[62] Representation becomes then an event with a performative dimension. The

---

[59] Michael Saward, *The Representative Claim* (Oxford University Press 2010) 11 (hereafter Saward, *Representative Claim*).
[60] ibid 20–21.
[61] ibid 32–33.
[62] ibid 36.

constructivist (and performative) quality of the new paradigm consists in the fact that both the representative (the subject of representation) and the constituent (considered as the object of representation) are *constructions*, propounded by a 'maker', who may or may not be the same as the representative, and they differ from the empirical, embodied reality of who the representative *qua* maker, and the constituent *qua* concrete referent, actually are. Furthermore, the offer and acceptance of a constructed subject (distinct from the maker of the claim) and of a constructed object (distinct from the observable referent) take place before the eyes of an *audience*, which must always be presupposed. Thus, for example, an 'MP (maker) offers himself or herself (subject) as the embodiment of constituency interests (object) to that constituency (audience). The referent is the actual, flesh-and-blood people of the constituency. The object involves a selective portrayal of constituency interests'.[63]

With this rethinking the paradigmatic relation of 'representing' as claim-making,[64] Saward places such relation on a performative terrain. Because 'the world of political representation is a world of claim-making rather than the operation of formal institutions',[65] it follows that while Pitkin's and others' so-called presence approach equates representation with making present something that is absent, the 'event approach' propounded by Saward 'looks at claims that *give the impression of making present*'.[66] This Goffmanian terminology surfaces again and again in the text.[67] Representing is tantamount to successfully creating an impression of representing:

> Would-be constituencies, even relatively culturally homogenous ones, contain a huge variety of apparent and potential interests, many of which will cut across each other in complex ways, and will divide as much as unite. Would-be representatives, of whatever type, must of necessity pick and choose, propose and fabricate, a distinctive and limited vision of, or set of interests for, the constituency. The prospect that they can in some plausible sense represent a clear and encompassing set of constituency interests is remote, at best. Would-be representatives have to make claims, about themselves and their would-be constituencies, and use these claims in order to try to impose, or encourage a belief in, a particular set of 'interests' as an unavoidable precondition of speaking for those interests. In this sense, representation is as much constitutive as reflective of facts about interests and capacities. And it is through the process of claim-making that the work of constituting is pursued.[68]

This interplay of would-be representatives and would-be constituencies always takes place—Saward adds—before an *audience*: 'There is little political point in a claim that does not seek to address a specified (national, local, ethnic, religious, linguistic, class, or other) audience, and more to the point, to attempt to induce in potential

---

[63] ibid 37.
[64] The same term is used by Laclau, when he identifies the transition from local 'request to claim' as the initial building block of the populist process of constructing the people's bid for hegemony. See Ernesto Laclau, *On Populist Reason* (Verso 2005) 73 (hereafter Laclau, *Populist Reason*).
[65] Saward, *The Representative Claim* (n 59) 43.
[66] ibid 42 (emphasis in original).
[67] See ibid 67–68.
[68] ibid 44–45.

audiences and constituencies notions of themselves *as* audiences or constituencies'.[69] Audiences are no less a product of construction and impression management:

> The intended audience may be coterminous with the intended constituency, or it may include the intended constituency plus other citizens and influentials. It may also be just one segment of the intended constituency, or combine such a segment with some outside the intended constituency. Which of these alternatives is involved in a given case depends on context, purposes, and resources of claimants.[70]

To sum up:

> representative claims are invariably, to one degree or another, constitutive claims; they construct in some measure the groups that they purport to address (audience), along with the groups that they purport to speak for or about (constituency). Claim-makers, of course, do not generally want to reveal this fact; they prefer to be seen to be addressing preexisting, natural or fundamental interests that are already 'out there'.[71]

The price to be paid for this change of paradigm is no less than the complete loss of all normative perspective. A normative assessment of the quality of any single representative claim is de facto undermined by Saward's adoption of a performative, instrumental perspective from which one can only make sense of the success or failure of the representative claim, not of its *deserving* success or failure. Within Saward's theoretical framework, just as within Laclau's populist quest for hegemony, little can be said about the quality of a representative claim, other than the claim has either been accepted by referent and audience, or that it has been rejected or ignored. Given the nexus of successful representative claims and democratic legitimacy, the same bias comes to affect the notion of legitimacy embedded in Saward's constructivist paradigm. All that Saward can say about democratic legitimacy, in fact, is that it amounts to ' "perceived legitimacy" as reflected in *acceptance* of claims over time by appropriate constituencies under certain conditions'.[72]

---

[69] ibid 48.
[70] ibid 49.
[71] ibid 54. For a similar point, namely that representation 'is the primary terrain of constitution of social objectivity', see Laclau, *Populist Reason* (n 63) 163. Some sympathetic commentators urge Saward to go even further along the path of making the representative claim entirely 'constructivist', that is, to emphasize more decidedly that 'the relationship between representative and constituency is arbitrary, conventional and mutually constitutive' and to acknowledge, in relation to the concept of 'referent', that the materiality of the referent (people and groups as existing apart from and prior to 'evocation') is also somehow 'discursively constituted': see Lisa Disch, 'The "constructivist turn" in political representation' (2012) 11/1 Contemporary Political Theory 117. Other commentators, instead, aptly remind Saward of Pitkin's fundamental insight into the indispensable mutual independence of represented and representative, and wonder whether the constructive quality of the 'representative claim' risks sacrificing that mutual independence to the idol of 'constructiveness'. See Dario Castiglione, 'Giving Pitkin her due: What the "representative claim" gets right, and what it risks missing' (2012) 11(1) Contemporary Political Theory 122.
[72] Saward, *The Representative Claim* (n 59) 84. For a 'charitable' and sympathetic, though ultimately unconvincing, attempt to show that Saward's constructivist approach to representation leaves room for some kind of normative, theory-based assessment of the conditions that corroborate as prima facie valid a constituency's acceptance of a representative claim, see Lisa Disch, 'The "Constructivist Turn" in Democratic Representation: A Normative Dead-End?' (2015) 22(4) Constellations 487–88. For a similar argument applied to Saward's concept of legitimacy, see ibid 495–96.

c. Rehfeld's eightfold typology of representation

Over and beyond Mansbridge's and Saward's approaches, many interesting new contributions to the understanding of representation have created a variegated field that perhaps still awaits a new synthesis. Let me mention again Dryzek's idea of 'discursive representation', Urbinati's view of 'representation as advocacy', Young's revisitation of descriptive representation, and Castiglione's and Warren's comprehensive 'new ecology of democratic representation'.[73] The most groundbreaking conceptual innovation of the post-Pitkin era, however, is Andrew Rehfeld's eightfold typology of relations of representation. Whereas only anticipatory representation—among Mansbridge's four notions of *promissory, anticipatory, gyroscopic,* and *surrogate* representation—introduces significant elements of novelty, but incurs the difficulty of forfeiting all normative dimension; and whereas Saward's constructivist turn empties his 'representative claim' of all normative import and reduces it to a successful performative effect; Rehfeld's new understanding of representation preserves the valuable Pitkinian normative emphasis on reconstructing the ingredients of good representing as the practice of acting for another.

Rehfeld starts by observing that the pivotal distinction between the 'independent/ trustee' and 'mandated/delegate' models of representation in fact obscures three other important distinctions. *First*, regardless of whether he acts as trustee or delegate, the representative may aim at the good of the whole or of a part of the body politic. *Second*, regardless of whether he acts as trustee or delegate, the representative may rely either on his own or his constituents' judgment in order to determine the good (common or particular) to be pursued. *Third*, he may pursue such good (general or particular), identified through his or someone else's judgment, on the basis of internal motivations or for the sake of external rewards, most notably re-election.[74] Thus the classical opposition of trustee- and delegate-conceptions of substantive representation captures only two among eight distinct possibilities: namely, it captures the opposition of (i) a representative—called 'Republican' by Rehfeld—who aims at the general interest as defined *by him* and is motivated by internal, virtue-derived reasons, and (ii) a delegate—called a 'Pluralist', to evoke Dahl's idea of polyarchy— who aims at the constituents' interest, as understood *by them* and in view of the benefit of re-election.

Many more cases, some of which embodied by historical figures, other merely hypothetical, can be imagined. Rehfeld organizes his typology by modifying one variable at a time. Thus, assuming a constant orientation to the general interest, a representative may embody an ideal type which is a variant of the Weberian 'civil

---

[73] See Dryzek and Niemeyer, 'Discursive Representation' (n 30); Nadia Urbinati, 'Representation as Advocacy: A Study of Democratic Deliberation' (2000) 28 Political Theory 758; Young, *Justice and the Politics of Difference* (n 9) and *Inclusion and Democracy* (n 9); Dario Castiglione and Mark Warren, 'A New Ecology of Democratic Representation? Eight Theoretical Issues' (2013) 2(2) Intrasformazione: Rivista di Storia delle Idee 155.

[74] See Andrew Rehfeld, 'Representation Rethought' (n 54) 215.

servant', oriented to the general interest as defined by the public he serves and relatively unresponsive to external incentives.[75] Differently than for Weber, this kind of civil servant receives the defining view of the general interest not from hierarchically (and usually elected) superordinate officials, but from the public to which his activities are oriented. Then next on the scale of publicly spirited representation come representatives motivated primarily by external incentives (re-election, career building). When they rely on their own judgment concerning the general interest, Rehfeld identifies them as 'Madisonian lawmakers', and when they defer to their constituents' judgment Rehfeld qualifies them as 'Anti-Federalists'.[76] The latter label may strike us as peculiar, but Rehfeld defends it by observing that 'although Anti-Federalists were more concerned overall with the particular interests of local communities, there was a strain that defended instructions with legal sanction in order to pursue the national good'.[77]

Another spate of four diverse kinds of representatives can be distinguished if we hold fast to the hypothesis of a representative oriented to pursue the good of her constituents. This 'pluralist' representative may rely solely or mainly on her judgment in defining such partial good and be internally motivated (and unresponsive to electoral sanction): a typical example would be offered by a 'tin-eared, passionate volunteer working to better a community as he or she judges it would improve without regard to what the community believes is right and undeterred by the fact that he or she will soon be asked to leave'.[78] Many vanguard-type forms of representation are of this sort. When these two variables—orientation to a partial good and internal motivation unaffected by incentives—are held constant and we shift from autonomous determination of the constituents' good to deference to the constituents' own judgment, we encounter a sixth type of representative: an ambassador. Ambassadors 'want to advance their home nations' interests, as judged by the government they serve, but [they] are motivated by an internal sense of purpose ('service to country') rather than [by one] induced by threat of sanction'.[79] A final oppositional pair can be generated when, along with the pursuit of a particular good, we hold constant the representative's responsiveness to external sanctions and rewards (material or reputational). Then at one end of the spectrum we encounter the examples of professional representatives (lawyers, doctors, financial advisors) who rely on their own judgment as to the best interest of the person they represent. At the other end, we encounter what Rehfeld describes as the most radical version of the delegate model: 'someone who pursues the good of his or her constituents as his or her constituents see it, motivated simply by his or her desire for external reward (ie re-election)'.[80] Another example could be the low-level, self-serving professional who considers her client or patient a mere source of revenue, is totally motivated by external rewards, and defers to the client's judgment.

---

[75] See ibid 224.
[76] ibid.
[77] ibid.
[78] ibid.
[79] ibid.
[80] ibid.

3. Grounding Sequential Sovereignty: Time and Representation

It is time to take stock of the distinct relations of representation generated by these diverse theoretical frameworks, in order to make sense of the ways in which the people and the electorate can be represented by the institutions therewith entrusted. In this concluding section, that task will be carried out in two steps. First, by correlating forms of representation with the temporal dimension of the represented constituency: the larger the temporal extension of the constituency, the more representation will tend to take the form of trusteeship, but then also different subtypes of trusteeship can be envisaged, that correspond to alternative active or quiescent, assertive or tolerant dispositions of the representative, and to diverse forms of institutionalizing the practice of representing the people. Second, I will highlight the difficulties incurred by political philosophical accounts that fail to properly reflect the temporal gap between the voters and the people and to account for the sequential embeddedness of the voters within the people, thus in the end incurring the difficulties of a serial view of popular sovereignty.

a. Representing 'the people' and the electorate

Let me recapitulate the initial stipulations and questions, now in the light of the conceptually differentiated notion of representation that we have reconstructed. The starting point for a reflection on the distinction of representing the people and representing the electorate is that only the voters, *qua* living segment of the people, are possessed of political agency. Only they can assent and dissent through their vote, through their feet when they take to the streets, or through their voice when they enliven the public sphere. The people cannot assent or dissent in a direct way. Generations of the people no longer alive manifest their agency as a normative legacy, deposited in the documents of constitutional significance: the founding constitution (whenever available), the subsequent amendments to it, possibly other testimonies. Generations of the people that are not yet on the political scene do not have political agency, and no one can represent 'not yet existing intentionality'. What *can* be represented and protected, however, is their interest in exercising agency on an equal footing to that of the previous generations. Why? Because future generations in due course *will* be part of the people and for the people to include segments with diminished rights and entitlements inevitably detracts from the overall quality of its democratic identity and from consistency with the initial constitutional-democratic project. This entwinement of temporality and the people generates two important consequences for representation.

First, it spawns a reduction in number of the relevant types of representation within the post-Pitkinian picture. To begin with the voters, they are by and large represented by three kinds of institutional representatives: members of parliament, appointed prime ministers, and elected presidents. From a national constituency presidents obtain a mandate that does not depend on a confidence vote, thus they are subject to a lesser pressure to represent their constituency in the guise of delegates—except surreptitiously, for example when a president is rumoured to *really* represent financial capital, the oil industry, the military, or in a merely rhetorical way, as for example when populist presidents like Chavez, Morales, or Trump claim that through their being in power 'the common people rule'. Thus, by virtue of the nature of their mandate, presidents tend to be closer to the trustee end of the spectrum than representatives in legislatures. However, as documented by the increasing influence of opinion polls on the shaping of executive action, presidents may be ever more tempted to defer to the oscillations of public opinion concerning the issues of the day.[81]

The same happens with prime ministers in parliamentary systems. Although they depend on a parliamentary majority, often composed of litigious parties, and are not directly elected, they tend—just as presidents do—to lean towards the trustee end of the spectrum, though occasionally they may turn into 'delegates of public opinion'. Thus, in the case of top executive officials, most of Rehfeld's variants of representation (exemplified by civil servants, volunteers, ambassadors, professionals, pared-down delegates) do not apply and we are left with the old tension between Burkean trustees and Madisonian representatives.

Members of parliament have more flexibility concerning the patterns of representation available to them: differently from presidents and prime ministers, they may openly pledge to pursue the good of their own particular constituency or even act as Rehfeld's 'pared-down delegates'. In so doing, they might perhaps forfeit their chance to go down in history as Madisonian 'enlightened statesmen' but may still win re-election. Populist members of parliament often embody the extreme version of this delegate model of representation. MPs belonging to the *Five Star Movement* in Italy have been pressured to conform to the policy indications voted on by militants of the movement on a website named 'Rousseau'. Although this practice runs contrary to Article 67 of the Constitution of Italy,[82] it has not been legally challenged thus far, perhaps also because the downturn of the electoral fortunes of the Movement in 2020 has loosened the grip of the leadership on the parliamentary group. Anticipatory representation is by definition beyond the reach of second-mandate presidents, but is widely practiced among members of parliament.

The point, however, is that even when propelled into office by wide, and even in the unlikely case that they interpret their mandate as enjoining them to act as Burkean, gyroscopic trustees who pursue the common good by relying on their own judgment and without craving external rewards, elective heads of the executive branch and members of parliament understand the temporal span of the 'good of the whole polity' as encompassing their term in office or, at most, the present historical juncture.

The people, instead, has a much more extensive temporal existence, often several generations and in some illustrious cases a historical span of centuries. The good of

---

[81] On this point, see Bruce Ackerman, *The Decline and Fall of the American Republic* (Harvard University Press 2010) 24–28.

[82] 'Each Member of Parliament represents the Nation and carries out his duties without a binding mandate', Article 67 of the Constitution of Italy.

the whole polity *at a given point in time*, then, cannot be assumed to be automatically equivalent to the good of the entire people in its transgenerational existence. Although nothing in principle prevents top executive officials and members of parliament from voicing a 'representative claim' to the effect that they represent the people as such, in its historical full extension, usually these claims are little more than propaganda pitches that occasionally usher in catastrophe—as was the case with Hitler's claim to represent the German people and not just a majority of voters. At certain special junctures, heads of government may rise to represent constituencies larger than the present electorate—Roosevelt during the New Deal, Churchill during the Second World War, Kohl at the time of the reunification of Germany. Ordinary language reserves the terms 'statesmen' to signal that special stature. However, failure to rise to that exceptional status does not amount to failing the mandate. If we remember and honour the exceptions, that's evidence for the existence of a rule that points in a different direction.

Because of the possibility that the *majority of the voters* may, at some point, favour policies that run against the guarantees, rights, and entitlements that the historical *majority of the people* intended to grant to all free and equal citizens of the polity, regardless of the historical time when they happened to live, then that 'will of the (transgenerational) people', as distinct from the will of the voters, must be represented as well. Who should represent it? Contrary to what has been suggested by political constitutionalists, the assessment of the alignment of the will of the voters with the will of the broader people cannot be left for the voters and their direct representatives to determine. The latter would then act as judges in their own cause.[83] The people must be represented by some other institution.

Different solutions have been and could in principle be envisaged for solving this problem, but within contemporary constitutional democracies the function of representing the people has most frequently been understood as a high, supreme, or constitutional court's mandate of interpreting the people's will, as registered in a constitutional document. Other institutional possibilities could exist (eg a permanent constitutional assembly),[84] and in the next subsection Samuel Freeman's interesting proposal for repositioning constitutional courts outside the judicial branch will be engaged. However, this is a complex subject that deserves a dedicated monograph. For my present purpose of outlining a political-liberal understanding of how the transgenerational people, endowed with democratic sovereignty, should properly relate to the living segments of voting citizens, that issue will be bracketed and the mandate of representing the people will be discussed *as though* by default it were the prerogative of a high, supreme, or constitutional court.

Having said this, what kind of principal is represented by a constitutional court? The people is a principal that includes three distinct segments. In relation to its *future* generations, a court can only play the role of a trustee of their best interests and not

---

[83] For an argument in defence of vesting legislatures with the prerogative to self-monitor the constitutionality of their legislation, see Jeremy Waldron, 'Legislatures Judging in their own Cause' (2009) 3(1) Legisprudence 125.

[84] For a discussion of this possibility in relation to the EU, see Markus Patberg, *Constituent Power in the European Union* (Oxford University Press 2020), 197–214.

of a delegate. In relation to *past* generations, a court can play the role of interpreter of their constitutional will, as expressed in the constitution. The people, however, also includes the *presently living* generations, and a court should also represent their constitutional will, though not exclusively, as the other institutional actors may legitimately do. Typically, populist forces urge constitutional courts to act as delegates of the present generations, but when courts position themselves in that role, they fall short of fulfilling other aspects of their mandate.

As illustrated in Chapter 2, the Conseil Constitutionnel of France, when asked to pronounce on the constitutionality of the referendum of October 1962, convened by President de Gaulle for the purpose of making the presidential office elected by popular vote, argued that it could not review the constitutionality of measures adopted by referendum, because a referendum 'constitutes the direct expression of national sovereignty'.[85] The court depicted itself as a delegate of the living segment of the people, expressing its will in a referendum. Interpreting the mandate of representing the people in quite a different way, the Supreme Court of India articulated the doctrine of the 'basic structure' of the constitution. Within a constitutional order that attributes constituent power to Parliament (Article 368), allows it to amend the Constitution with a majority vote of each House on the condition that at least two-thirds of the members are present, and identifies no matter as beyond amendability, in the landmark case *Kesavananda Bharati Sripadagalvaru v State of Kerala* ((1973) 4 SCC 225), the Court, with a tight majority vote, established that the amending power, as invested in the legislators elected by the voters, should be interpreted as the power to modify, but not to disfigure, the normative core of the Constitution, its so-called basic structure—which includes

> (1) the supremacy of the Constitution; (2) republican and democratic form of Government and sovereignty of the country; (3) secular and federal character of the Constitution; (4) demarcation of power between the legislature, the executive and the judiciary; (5) the dignity of the individual [...]; (6) the unity and the integrity of the nation.[86]

The Supreme Court of India acted as a trustee of the people of India vis-à-vis the voters who elected the Parliament. It subsequently intervened again to consolidate its own role of trustee of the Indian people by interpreting the Constitution as prohibiting parliamentary overrule of the Supreme Court's pronouncement of unconstitutionality.[87]

---

[85] Bruce Ackerman, *Revolutionary Constitutions* Bruce Ackerman, *Revolutionary Constitutions. Charismatic Leadership and the Rule of Law* (Harvard University Press 2019)192.

[86] *Kesavananda Bharati Sripadagalvaru v State of Kerala* ((1973) 4 SCC 225), § 620, 150.

[87] In *Minerva Mills Ltd v Union of India* (1980 AIR 1789), the Supreme Court of India reaffirmed and extended the doctrine of the Basic Structure, when it declared unconstitutional sections 4 and 55 of the Constitution (Forty-second Amendment) Act 1976, voted by the majority of Indira Gandhi. The Congressional amendment asserted the possibility for the legislature to overrule the Court's pronouncements and to reaffirm a constitutional amendment declared unconstitutional by the Court. The Court's new pronouncement denied that the lack of explicit limitations imposed by the Constitution onto the constituent power of Parliament to amend the Constitution could allow misrepresenting the meaning of 'amending power' as including also the power to subvert, repeal, destroy, or alter the 'basic and essential features' of the Constitution.

In so acting the Court exercised its own judgment as a Burkean trustee of the people, no less than the Supreme Court of the United States did in *Marbury v Madison* (1803) when it claimed the right to review legislation for compliance with the Constitution,[88] and later the Courts of Colombia and Taiwan.[89]

Second, the entwinement of temporality and the people enjoins us to consider not only which institution should represent the people and which the voters, but also to reflect on the different ways in which a high, supreme, or constitutional court could fulfil its mandate of 'representing the people'. These different ways do not derive from the disjunctions evidenced by Rehfeld. After all, a court cannot choose to rely on the people's *explicit* judgment because the only judgment that can be actively expressed is that of the living segment of the people. Thus, it must rely on its own interpretation of the people's judgment as inscribed in the constitutional document and its amendments, and can only metaphorically rely on external incentives, mainly of a reputational nature, because they can only come from future generations, not from the present one, lest we fall back into the aberration of a 'delegate' court.

In order to distinguish the different ways in which the court can exercise its trusteeship, we can draw on Michelman's reflection on three facets of a court's relation to its mandate. A court may execute its representative function in a *quiescent* or *activist* mode: in the first case a court will tend 'to narrow the range of social disputes on which [it] will see fit to pronounce in the constitution's name'.[90] An *activist* court, on the contrary, will tend to publicly articulate the point of view of 'the people', as derivable from interpreting the constitution, much more frequently, in the most extreme case every time the legislative power expresses the will of the electorate through statutes of large consequence.

Furthermore, a constitutional court may represent the people with *tolerance* or with *assertiveness* vis-à-vis the representatives of the voters. Tolerance, in Michelman's terminology, refers to a court's willingness to provisionally abstain from imposing (often by a majority vote) onto the electorate its own vision of the 'most reasonable' among a plurality of balance-judgments concerning basic liberties and rights, provided that the competing balance-judgments—favoured by legislative and executive institutions or by associations of citizens—pass the threshold of being at least reasonable.[91] Assertiveness, instead, refers to a propensity for closure and to an institutional impatience with pronouncements, on the part of the branches that reflect the opinion of the voters, when such pronouncements and orientations fall short of 'most-reasonableness', though largely remaining within the range of the at least reasonable.

---

[88] *Marbury v Madison* (1803), 5 US 137. On Justice Marshall's argument for deducing the power of judicial review from Section 2 of Article Three of the Constitution of the United States, see Alexander Bickel, *The Least Dangerous Branch: The Supreme Court at the Bar of Politics* (first published 1962, 2nd edn Yale University Press 1986) 4–14.
[89] For a discussion of the doctrine of the Supreme Court of India and later of the Courts of Colombia (2003) and Taiwan, see Richard Albert, *Constitutional Amendments: Making, Breaking, and Changing Constitutions* (Oxford University Press 2019) 151–56.
[90] Frank Michelman, 'Political-Liberal Legitimacy and the Question of Judicial Restraint' (2019) 1 Jus Cogens 61.
[91] ibid 72.

Finally, the court's representative role can be exercised in a *weak form* if the constitutional provisions render the court's pronouncements not ultimately binding for the other branches, but simply authoritative intimations to reconsider the contested matter. This weak form of judicial review falls short of satisfying the requirement, embedded in Rawls's liberal principle of legitimacy, that constitutional essentials, if fixed beyond uncertainty, function as benchmarks of legitimacy. In full coherence with the political liberal paradigm, however, Michelman has ingeniously suggested the possibility of approximating the un-occlusiveness of weak-form judicial review by acting on the *temporal* dimensions of the role of the court as the people's trustee: 'case-bound determinations of constitutional meanings and applications from an undoubtedly strong-form court need not take full and legal control from the instant of their first utterance'.[92] A convenient time span between the 'first utterance' of a pronouncement and its final binding effect, in combination with attitudes of *quiescence* and *tolerance* on the part of the court, may provide a chance for a constitutional dialogue with the other branches and offer an instrument more flexible than amending the constitution for minimizing the risk of judicial occlusion of the democratic will.

Michelman's suggestion opens up a new perspective on an old issue. By definition the role of a high, constitutional or supreme court as representative of the transgenerational people may generate a tense relation of the court with the institutions that normally, though not exclusively, represent the will of the voters or the electorate. However, by distinguishing different dimensions of the trustee quality of the court's representative role and different ways of playing that role we can, along with Michelman, identify ways of allaying that tension as far as possible.

A quiescent and tolerant court that injects a large temporal gap, possibly measured in years, between the time when a question of constitutional salience emerges and the final choice of one among its alternative answers as 'the most reasonable'—a choice which ultimately, and consistently with the paradigm of political liberalism, cannot but rest with the representatives of the transgenerational people—is a court that allows for the most fruitful possible dialogue between the people and the electorate and minimizes the risk of unnecessarily occluding the democratic will of the voters.

b. Judicial review as representing the transgenerational people

The strategy of conceptualizing the difference between representing either the people or its pro-tempore living segment as a diverse relation of time and representation allows us to fine-tune one aspect of political liberalism most in need of further elaboration in the present historical context. In 'Constitutional Democracy and the Legitimacy of Judicial Review',[93] Samuel Freeman argues that the practice of judicial review can be defended in terms of a social-contract theory of democracy. Drawing on Rousseau, the gist of Freeman's argument is that the founding of a democratic polity should be conceived as a two-step process.

---

[92] ibid 71.
[93] Samuel Freeman, 'Constitutional Democracy and the Legitimacy of Judicial Review' (1990) 9/4 Law and Philosophy 327 (hereafter Freeman, 'Constitutional Democracy').

In the first stage, a commitment is made to a constitutional pact that can preserve the initial freedom and equality of the consociates and then, after that pact is accepted, the consociates may want to establish a procedure of judicial review designed to safeguard them in the future against the erosion of their sovereignty, rights, freedom, and equal status by the ordinary functioning of the institutional order that they are going to set in place. Thus the 'counter-majoritarian' aspect of judicial review is not antidemocratic, according to Freeman, because the practice reflects a 'pre-commitment' of the democratic sovereign, no less than Ulysses being kept tied to the mast by his crew reflects a pre-commitment freely made by himself not to give in to the siren song.[94]

In Freeman's words, judicial review

> is the device that free and sovereign persons might rationally agree to and impose, in light of their general knowledge of social conditions, as a constraint upon majority legislative processes, to protect the equal basic rights that constitute democratic sovereignty. Judicial review limits the extent of the exercise of equal rights of political participation through ordinary legislative procedures. Since it invokes a non-legislative means to do this, it may well be a constitutional measure of last resort. But this does not imply that it is undemocratic. For it is not a limitation upon equal sovereignty, but upon ordinary legislative power in the interest of protecting the equal rights of democratic sovereignty.[95]

This understanding of judicial review presupposes a 'political liberal' version of the distinction of constituent and constituted power and a dualistic view of democracy as the conjunction of procedures that ensure (i) equal participation of all citizens in the formation of the communal will (majority rule being the best institutional solution to ensure that outcome), and (ii) equal protection of every citizen's constitutional rights and share of sovereignty from being curtailed by majoritarian legislation. The second function, integral to the idea of a *constitutional* democracy, needs to be entrusted to some institutional procedure, and judicial review is one of these procedures.

These two functions are assigned to specific institutions by constituent power. Legislative authority is 'a delegated power of government, to be exercised by representatives in accordance with constitutional conditions and for the good of each citizen. As delegated, it is an ordinary power of government, not to be confused with the constituent power that creates it'.[96] Legislative authority is but one of several separated powers and gives then rise to the need for an 'authoritative interpretation of the constitution in order to coordinate these diverse powers and resolve persistent disputes, avoid conflicting demands from being placed on citizens' conduct, and insure that constitutional forms are being respected and adhered to by the ordinary powers of government'.[97]

---

[94] For two diverse critical appraisals of Freeman's argument, see Zurn, *Deliberative Democracy* (n 4) 131–41 and Jeremy Waldron, 'Freeman's Defense of Judicial Review' (1994) 13 Law and Philosophy.
[95] Freeman, 'Constitutional Democracy' (n 93) 353.
[96] ibid 357.
[97] ibid.

Then the mandate of a supreme or constitutional court is described by Freeman as 'distinct from the ordinary powers of the legislative, judicial and executive functions'. This final power

> is also a delegated and institutional power, and is not to be confused with either the ordinary powers of government or with ultimate constitutional authority, which always resides in the sovereign body politic. Somewhat like institutional procedures for amending the constitution and a bill of rights, the final authority of interpretation might be seen as an institutional expression of the constituent power of sovereign citizens.[98]

Freeman's account of judicial review includes an aspect which needs further consideration. From the twin assumptions (i) that the separation of powers vests the power to interpret the law in the judiciary and (ii) that the constitution is the fundamental law, Freeman argues, one cannot derive the conclusion that offering a final interpretation of the constitution is a function of the judicial power—as Hamilton suggests in n 78 of *The Federalist Papers* or as stated in the Supreme Court's opinion in *Marbury v Madison*. This unwarranted conclusion obscures the fact that

> the constitution of a political regime is not just so much more ordinary law for courts to interpret. It is rather the highest order system of rules for making those institutional rules that are recognized as ordinary laws.... Nothing is law, and no institution has any powers, except as it accords with the constitution. And there is nothing about the ordinary powers of courts granted under the constitutional separation of powers that would grant to the judiciary (or any other branch) the authority to interpret those exceptional rules that constitute the three powers of government and assign to them their ordinary powers.[99]

Drawing on Rousseau's theory of the 'tribunate'—an institution entrusted with protecting the sovereignty of the people from its constant erosion by government[100]—Freeman argues for a constitutional court separate from the ordinary judicial system. The supreme function of interpreting the constitution, according to him, is 'not a peculiarly judicial power; it is rather the exercise of a conserving power. Whoever exercises this final authority acts as the conservator of the constitution'.[101]

This line of thinking implies a rejection of the idea that judicial review is antidemocratic because it is countermajoritarian. The flaws in that idea will be the object of closer scrutiny below.[102] To follow Freeman's argument for the time being, there is no single ingredient of the democratic rule of law (be it accountability, majority rule, equal participation, etc) that by itself exhausts the meaning of democracy, but for judicial review to count as 'antidemocratic' a balanced judgment that takes all these and

---

[98] ibid.
[99] ibid 358–59.
[100] See Rousseau, *Social Contract* (n 44) Book IV, Ch V, 128–30.
[101] Freeman, 'Constitutional Democracy' (n 93) 359.
[102] See Chapter 6, Section 1.

other aspects into account is required. Furthermore, adverse judicial review resulting in the unconstitutionality of a statute is only a 'pro-tempore' final pronouncement. Nearly all constitutions embed provisions for amending the text, usually on the basis of a supermajority. Judicial review is then not a final unappealable verdict but simply a shifting of the majority bar, for realizing the will of the electorate, a notch higher than simple majority.[103]

However, although it ingeniously avoids the foundationalist trap of naturalizing fundamental rights or positing them as externally binding on the sovereign democratic will, Freeman's political liberal defence of judicial review ends up conveying a disputable understanding of the temporal relation of the people as author of the constitution and the living segment of it. Questioning all originalist approach to constitutional interpretation and questioning the idea that the written Constitution may silence the 'material' or 'living' constitution, Freeman writes:

> Our forebears' intentions can be of little relevance to constitutional interpretation in a democracy. For it is now *our* constitution; *we* now exercise constituent power and *cannot be bound by our ancestors' commitments*. Only *our* intentions, as free and equal sovereign citizens, are then relevant in assessing the constitution and assigning a role to the document that bears that name. And we cannot do this without ultimately looking to the requirements of a just democratic constitution.[104]

This statement deserves closer inspection, because it casts light on the central opposition of a *serial* and a *sequential* understanding of popular democratic sovereignty—an opposition that allows us to lay bare the unexpectedly deep roots of contemporary populism.

In unwitting consonance with political constitutionalists and other adversaries of judicial review, Freeman envisages the relation that binds the succeeding generations of a people along *serial* lines. Just as the subsequent owners of a piece of property—be it real estate or simply an automobile—exert their entitlement to use and dispose of the property as they please, with no obligation whatsoever to have their use of the property fit or comport with the use to which the same piece of property was put by the previous owners, likewise when our ancestors' constitution finally becomes *our* constitution, we are free to make it reflect our sovereign will. To be sure, the simultaneously living generations of the people—the voters or the electorate—are supposedly bound, no less than all the previous and the future generations, by 'the requirements of a just democratic constitution'. However, this common point of reference, valid for all generations, appears to be too thin, abstract, and subject to divergent interpretations to prevent wide oscillations, across generations, of the way in which the requirements of a just democratic constitution, once duly considered, are then actually translated into law.

Conceiving popular sovereignty as exercised *serially* by each living segment of a people, as opposed to considering it exercised *sequentially* by all free and equal

---

[103] See Freeman, 'Constitutional Democracy' (n 93) 362–64. The same point is made by Rawls, *PL* 237–38.
[104] Freeman, 'Constitutional Democracy' (n 93) 370 (emphasis added).

generations of a transgenerational people, leads to the impossibility of blocking three deeply problematic implications. But before exploring these implications, which by themselves establish the case for the competing sequential conception of popular sovereignty, it might be worth reconstructing the genealogy of the serial or proprietary view.

c. Three flaws of serial sovereignty

Serial democratic sovereignty has an illustrious pedigree. In Chapter 2, an important tributary to the imposing flow-rate of the populist stream was traced to the serial understanding of popular sovereignty *implicitly* taken for granted by Rousseau and Sieyès. Both understood the generations of the people or the nation as severally possessed of the full right to reshape entirely 'the present form of government', without any normative limits other than formal presuppositions or natural law. Certainly, no limits rooted in extant constitutional provisions or other legal constraints stemming from the previous generations' will were thought to apply, for they would detract from the present generation's sovereignty. At the end of the eighteenth century some *explicit* theories of serial sovereignty were articulated, among others, by Condorcet, Thomas Jefferson, and Tom Paine.

In 1789 Condorcet raised the question 'How could humans possibly be equals in rights, how could the law be the expression of the general will, if children were forced to submit themselves to the constitutions that their grand-fathers would have written?',[105] and in a famous letter of the same year to James Madison, Thomas Jefferson made the same point in a much more detailed argument. Addressing the question 'Whether one generation has a right to bind another', Jefferson starts out with the transmissibility of proprietary rights over generations. Being 'self-evident' that 'the earth belongs in usufruct to the living'[106] and that 'the dead have neither powers not rights over it', Jefferson argues that the portion of the earth possessed and occupied by each human being returns in possession of society upon his or her death. Inheritance rights are positive rights, created by society, not natural rights. In the absence of appropriate legislation, the land of the deceased can be 'taken by the first occupants'.[107]

Similarly, considering the property of an aggregate population of individuals, if Louis XIV and Louis XV had hypothetically 'contracted debts in the name of the French nation to the amount of 10,000 milliards of livres',[108] loaned by Genoan bankers, and if they had negotiated that such amount be paid back after nineteen years, would the subsequent generation be under the obligation to honour the debt incurred by their predecessors? Jefferson's answer is clear-cut: 'Not at all'.[109] Once again, the belief that the inheritance of an estate is conditional upon paying the deceased's

---

[105] Condorcet, M de, August 30, 1789. *Lettre de M de Condorcet à M le compte Mathieu de Montmorency.* see https://gallica.bnf.fr/ark:/12148/bpt6k41732k/f12.item.texteImage, accessed 6 February 2021.
[106] Thomas Jefferson, *The Portable Thomas Jefferson*. Edited by Merrill D Peterson (Penguin 1977), 445 (hereafter Jefferson, *Letter to Madison*).
[107] ibid.
[108] ibid 447.
[109] ibid 448.

debts rests on a 'municipal', not natural, obligation, not binding beyond convention. Thus, the descendants of the French subjects of Louis XIV and XV would not be obliged to repay the debt to the Genoan bankers. These property-related examples pave the way to Jefferson's case against the *sequential* or 'perpetual constitution':

> On similar ground it may be proved that no society can make a perpetual constitution, or even a perpetual law. The earth belongs always to the living generation. They may manage it then, and what proceeds from it, as they please, during their usufruct. They are masters too of their own persons, and consequently may govern them as they please. But persons and property make the sum of the objects of government. The constitution and the laws of their predecessors extinguished then in their natural course with those who gave them being.... Every constitution then, and every law, naturally expires at the end of 19 years. If it be enforced longer, it is an act of force, and not of right.[110]

A similar point is made in 1791 by Tom Paine in his pamphlet *Rights of Man*:

> The parliament or the people of 1688, or of any other period, had no more right to dispose of the people of the present day, or to bind or to control them in any shape whatever, than the parliament or the people of the present day have to dispose of, bind or control those who are to live a hundred or a thousand years hence. Every generation is, and must be, competent to all the purposes which its occasions require. It is the living, and not the dead, that are to be accommodated. When man ceases to be, his power and his wants cease with him; and having no longer any participation in the concerns of this world, he has no longer any authority in directing who shall be its governors, or how its government shall be organized, or how administered.[111]

The proprietary or serial view of sovereignty—based on the idea that each segment of the people is a separate 'owner' of democratic sovereignty and therefore fully exercises 'pro-tempore constitutional authorship'—may give rise to, or in any event is not in a position to block, three consequences that undermine its normative cogency. Let me call them the 'wanton republic', the 'indistinct republic', and the 'underdetermined republic'.

Concerning 'the wanton republic', imagine a democratic polity over a span of six generations, say roughly 200 years. Imagine that Generation 1, as a founding generation, ratifies a constitution that establishes a basic structure similar to that of the United States. Generation 2 then abolishes the presidency in order to create a Westminster-style parliamentary system, with a cabinet and a prime minister voted in by Congress. Generation 3 abolishes the Senate while retaining a now monocameral parliamentary system. Generation 4 returns to bicameralism and establishes a plurality of Christian churches. Generation 5 restores the presidency but abolishes again the Senate and disestablishes religion while constitutionalizing social rights within the

---

[110] ibid 449.
[111] Tom Paine 'Rights of Man' (1791) in Philip Foner (ed) *The Life and Major Writings of Tom Paine* (Citadel 1961) 251.

basic structure. Generation 6, finally, returns to bicameralism but abolishes once again the presidency in favour or a parliamentary regime and de-constitutionalizes social rights but instead constitutionalizes proportional representation.

Nothing in the model of serial sovereignty allows us to raise doubts about the legitimacy of this polity, which in fact levels down the regulatory function of the constitution to a virtual null point. The constitution has become just the reflection of the preferences of each of the six generations. Recall what Aristotle said of the polis in which the assembly is swayed by the demagogues to the point that its decrees only last the time that their motivating political sentiment persists.[112] Similarly, this 'wanton republic' also, strictly speaking, no longer has a constitution. Because it fails to project any trans-contextual cogency, higher law becomes indistinguishable from ordinary law and indeed from prevailing sentiment: in order to avoid a so-called tyranny of the past, the serial model of sovereignty makes the polity fall prey to the 'tyranny of the momentary political sentiment'. Thus, serial sovereignty ends up undermining the very idea of a constitution.

Along similar lines James Madison objected, in his reply to Jefferson:

> Would not a Government so often revised become too mutable to retain those prejudices in its favor which antiquity inspires, and which are perhaps a salutary aid to the most rational Government in the most enlightened age? Would not such a periodical revision engender pernicious factions that might not otherwise come into existence? Would not, *in fine*, a Government depending for its existence beyond a fixed date, on some positive and authentic intervention of the Society itself, be too subject to the casualty and consequences of an actual interregnum?[113]

Serial sovereignty models of the relation of the people to their constitution have a serious difficulty in helping us grasp why these extreme forms of cross-generational iterative discontinuity would reflect negatively on legitimacy.

There are two separate components to this projected negative impact of possible discontinuity on political legitimacy. On one hand, a constitution is the symbolic vehicle of the *political* identity of a people; it enshrines the 'political ideal of a people to govern itself in a certain way' or, in other words, the sense of who we are, politically. 'Political' though it may be, such identity functions like *any* identity: a patterned cluster of flexible qualities that relate to a normative, definitional core which, though not unchangeable, changes much less than the more peripheral aspects of the identity. When the core or basic structure is unstable, as in our example, that instability detracts from the coherence, and thereby from the overall quality, that *any* felicitous identity, political or non-political, must possess in order to demarcate itself from what does not belong within its precinct.[114] The 'non-perpetual constitution' imposes that cost on

---

[112] See Chapter 1, n 87, above.

[113] *The Papers of James Madison*. Edited by William T Hutchinson et al (University of Chicago Press 1962–77) Volume 1, Chapter 2, Document 24 http://press-pubs.uchicago.edu/founders/documents/v1ch2 s24.html.

[114] To cast this point in terms of 'self-constitution', the commitments through which a subject (be it an individual or a *demos*) defines itself: (i) cannot be logically inconsistent or even empirically incompatible, without detracting from the fulfilment of such identity, relative to an identity shaped by commitments consistent 'over time'; and (ii) cannot, even if not inconsistent or incompatible, fail to add up to an intelligible

the self-constituted people. On the other hand, with a thorough institutional reconfiguration of the basic structure taking place as each segment of the people amends the constitution in accordance with its preferences, the constitution would forfeit its regulatory function and would be reduced to a projection of the pro-tempore popular sovereign's inclinations. The wanton republic that a serial understanding of popular sovereignty may fail to block would merely have a nominal constitution with null regulatory force and would consequently lack not only stability—as Madison points out—but also a recognizable political identity properly recognizable *over time*.[115]

Two objections can be raised against this criticism of 'serial sovereignty'. A transgenerational cogency of the constitution is what Jefferson rejects, so holding its lack of regulatory function against the non-perpetual constitution is at best a purely external criticism. Secondly, constitutions change all the time, over and beyond being formally amended, because their necessarily general provisions speak to us only when duly interpreted, and their interpreted meaning changes with the historical situatedness of their authoritative judicial interpreter. One dramatic instance of change by slippage of meaning (discussed below in Chapter 7, Section 3.d) is offered by the modification of the earlier understanding of the Second Amendment to the Constitution of the United States as a collective right to form a militia in order to resist all forms of tyranny, to the later and contemporary understanding of it as an individual right to 'keep and bear arms' for protecting one's own person, family, and property. On account of this ubiquitous slippage of the meaning of constitutional provisions, then, it would be unfair to hold lack of regulatory force against the 'non-perpetual constitution'.[116] In response to the first objection, while it is true that the transgenerational regulatory function is excluded by Jefferson from those that a constitution should perform, nonetheless his usage of the term arguably commits him to the assumption that a constitution is distinct from ordinary law and its point is (though not exclusively) to regulate what ordinary law may prescribe or prohibit— only the proper time frame of such regulatory function being contested. The critique of the serial model of sovereignty calls into question that nexus of 'non-perpetuity' and distinctness from ordinary law: the constitution cannot be meaningfully held to outrank ordinary law if ordinary law can outlast the constitution and possibly offer the benchmark for amending the constitution.

---

answer to the question 'what political ideal do we want to govern ourselves by?'. To be sure, one could conceive of identities centred around a commitment to accommodating as much diversity as possible, on the basis of some libertarian programme or of some post-structuralist philosophy of difference. But such move would indirectly corroborate the point: the individual self or body politic that chooses to accommodate as much diversity as possible and to try out over time as many 'constitutional projects' as possible *is* indeed constituting itself around a central normative core, that is, the desirability of opening up the identity (individual or political) to as much synchronic and diachronic variation as possible. On this point, see Alessandro Ferrara, 'Authenticity Without a True Self' in Philip Vannini and J Patrick Williams (eds) *Authenticity in Culture, Self, and Society* (Ashgate 2009) 31–33.

[115] See 'Introduction', above, n 2.
[116] I'm indebted to Steven L Winter for having brought these two objections to my attention. He would not necessarily agree with my response to them. On the slippage of legal meanings and its impact on the application of provisions, see his *A Clearing in the Forest: Law, Life, and Mind* (University of Chicago Press 2001) 186–222.

In response to the second objection, a comparison with language will illustrate my rejoinder. Languages too, no less than legal orders and constitutions, are in constant flow. It has been said by Jack Balkin, in a sense elucidated in the next chapter, that 'you cannot step into the same Constitution twice'.[117] Much in the same way, it could be argued that you never speak the same language twice, because the frequency of the words and the positional value of their meaning in relation to one another changes and some speaker may borrow some new word from another language or introduce some new manner of speaking. However, this is the descriptive point of view of an *observer* of linguistic facts. From the point of view of an active *participant* in a system of rules—be they linguistic or legal—this undeniable fact does not eliminate the need to choose among alternatives, which may or may not fall within the range of acceptability. The ongoing transformation of spoken languages does not change the basic normative assumption that at any time competent native speakers attribute grammaticality or ungrammaticality to any given sentence, with some relatively small area of undecided cases. Similarly, even if an observer could describe the constitution as constantly evolving (as the metaphor of 'the living constitution' suggests) due to the sum total of interpretive acts that affect the meaning of its provisions, nonetheless it is usually not considered a futile exercise for a supreme or constitutional court to say what the most reasonable interpretation of the constitution is. If that exercise is not deemed futile, that corroborates the conclusion that the evolution of the living constitution no more undermines the sensibleness of the regulatory function of the constitution than the constant evolution of a natural language undermines the sensibleness of the attempt to reconstruct its grammar.

Concerning the rise of 'the indistinct republic' as a possible consequence of serial sovereignty, imagine two neighbouring polities with intense economic, social, and cultural exchanges, as for example France and Italy. Assume that one of these is the wanton republic described above. If each generation is completely unbound by the commitment of the preceding ones, why should Generations 5 and 6, for example, relate to Generations 1 and 2 as *their* political predecessors in any closer sense than they relate to the Generations 1 and 2 of the neighbouring polity? Later generations will feel equally unbound by the commitments of the citizens that have preceded them. Whatever greater closeness Generation 6 can feel with respect to Generation 1 of *their* polity will not originate by Generation 6's and Generation 1's sharing a *political* identity, but merely by their sharing an ethnic or cultural one. If we, as the living segment of our people, feel no more bound by *our* ancestors' commitments than by the commitments underwritten by the previous generations of other polities, then our own democratic polity—regardless whether its basic structure happens to be renewed or not renewed as it randomly pleases the will of the living citizens—fails 'over time' to demarcate itself from the other neighbouring polity in any sense attributable to anything other than happenstance.

After all, Jefferson did not shy away from acknowledging that 'by the law of nature, one generation is to another as one independant nation to another'.[118] If there is no closer relation of a generation to its own, as opposed to other people's

---

[117] See Chapter 6, n 53.
[118] Jefferson, *Letter to Madison* (n 106) 448.

ancestors, the serial republic—the product of 'generational federalism' rather than of transgenerational constitutional authorship—is irreparably indistinct. It fails to be individuated *along political lines*.

What's wrong with indistinctness? If the citizens are not able to develop any sense of being somehow—as Habermas once felicitously put it—'in the same boat as their forebears'[119] in relation to a transgenerational democratic project, then their identification with their forebears can develop only along *ethnic* lines, with all the dangers thereto associated, but not in terms of the Rawlsian 'political ideal of a people to govern itself in a certain way'. Serial sovereignty breeds and indirectly sustains the ethnicization of collective identity. It doesn't matter that a *demos* may *draw inspiration* from the 'political ideal' of a previous constitution-making actor, as the case might be with the Athenian polis and the Roman republic functioning as sources of identification for the American and French framers. The feeling of being inspired by such exemplary models is different from that of feeling bound by commitments made by predecessors with whom we want to be in the same constitutional boat.[120]

Finally, the serial understanding of democratic sovereignty contributes to generating 'the underdetermined republic'. Because it lacks a distinction between the constituent power to enact the constitution and the subsequent power to amend it, the serial view leaves the democratic polity vulnerable to the risk that the diverse generations of the same *demos* might come to be possessed of very different degrees of freedom. A clarification is here in order. From an empirical point of view, it is certainly true that the different generations of a people may enjoy different degrees of freedom. New rights, new interpretations of previously established rights, or new principles and standards may be introduced, resulting in dimensions of freedom unknown to previous generations of citizens. That said, prolonged emergencies in the areas of security, health, the economy, or climate may necessitate measures that reduce the freedom and rights of certain cohorts of citizens. From a normative point of view, however, there is something counterintuitive in the idea of a legitimate constitutional amendment designed to make future generations less free than the present ones. Even when certain prerogatives are intentionally curtailed—for example, when an amendment inserts in the constitution the requirement of a balanced budget, thereby abridging the future voters' freedom to support debt-creating policies—still the legitimacy of the new provision must rest on its serving the purpose of *equalizing* the spending capacity of all the generations, present and future.

It is counterintuitive, from a democratic point of view, that some generations of citizens may become less equal than others due to the unnecessitated, intentional, and unbridled exercise of amending power by preceding generations. Serial views of democratic sovereignty, through their empowering the presently living citizens to reshape the constitution according to their orientations and preferences, fail to offer a normative safeguard against such vulnerability.

Going back to Freeman's account, a constitutional court, as 'conservator of the constitution', must represent the *entire* multi-generational people, without letting the

---

[119] See Jürgen Habermas, 'Constitutional Democracy—A Paradoxical Union of Contradictory Principles?' (2001) 29(6) Political Theory 775.
[120] Again, I thank Steven L Winter for having prompted this reflection through one of his objections.

constitutional agency of the past generations evaporate as the commitments of the presently living segment of the people emerge and prevail. In the latter case, the 'conservator of the constitution' would risk turning into a delegate of the electorate, as opposed to a trustee of the transgenerational people and of the integrity of its constitutional project. Consequently, the degree of political autonomy possessed by a generation of citizens could be severely curtailed by the lawmaking and constitution-amending of previous ones. If the 'political project' scripted in the constitution fails to fixate the autonomy and rights possessed by future generations of citizens, the republic becomes 'underdetermined'.

Alongside these three *normative* flaws, a different set of *empirical* flaws undermine the attractiveness and practicability of serial sovereignty. Already pointed out by contemporaries of Jefferson,[121] these flaws have been highlighted again in contemporary literature. Whether it includes a self-expiring constitution or simply leaves the constitution at the entire disposal of each generation, a serial understanding of democratic sovereignty undercuts the possibility of conceiving long-term political, institutional, and economic projects, including large-scale philanthropic endeavours, which require multi-generational stability. Thus, serial democratic sovereignty indirectly negatively affects the prosperity of the polity.[122] Over and beyond these empirical flaws, however, the three normative implications generated by the serial conception of democratic sovereignty—that in our times has become the normative core of right-wing and left-wing populism—are decisive for warranting its rejection in favour of a *sequential* view of the relation among succeeding generations of the same *demos*.

However, constructing the sequential view of popular sovereignty *ex negativo*, on the basis of rejecting serial sovereignty, will not suffice. A political-liberal constitutional theory built on *Political Liberalism* needs also to engage in a *pars construens*: it needs to outline the proper relation between the 'pro-tempore final' interpretation of the constitution offered by its 'conservator' and the amending power vested in the presently living citizens. The elucidation of this relation will be at the centre of the next two chapters.

---

[121] See James Madison, 'Letter to Thomas Jefferson' (4 February 1790) in PB Kurland and R Lerner (eds), *The Founders' Constitution* (University of Chicago Press 1986) 70–71.

[122] See Víctor Muñoz-Fraticelli, 'The Problem of a Perpetual Constitution' in Axel Gosseries and Lukas H Meyer (eds) *Intergenerational Justice* (Oxford University Press 2009) 386–87.

6
Representing 'the People' by Interpreting the Constitution

> The conversation between past commitments and present generations is at the heart of constitutional interpretation. That is why we do not face a choice between living constitutionalism and fidelity to the original meaning of the text. They are two sides of the same coin.
> (Jack Balkin, *Living Originalism* 20)

> I think that the distinction between enumerated and unenumerated rights... is bogus.
> (Ronald Dworkin, *Freedom's Law* 72)

In Chapter 5, the function of representing the people, as distinct from the function of representing the electorate, was discussed in relation to (i) the nature of the act of representing, as theorized by Pitkin and recent contributors; (ii) the diverse temporal dimensions of the people and the electorate; and (iii) the consequences of neglecting the distinction of people and electorate. It is now time to build on the suggested association of 'representing the people' and judicial review, and to consider the *justification*, the distinct *variants*, as well as the *standard of validity* applicable to judicial review.

1. The Democratic Legitimacy of Judicial Review Revisited

Before reconstructing what political liberalism can say about the function of representing the people by interpreting the constitution, we need to review the democratic credentials of judicial review. In *Political Liberalism* those credentials are simply taken for granted, but in view of the criticisms ongoingly levelled against them by populism and political constitutionalism, it is worthwhile to spell out the reasons why these objections leave the democratic standing of judicial review unscathed.

In contrast to several political constitutionalists' intimation of an intrinsic connection of judicial review with the supremacy of the judicial branch among the separated powers,[1] Rawls carefully separates the case for judicial review, fully endorsed by him,

---

[1] See, for example, Jeremy Waldron, *Law and Disagreement* (Oxford University Press 1999) 244 and 291 (hereafter Waldron, *Law and Disagreement*), and Richard Bellamy, *Political Constitutionalism: A Republican Defence of the Constitutionality of Democracy* (Cambridge University Press 2007) 40 (hereafter Bellamy, *Political Constitutionalism*).

from the notion of *judicial supremacy*, which he emphatically rejects.[2] His view is expressed in a passage where he writes

> A supreme court fits into this idea of dualist constitutional democracy as one of the institutional devices to protect the higher law. By applying public reason the court is to prevent that law from being eroded by the legislation of transient majorities, or more likely, by organized and well-situated narrow interests skilled at getting their way. If the court assumes this role and effectively carries it out, it is incorrect to say that it is straightforwardly antidemocratic.[3]

We need to elucidate the reasons why a supreme or constitutional court's discharging the role of preventing higher law from being eroded 'by the legislation of transient majorities, or more likely, by organized and well-situated narrow interests skilled at getting their way' is *not* anti-democratic.

Before doing so, it is worth clearing away a misleading attribution of the opposite view to Alexander Bickel, on account of his influential 'counter-majoritarian objection', articulated in *The Least Dangerous Branch*: 'when the Supreme Court declares unconstitutional a legislative act ... it thwarts the will of the representatives of *the actual people of the here and now* '.[4] Bickel's thesis amounts to the literal meaning of that famous sentence: primarily affected by the Supreme Court's pronouncing a legislative provision unconstitutional are 'the representatives of the actual people of the here and now', not the representatives of the people of the past, of the 'there and then', unless one assumes uncharitably that the sentence is slackly formulated or that the 'people of the here and now' are all that matters for democratic legitimacy. In fact, if freely reformulated in the light of the distinction of people and electorate, Bickel's dictum would run: 'when the Supreme Court declares unconstitutional a legislative act ... it represents the majority of the people, *qua* author of the constitution, thwarting the will of the representatives of *its living segment*'.

The thesis that judicial review is not just counter-majoritarian, but more thoroughly *anti-democratic* has been spelled out by Waldron and Tushnet. According to Waldron, 'by privileging majority voting among a small number of unelected and unaccountable judges, it disenfranchises ordinary citizens and brushes aside cherished principles of representation and political equality in the final resolution of issues about rights'.[5] Similarly, Richard Bellamy argues that

> talk of courts employing rights considerations to 'trump' legislative decisions seems misconceived if we consider that rights considerations have already figured in the legislature. For, can trumps trump trumps? True, the legislative decision may well have

---

[2] As Rawls puts it, 'the Constitution is not what the Court says it is. Rather, it is what the people acting constitutionally through the other branches eventually allow the Court to say it is', PL 237.
[3] ibid 233–34.
[4] Alexander Bickel, *The Least Dangerous Branch: The Supreme Court at the Bar of Politics* (first published 1962, 2nd edn Yale University Press 1986) 16–17 (emphasis added).
[5] Jeremy Waldron, 'The Core of the Case Against Judicial Review' (2006) 155 Yale Law Journal 1353 (hereafter Waldron, 'Against Judicial Review').

been taken by majority rule. But then, so may the court's.... In both cases, majority rule is a closure device for reaching a decision when all trumps have been played.[6]

Mark Tushnet opens one chapter of his *Taking the Constitution Away from the Courts* with an ingenious thought experiment: what would happen if the Supreme Court unilaterally decided to renounce its hard-won prerogative to review congressional legislation? He suggests that 'doing away with judicial review would have one clear effect: It would return all constitutional decision-making to the people acting politically',[7] as though the Supreme Court was not also representing the people, within a scheme of separated powers.

It must be specified that Waldron and Tushnet carefully distinguish *strong* and *weak* forms of judicial reviews, addressing their objections against *strong* forms only, which include a supreme or constitutional court's 'authority to decline to apply a statute in a particular case ... or to modify the effect of a statute to make its application conform with individual rights' or 'to establish as a matter of law that a given statute or legislative provision will not be applied', or even, in some jurisdictions, the authority 'to actually strike a piece of legislation out of the statute-book altogether'.[8] Both leave open the possibility of weak forms, and Tushnet actively explores different variants of that possibility.[9]

The case against judicial review, then, turns in the end on *one* pivotal point. Judicial review is anti-democratic because in settling disagreements about rights, which can be understood as the expectable product of the burdens of judgment, it groundlessly privileges—against the intuitive primacy of legislative institutions that represent the voters—the authority of a 'scholarly or judicial elite, on the ground that they are more likely to get the matter right'.[10] An *epistocratic* residue is here operative,[11] sometimes based on an unfair comparison of courts at their best, as fora of principle (Dworkin) and public reason (Rawls), and legislatures at their worst, as horse-trading market grounds for striking compromises. Instead, if both judicial and legislative institutions are compared at their best, people, when reasonably disagreeing about rights, 'need to adopt procedures for resolving their disagreements that respect the voices and opinions of the persons—in their millions—whose rights are at stake in these disagreements and treat them as equals in the process'.[12] Whereas there is no reason, except prejudice, to suppose that legislative institutions at their best cannot do this,

---

[6] Bellamy, *Political Constitutionalism* (n 1) 37–38.
[7] Mark Tushnet, *Taking the Constitution Away from the Courts* (Princeton University Press 1999) 154 (hereafter Tushnet, *Taking the Constitution Away*).
[8] Waldron, 'Against Judicial Review' (n 5) 1354. See also Tushnet, *Taking the Constitution Away* (n 7) 154–76. See also Kramer's definition of judicial review as 'the practice of regularly submitting constitutional disputes to judges for resolution in the context of ordinary legislation', Larry Kramer, *The People Themselves: Popular Constitutionalism and Judicial Review* (Oxford University Press 2004) 19.
[9] See Mark Tushnet, *Weak Courts, Strong Rights: Judicial Review and Social Welfare Rights in Comparative Constitutional Law* (Princeton University Press 2008) 18–42.
[10] Waldron, *Law and Disagreement* (n 1) 244.
[11] On this point see Cristina Lafont, *Democracy Without Shortcuts: A Participatory Conception of Deliberative Democracy* (Oxford University Press 2020) 221 (hereafter Lafont, *Democracy Without Shortcuts*).
[12] Waldron, 'Against Judicial Review' (n 5) 1346.

an additional layer of final review by courts adds little to the process except a rather insulting form of disenfranchisement and a legalistic obfuscation of the moral issues at stake in our disagreements about rights. Maybe there are circumstances—peculiar pathologies, dysfunctional legislative institutions, corrupt political cultures, legacies of racism and other forms of endemic prejudice—in which these costs of obfuscation and disenfranchisement are worth bearing for the time being. But defenders of judicial review ought to start making their claims for the practice frankly on that basis—and make it with a degree of humility and shame in regard to the circumstances that elicit it—rather than preaching it abroad as the epitome of respect for rights and as a normal and normatively desirable element of modern constitutional democracy.[13]

The questionable element in Waldron's critique of the loss of self-government generated by letting unelected courts assess legislation on rights concerns the correct identification of what he calls 'the persons—in their millions—whose rights are at stake in these disagreements' over the implications of legislative measures and who deserve being treated as equals. Who exactly are these persons? They cannot just be the contemporaries of those included in, and represented by, the legislative majority that approved the contested provisions. That over-restrictive identification would instantly make the rights exercised by past generations of citizens evaporate into irrelevance: those rights would no longer count in the equation, as though their bearers, no longer belonging to living generations, had thereby fallen outside the count of who belong to the self-governing people. Furthermore, that over-restrictive identification would empty out the relevance of the rights of unborn citizens and of minors, who are not represented in legislative institutions because they cannot yet vote.

Similarly to what we have observed in populism, Waldron's solution for settling reasonable disagreements about rights turns the living segment of the people—endowed with agency and franchise—into the sole arbiter of the implications of policies and statutes for rights. As it was the case with Freeman, a staunch advocate of judicial review, also Waldron, who instead militates among its critics, understands the constitution as owned exclusively by the living portion of the people, in a pattern of *serial sovereignty* potentially, though not necessarily, conducive to the 'wanton', the 'indistinct', or the 'underdetermined' republic.[14]

However, even when they concede that democratic sovereignty cannot sensibly be understood along serial lines, critics of judicial review often raise a counter-objection. Why couldn't legislative institutions represent the transgenerational people as well, and not only the electorate?

Two reasons suggest a negative answer. From an empirical point of view, it is unreasonable to expect that interests and claims that no longer result in votes, and thus in chances to rule the polity, or that will generate votes at such a later point in time, when the present protagonists will have left the scene, would carry as much weight, in the consideration of *present-day* representative bodies, as the interests and claims that *do* exert electoral influence.

---

[13] ibid.
[14] See above, Chapter 5, Section 3.c.

From a normative point of view, to have members of the legislative institutions represent both the will of the majority of the voters and the will of the constitution-making people as creator of the rights hypothetically encroached by the policies or measures under assessment would instantly turn the voters, and their direct representatives, into judges in their own cause—namely, in a case that concerns the consistency of their own will, *qua* voters, with the people's will.

Elsewhere Waldron has rebutted this critical objection by claiming that in matters of rights, as well as in matters of consequential decisions, such as breaking the electoral tie of *Bush v Gore, all citizens*—thus including the Justices of the Supreme Court—have a stake in the matter, not just the members of a legislature.[15] Consequently, Waldron argues, if legislatures are accused of infringing the *nemo judex* principle, courts are in no better position. Each Justice has a personal stake, as a citizen, in upholding a certain version of free speech as opposed to another, not to mention the political benefit, depending on his or her inclination, of breaking the electoral tie in favour of Al Gore or George W Bush.

The flaw in Waldron's rejoinder consists in his conflating two sets of interests that need to be distinguished: (i) having a *generic* stake in a clash of two rights or interests (ie a stake applicable to each and every citizen), and (ii) having a *group-specific* advantage to be obtained from the outcome. For example, members of legislative assemblies, both individually and as members of parties, could gain an electoral advantage from a decision about rights that Justices of the Supreme Court are in no position to obtain. The first kind of interest in a controversy over rights, insofar as it is an interest that *all* citizens individually have, constitutes no ground for excluding anyone from deciding the matter: simply, *no one* would be above that kind of interest. Instead, the second kind of interest, being shared solely by specific groups of citizens, because of their location in the social stratification and division of labour, unduly influences the decision at issue and should then be neutralized by excluding the relevant group of citizens from the decision-making process.

From the angle of political-liberal constitutionalism, then, the argument in favour of judicial review is that the majority-based power exercised by legislative institutions that represent the electorate is a *constituted* power. As such, it generates legitimate outcomes only when it operates *within* the constitutional tracks drawn by what Rawls calls 'the constituent power of the people'. In observance to the *nemo judex* principle, the assessment of that compatibility cannot be entrusted to the holders of constituted law-making power. A *different* institution ought to represent the point of view of the transgenerational people. This normative conclusion does not rest on such institution's presumed superior familiarity with 'matters of principle', as an epistocratic defence of judicial review would have it, but on its greater degrees of *independence* from the configuration of interests that animate the political arena.

When this different institution—a high, supreme, or constitutional court[16]—finds that some legislative outcome of the representatives of the electorate falls outside the

---

[15] Jeremy Waldron, 'Legislatures Judging in their own Cause' (2009) 3(1) Legisprudence 125.
[16] A separate argument is needed to establish that such an institution should be a supreme or constitutional court, as opposed to an elective and permanent constitutional assembly or convention, a special body composed of representatives from the three branches of separated power or any other differently designed

tracks established by the constituent power of the people, and therefore fails to be valid law, the institution certainly thwarts or frustrates the majoritarian will of the electorate and its representatives, but does not thwart the democratic process, because that process cannot be reduced to the implementation of the majoritarian political will of the living segment of the people without thereby undermining the very notion of *constitutional* democracy and generating the three potentially negative implications of serial sovereignty.

This thesis constitutes the backbone of a justification of the democratic significance of judicial review, but does not exhaust its relevant facets. Other facets of the contribution of judicial review to the legitimacy of the democratic process have been highlighted by Cristina Lafont. Contrary to those who claim that judicial review detracts from the quality of the democratic process by juridifying political divides[17] and encouraging the removal of contentious issues from the arena of democratic deliberation, Lafont rightly emphasizes two points.

First, a constitutional court is activated by a legal claim brought before its attention by single individuals or groups of citizens, often backed up by NGOs, advocacy groups, movements, and political organizations. Thus, it is misleading to depict the court as confronting the 'will of the electorate', let alone that of the people. The court's pronouncement, instead, testifies to the divisiveness of the issue and to the existence of a plurality of contrasting orientations. Instead of opposing a monolithic will of the electorate, a constitutional court's sentence establishes which side of that *already divided* will best comports with the broader will of the transgenerational people.[18]

Second, political constitutionalists often lament the *depoliticization* of public debate that results from judicial review. As Bellamy claims,

> it is not always particularly profitable to discuss all these issues [disagreements over the substance, scope, sphere, and subjects of rights] in terms of which formulation best interprets the wording of the right in a given document. Think, for example, of the way American debates concerning defamation, incitement, libel, pornography, commercial advertising and the like all get distorted by terminological disquisitions over what counts as 'speech'. It would seem much more fruitful to discuss the pros and cons of particular policies head on in terms of the interests and values at stake.[19]

On the contrary, it can be argued that, far from *depoliticizing* the question at hand, the pronouncement of a court, together with the sometimes long and public debate that precedes it, contributes to ameliorate the democratic quality of that debate, by framing it as an issue of principle and of the balancing of rights. In Lafont's words, 'secret ballots might be blind. Public deliberation can't be'.[20] This means that judicial review contributes to 'the constitutionalization of political debate' and does so 'by structuring

---

institution. I will not provide such argument but will simply follow the consolidated custom of identifying such an institution as the highest judicial court, entrusted with the role of interpreter of the constitution.

[17] Philip Pettit 'Depoliticizing Democracy' (2004) 17(1) Ratio Juris 52.
[18] Lafont, *Democracy Without Shortcuts* (n 11) 227.
[19] Bellamy, *Political Constitutionalism* (n 1) 50.
[20] Lafont, *Democracy Without Shortcuts* (n 11) 214.

political discourse about fundamental rights and freedoms' as a 'matter of principle', as opposed to the balancing of interests that forms the texture of ordinary politics.[21]

A separate problem in this discussion of the merits of judicial review concerns the relation of judicial review to *equality*. Nominally meant to ensure that the rights of free and equal citizens be respected and that the institutions of a democratic state address all the citizens, to use Dworkin's eloquent phrase, 'with the same voice', in fact, Waldron argues, judicial review is activated by individual citizens, or groups thereof, in order to obtain via judicial rulings a 'greater weight for their opinions than electoral politics will give them'.[22] Lafont correctly observes that equality is reflected in the *equal* right of any citizen to set judicial review in motion, provided that a well-grounded reason for doing so exists. However, in no way can that prerogative sensibly be understood as amounting to a greater chance to obtain the desired ruling from a supreme or constitutional court. What Waldron depicts as the quest for a supposed 'greater weight' of one's opinion relative to what the political process would afford must instead be understood as a greater chance to receive the kind of *scrutiny* that the citizens starting a lawsuit deem owed to them and might experience difficulty in receiving within majoritarian legislative institutions.[23]

Lafont's defence of judicial review also constitutes an improvement over Dworkin's and Pettit's versions, in that judicial review's democratic credentials are said to rest not on the fact

> that it makes possible to answer questions about the constitutionality of a contested statute or policy *in isolation from political debate*. To the contrary, the important contribution of the courts—which are indeed 'depoliticized in the sense of being a forum of principle …'—has nothing to do with isolating their decision from the political debate among all citizens in the public sphere.… The main contribution of the institution [of judicial review] is that it empowers citizens to call upon the rest of the citizenry to publicly debate the proper scope of the rights and freedoms they must grant one another in order to treat each other as free and equal.[24]

This call to participation comes with a condition, however. It would be pointless, in fact, for the attempt of the highest judicial interpreter of the constitution to settle, via public reason, the clash of rights and liberties involved in a certain legislative measure to be undermined by the clash of sectarian armies of citizens brandishing their own polarized comprehensive conceptions. The call of the plaintiffs of the day to fellow citizens is a call, as Lafont rightly highlights, to '*put on their robes*'[25] and enter a productive interlocution—also mediated ideally by public reason—with their fellow other-minded citizens, their advocates in the public sphere, and the court, over the question of how certain policies and legislative measures affect the equal protection of

---

[21] ibid 228.
[22] Waldron, 'Against Judicial Review' (n 5) 1395.
[23] See Lafont, *Democracy Without Shortcuts* (n 11) 237.
[24] ibid 238.
[25] ibid 240 (emphasis in original).

the fundamental rights of *all*. The constitutionalization of political debate induced by judicial review is ultimately the flywheel of public reason among the citizens.

2. Interpreting the Constitution: the Mandate of the Interpreter

To recap: from the perspective of political liberalism, the people *qua* author of the constitution is represented, within a democratic polity, by the supreme or constitutional court that acts as its trustee primarily by way of interpreting the constitution. This is not to exclude that someone else, for example elected officials and parties, may at a given time represent the people. For instance, parliaments, presidents, or prime ministers may represent 'the people' when, pursuant to the formal provisions for amending their constitution, they are entitled to put forward or actually enact amendments to the constitution. Parties can represent 'the people' when they advocate such amendments, or even at times of normal politics, when they elaborate and implement platforms that inflect, from the specific angle of the party's comprehensive conception and within the limits of public reason, the 'political values' embedded in the constitutional essentials and distinctive not of one sector of the electorate, one class, one group of citizens, but of 'the people' as a whole. In fact, political forces and, at certain 'constitutional moments', social movements sometimes address constitutional values, advocate innovation, and mobilize in the name of certain changes or certain new meanings to be attributed to such values, as the New Deal, the Civil Rights era, and later the feminist movement attest. In those cases, movements, parties, and political leaders claim to speak, as the living generation of the people, not just for themselves but for the entire transgenerational people, and they do have an important impact. Constitutional courts, although activated by litigation, do take inspiration and encouragement to reinterpret the constitution differently from the heightened climate of mobilization and constitutional debate generated by these forces.[26]

The crucial difference, however, is that while these actors, institutional or 'partisan', may or may not choose to represent 'the people', and in any event cannot be blamed for simply representing the electorate or even just segments of it, a constitutional court is an institution *defined* by the mandate to represent 'the people' rather than the electorate. Whilst others may, rightly or wrongly, claim to represent the people, no one other than a constitutional court has that mandate as its *raison d'être*, and thus can be said to have failed as an institution when failing to fulfil it.

It is now time to specify what that mandate includes. In Chapter 5, Section 3 its *external* modalities—that is, how the court's mandate may relate to other institutions—have been addressed. Drawing on Michelman's effort to build a political liberal theory of judicial review, a court has been found able to exert its mandate in an *active* or

---

[26] See We the People. Volume 3, *The Civil Rights Revolution* (Harvard University Press 2014) 75–76, 229–30 (hereafter Ackerman, *Civil Rights Revolution*). See also Jack M Balkin, *Living Originalism* (Harvard University Press 2011) 284 and 321 (hereafter Balkin, *Living Originalism*).

quiescent, assertive or *tolerant, strong* or *weak* mode.[27] What is needed now is a specification of the *internal* modalities according to which a court may understand its own mandate.

a. Reconciling the tension between two versions of the interpreter's mandate

Once again, it is possible to draw on Michelman's reflections as a starting point.[28] He condenses a number of inhospitable conditions that affect the democratic process in contemporary societies[29] into two ideal-typical complex predicaments designated as (i) 'occlusion of authorship', namely, a decline of the citizens' control over the regulatory legal order confronting them; and (ii) 'shortfall of agreement', namely, a persisting, widespread, crisis-ridden widening of the gaps among the political, moral, social, and religious conceptions endorsed by citizens, a predicament that elsewhere I have defined as 'hyperpluralism'.[30]

The point of Michelman's two ideal-typical adverse conditions for democracy is to highlight different conceptions of an apex court's interpretive mandate, correlated with the court's perception of a more pressing urgency of either the 'shortfall of agreement' or the 'occlusion of authorship' among the inhospitable conditions.

More specifically, if we take occlusion of authorship as the condition primarily in need to be remedied—the remedy consisting of reframing the traditional liberal standard of the 'consent of the governed' as a dualistic scheme of 'legitimation-by-constitution'—then there follows a tendency to understand the function of the court as 'to "protect" the higher law *as historically enacted by the people*'[31] and to aim its interpretive mandate at developing 'some mode or method, be it ever so highly abstracted or extenuated, of extracting from enacting history *the actual legislative will of the people themselves*'.[32]

Should we, on the other hand, tend to prioritize remedying the shortfall of agreement rather than the occlusion of authorship, then, according to Michelman, 'the corresponding call for overseeing courts can only be to bend both the scripted constitutional essentials and the doctrines of their application as far as possible toward values that the judges "believe in good faith … that all citizens as reasonable and rational" could endorse'.[33] This different function assigned to the highest interpreter of the constitution can be discharged only by testing controversial laws against some general conception of political rightness—hence a penchant for 'the so-called

---

[27] See above, Chapter 5, Section 3.a.
[28] The ideas presented here are articulated by Michelman in Ferrara and Michelman, *Legitimation by Constitution: A Dialogue on Political Liberalism* (Oxford University Press 2021) 81–89 (hereafter Ferrara and Michelman, *Legitimation by Constitution*). In this section I draw on my own response in ibid 90–95.
[29] Frank I Michelman, 'How Can the People Ever Make the Laws? A Critique of Deliberative Democracy' in James Bohman and William Rehg (eds) *Deliberative Democracy* (MIT Press 1997).
[30] Alessandro Ferrara, *The Democratic Horizon: Hyperpluralism and the Renewal of Political Liberalism* (Cambridge University Press 2014) 88–92.
[31] Ferrara and Michelman, *Legitimation by Constitution* (n 28) 88.
[32] ibid (emphasis added).
[33] ibid.

"philosophical" approach to constitutional interpretation, which currently stands as originalism's polemical opposite'.[34] According to Michelman, this tension is hard to reconcile: the 'philosophical' approach required to remedy of shortfall of agreement is bound to clash with the more originalist approach required for retrieving the will of the people as author of the constitution.

But is it really so or can these two versions of the mandate of the highest judicial interpreter of the constitution ultimately be reconciled? I believe it is not impossible to articulate a notion of the mandate that remains consistent with political liberalism and yet allays that tension. For that purpose, we need first to reconstruct the deeper layer of conflicting elements that oppose the two approaches. The primary task of a supreme judicial interpreter entrusted with 'unblocking occlusion' necessarily must include reference, according to Michelman, to some trace of the sovereign will, reconstructed either from the duly interpreted original constitution or from some subsequent constitutional moment—a task from which a supreme judicial interpreter entrusted with the alternative task of remedying the 'shortfall of agreement' in a reasonably non-rejectable way is exempted. In the first mode, the highest interpreter of the constitution is asked to tell the public what the sovereign people *did* will, in the second to articulate what it *should* will.[35]

This rift need not sink the prospect of a unified view of the mandate of the interpreter of the constitution. The key to bridging the divide consists in realizing that whatever the people wills—whether by way of enacting a constitution or by its subsequent modification—is always necessarily willed *against a set of background assumptions*, of a cognitive nature, themselves not immune from critical scrutiny. As an example, let me offer the transition from *Plessy v Ferguson* to *Brown v Board of Education* as indicative of two quite different applications of the equal protection clause of the Fourteenth Amendment, both offered by the highest interpreter of the Constitution of the United States respectively in 1896 and 1954.[36]

Even if we imagine, along with Michelman, that the priority of unblocking the occlusion of authorship commits one to think that the Supreme Court in *Brown* should have anchored its opinion in the reconstruction of an unequivocal, historical act of will of the democratic sovereign, still one could think that the democratic sovereign did endorse 'equal protection' since the time of the Fourteenth Amendment, but whereas in 1868, and as late as in 1896, the 'badge of inferiority' associated with racial separation was described as non-existent (or existent 'solely because the colored race chooses to put that construction upon it', as the Court stated in *Plessy*),[37] half a century later the interpreter of the constitutional script found, in the light of evidence partly of a social-scientific nature, that 'separate educational facilities are *inherently* unequal'

---

[34] ibid.
[35] See Frank I Michelman 'Political Liberalism's Constitutional Horizon: Some Further Thoughts' (2017) 4 Rivista internazionale di filosofia del diritto 607.
[36] See *Plessy v Ferguson*, 163 US 537 (1896) and *Brown v Board of Education*, 347 US 483 (1954).
[37] *Plessy v Ferguson*, 163 US 551 (1896). Of course, that was the official claim in the Court's opinion. Whether that claim was sincerely believed is contested. Justice Harlan's dissenting opinion inclines us to suspect that it might not have been sincere. For an insightful discussion, see Steven L Winter's account of the transition from *Plessy* to *Brown*, in his 'Indeterminacy and Incommensurability in Constitutional Law' (1990) 78 California Law Review 1441 1527–34.

and violate the 'equal protection of the laws', because segregation is '*usually* interpreted as denoting the inferiority of the negro group'.[38]

On segregation, then, the Warren Court neither articulated what the people *should* will (thus making itself vulnerable to the charge of itself occluding the citizens' authorship of the laws) nor violated historical evidence by attributing to the people a non-segregationist, substantive understanding of 'equal protection', foreign to nineteenth-century America. Indeed, the background assumptions under which that democratic will to provide 'equal protection of the laws' was formed—including the assumption that segregation along racial lines could be compatible with equal citizenship—had not yet been conclusively challenged.[39] Thus the Supreme Court can be argued to have taken *a third course*, not contemplated in Michelman's disjunctive rendering of the two possible judicial mandates. In *Brown v Board of Education*, the supreme constitutional interpreter did rightly impute an actual and original act of will to the democratic sovereign—namely, the historical act of establishing 'equal protection of the laws' earlier in 1868—but at the same time, in the same act of adjudication, updated, in the light of a changed historical context, the *cognitive assumptions* against which such original will was formed. This view is partially supported by what was later asserted by the Court in *Casey*: although they clarify that for them '*Plessy* was wrong the way it was decided', the Justices state that 'Society's understanding of the facts upon which a constitutional ruling was sought in 1954 was thus fundamentally different from the basis claimed for the decision in 1896'.[40]

---

[38] *Brown v Board of Education*, 347 US 494 (1954), quoting a finding by a Delaware court (emphasis added).

[39] As historical research shows, however, in the wake of the enactment of the Fourteenth Amendment and during the preparatory stages of the Civil Rights Act of 1875, some congressmen and senators already advocated desegregation of schools in legislation on the ground that segregated public schools violated the Fourteenth Amendment. See, Michael McConnell, 'Originalism and the Desegregation Decisions' (1985) 81 Vermont Law Review 947. See also Balkin, *Living Originalism* (n 26) 105.

[40] *Casey v Planned Parenthood* 505 US 833 (1992) 863. Thanks are due to Steven L Winter for having brought to my attention this reference to *Plessy* included in *Casey*, though he might not agree with the implications that I draw from it. In 'Bridges of Law, Ideology, Commitment' 2022 37 Touro Law Review, quoting Robert Cover, he objects that law and constitutions constantly change. Then, presumably by virtue of the positional view of meaning, 'equal protection as allowing segregation' (in *Plessy*) and 'equal protection as prohibiting segregation' (in *Brown*) do not amount to different variants of the same agreed-to clause as in my account, but to two radically opposed, self-standing constructions of the Fourteenth Amendment: namely, 'a constitutional provision that "condones" segregation is not "the same" as one that condemns it', Steven L Winter, personal communication, email of 8 January 2022, on record with the author. Two rejoinders come to mind. *First*, as Heidegger observed of the prisoners in Plato's cave, who only from *our* perspective can be said to see 'mere' shadows, because in their world shadows are not distinct from objects but are all that is perceived, so one could argue that 'segregation' (as in the phrase 'a constitutional provision that "condones" segregation') is taken as such only from the later evaluative standpoint, which considers segregation impermissible. To deny that there is a perceivable separation of citizens along racial lines, which in light of the Fourteenth Amendment is reputed permissible at t_1 and impermissible at t_2, seems to me as odd as denying that an Aristotelian and a Newtonian observer could agree that the same body is falling, only because they radically disagree on the explanation of that motion. *Second*, the point that law and constitutions constantly change reflects the perspective of an observer. It offers little help to the participant, who must constantly form a judgment concerning whether a given practice is compatible or incompatible with a given provision taken as in force. The same point can be clarified in relation to language. The fact that languages are also in constant flux does not prevent speakers and hearers from having to assess the grammaticality of utterances at the time when they are exchanged.

In sum, the two alternatives presented by Michelman as destined to endlessly clash admit of bridging, along the following lines: In the process of recalibrating its interpretation of the Constitution in the light of a new historical context, the highest judicial interpreter *neither* imputes to the people an original intent to desegregate schools and a substantive conception of equality (a will and a conception certainly not existent at time of the Founding and of the enacting of the Fourteenth Amendment) *nor* develops a non-rejectable philosophical argument about how the equal protection clause *should* henceforth be interpreted. By modifying the *background cognitive assumptions* relevant for interpreting the Constitution, the highest judicial interpreter shows the way in which it is possible to bridge the gap between the two kinds of mandate.

The same line of reasoning can be applied to *Obergefell v Hodges*.[41] In this case the judicial interpreter is not so much trying to convincingly show that the people *actually willed* same-sex marriage, but that the people's historical will to grant equal protection was formed in a context where certain assumptions (about sexual preference) still seemed tenable, and therefore led to legal conclusions that now, in the light of contrary evidence, deserve being reversed.

To put the point in more general philosophical terms: 'we', as one generational section of 'the people', acting through the constituted power of the highest judicial interpreter of the constitution, can be bound by the *normative will* of our predecessors, for example their will to ground our communal political life in freedom and equality, as secured under a certain list of enumerated rights, but cannot be bound by their *cognitive horizon*. Through that understanding we can offer relief to Michelman's worry that by interpreting the constitution with a view to aligning it to principles reputed 'reasonably non-rejectable', a constitutional court thereby contributes to occluding democratic authorship. The third course outlined above and exemplified by *Brown* and *Obergefell* relieves this concern.

My alternative understanding of the mandate of the highest judicial interpreter—bound by the normative commitments of the transgenerational people, but not by its cognitive presuppositions—matches with Rawls's paradigm for a well-ordered constitutional democracy, in which no branch of government is above challenge. In light of Rawls's equal rejection of judicial as well as parliamentary supremacy, any 'philosophical' interpretation, for example of 'equal protection' provided by the higher judicial interpreter, must be taken as at least *putatively* reflective of the will of the people—even if only in a fallibilistic sense, unless and until the people (through the other branches and according to the procedures provided by the constitution) sets the amending procedure underway and corrects some erroneous, partial, or otherwise unwelcome interpretation on the part of the court. 'Judicial occlusion', as it were, must always remain temporary and ways to offset it must be provided by the constitution.

Unconvinced by this strategy for reconciling the tension between the two versions of the mandate, which in his opinion ultimately fails to do justice to the 'originalist horn' of the dilemma,[42] Michelman then suggests a different approach to bridging the same gap. Sceptical about the possibility of bridging that gap conceptually, Michelman urges political liberals to avoid pitting these two understandings of a constitutional

---

[41] *Obergefell v Hodges*, 576 US (2015)
[42] See Ferrara and Michelman, *Legitimation by Constitution* (n 28) 102.

court's mandate one against the other as institutional alternatives between which one should *choose*. They should rather be brought 'together in a unified coherent practice of constitutional-legal application'.[43]

Michelman's different approach rests on distinguishing the 'regulatory' and the 'proceduralizing' function of a constitution. The regulatory function aims at ensuring that law-making, and more generally all the binding legislative, judicial, or administrative decisions, comport with certain guidelines that respond, in turn, to the principles of a 'political conception of justice' supported by 'overlapping consensus'. This regulatory function ensures that the normative infrastructure of the polity be responsive to the constitutional essentials: for example, a constitutional right to 'free speech' ensures that no ordinary regulation unduly limits freedom of expression.

The 'proceduralizing' function, instead, aims at preserving openness and legitimacy in contested areas, where reasonable disagreement is the normal predicament, and thus aims at avoiding that majorities highjack the democratic process, tilt the scales in favour of their preferred outcomes, and ultimately undermine the perception of legitimacy of the polity on the part of dissenters.

Michelman then considers his two versions of the interpretive mandate of a supreme or constitutional court (linked with an assumed priority of either the regulatory or the proceduralizing function of the constitution) 'joined together by the obvious and simple truth that the proceduralizing aim cannot get off the ground without presupposition of a regulatory success'.[44] As he concisely puts it: 'proceduralizing ambition presupposes regulatory effect'.[45]

Underlying both Michelman's and my approach is the perception of a pressing need to bridge the divide between the two versions of the interpretive mandate of a constitutional court, a divide that may possibly rest on postulating a split between *descriptive* reconstruction (of historical traces of the will of the people) and *evaluative* assessment (of the desirability of constitutional interpretations, in light of their potential for cutting across controversial substantive orientations) on which recent philosophy has cast doubt.[46]

b. Living originalism as 'political originalism'

The distinction between the binding normativity of the constitution and the not-binding cognitive presuppositions that undergird adjudication prompts us to examine closer the nature of a constitutional court's interpretive mandate. Drawing on Jack Balkin's theory of 'living originalism', we can distinguish a *restrictive* and an *expanded* way of understanding constitutional interpretation. This distinction touches on the 'originalist' and 'philosophical' alternatives mentioned by Michelman, but at the same time recasts them in a way worth exploring further and suggests another distinction

---

[43] ibid.
[44] ibid 101.
[45] ibid.
[46] See Hilary Putnam, *The Collapse of the Fact/Value Dichotomy* (Harvard University Press 2002).

which will have a bearing on the discussion of the standard of interpretation, in Section 3.

With the intent to supersede the opposition of originalism and living constitutionalism, Balkin argues that a basic dimension of 'fidelity to the constitution'—understood as 'accepting and seeking to follow its plan for government as our plan'[47]—is indispensable for all constitutional interpretation. In his words, 'the conversation between past commitments and present generations is at the heart of constitutional interpretation' and for this reason 'we do not face a choice between living constitutionalism and fidelity to the original meaning of the text. They are two sides of the same coin'.[48] Borrowing from Rawls's terminology, let me call this living originalism 'political originalism'. Balkin distinguishes two opposite ideal types of originalism in relation to the object of interpretation and a different pair of opposed originalisms in relation to the way the constitution shapes the polity.

Concerning *interpretation*, Balkin's 'framework originalism' recasts the requirement of constitutional fidelity in terms of capturing the original meanings of rules, standards, and principles found in the text but denies 'that the original meaning of the text includes principles stated at a level that captures most of the public's—or the framers'—*expected applications*'.[49] From the perspective of 'framework originalism', the original meaning of 'equal protection of the laws' does not include the historically expected application of this principle in the pre-Brown era as allowing segregation and the prohibition of interracial marriage. 'Conservative originalism', instead, comes in a variety of forms that embed a much more restrictive understanding of the fidelity-requiring elements. Initially linked with the notion of recovering the intention of the framers, conservative originalism, on the spur of criticism levelled by Dworkin and others against the 'authorial-intention' view of meaning,[50] moved on to link interpretation with the original *general* meaning or 'original understanding' of the terms used. Yet, in so doing, conservative originalism, Balkin argues, quickly tended 'to conflate the question of original meaning with constructions based on expected applications'.[51]

Concerning, instead, *the way the constitution institutionally shapes the polity*, Balkin distinguishes his own 'framework originalism' and so-called skyscraper originalism:

> Skyscraper originalism views the Constitution as more or less a finished product, albeit always subject to later Article V amendment. It allows ample room for democratic lawmaking to meet future demands of governance; however, this lawmaking is not constitutional construction. It is ordinary law that is permissible within the boundaries of the Constitution. Framework originalism, by contrast, views the Constitution as an initial framework for governance that sets politics in motion and must be filled out over time through constitutional construction. Put in terms of Article V, skyscraper originalism views amendment as the only method of building the Constitution; by contrast, framework originalism sees a major role for

---

[47] Balkin, *Living Originalism* (n 26) 39.
[48] ibid 20.
[49] ibid 228.
[50] See ibid 102 and Ronald Dworkin, *Freedom's Law: The Moral Reading of the Constitution* (Harvard University Press 1996) 13, 291–92 (hereafter Dworkin, *Freedom's Law*).
[51] Balkin, *Living Originalism* (n 26) 101.

constitutional construction and implementation by the political branches as well as by the judiciary.[52]

By bringing together the two distinctions, we can now locate conceptions of the interpretive mandate on a spectrum, at one end of which we find a *restrictive* view, that understands fidelity as directed to the 'expected application' of the basic rules, standards, and principles of the constitution as they can be attributed to the framers of the constitution and understands 'the constitution' as a written documented supplemented by the duly approved amendments. At the opposite end of the spectrum, we find an *expanded* view of the mandate, which understands fidelity to the original meaning of the constitution's rules, standards, and principles as constructed in the light of knowledge, moral assumptions, and urgencies of today. As Balkin eloquently puts his point, each generation's fidelity to the original constitution's text and principles does not eliminate the fact that 'you cannot step into the same Constitution twice', not 'because the Constitution is always changing', but 'because you and the position from which you interpret the Constitution are always changing'.[53]

I call this view 'political originalism' not in order to suggest that Rawls has endorsed it in *Political Liberalism* but because it fits with his idea that the constitution 'is what the people acting constitutionally through the other branches eventually allow the Court to say it is'.[54] Such originalism is 'political' in the sense that even though it presupposes that the mandate of a constitutional court is to maintain fidelity to the original commitments embedded in the constitution, it neither restricts the meaning of these commitments to the original underlying assumptions, nor embraces the views of the living segment of the people. Rather, as in the exemplary case of 'equal protection', 'political originalism' recasts the original and the present-time views as a *reformulation of the same commitment*:

> when we ask about the 'meaning' of the equal protection clause, we could be asking (1) what concepts the words in the clause point to; (2) how to apply the clause; (3) the purpose or function of the clause; (4) the intentions behind the clause; or (5) what the clause is associated with in our minds or, more generally, in our culture. Fidelity to 'original meaning' in constitutional interpretation refers only to the first of these types of meaning: the semantic content of the words in the clause. Fidelity to original meaning does not, however, require fidelity to any of the four other types of original meaning.... Fidelity to original meaning as original semantic content does not require that we must apply the equal protection clause the same way that people at the time of enactment would have expected it would be applied. It does not require that we must articulate the purposes or functions of the clause in exactly the same way the framers and ratifiers would have, or that we apply it only according to their intentions. Finally, it does not mean that the clause can only have the same associations for us that it had for the adopting generation. Today, for example, the clause is associated with many things in our minds and our political culture—like Dr Martin Luther King

---

[52] ibid 21–22.
[53] ibid 269.
[54] Rawls, *PL* 237.

Jr and the civil rights revolution—that the adopting generation could not have known about.[55]

c. Modulating constitutional interpretation: strictures and amplitudes

A constitution is no monolith. The fact that it embeds certain defining commitments that shape the *demos* no less than the demos made them—to 'form a more perfect Union', to the 'free exercise' of religion, to 'freedom of speech, and of the press', to 'equal protection of the laws', just to mention a few from the Constitution of the United States—does not mean that all of its component parts are of that tenor, or subject to the same kind of interpretive construction.

Following Balkin, it is possible to distinguish *rules*, *standards*, and *principles* within a constitution, as well as structure-forming provisions that shape the polity. Rules are used in order to bind the judgment of future generations by strict directives subject to virtually zero interpretation: no person is eligible for the office of President of the United States 'who shall not have attained to the Age of thirty five Years' (Article II).[56] Instead, the use of terms that refer to general or abstract concepts indicates that the framers 'sought to embody general and abstract principles of constitutional law, whose scope, in turn, will have to be worked out and implemented by later generations'.[57] Sometimes that content takes the form of a standard (eg 'cruel and unusual punishment'), in other cases of a principle ('equal protection of the laws' or 'free exercise of religion'), and in both cases we need to construct 'subsidiary principles' that can help us to make sense of or contextualize the main principle.[58]

Finally, there are implicit, unstated or *underlying* principles that can be constructed from the constitutional clauses and the general architecture of the text. Their function is to orient our reflective judgment about the 'political ideal of a people to govern itself in a certain way'.[59] Examples of such principles are the separation of powers, the idea of checks and balances, the democratic principle, or the principle of laicity or religious neutrality in the Constitution of Italy. There is no explicit provision that refers to the

---

[55] Balkin, *Living Originalism* (n 26) 12–13. Balkin argues that the adoption of a general concept such as 'equal protection of the laws' was also partly due to contingent political urgencies: 'The Fourteenth Amendment served as the Republicans' platform for the elections of 1866', and 'the Republican Platform for 1866 had to be sufficiently ambiguous and broad to attract quite divergent segments of the nation's electorate. Moderates and radicals chose open-ended "language capable of growth" that papered over their differences and allowed them to present a unified front that would appeal to a wide range of constituencies. Moderates could report to their constituents that phrases like "privileges or immunities" and "equal protection" did not require integrated facilities and did not threaten laws against interracial marriage; radicals could point to the broad guarantees of equal citizenship to push for future reforms. By deliberately using language containing broad principles, specific applications would be left to future generations to work out', ibid 26.

[56] 'When the text provides an unambiguous, concrete and specific rule, the principles or purposes behind the text cannot override the textual command. For example, the underlying goal of promoting maturity in a president does not mean that we can dispense with the thirty-five-year age requirement. The language creates a rule and must be applied accordingly', ibid 14.

[57] ibid.
[58] See ibid.
[59] Rawls, *PL* 232.

'separation of powers' or 'checks and balances' in the Constitution of the United States or to the religious neutrality of the Italian State. Nevertheless, as Balkin puts it, 'we ascribe these principles to the Constitution.... We say that they "underlie" the text, in the sense of supporting it and making sense of it'.[60] The most important is perhaps the principle of democracy, not mentioned in the Constitution of the United States on account of the generalized mistrust for democracy during the time of the Founding, republicanism and representative government being the terms of choice for designating what is today understood as constitutional democracy.

These underlying principles perform two functions. *First*, some of them, including federalism, equal citizenship, equality before the law, and the rule of law, 'explain the functions of government and how the constitutional system is supposed to operate'.[61] *Second*, other underlying principles are expressed through formulas, like freedom of speech, to which a meaning must be assigned. It is important to keep the substance of principles distinct from the literal expressions of the constitutional text: 'they do not *constitute* the text, as the words "equal protection of the laws" do. They are *constructions* that support and help explain the point of the text, and they do not exhaust either its meaning or its effect'.[62]

'Political originalism' posits then an inverse relation between the gradient from constitutional strictures (ie the rule-determined length of term of the different top executive and legislative offices) to such amplitudes as stated standards or principles subject to interpretive construction (ie no 'cruel and unusual punishment', 'due process', 'equal protection of the laws') and, on the other hand, the demandingness of the procedural requisites for changing the constitution. In order to change rule-determined aspects such as voting age, length of terms for elected officials, term limits, direct or indirect electability, or to change significant structural aspects of the institutional framework (eg to abolish the Electoral College in the United States), no less than a formal constitutional amendment is required, in compliance with the amendment provisions found in the constitution. That said, original standards and (explicit or implicit) principles can be modified and brought into alignment with new cognitive assumptions, techno-scientific achievements, and moral sensibilities by way of *differently constructing* the relevant constitutional essentials on the part of the judicial representative of 'the people'. This interpretive avenue for constitutional change remains open to formal amendment as well (as the case of voting extended to women attests). Finally, underlying principles have a structural, defining quality—they are what the Supreme Court of India has qualified as the 'Basic Structure' or the Italian Constitutional Court as a 'constitutional architrave'—and are as implicitly unamendable as provisions entrenched by 'eternity clauses'. As Schmitt and Rawls jointly acknowledge, they cannot be modified without thereby introducing a constitutional rupture that extends beyond Ackerman's 'unconventional adaptation'. In Section 3, the standard of validity that applies to the interpretation of these diverse constitutional elements will be discussed.

---

[60] Balkin, *Living Originalism* (n 26) 259.
[61] ibid.
[62] ibid 260 (emphasis added).

d. The contribution of judicial review to constitutional authenticity

Finally, judicial review revisits and revamps the sources of 'constitutional authenticity'. Many of the standards and principles embedded in a constitution are rooted in widely shared notions of public law or *droit politique*: the separation of powers, the rule of law, democracy, the separation of religion and politics, federalism, checks and balances. In the constitution of virtually every democratic polity we find local iterations of these principles. Can these standards and principles fulfil (i) the *expressive* function (addressed in Chapter 4, Section 3.a) of providing the focal point of a unique political identity and (ii) the *integrative* function of gathering affective identification with the unique distinctiveness of the commitments posited by citizens as irrecusably defining of themselves?

In some cases, the wording of constitutional clauses evokes such uniqueness in ways related to specific national episodes of historical affirmation of what at first sight might not look unique: 'freedom of speech, or of the press', the 'free exercise of religion', 'equal protection of the laws', etc. But in other cases, perhaps the most significant, it is both the verbal formula and the wording-independent substance that together play that role: the Italian democratic republic 'founded on labour', the 'more perfect Union', the 'right to keep and bear arms', 'Liberty, Equality, Fraternity', 'government of the people, by the people and for the people'.

We can understand this aspect of the constitution as its being 'our law', in Balkin's vocabulary, in addition to its being the 'basic law' of a country. As 'basic law', a constitution 'sets up a basic framework of government that promotes political stability and allocates rights, duties, powers, and responsibilities', then also provides 'a plan for ordering political life and offers ways of implementing, expanding, or modifying the plan over time', and, finally, counts as 'foundational law (or supreme law) that trumps other law to the contrary'.[63] The constitution 'trumps ordinary law not simply because it is legally or procedurally prior to it, but because it represents important values that should trump ordinary law, supervise quotidian acts of governmental power, and hold both law and power to account'.[64]

However, a constitution also functions as 'our law' or, in my vocabulary, projects 'constitutional authenticity', when the citizens understand it as their achievement as a people, 'which involves a collective identification with those who came before us and with those who will come after us'.[65] As a result, a constitutional narrative coalesces 'through which people imagine themselves as a people, with shared memories, goals, aspirations, values, duties, and ambitions'.[66] The dimension of historical temporality is brought in once again:

> The idea of the Constitution as our law ... requires an identification between ourselves, those who lived in the past, and those who will live in the future. And it

---

[63] ibid 59.
[64] ibid.
[65] ibid. See also Rawls, *PL* 204.
[66] Balkin, *Living Originalism* (n 26) 68.

requires faith that the Constitution is either good enough as it is to deserve our respect and attachment or that it eventually will be redeemed so that it is deserving.[67]

As in all notions of authenticity, so too in the case of constitutional authenticity the *factual* uniqueness of 'our' history, namely how 'our' Constitution has come into being and has evolved, in and of itself is not enough. That uniqueness must also be valourized by a sense of its realizing some significant aspect of justice, and not just being a technique for living together with a manageable conflict:

> When people critique the Constitution-in-practice in the name of the Constitution—or in the name of what the Constitution truly stands for—they implicitly make this distinction. They are advocating a restoration or a redemption of an ideal or true Constitution that may never have existed fully or completely in practice, but that they view as their goal.[68]

This aspirational moment is called 'redemptive constitutionalism' by Balkin. Redemptive constitutionalism cannot be reduced to successful adaptation to changing historical conditions. Inherent in it is the notion of the fulfilment of a promise embedded in the normative core of the constitution, bound to remain an unfinished project because of the imperfection of human institutions, and the intrinsic connection—highlighted by Rawls—of freedom and plurality.

Along similar lines, Dieter Grimm argues that 'a constitution is subject to expectations that extend far beyond its normative regulatory function' and is expected by citizens 'to unify the society that it has constituted as a polity' and to provide 'the fundamental consensus that is necessary for social cohesion'.[69] Grimm points to 'constitutional authenticity' when he distinguishes the *integrative* from the *normative* function of a constitution, and in a sceptical vein, contrasting the constitutions of the Weimar Republic and the United States, questions the assumption that the integrative function might be fulfilled by the mere ongoing existence of a constitution.[70] Law can produce compliance, but not identification: 'a norm that would require a constitution to have an integrative effect would be a norm without a regulatory value',[71] just as would be the case for a law requiring spouses to love each other.

If then 'a constitution may fail to have an integrative function despite its legal efficacy',[72] the question arises: what factors can favour the constitution's potential for playing that function? In a different vocabulary, Grimm converges on the authenticity thesis when he states that 'A constitution will have an integrative effect if it embodies a society's fundamental value system and aspirations, and if a society perceives that its constitution reflects precisely those values with which it identifies and which are the sources of its specific character'.[73] The substantive capacity to 'integrate' or favour

---

[67] ibid 70.
[68] ibid 69.
[69] Dieter Grimm, *Constitutionalism: Past, Present, and Future* (Oxford University Press 2016) 144.
[70] See ibid 145.
[71] ibid 145–46.
[72] ibid 146.
[73] ibid 148.

identification, according to Grimm, is favoured by recourse to 'open wording', or standards and principles as opposed to rules, because open wording 'helps to prevent competing ideas about the meaning of the text from undermining the citizenry's identification with it'.[74]

Thus, over and beyond revisiting and updating the meaning of constitutional standards and principles, the function of judicial review is also to kindle the authenticity of a constitution through three aspects of its operation. *First*, the court's constant revisiting of the constitution's key normative terms, which are the ones most likely to give rise to controversy about their implications, makes them all the more salient in public discourse. *Second*, the court is usually led by the internal dynamics of adjudication to articulate new meanings for those older normative terms, and by that move it indirectly evidences the *vitality* of the constitutional project and its potential for bringing together the past, the present, and the future in a necessarily always imperfect attempt at synthesis. *Third*, judicial review safeguards constitutional authenticity by stemming the opposite risk of giving in to contemporary pressures, coming from special interests and transient ideologies, that might compromise the constitution by way of hyper-adaptation.

Indirectly, then, judicial review contributes to averting the problem of a perceived under-individuation of the polity, connected with the serial idea of sovereignty, by way of strengthening, via the judicial elaboration of the key standards and principles, the chain of sequential sovereignty that links the living segment of the people with the past generations *of the same people*. At the same time, through its inherently future-oriented effort to recalibrate the constitutional commitments and project of self-government for the future generations of the people, judicial review contributes to strengthening the bond that connects present and future generations of the same people.

The strengthening not only of the normative ties, but also of the affective relation of the diverse generations of a people with the project for self-government embedded in the constitution, is a major contribution offered by judicial review to the flourishing of a *political* identity, *reflective* and not hostage to factual ethnical contingencies:

> To regard myself as part of the same 'We the People' as James Madison and a twenty-fifth-century person who will not be born for centuries, I do not have to assume any biological, ethnic, or mystical connections. All I need do is understand the three of us as working on a common project of self-governance.[75]

If these are the functions fulfilled by the judicial representative of the entire people, and if these functions are carried out by way of interpreting the constitution, we now need a sense of validity in interpretation. In fact, the point of understanding representation as 'acting for', in Chapter 5, was to enable us to assess the *quality* of representation. If the function of representing the people consists of interpreting anew the 'project for a political life together', then the question 'When does the representative of the entire people represent it well?' is transformed into the question: 'What makes an

---

[74] ibid 149.
[75] Balkin, *Living Originalism* (n 26) 57.

interpretation of the constitution a valid one?' This question will be addressed in the next section.

3. The Normativity of the Most Reasonable and the Line between *Interpreting* and *Transforming*

In order for the democratic process to operate, it is then crucial that constitutional rules, standards, and principles, part and parcel of the 'political ideal of a people to govern itself in a certain way', be interpreted *in light of*, though not in lockstep with, present-day assumptions and historical experiences, because these constitutional essentials are the benchmark against which the legitimacy of governmental activities is assessed. As elucidated above,[76] one of the central tenets of political liberalism is that the 'consent of the governed', a crucial ingredient of the legitimacy of any liberal-democratic order, cannot be expected to bless all the details of the legislative, administrative, and judicial acts that take place in a complex society. According to the 'liberal principle of legitimacy', no legislative and administrative details, but only 'constitutional essentials', can aspire to be the object of the consensus of free and equal citizens *on the basis of reasons of principle*. From these essentials, taken as 'rational and reasonable', legitimacy can then cascade on all the exercises of legislative, administrative, and judicial authority that conform with them.

In order for 'legitimation by constitution' to operate, then, it is necessary to posit one 'pro-tempore ultimate' interpreter of constitutional provisions, entrusted with the function of decoding and updating the meaning of formulae such as 'equal protection of the laws', 'due process', 'free speech', and 'cruel and unusual punishment'.

The question then arises: what makes of the court's interpretation of these formulae a good interpretation and thus attests that the court has validly acted as representative of the transgenerational people?

This question includes three more specific ones. *First*, how are we to make sense of good interpretive judgment? *Second*, how can we distinguish an *interpretive* judgment from a *transformative* rendition of the constitutional text, which exceeds the jurisdictional sphere of the court and should be left for the living segment of the people to effect? *Third*, what institutional leeway should judicial review leave open for correcting the court's interpretive pronouncement?

It may happen, and it often does, that individuals, movements, and political parties legitimately dissent over the pronouncements of a constitutional court. Are they then subjected to the domination of a small number of judges dressed in robes, the 'five lawyers' referred to by the dissenters of *Obergefell*? The possibility of answering in the negative, contrary to what political constitutionalists claim, rests on the fulfilment of three conditions: (i) the constitutional court's pronouncement rests on the most reasonable way of interpreting the constitution; (ii) that pronouncement does not overstep the bounds of *interpreting* the constitution, as opposed to unduly *transforming* it; and (iii) practically viable avenues remain available for correcting the

---

[76] See Chapter 1, Section 1.b.

court's interpretation by way of amending the constitution. Let us examine these three conditions.

a. The standard of the most reasonable applied to adjudication

To interpret the constitution, as we have seen above in Section 2.c, means to navigate *strictures* and *amplitudes*. Strictures pose fewer challenges. On one hand, provisions that have the form of 'rules'—for example, a citizen must be at least fifty years old in order to be eligible as President of the Italian Republic and at least thirty-five to be eligible as President of the United States; or, the Italian Senate is composed of 200 members and that of the United States of 100 members—fall under the scope of what Kant called 'determining judgment'.[77] A case under scrutiny can be subsumed without significant semantic loss under an antecedently posited concept. Knowing the age of a citizen allows anyone to conclude with certainty whether that person is eligible for the office of President of Italy or of the United States.

Likewise, provisions that structure the form of government, provided that they are not ambiguous, raise few challenges for the highest judicial interpreter. Article 60 of the Constitution of Italy fixes at five years the length of the term for both Houses of Parliament, and Article 1, Section 3 of the Constitution of the United States provides that the Senate 'shall be composed of two Senators from each State', for a mandate of six years. Rule-like formulations are not just confined to technical requirements. Matters of great moral import may be regulated by rule-like provisions: Article 27 of the Constitution of Italy provides that the 'Death penalty is prohibited'.

Amplitudes, instead, raise the greatest challenges. They fall into three distinct cases, but the basic difficulty is similar. The *first* is the case of *standards*: 'cruel and unusual punishment' is a standard, mandated by the Eight Amendment of the Constitution of the United States, that regulates the acceptability of forms of punishment; 'efficiency' and 'impartiality' are the standards by which Article 97 of the Constitution of Italy requires that 'public officers' should exercise their administrative activities. What then counts as cruel, or unusual, and what counts as efficient or impartial, evidently cannot be brought under conceptual subsumption as easily as age requirements.

The *second* is the case of *principles*: relevant examples are the principles of 'freedom of speech, and of the press', 'equal protection of the laws', and also that 'All citizens have equal social dignity and are equal before the law, without distinction of sex, race, language, religion, political opinion, personal and social conditions' (Article 3 of the Constitution of Italy) or that 'All religious denominations are equally free before the law' (Article 8 of the Constitution of Italy). The complex discussion of how 'equal protection of the laws' should be understood, cursorily reported above, attests the range of diverse interpretations in these matters of principle.

However, before addressing the question of the standard of interpretation, one *third* class of amplitudes needs to be mentioned: *underlying* or *implicit* principles. The Italian Constitutional Court, in a landmark pronouncement of 1989, established

---

[77] Immanuel Kant, *Critique of the Power of Judgment* (1790), edited by Paul Guyer (Cambridge University Press 2001) § 4, 67 (hereafter Kant, *Critique of Judgment*).

'the overriding principle of the secularity of the State, which is one of the aspects of the form of State outlined in the Constitution of the Republic'.[78] 'Secularity', or religious neutrality, is not mentioned explicitly in any Article of the Constitution of Italy, yet is declared by the Court to be an 'overriding principle' that undergirds the 'form of State' created by the Constitution. Another famous example is the doctrine of the 'Basic Structure', articulated by the Supreme Court of India in *Kesavananda Bharati Sripadagalvaru v State of Kerala* and *Minerva Mills Ltd v Union of India*.[79] A third example is the general principle of the separation of powers, underlying the government structures of all democratic polities but rarely made explicit.[80]

Standards and (explicit or implicit) principles pose the greatest challenge for a normative assessment of how well a constitutional court represents the people. The question 'what makes one act of adjudication better than another?' is prohibitively too complex to be answered in one section of a chapter, but here my aim is, more modestly, to highlight the contribution that political liberalism can offer towards such an answer.

Rawls's implicit view of interpretation arguably leans not towards a strictly 'textualist' but towards a somehow *inclusive* understanding of the constitution that encompasses, beyond the text, also the Declaration of Independence and the implicit principles of constitutional democratic government. We can, furthermore, consider Rawls's conception as leaning towards a 'living constitution' as opposed to a fixed, let alone strictly originalist, understanding of the constitution. Finally, his conception inclines more towards a notion of the constitution as a 'vision' than as a set of rules.[81]

Political liberalism's most important contribution to constitutionalism, however, concerns the standard of validity. That standard is located at a level of abstraction positioned higher than the criteria of 'literal interpretation', 'inductive reasoning', 'original intent', 'stare decisis', or 'balancing', which are usually adopted by standard constitutionalism.[82] It competes with Dworkin's criterion of 'integrity', understood as 'making the most'[83] of a polity's past legal and jurisprudential history on the part of judges who see themselves as chain-novelists, and it competes with Balkin's 'text and principle' method for correct interpretation.[84]

Political liberalism can contribute a dual standard of the 'reasonable' and, more importantly, of the 'most reasonable'. Rawls famously identifies the supreme or constitutional court as the exemplar of public reason,[85] namely of a mode of reasoning (about matters concerning the basic structure, the constitutional essentials, and all the

---

[78] Constitutional Court of Italy, Judgment number 203 of 1989, English translation published on line at https://www.cortecostituzionale.it/actionSchedaPronuncia.do?anno=1989&numero=203, accessed 25 June 2020.
[79] See Chapter 3, n 64; Chapter 5, nn 86 and 87.
[80] See Balkin, *Living Originalism* (n 26) 142.
[81] For an articulation of these three polarities as descriptive of the major partitions of the field of constitutional interpretation, see Walter F Murphy, James E Fleming, and William F Harris II, *American Constitutional Interpretation* (Foundation Press 1986), 289–90 (hereafter Murphy, Fleming, and Harris, *Constitutional Interpretation*). See also Philip Bobbit, *Constitutional Interpretation* (Blackwell 1991).
[82] See Murphy, Fleming, and Harris, *American Constitutional Interpretation* (n 81) 302–13.
[83] See Dworkin, *Freedom's Law* (n 50) 10–11 and *Law's Empire* (Harvard University Press 1986), 228–32.
[84] See Balkin, *Living Originalism* (n 26) 6–7.
[85] Rawls, *PL* 231–40.

constitution's standards and implicit principles) that proceeds *from premises shared by all the participants*, as opposed to reasoning from what we, unilaterally and on the basis of some comprehensive conception, see as 'the whole truth'. Public reason tries to draw shareable conclusions from shared premises. These conclusions are not logical derivations—as in the legal-positivist Enlightenment dream of Cesare Beccaria, who famously argued that, in adjudication, a court's sentence is the conclusion of a syllogism that has the law as the major premise and the facts of the matter as the minor premise.[86] Public reason, instead, consists of practical arguments that, differently from those concerning constitutional *rules*, cannot rely on the closure of determinant judgment and thus are in no position to force the addressees to consent under penalty of being irrational if they don't. Thus, public reason leaves room for reasonable disagreement occasioned by the burdens of judgment.

Having said this, the normative import of public reason consists, no less than Kant's 'merely reflecting' judgment,[87] of its reaching conclusions whose validity does not depend on the factual coalescing of consent but places the addressees under an 'ought' to consent. The question is: what does this 'ought' rest on? A standard legal-positivist answer runs: such 'ought' rests on the fact that the judgment in questions is proffered by a constitutional court, the one authorized highest interpreter of the constitution. Under that positivist view, the court cannot be mistaken, which runs counter to experience and implicit admission by a supreme court itself when it overrules its previous opinions. Another answer is Dworkin's famous standard of Hercules, who in adjudicating 'makes the most of the entire jurisprudential body of the polity'.

Rawls offers a different answer: when a supreme or constitutional court acts as an exemplar of public reason, its (re-)interpretation of a constitutional standard or principle commands consent because it is *the most reasonable*. Only up to a point can we gather the meaning of this crucial standard from Rawls's texts. Rawls defines the reasonable indirectly, as the property of an argument, a doctrine, a constitutional essential, a political platform, and, in our case, an interpretation of the constitution, to be endorsable by reasonable persons, that is, persons willing to propose and abide by fair terms of cooperation and to recognize the burdens of judgment. That is a necessary but not yet sufficient step. Sound and unsound, valid and not valid arguments, interpretations, and doctrines may equally be reasonable. We have then only a baseline for defining when a constitutional interpretation, produced from within the circle of its members or by external advocates, is *worth considering* by the court: it must be 'at least reasonable'. Such a standard eliminates a lot of comprehensive arguments that fall short of reasonability, on account of their unshared premises or their implications. But the standard of the reasonable cannot enable the highest judicial interpreter to identify *which* interpretation, among the plurality of the at-least reasonable ones, deserves to become—for reasons other than the subjective preference of the proponent—the single *most reasonable* one. For that purpose, we need to specify what, consistently with political liberalism, something being more reasonable than something else or actually most reasonable may possibly mean.

---

[86] See Cesare Beccaria, *Of Crimes and Punishment and Other Writings* (Cambridge University Press 1995) 14.
[87] Kant, *Critique of Judgment* (n 77) § 4, 67.

As suggested in Chapter 1 (Section 1.c), for Rawls the status of being the most reasonable within a family of 'at least reasonable' liberal and political conceptions of justice applies to justice as fairness not on account of its 'being true to an order antecedent to and given to us', but on account of justice as fairness's 'congruence with our deepest understanding of ourselves and our aspirations' and with 'our history and the traditions embedded in our public life'—an expression more or less equivalent to justice as fairness's congruence with 'who we are, politically and historically'.[88]

We need to translate that expression into the vocabulary of self-constitution outlined above.[89] It cannot be the case that *factual* aspects—for example, 'our history and the traditions embedded in our public life'—determine what we ought to regard as the most reasonable political conception of justice for us. That would undermine our autonomy. Indeed, one of the semantic indicators that Rawls does not contemplate such a rendition comes from his reference to the congruence of a conception of justice 'with our deepest understanding of ourselves and our *aspirations*'. Thus, it must be assumed that to consider justice as fairness as the most reasonable political conception of justice for us means that on the basis of a reflective judgment in which we take stock of our history, our traditions, but also of our future-oriented aspirations, we develop, in a reflective equilibrium encompassing all these aspects, a sense of the *irrecusability* of justice as fairness as the 'most reasonable' political conception of justice that we can hold.

As though we were re-enacting Luther's stance, we form a sense that we 'can do no other' than to select justice as fairness as 'most reasonable' among a number of 'at least reasonable' political conceptions of justice. In the contemporary vocabulary of self-constitution, we come to feel that we cannot but 'reflectively endorse' justice as fairness, 'wholeheartedly identify' with it, and that the normativity that we obey in that act of endorsement, judgment, or wholehearted identification manifests itself as 'irrecusability': 'we can do no other', as opposed to 'we don't want to do any other'. The normativity of the 'most reasonable' is neither a transcendent normativity forcing itself upon us, nor is it entirely at our disposal as the normativity of a preference.

In our reformulated allegory of the cave,[90] sideways at the entrance of the cave, the philosophers would come to understand the self-imposed pluralism-safeguarding prohibition against using coercive power to affirm controversial accounts of the outside of the cave as being neither discovered outside the cave nor one of the opinions inside the cave. Likewise, for Rawls our selecting justice as fairness as the most reasonable political conception of justice responds neither to an external, transcendent, autonomy-crushing normativity nor to an arbitrary preference. Internal, non-cognitive necessitation, irrecusability, 'can't do no other', are all approximations to this *sui generis* normativity rooted in self-identity or 'who we are'.[91]

---

[88] See John Rawls, 'Kantian Constructivism in Moral Theory' (1980) 88 The Journal of Philosophy 519.
[89] See Chapter 4, Section 2.d.
[90] See Chapter 1, Section 1.c.
[91] As pointed out in Chapter 3 (Section 4.b), an important forerunner of this notion of situated, singular normativity is Rousseau's 'legislator', see Jean Jacques Rousseau, *The Social Contract* (1762), translated and with an introduction C Betts (Oxford University Press 1994) Book II, Chapter 8, 46. In the twentieth century, a similar view of situated, singular normativity resurfaces in Simmel's 'individual law': see Georg Simmel, 'Das individuelle Gesetz,' (1913), in *Das Individuelle Gesetz: Philosophische Exkurse* (Suhrkamp 1987) 174–230.

This model of normativity can be applied to the interpretation of constitutional standards and principles, explicit and implicit, by a supreme or constitutional court. The best rendition of 'equal protection of the laws' or 'freedom of speech' or the 'free exercise of religion' or, in another context, the Italian Republic's 'duty to remove those obstacles of an economic or social nature which constrain the freedom and equality of citizens, thereby impeding the full development of the human person', is the one *construction* that, among the 'at least reasonable' ones available, appears to the majority of the constitutional or supreme court worth endorsing as the 'most reasonable'.

In a specific case, being the 'most reasonable' means, for the interpretation of a contested standard or principle, that the majority of the court endorses offering that interpretation—which, for example, extends 'equal protection' to exclude segregation or to allow same-sex marriage—as an 'irrecusable' commitment that 'the people', including its living segment, *cannot but make* lest it would endanger its permanence as the self-same people who authored the political project outlined in the constitution. In this case, qualifying some legal interpretation as the 'most reasonable' is equivalent to the court's addressing the people by saying 'we'—because the members of the court are part of the people—'can do no other' than interpret the controversial constitutional standard or principle in this way, if we want to continue to live within the constitutional project that regulates our political life.

Dissenting opinions dispute this asserted non-cognitive necessitation and maintain, instead, that the 'most reasonable' interpretation is 'just reasonable' and is arbitrarily upgraded on the scale of normativity by the majority of the court.

It is worth emphasizing that this political liberal standard of correct constitutional interpretation produces the same result as Dworkin's standard of 'making the most' of the integrity of the constitutional project underlying a polity's life, but without indulging in the epistemic fantasy of burdening the best judicial interpretation with the claim to be tracking 'the one correct answer', in a cognitive sense, to the disputed matter. The distance between tracking the one correct answer and making the most reasonable *commitment* is what separates the standard of correct constitutional adjudication derivable from political liberalism from Hercules's epistemic tour de force.

b. The red line between interpretation and transformation

This reconstruction of the political-liberal standard of correct constitutional interpretation offers an additional advantage over epistemic models of either an originalist or a constructivist ilk. A simple change of modality illustrates where the conceptual red line between *interpreting* and unduly *transforming* the constitution lies. That line runs across two diverse modalities that suffice in order to sort out all the five possible types of legal developments from a constitutional text.

According to Sanford Levinson, all possible legal developments of an extant constitutional text fall into one of five cases. First, the instance considered can be 'simply a recognition, called "interpretation", of what was already immanent within the existing body of legal materials'. Second, it could be a permissible exercise 'of the powers allowed governmental actors by the Constitution' (eg a statute, an executive order, an administrative regulation). Third, the development in question, falling into neither of the previous cases, could count as a 'genuine', albeit not essential, change of the constitutional provisions and thus could be 'unproblematically described as an "amendment"'. Fourth, the alteration could be of such magnitude as to deserve being described as a 'revision', namely an *important* amendment 'congruent with the immanent values of the constitutional order' and thus 'unproblematic, assuming compliance with whatever constitutional procedures are established in regard to such "revisions"'. Fifth, the development may finally represent a change of such fundamental dimension 'as to be best described as "revolutionary"' and thus taken out of the language of amendment and legitimated, if at all, by some extraconstitutional set of events'.[92]

Only the first two cases fall under the heading of 'interpretation'; the remaining three count as instance of 'transformation', the legitimacy of which will be discussed in the next chapter. What unifies each of these two groups of legal instances is the mode of normativity associated with it. When some constitutional standard or principle posits a normative commitment (eg rejecting 'war as an instrument of aggression against the freedom of other peoples and as a means for the settlement of international disputes', or refraining from 'abridging the freedom of speech, or of the press'[93]) as one that the people *cannot but make*, in order to remain faithful to its political identity as defined by its self-authored constitution, we are in the domain of *interpretation*.

When instead some constitutional standard or principle is understood as a commitment that the people *may want* to make, in order to improve or somehow update their constitutional project, there we enter the domain of *transformation* and we leave the jurisdiction of a court. The authority to make or reject such a new commitment is duly vested solely in the democratic sovereign, the people, in ways that remain to be discussed.

Waldron, Bellamy, Tushnet, and others who lament a judicial occlusion of democratic authorship do have a point—not so much when they refer to the *magnitude* of change, as though a threshold of social impact existed (why would desegregation exert a lesser impact than same-sex marriage?) above which only legislatures are authorized to decide—but when they raise the challenge of distinguishing the *interpretation* of the constitution from its *transformation*. Even defenders of the democratic propriety of *Obergefell*, among which I count myself, readily acknowledge that anti-discrimination arguments under the Fourteenth Amendment could not justify, at least in our historical time, overturning statutes prohibiting polygamy. How to describe the different legal standing of the possibly equally strong subjective feelings of exclusion from marriage experienced by a gay couple and by a polygamous community? The difference cannot rest on the readiness of the larger public to accept the practice in question, lest we forfeit the constitutional character of the Constitution.

Perhaps the difference between 'interpreting' and 'transforming' cannot be captured by a *concept* at all, any more than the difference between an artwork that barely deserves the name and one that breaks new ground can be captured *conceptually*. In

---

[92] Sanford Levinson, 'How Many Times Has the United States Constitution Been Amended? (A) < 26; (B) 26; (C) 27; (D) > 27: Accounting for Constitutional Change' in S Levinson (ed), *Responding to Imperfection: The Theory and Practice of Constitutional Amendment* (Princeton University Press 1995) 20–21 (hereafter Levinson, *Responding to Imperfection*).

[93] Constitution of Italy, Article 11. Constitution of the United States, First Amendment.

spite of the impossibility of fixing it with a concept, standard, or criterion, that difference exists, exerts normative force, and, far from reflecting the empirical convergence of our judgments, it grounds what our judgments *ought to* recognize. Just as a work of art possessed of the quality of exemplarity—to avoid the Kantian term 'beauty', too internal to *one* specific (and not necessarily the most promising) aesthetic paradigm—produces a sense of the 'promotion of life' in those who come in contact with it,[94] so the interpretation that 'enlivens' the constitutional text and brings it into creative contact with our context produces a sense of promoting and enriching our political life in a stable and just society of free and equal citizens. In Kant's terminology, these judgments are called 'purely reflecting' and not determining. We can further refine that binary of 'determining' and 'purely reflecting' judgments by understanding the interpretive judgments pronounced by a constitutional court as 'oriented reflecting judgments'.[95] While 'merely reflecting' are judgments in which 'only the particular is given' and we look for a principle under which to make sense of the matter at hand, without being able to derive it from experience or conceptual analysis, in the case of constitutional adjudication—as in many other human practices—the search is 'oriented', guided by constitutional standards and principles, constitutional essentials, precedents, and other factors. These factors guide our judgment without 'dictating' or determining its final outcome.

If the judgment of whether the line separating interpretation from undue transformation has been crossed cannot be brought to a closure susceptible of demonstration, as though it was a syllogism, then although a constitutional court will always claim that its pronouncement *is* duly within the bounds of interpretation, that claim will often be contested. Consequently, the best remedy for minimizing the risk of judicial occlusion of the democratic will is to preserve the openness and viability of strategies for the people to *correct* the pronouncement of the supreme interpreter of its constitutional will.

This observation leads to the third condition that must be fulfilled in order to reject the conflation of judicial review and judicial supremacy.

c. Correcting the highest interpreter: author and interpreter of the constitution in conversation

Instances of constitutional adjudication found wanting, either in substantive terms or in arbitrary timing, can be remedied and rectified only by an exercise of the people's will. This can happen either in the forms canonically established by the constitution or through more unconventional ways. But if the ideal equilibrium envisaged by liberal-democratic constitutionalism—that is, the highest interpreter is entrusted with saying 'what the constitution says', but the people *qua* author of the constitution in some way or other can correct that interpretation by amending the constitution—has been

---

[94] Kant, *Critique of Judgment* (n 77) § 23, 128.
[95] On 'oriented reflective judgment' (thus called according to the then used James C Meredith translation (Oxford: Clarendon Press, 1986)), see Alessandro Ferrara, *Justice and Judgment: The Rise and the Prospect of the Judgment Model in Contemporary Political Philosophy* (Sage 1999) 193–94.

altered by historical circumstances, and if consequently the living co-author of the constitution incurs greater difficulties in making its voice heard, then a new balance must be found.

Rawls's paradigmatic formulation for avoiding judicial supremacy, in *Political Liberalism*—'the constitution is not what the Court says it is. Rather, it is what the people acting constitutionally through the other branches eventually allow the Court to say it is'[96]—needs to be further specified in relation to different gradients on the scale from ideal to non-ideal cases.

My suggestion is to understand the relation between the people and a constitutional or supreme court as the conversation of an author—the author of 'the Constitution'—and its interpreter over the meaning and implications of a text. When presented with interpretations, the author (i) may tacitly *accept* the interpretation offered; (ii) may *dispute* it by raising legal claims in the same or in neighbouring areas that bear on the issue and could lead to a qualified, hedged, or modified version of the earlier interpretation; or (iii) may *reject* the interpretation altogether and formally or informally amend, *qua* author, the constitution in such a way that the rejected interpretation is overridden or emptied by the newly revised constitutional script. The problem is that 'the people' is a construction, though not a fiction, and as construction is contested among rival parties. The really living, embodied elements of 'the people' are only the judges and the electorate. Thus, a number of indicators have to be singled out that offer evidence that any of those three cases is materializing.

The claim that the author of the constitution *accepts* the interpretation offered by the interpreter can be gleaned from the fact that, absent any oppression, no segments of the political arena address the electorate or mobilize in the public sphere in order to oppose the pronouncement. There is room here for a normative reflection, not to be pursued here, on the conditions of validity of the people's tacit consent.

More complicated is the second possibility: to say that the author of the constitution *disputes* aspects of the Court's interpretation really means that segments of the presently living citizenry activate themselves as legal subjects, often on the spur of advocacy groups, in order to bring new constitutional cases to the attention of the interpreter—as when in a conversation new aspects of a topic are brought up for consideration. Lawsuits are filed and in the public sphere attention is increasingly called to the contested aspects of the Court's pronouncement—by professionals, politicians representing segments of the electorate, advocacy groups, media actors, and concerned citizens. In the course of that legal conversation, and in its subsequent official pronouncements, the court may or may not heed the intimations that, equally on behalf of 'the people', those actors are trying to press on it, thereby leading the conversation back to the first case, as described above, or to the third case, to be described next.

In the third case, the interpreter offers an interpretation of the constitutional script that the author finds unacceptable and wishes to rebut. The legal conversation here takes a different course. Sectors of the citizens, who are the only subset of 'the people' endowed with agency, find it unpromising to limit their opposition to the filing of new lawsuits in the hope that constitutional litigation will lead the supreme or

---

[96] Rawls, *PL* 237.

constitutional court to overrule its previous opinion. These social and political movements want to bind the interpreter, oblige the Court to heed the constitutional author's own sense of what the contested constitutional standards or principles entail about a certain subject matter. In this case, the citizens and sectors of the electorate, along with or simply through their representatives, may want to activate the formal procedures—in the various forms they take in each constitutional regime—for amending the constitution in such a way that the desired normative substance is unambiguously stated in the amended provisions.

It could be objected that the formal mechanism for amending the constitution, in the case of the United States, during the twentieth and twenty-first centuries has become prohibitively difficult for the living segment of 'the people' to operate, as documented by Ackerman in *The Civil Rights Revolution*.[97] Such alteration of the constitutional picture—due to historical causes that include the rise of the Presidency to a prominent constitutional role, the acceleration of time, and several other factors impossible to fully enumerate here—produces a new predicament in which the mere lack of an amendment procedure underway in response to a pronouncement of the Supreme Court is less indicative of citizens' acceptance than it used to be until the *New Deal*. Such objection certainly raises a serious problem. Given the increasingly reduced accessibility of the formal amendment procedure, in the case of the United States and of many other democratic polities, the power of the judicial interpreter of the constitution has been enhanced and awaits rebalancing in order for judicial occlusion of the democratic will to be forestalled. This discussion is totally open and could be next, along with the separation of powers, on the ongoing agenda for rethinking the paradigm of political liberalism.

---

[97] See Ackerman, *Civil Rights Revolution* (n 26) 40–41. In fact, the amending pathway provided by Article V has functioned only in a limited number of cases over a bicentennial time span. Thirty-three amendments have been proposed, and twenty-seven ratified. Of these twenty-seven, only four have been conceived in order to overturn an interpretation of the Constitution rendered by the Supreme Court. Specifically, 'the Eleventh Amendment reversed the Court's opinion in *Chisholm v Georgia*, 2 US 419 (1793); the Fourteenth Amendment overturned *Dred Scott v Sandford*, 60 US 393 (1857); the Sixteenth Amendment overturned *Pollock v Farmers' Loan & Trust Company*, 158 US 601 (1895); and the Twenty-sixth Amendment modified the result that would have otherwise prevailed in *Oregon v Mitchell*, 400 US 112 (1970)', John R Vile, 'The Case against Implicit Limits on the Constitutional Amending Process', in Levinson, Responding to Imperfection (n 92) 210, n 91.

7
Amending Power
Vertical Reciprocity and Political Liberalism

> You cannot step into the same Constitution twice, but this is not because the Constitution is always changing; it is because you and the position from which you interpret the Constitution are always changing.
> (Jack M Balkin, *Living Originalism* 269)

One additional aspect of the constitutional theory implicit in political liberalism remains in need of clarification at this point. The transgenerational people, unpossessed of agency except for its living segment, needs representation by a judicial interpreter of its will, and the quality of such 'substantive representation' rests on the apex court's offering the 'most reasonable' interpretation while avoiding usurpation of the prerogative to *transform* the constitution. But the 'most reasonable' interpretation rests on an oriented reflective judgment, not susceptible to offering *more geometrico* demonstrations. The burdens of judgment are never inoperative and consensus cannot be forced on anyone, not even via the Habermasian uncoercive coercion of the better argument. Under these conditions, then, judicial review can avoid resulting in democracy-occluding judicial supremacy only if the court's pronouncements remain open to correction by the present and future living segments of the people. For this reason, the exercise of *amending power* on the part of voters who self-activate, either directly or through their legislative and executive representatives, in response to pronouncements of the judicial interpreter of higher law or *motu proprio*, constitutes a fundamental aspect of the democratic quality of a regime and we need to reconstruct what political liberalism can say about it.

Few questions are harder to answer, in constitutional theory and political philosophy, than the one concerning the nature, internal differentiation, bearer, and proper limits of secondary constituent or amending power. In this chapter, those questions will be addressed from the angle of the relation of a people to its living segment.

'Amending power' has its home in a territory left unexplored by classical political philosophy. Locke and Rousseau only addressed the distinction between the constituent power of the people or the nation and the constituted power of governmental officials. Likewise, in *Political Liberalism* Rawls distinguishes 'constituent power from ordinary power as well as the higher law of the people from the ordinary law of the legislative bodies'.[1] On a factual plane he notes that 'in the long run a strong majority *of*

---
[1] Rawls, *PL* 233.

the electorate can eventually make the constitution conform to its political will'[2] and amend it in radical ways—a crucial point to which I will return in Section 3.d—but beyond his discussion of implicitly entrenched rights, Rawls offers no explicit reflections concerning the proper exercise of amending power. The object of this chapter is to fill this lacuna that compounds the lack of a political conception of the people, by outlining a normative view of amending power consistent with political liberalism and reflected in a distinct principle of legitimacy.

1. The Concept of Amending Power

To begin, it must be noted that secondary constituent or amending power occupies 'a twilight zone between authorizing and authorized powers' and 'is simultaneously framing and framed, licensing and licensed, original and derived, superior and inferior to the constitution'.[3] On one hand, being the power to revise the constitutive rules of the political game, it is formally regulated, as far as its mode of exercise is concerned, by the constitutional provisions dedicated to amending procedures. On the other hand, insofar as it may transform the constitution, amending power is *superordinate* relative to the constitution and thus cannot derive from it. Its source has traditionally been traced to 'the people', though amending power actually belongs only to the living segment thereof. As Holmes and Sunstein correctly observe,

> It is almost as if the electorate, through its residual right to initiate and ratify constitutional amendments, retains some of its original authority to choose the nature of the political regime, to lay down the ground rules of subsequent decision making, and to establish the limits and legitimate aims of government action.[4]

a. The function of amending power for democratic legitimacy

Without presupposing such power to modify the constitutive rules of the game, the subsequent generations of the people would live in the shadow of the founding one, executing a programme that they have not scripted. It is this normative grip of the dead over the living generations that Rousseau and Jefferson had well in mind when they both suggested that periodically each generation should be offered the possibility of reassessing the constitutional pact and the form of government—thereby feeding into the contemporary populist myth of a 'will of the living people' endowed with full-scale constituent power. Crystallized institutional arrangements could claim no democratic legitimacy. Their legitimacy rests, *inter alia*, on the people's persisting

---

[2] ibid (emphasis added).
[3] Stephen Holmes and Cass R Sunstein, 'The Politics of Constitutional Revision in Eastern Europe' in Sanford Levinson (ed), *Responding to Imperfection: The Theory and Practice of Constitutional Amendment* (Princeton University Press 1995) 276 (hereafter Levinson, *Responding to Imperfection*).
[4] ibid.

'right to change or not to change fundamental value commitments and the rules of the game'.[5] Yet the picture is more complicated.

The power to amend the constitution can only derive from the constituent power of 'the people', but the transgenerational people possesses no agency and can appoint no representative. Its living segment is the only one endowed with agency but neither can it be equated with the whole people, nor can it 'represent' the whole people, because it is a self-interested voice, specifically situated, within it. Thus, when it comes to amending the constitution, those who have agency are *not* the people, and the real, transgenerational people *does not have agency*: the transgenerational people is a construction of the mind, necessary for the working of the idea of a self-governing 'just and stable society of free and equal citizens'.[6] The question then must be addressed: Whence does the amending power of the living segment of the people originate?

It is a power both internal and external to, and continuous and discontinuous with, the constituent power of the people. The electorate derives its entitlement to transform the constitution from its being a co-owner—along with past and future segments of the people—of the constitution in a *sequential*, as opposed to *serial*, pattern in which owning something 'sequentially' entails owing something to the previous and the future co-owners. In other words, the electorate derives its entitlement to transform the constitution from its co-participation in a normative conversation about the *nomos*[7] that should preside over the conduct of things political within a certain space.

Amending power, however, is dissimilar from the power vested in other forms of co-participation. Living human beings are co-participants in joint structures of interaction that are transformed through aggregated preference and patterned slippage. For example, we co-determine the fluctuations of the market through the use of our share of resources. Likewise, through patterned slippage of the meaning assigned to signifiers, we co-determine changes in the life-world and in the language wherein we are immersed. Deep changes, and often also the transient fluctuations, in the market structure, as well as long-term transformations of our language and life-world, are certainly produced by the living generations, yet they are hardly the product of conscious design. They can be imputed to the agency of the living generations, as one of its consequences, but do not flow from their conscious intentions. They result from individual conscious intentions that combine with one another in a pattern that belongs to no one.

---

[5] ibid 277.
[6] Notice how the ontological status of the holder of constituent power for Kelsen and of the transgenerational people as intended here do overlap somewhat but are not the same. Whereas for Kelsen constituent power and its holder are 'necessary presuppositions' of existing law taken as valid and effective (if we have this valid and effective set of laws, someone must have enacted the supervenient constitution according to this hypothetical basic norm), my transgenerational people is a more differentiated construction, insofar as it combines three segments: (i) past generations, that have authored the constitution from the founding to the present and whose constitutional will can be interpreted, contended over, attested by evidence; (ii) a living segment, endowed with autonomous agency, which is by no means a construction of the mind; and (iii) future generations, again a pure construction, endowed with a virtual presumed will basically equivalent to a reasonable propensity to command the same autonomy as the previous generations. I am grateful to Frank Michelman for having prompted this comparison.
[7] See Robert M Cover, 'The Supreme Court, 1982 Term—Foreword: Nomos and Narrative', *Faculty Scholarship Series*. Paper 2705, http://digitalcommons.law.yale.edu/fss_papers/2705, 4–6.

The agency of the living segment of a people, when it transforms the constitutive rules of politics, is different. Being part of the people, the electorate is definitionally possessed of the two political capacities of engaging in intentional political collective action and self-regulating its action via constitutive rules.[8] But, differently from in the case of the people, the constitutive rules through which an *electorate* acts in ordinary and constitutional politics are not of its own making: they are inherited from the common script that charters the communal political life of *all* the generations of the people. As in a conversation or in a structured game, also in the case of politics it lies within the purview of each free and equal participant to call for a suspension of the regular flow of rule-governed moves, and to offer the fellow participants a proposal for reshaping the constitutive rules of the common practice. In both cases, only upon acceptance of the proposal by all (or a supermajority of) the other participants can the new rules take effect.

Thus, differently from the cases of the market, the life-world, and natural language, and in consonance with how the rules of a structured game are transformed, in *formal* constitution-amending, as opposed to the slippage that the 'material' or 'living' constitution is constantly subjected to, there is an actual single moment when transformation becomes the object at first of deliberation and, then, of conscious decision-making.[9] The entitlement of the electorate to operate *that* transformation comes from its being 'internal to' or 'a subset of' the author of the constitution—that is, the people. An *external* political subject, unconnected with the people, could not legitimately alter the constitution, at least not within a liberal-democratic framework.

b. The specificity of amending power

However, the crucial difference relative to a structured game or a conversation is that in the case of constitution-amending the consent that validates a proposal, and turns it into a legitimate transformation of the rules, comes from a subject—again, the people—*not* directly present at the scene of deliberation in the same way as the proponent. The proponent of rule-change is present, but the provider of validating consent is not. Since 'the people' cannot be reductively equated to its living segment without incurring the three problematic consequences of serial ownership,[10] the specificity of amending power consists of the fact that the electorate, as distinct from the people, can never be fully sovereign and yet must be entitled to *transform* the constitutive rules of the polity, because the highest judicial representative of the people can only *interpret* them. How can the constitutive rules of politics be transformed by a less than fully sovereign subject?

Amending power, consistently with the paradigm of political liberalism, is not unbound—it would be illogical that the power of amending a constitution were more unbound than the power of framing it. Furthermore, the living proponents of

---

[8] See Chapter 4, Section 2.a.
[9] For a classical formulation of this distinction, though couched in a different vocabulary, see Georg Jellinek's 1906 essay *Verfassungsänderung und Verfassungswandlung* (Adamant Media Co 2005).
[10] See Chapter 5, Section 3.c.

constitutional transformation are not sovereign, in that it does not lie within their power *alone* to bring about *legitimate* constitutional transformations. The members of a living generation *become* sovereign when their constitutional will really becomes 'the will of the people'—the sole subject to whom authorship of the constitution can be attributed. And when does the constitution-transforming will of the electorate become the will of the people?

Here's the rub. That momentous upgrade, from 'will of the voters' to 'will of the people', cannot simply coincide with the official enactment of a constitutional amendment, duly approved in a referendum or by a representative legislative assembly, on the part of a judicial body entrusted to represent the entire transgenerational people. That constituted judicial power would then be more sovereign than the segment of the people proposing and ratifying an amendment to the constitution. Thus, the attestation of the consistency of the will of the living segment of the people and that of the entire transgenerational people can only be a *necessary* condition.

What then is a *sufficient* condition for the will of the electorate to count as that of the people? The answer is *temporal continuity*, or not being rejected by subsequent generations of the same people. When the amending will of the electorate, over and beyond being validated as consistent with the will of the people inscribed in the constitution and represented by its highest judicial interpreter, is explicitly or tacitly *accepted* by subsequent generations of the people, then the will that has modified the constitutive rules can be legitimately attributed to a subject larger than the electorate.

An illustration of this triadic relation of the people, its highest judicial interpreter, and the electorate comes from the approval, and subsequent repeal, of the Eighteenth Amendment to the Constitution of the United States, establishing 'prohibition'. Proposed on 18 December 1917 and ratified on 16 January 1919, the Amendment expressed the will of the majority of the electorate to the effect that 'the manufacture, sale, or transportation of intoxicating liquors within, the importation thereof into, or the exportation thereof from the United States and all territory subject to the jurisdiction thereof for beverage purposes' be prohibited. It was an *addition* to other constitutive rules of the American polity, contested by some as not of constitutional import, but anyway duly registered as the will of the electorate, not inconsistent with that of the people of the United States as of the year 1919. However, the will of that living segment can be described as coinciding with the will of the people of the United States only for a period of about fourteen years—less than a generation.

On 20 February 1933, with the required supermajority Congress proposed a Twenty-First Amendment to repeal the former Eighteenth Amendment. The new amendment was ratified on 5 December 1933. The example illustrates the dynamic of amending power. 'The will of the people' cannot be directly observed—it can only be inferred from interpreting the constitution—and certainly cannot contradict itself. Thus, two subsequent expressions of the will of the electorate, one affirming and the other repealing an amendment, must be taken as evidence that the will of the people has changed, in this case within a span of fourteen years. The requisite of consistency with the basic design of the constitution is only a necessary condition, but the *sufficient* one for the holder of amending power to succeed in legitimately transforming constitutional provisions is that the new rules be lastingly accepted by subsequent generations—an acceptance which in this case failed to materialize.

Based on this general outline, the correct exercise of 'amending power' comprises four distinct facets, to be considered from the angle of political liberalism and concerning the 'when', the 'what', the 'who', and the 'where' of the amending process. After considering these aspects, the key issue of the *limits* of amending power will be addressed and, finally, a liberal principle of its legitimate exercise will be introduced.

2. Four Facets of the Exercise of Amending Power

A caveat is in order, before highlighting these four facets. The elucidation of secondary or amending power will be approached from a *normative* point of view, which is not to imply that descriptive accounts cannot be illuminating, as attested by the magisterial account, offered by Bruce Ackerman in his trilogy *We the People*, of how amending power actually operated beyond the formal guidelines of the Constitution of the United States. The New Deal and the Civil Rights Revolution, two major constitutional moments in the history of the country, have transformed the Constitution without relying on formal amendments, with the exception of the Twenty-Fourth Amendment (1964), which however concerned only a very specific aspect of the new affirmation of civil rights. The previous transformation—the Reconstruction, after the Civil War—did occur through formal amendments, but in the context of a number of 'unconventional adaptations'. Ackerman's account focuses on the actual transformative processes and the reasons for their final successful outcome. This chapter focuses on the normative question: how is the legitimacy of an exercise of amending power to be understood?

a. Time for a change: when is amending needed?

The first facet of this complex question can be captured as a 'when' question: under what conditions should the power to amend the constitution be activated? Are there cases when it was activated and it shouldn't have been? Are there opposite cases, when it should have been activated but failed to be? Furthermore, what conditions justify the activation of amending power *within* the formal guidelines provided by the constitution? What conditions suffice to justify its activation *beyond* the locally applicable constitutional guidelines for amendment? Are there decisive arguments in favour of excluding that legitimate constitutional change can occur outside the formal provisions by which a constitution regulates the proposal and ratification of amendments, or can we follow the line of procedural 'non-exclusivism' and acknowledge that legitimate constitutional change may occur in ways (important statutes, crucial pronouncements, executive orders that modify the relation among the separated powers, etc) other than those formally provided by the constitution?[11]

---

[11] With reference to the United States, on 'Article V non-exclusivism', Bruce Ackerman has observed that none of Article V's '143 words says anything like "this Constitution may only be amended through the following procedures, and in no other way." The Article makes its procedures sufficient, but not necessary, for the enactment of a valid constitutional amendment', Bruce Ackerman, 'Higher Lawmaking', in Levinson, *Responding to Imperfection* (n 3) 72. Along converging lines, Akhil Reed Amar claims that one thing that

The general 'when' question also includes more specific ones: Are there reasons for barring the proposing or ratifying of amendments during certain specific times? The Constitution of France prohibits amending the constitutional text when 'the integrity of national territory is placed in jeopardy', that of Greece 'before the lapse of five years from the completion of a previous revision', that of Brazil 'during federal intervention, state of defence or stage of siege', and that of Spain 'in time of war' or during 'states of alarm, emergency and siege'.[12] Are there reasons of principle for connecting the exercise of amending power to certain junctures of democratic life (for example, tying referendums to general elections, due to the increased potential for voter mobilization)? Are there arguments that run in the opposite direction and forbid the overlapping of elections and referendums on constitutional matters (eg a greater risk of ideological polarization and politicization of constitutional matters)?

Another aspect of the 'when' question concerns the *expiration* of the amending process, a question raised by the vicissitudes of the Twenty-Seventh Amendment of the Constitution of the United States, proposed in 1789 and approved, upon ratification by the required thirty-eighth state, over two centuries thereafter, in 1992. Should the formal process be considered open-ended or enclosed within temporal brackets? If so, what principles should orient the identification of temporal limits? The question cannot be answered here, but two opposing arguments can be mentioned. In favour of a temporal limitation militates the idea that deliberation ought to take place in the context where as many background assumptions are shared as possible. For this reason, the Congress of the United States in the twentieth century has started setting a time limit of seven years for the ratification of a proposed amendment, prolonged to ten in the case of the Equal Rights Amendment. On the other hand, the longer the span of time taken by deliberation, the narrower the temporal gap between the will of the electorate and that of the people: no other Amendment to the Constitution of the United States can lay a stronger claim to resting on 'the will of the people' than the Twenty-Seventh Amendment.

More generally, unless the question 'When does a constitution need amending?' is understood in strictly subjectivist terms—that is, a constitutional amendment is legitimate whenever the holders of constituent amending power, be they officials or sectors of the electorate, form a political will to that effect—can a normative paradigm pinpoint contexts in which amending is *called for* or, on the contrary, *unwarranted*, independently of that will?

A general consideration that political liberalism can offer in that respect consists in pointing to the embeddedness of the political will of the holders of amending power within a larger context of beliefs. It is the combination of a general orientation and a set of beliefs that renders a concrete amendment to a given constitution deserving

---

Article V does not say is 'that it is the *only* way to amend the Constitution', see his 'Popular Sovereignty and Constitutional Amendment', in ibid 90. More generally, Amar claims that 'We the People of the United States have a legal right to alter our government—to amend our Constitution—via a majoritarian and populist mechanism akin to a national referendum, even though that mechanism is not explicitly specified in Article V'—ibid 89. For an enlightening discussion of this and the opposite, exclusivist thesis, see Frank Michelman, 'Thirteen Easy Pieces' (1995) 93(6) Michigan Law Review 1297.

[12] See the Constitution of France, Article 89; Constitution of Greece, Article 110/6; Constitution of Brazil, Article 60, § 1; Constitution of Spain, Part X, Sections 169 and 116.

of endorsement. For example, a controversy over the meaning or application of a standard or principle included in the constitution may have been solved by the highest judicial interpreter in a way considered deeply erroneous by the living segment of the people or large sectors thereof. Correction of such a contentious interpretation warrants the activation of amending power. The history of the United States provides examples of at least four such cases.[13]

In addition to this remedial use of amending power, it can generally be said that amending power ought to be activated whenever a sector of the electorate or an authorized institutional actor believes that a desirable new rule, standard, or principle cannot be generated via construction or, in other words, lies 'beyond interpretation'. A distinction ought to be made. Rules are so specific that their modification can hardly be obtained by interpretation or construction: for example, a minimum age for eligibility to a given office or a limit to the terms that a president can serve, if set by a constitutional provision, can only be changed via the use of amending power. The case is different with standards and principles, for they can be updated both by reinterpretation (as exemplified by the judicial interpretation of 'equal protection of the laws' in *Plessy* and in *Brown*) or by amending the constitution (as exemplified by the extension of the principle of equality to include the right to vote, through the Fifteenth Amendment (1870): 'the right of citizens of the United States to vote shall not be denied or abridged by the United States or by any State on account of race, color, or previous condition of servitude').[14]

The line between an extensive judicial interpretation of constitutional principles and their transformation is very tenuous and not susceptible to being subsumed under a concept, as clarified in Chapter 6, Section 3.b. For this reason, the legitimacy of a constitutional democracy depends crucially on the actual and ongoing unimpeded viability of the institutional pathways for correcting pronouncements of the supreme or constitutional court deemed to be unduly transformative. Consequently, the ideal-typical sufficient condition for legitimately activating amending power—that is, a perceived need for a constitutional transformation that exceeds the boundaries of construction and interpretation of the extant text—is not strictly imperative. During the New Deal, innovative legislation of constitutional salience was pursued, as documented by Ackerman, while deliberately discarding the path of amending the Constitution, on account of the urgency of anti-crisis legislation, of the temporal extension of the amendment process in the United States, and of the efficacy of the political pressure on the Supreme Court. Yet, in terms of ideal theory it might be claimed that innovative constitutional contents are more legitimately introduced via

---

[13] See Chapter 6, Section 3.c (n 97).

[14] In the context of a broader argument about the irrelevance of formal amendments to the regulatory function of the Constitution, David Strauss has argued that the formal ratification of the Fifteenth Amendment changed nothing on the ground and failed to achieve the goal of enfranchising African Americans. As he observes, 'to a limited degree, the Union army and the political changes imposed on the South in the aftermath of its occupation did [enfranchise them]; but when those effects faded, the Fifteenth Amendment might as well not have been part of the Constitution. Not until one hundred years later did the Voting Rights Act—itself the product of long-term social and economic forces—genuinely enfranchise blacks. The Constitution, in practice, did not change with the Amendment. It changed only when deeper changes occurred in society', David A Strauss, 'The Irrelevance of Constitutional Amendments' (2001) 114 Harvard Law Review 1483.

the amendment process than via packing, or threatening to pack, the highest court in order to obtain the desired 'interpretation'.

Within the larger set of innovative standards and principles a more specific subset includes those that are *entirely new*, linked not so much to the extension of already accepted principles but rather to the rise of new sensibilities among the citizens: for example, constitutional amendments that provide for environmental protection (newly introduced as Article 21 in a 1983 revision of the Constitution of the Netherlands) or a balanced budget (introduced as an amended Article 81 in the Constitution of Italy).[15] The time when new areas of public concern emerge, as today might be the case with climate change, mass migration, or global pandemics, seems the most appropriate for new exercises of amending power. The 'when' facet of our question naturally then leads to the 'what' facet.

b. Corrective and ameliorative amendments

The use of amending power also raises a 'what' question. What matters can be subjected to amendment and, more specifically, is amending power internally differentiated? Intuitively, all the different motives for transforming a constitution seem to fall under two large headings: (i) the correction of inadequacies of the extant constitution, and (ii) the insertion into the constitution of new areas or concepts hitherto ignored or neglected and the affirmation of previously unenumerated rights.

As in the case of the 'when' question, in this case the natural starting point seems to be the tripartition of rules, standards, and principles.[16] A difficulty immediately arises. Standards such as the prohibition to inflict 'cruel and unusual punishment' and principles as 'equal protection of the laws' seem less likely to be matters for formal amendment than for judicial reinterpretation. Instead, constitutional provisions that take the form of rules—for example, provisions about the voting age, the number of legislative representatives, the method of election to a certain office, and the like—seem the ideal candidates for formal amendments.

However, that is a misleading impression. The distinction of 'strictures' and 'amplitudes' cuts across another distinction, related to the rationale for proposing a constitutional amendment: the distinction between 'corrective' and 'ameliorative' amendments. 'Corrective' amendments tend to remedy the perceived inadequacies of the extant constitution or, to borrow the title of an influential collection, to 'respond to imperfection'—for example, to remedy electoral mechanisms that fail to secure stability, certainty, tie-avoidance, inadequately separated powers that tend to interfere with one another, or age requirements that seem to have grown out of step with common sense. In that respect, there seems to be an elective affinity of the 'corrective' motivation and the amending of single constitutional rules.

---

[15] In the wake of the 2008 Recession, the Parliament of Italy amended the Constitution in order to introduce the principle of a balanced budget. Article 81 was the main amended provision, now mandating that 'The State shall balance revenue and expenditure in its budget, taking account of the adverse and favourable phases of the economic cycle', but at the same time Articles 97, 117, and 119 were also amended in order to reflect the same principle.
[16] See Chapter 6, Section 2.c.

On the other hand, standards and principles become the most frequent matter for 'ameliorative' amendments, motivated by the intention to 'constitutionalize' new standards (eg of accountability) or new principles or rights (right to privacy). Amplitudes are usually the stuff of amendments aimed at introducing new normative content. Principles related to environmental protection have been introduced in some form or other in 146 new constitutions,[17] but principles that concern privacy,[18] balanced budgets,[19] gender equality, and LGBTQ rights,[20] have also been the object of recent amendments.

Political liberalism offers no special criterion for correlating these two broad classes of amendments—corrective and ameliorative—to specific classes of actors, such as public officials or the electorate at large, and consequently to specific institutional venues, such as Parliaments, as opposed to referendums. Principles such as the prohibition of discrimination against same-sex marriage have been understood as interpretive constructions from pre-existent principles (eg 'equal protection of the laws') in the United States, but as transformative new principles, to be introduced into the Constitution via referendum, in Ireland. The reason is that structure-determining rules—such as number of terms in office, mode of selection of officials, eligibility or extension of franchise—may be as influential for the 'basic structure' as broader standards and principles. The most general point is that the more influential a given correction or innovation in relation to the basic structure, the larger should be the deliberative body that deliberates on and eventually enacts it. Legislative institutions and electorates are both constituted powers, according to political liberalism, but electorates—convened through referendums—seem to be one step closer to the holder of constituent power than their legislative representatives.

c. Who is to amend what?

Do these diverse aspects of a constitution generate different requirements for the legitimate exercise of amending power? Of interest is the mapping of diverse aspects of the constitution onto different kinds of holders of amending power. This is the 'who' facet of the legitimate exercise of amending power. Most constitutions vest amending

---

[17] See Roderic O'Gorman, 'Environmental Constitutionalism: A Comparative Study' (2017) 6(3) Transnational Environmental Law 435.

[18] Among the Constitutions that have included a general right to privacy, not reduced to the privacy of correspondence or domicile, see among others the Constitutions of Algeria (Article 77), Angola (Article 32), Bolivia (Article 21), Bulgaria (Article 32), the Dominican Republic (Article 44), Iceland (Article 71), Israel (Basic Law n 7), the Republic of Korea (Article 17), Mozambique (Article 41), the Netherlands (Article 10), Peru (Article 2), Portugal (Article 26), Slovakia (Article 16), Slovenia (Article 35), South Africa (Article 14), Spain (Section 18), and Switzerland (Article 13).

[19] Among the Constitutions that have introduced a mandatory principle of balancing the state budget are Austria (Article 13), Germany (Articles 109, 110, 115), Hungary (Article N), Italy (Article 81), Morocco (Article 77), Peru (Article 78), Slovenia (Article 148), Spain (Section 135), and Switzerland (Article 126).

[20] While 177 Constitutions include provisions that prohibit gender-based discrimination, only thirteen have introduced provisions that extend that prohibition to sexual orientation and thus variously protect LBGTQ rights. Among them are the Constitutions of: Bolivia (Article 14), Ecuador (Article 11), Malta (Article 32), Mexico (Article 1), New Zealand (Article 21, m), Portugal (Article 13), South Africa (Article 9), and Sweden (Articles 2 and 12).

power in institutions that nominally exercise separated constituted powers—mostly legislative institutions, but in some cases executive officers[21]—and under certain conditions require direct involvement, in referendums, on the part of the electorate. Does the diversity of these actors correlate with the diversity of rationales for amending the constitution, for example in the sense that officials are prima facie entitled to correct constitutional inadequacies but less entitled to introduce new matters, something that should remain the preserve of the living segment of the people?

Interesting reflections on the matter have been offered by William Harris and more recently by Yaniv Roznai. Both argue in favour of a direct relation between the importance of the object of amendment and the degree of representativeness of the authorized amending subject. In Harris's words,

> The less an amendment seemed to implicate the rights of the people, the more acceptable would be an amending route that centered on incumbent ... officials and 'bureaucratic' representatives.... Conversely, the more amendments encroach on the people's rights and powers, the more necessary it is to search out a plausible popular approval through the devices of such episodically extraordinary, special-purpose representative bodies as conventions.[22]

Yaniv Roznai has offered a similar argument. Observing that the Constitutions of Canada and of South Africa[23] provide formal procedures of increasing demandingness for distinct types of amendment, Roznai advocates a so-called spectrum theory of amending power, based on a gradient of demandingness along the following lines:

> The more similar the characteristics of the secondary constituent power are to those of the democratic primary constituent power described as the 'popular amendment power', the less it should be bound by limitations, including those of judicial scrutiny, and vice versa. The closer it is to a regular legislative power or 'governmental amendment power', the more it should be fully bound by limitations and judicial scrutiny.[24]

In both cases, the idea is that the more significant the matter for amendment, the closer the subject of amending power should be to 'the people' and, according to Roznai, the fewer limitations it should have. This seems a quite sensible idea, to be endorsed, and certainly consistent with the framework of political liberalism. Roznai's main intuition should, however, be reconciled with two additional observations. On one hand, very often rules have a direct, almost automatic impact on the life of the polity, which standards and principles may lack due to the possible attenuating effect

---

[21] Among the Member States of the European Union, amendments are to be formally proposed by Presidents in Bulgaria, Estonia, France, Poland and Romania, and worldwide in, among others, Afghanistan, Algeria, Angola, Ecuador, Egypt, Gabon, Kazakhstan, Madagascar, North Macedonia, Russia, Senegal, Serbia, Tajikistan, Tunisia, Ukraine, Venezuela, and Vietnam.

[22] William F Harris II, *The Interpretable Constitution* (Johns Hopkins University Press 1993) 194–95 (hereafter Harris, *Interpretable Constitution*).

[23] See Canada Constitution Act (1982), Part V, and the Constitution of South Africa, Article 74.

[24] Yaniv Roznai, *Unconstitutional Constitutional Amendments: The Limits of Amendment Power* (Oxford University Press 2017) 162 (hereafter Roznai, *Unconstitutional Constitutional Amendments*).

produced by subsequent judicial interpretation. This is the case, for instance, with the limitation of presidential terms, voting age, extension of the franchise, and number of allotted seats in a legislative or judicial institution. For this reason, the constitutional impact of the proposed amendment, and consequent demandingness in relation to the amending subject's representativeness, should not be correlated in any rigid sense with the distinction of rules, standards, and principles. On the other hand, officials who operate as constituted power holders may be in a better position, relative to parties and movements and associations representative of sectors of the electorate, to propose amendments, including rule-changing ones of whatever magnitude, related to the *institutional framework of the polity*—while the ratifying moment once again should be geared to an indirect or a direct (referendum-like) modality, depending on the relevance of the proposed reform.

To conclude, the normative indication that could be gleaned from the above considerations is to envisage a division of functions, whereby institutional actors should be primarily vested with the prerogative to enact amendments concerning *rules* or the organizational structure of the polity (save for high-impact rule-change), and the electorate with the prerogative to modify or introduce constitutional *principles*, with the area of constitutional *standards* falling in between.

d. The institutional venues of amending power

The answer to the 'who' question leads to another facet of the legitimate exercise of amending power, which concerns the specific institutional venue for designing, proposing, and ratifying an amendment. A legislative assembly or a president may propose an amendment according to procedures unfolding in very different institutional venues: for example, an amendment may be proposed in the legislative or executive institutions vested with the power for advancing such proposals, or within ad hoc conventions assembled through formal elections or appointment, and more or less open to popular participation. Call this the 'where' question. This question, strictly connected with the previous one, can be answered by indicating many alternative combinations, which fall in between the rigid alternative of either vesting amending power entirely in the institutional separated powers or bringing in the directly expressed will of the living segment of the people.

Article V of the Constitution of the United States exemplifies this possible degree of differentiation. It spells out four distinct possibilities for formal amendment, by combining two diverse alternatives at the proposing stage and two at the ratifying stage. First, an amendment can be proposed with a two-thirds majority in each House of Congress and then ratified by the legislatures of three-quarters of the States. This is a procedure in which only institutional actors of the legislative branch are active, similar to the amending procedures of many countries. Second, the amendment can be proposed as above, but ratified by conventions in three-quarters of the States. Third, the amendment can be proposed by a convention summoned by Congress on request of two-thirds of the States and ratified by the legislatures of three-quarters of the States. These two alternatives occupy an intermediate point on the spectrum: they combine ad hoc representative institutions ('conventions', convenable through a variety of procedures that set them in different relations of representativeness to the electorate) and routinely elected and functioning legislative institutions. Fourth, the amending proposal can be generated by a convention called by Congress on request of two-thirds of the States, with ratification also taking place through conventions in three-quarters of the States.[25]

Are there reasons for correlating, within the representative-institutions option, certain matters considered for amendment with the use of existent institutional venues or ad hoc conventions? Are there reason for correlating certain substantive matters with one kind of proposing institution and one kind of ratifying institution?

A theory of amending power needs also to consider the nature of the specific ad hoc conventions and the way they are convened. When their members are appointed, they can be assumed to reflect more or less closely the divisions inherent in the appointing institutions, and so their distance from the latter appears to be at a minimum. Choice of one type of amending pathway or the other is then less crucial, and little can be added to single contextual factors that favour one or the other choice. That said, when ad hoc conventions are elected, especially through a proportional electoral mechanism that makes them more representative of the electorate (particularly in contexts where first-past-the-post electoral laws prevail), then it makes sense to identify them as preferable institutional venues if the matter considered concerns essential elements of the constitution. Another factor that militates in favour of ad hoc conventions, when the matter for amendment touches important constitutional matters, is that they can be staffed (regardless whether their members are nominated or elected) with participants selected for their expertise and public-spiritedness and less influenced by the incentives of normal political life in representative institutions. Furthermore, the boundedness of their mandate may be more effective in insulating them from the pressure of unprincipled compromise-seeking.

In conclusion, a normative perspective on amending power inclines us to contend that the greater the salience of the matter under consideration—whether on account of its nature as new or reinterpreted standards or principles, or on account of its wide impact as rule-change—the more reasonable, *ceteris paribus*, it is to vest the amending power in ad hoc conventions at the proposing stage and in the electorate, through referendums, at the ratifying stage. However, in contrast to how it often happens in the literature on amending power, the relation of the salience of matters for amendment to the kind of actors or venues most appropriate for leading the amending process is best discussed separately from the issue of the *limits* applicable to amending power—a question that will be examined on its own, in the next section.

3. The Limits of Amending Power

The most important aspect of a reflection on the legitimate exercise of amending power concerns the limits of its use. We must distinguish explicit or formal unamendability, typically expressed in 'eternity clauses' included in specific constitutional provisions,

---

[25] See Harris, *The Interpretable Constitution* (n 22) 174.

and implicit or structural unamendability, not traceable to single positive provisions. The two forms of unamendability incur distinct difficulties. Explicit unamendability notoriously incurs the conundrum of the acceptability of a dual exercise of amending power, first in order to remove an unamendability clause and then in order to amend the desired matter.[26] Instead, *structural* or *implicit* unamendability poses possibly even more difficult problems, recalled above in connection with Rawls's discussion of the implicit unamendability of the First Amendment and with the doctrine of the Basic Structure put forward by the Supreme Court of India. These problems allow us to further elucidate the notions of sequential democratic sovereignty and of vertical reciprocity presupposed by Rawls's constitutional theory as it can be reconstructed from *Political Liberalism* and further expanded.

According to the view of constituent power discussed in Chapters 3 and 4, a constitution articulates a project for jointly living a political life over an open-ended time span, and it seems indefensible to affirm the right of a subset of the people, living during a limited time, to alter the design of the constitution in such a way that it becomes *incompatible* with the original one. Considered in quantitative terms, the living segment of the people is certainly not the majority of the entire people. Hence the legitimacy of the amendments it introduces, directly via referendums or indirectly through constituted institutions, depends on their consistency with the overall general commitments already inscribed in the constitution. That raises the question of who, in order to determine said consistency, should represent the entire people and interpret its constitutional commitments.

In Chapter 6, bracketing the independently interesting question concerning the preferability of such an institution over other possible alternatives, a supreme or constitutional court was simply stipulated to be representing 'the people' in its entirety. Whereas in that chapter the democratic standing of the judicial review of ordinary statutes and administrative acts was addressed, we should now focus on whether the legitimacy of *constitutional amendments*, as Rawls in passing suggested,[27] should be reviewed by a supreme or constitutional court. Should amendments be evaluated at

---

[26] The question whether all amendment-regulating provisions are to be considered *implicitly entrenched* (even if explicitly they appear to be constitutional provisions like any other) has been debated in a famous exchange between Herbert LA Hart and Alf Ross. Ross defended the view that Article V, if altered according to its own rules (but the argument can be applied to any amendment-regulating constitutional provision), would change into a new article that could no longer be regarded 'as valid because derived from it [Article V]': any norm presupposes 'the validity of the superior norm and thereby the continued existence of the same' and we cannot imagine that a norm 'which conflicts with the source of its derivation'. Alf Ross, *On Law and Justice* (University of California Press 1959) 82. Hart objected to both points, on the ground that Ross neglected to take the temporal dimension into account. According to Hart, while it may be true that a valid norm cannot be derived from a legal source with which it is in conflict, in the hypothetical case of amending Article V according to its own provisions, no such conflict would arise: 'the original procedure is to be used until it is replaced by the new, and the new procedure is to be used thereafter', Herbert LA Hart, 'Self-Referring Laws', in *Essays in Jurisprudence and Philosophy* (Clarendon Press 1983) 177. Contrary to Hart's view, the priority of substance over formal permissibility has been invoked, in the basis of the principle, articulated by the Supreme Court of the United States in 1867, 'what cannot be done directly cannot be done indirectly. The Constitution deals with substance not shadows', *Cummings v Missouri* (1867) 71 US 277, 325, quoted, along with other sources, in Roznai, *Unconstitutional Constitutional Amendments* (n 24) 139–41 where an interesting discussion of the intricacies of explicit unamendability can be found. See also Harris, *The Interpretable Constitution* (n 22) 181–91.

[27] See Rawls, *PL* 238.

the proposing stage? Referendums often consolidate momentous transformations on the ground as a *fait accompli*, as the cases of de Gaulle in 1962 and Erdogan in 2017 teach. Should a court be able to invalidate referendums *after* they have already been held and have putatively expressed the will of the electorate, if not of 'the people', as their proponents often claim? Judicial review has been defended as anti-majoritarian but not anti-democratic insofar as it leaves open the possibility for the living segment of the people to rebut the court's interpretation of the constitution, if deemed incorrect. In the case of a constitutional amendment, however, things are even more complicated. If we claim that the amendment's legal cogency depends on validation, preventive or ex post, by a court, are we not then causing the democratic process to be hostage to a judicial interpreter? How can we reconcile the avoidance of judicial supremacy over the democratic process and the prevention of the possibility of the electorate disfiguring the constitution by improperly amending it?

The starting point to answering this question is to assume that amending power is superordinate in relation to the constituted, separated powers, insofar as it can change the constitutive rules of politics that regulate the exercise of those powers, but cannot be considered on an equal footing with constitution-making power, unless we underwrite the serial-sovereignty foundational notion—itself, starting from Jefferson, Rousseau, and Sieyès, the largest tributary to the current populist climate—that the living segment of the people is for all practical purposes equivalent to the entire people as author of the constitution. But if amending power is conceived as a more limited power than primary constituent power, we need to outline its limits.

This task comprises three steps: (i) drawing a distinction between those constitutional rules, standards, and principles that can be changed by amending power, and those which cannot; (ii) justifying that distinction; and (iii) outlining the process through which intended amendments can be sorted out in legitimacy and formal compliance with the relevant constitutional provisions. These three steps will be separately addressed in the remainder of this section.

a. What can amending power *not* change?

What lies beyond the limits of amending power falls into three categories: (i) constitutional provisions of all sorts (rules, standards, and principles) *explicitly* posited by the text as 'unamendable'; (ii) constitutional provisions, as well as assumptions and principles, that are *implicitly* unamendable, even though nowhere in the text are they declared to be unamendable; and (iii) constitutional provisions that are unamendable out of 'constructive imperviousness'.

The *first* set is extremely variegated in scope and substance, but very easy to identify. For example, the Constitution of Italy and that of France both declare the 'republican form' of government unamendable.[28] Article 79 of the Constitution of Germany entrenches 'the division of the Federation into Länder, their participation on principle in the legislative process' and 'the principles laid down in Articles 1 and 20'. The Czech

---

[28] Constitution of Italy, Article 139; Constitution of France, Article 89.

Republic has chosen to entrench the democratic process: 'Any changes in the essential requirements for a democratic state governed by the rule of law are impermissible'.[29] The unamendability of these provisions, according to some constitutional theorists, can be circumvented via the double-amendment strategy, though at the cost of raising problems inherent the integrity of the process of amendment which are not of interest here.[30]

The identification of the *second* set of unamendables, instead, raises breathtaking challenges. Every political or legal philosopher who envisages principled limits to amending power outlines his or her specific catalogue. I will try to offer here as complete as possible a list, by including five subtypes of elements, to be counted within this category of 'structural unamendables'. First, provisions that fix key elements of 'the basic structure' in Rawls's sense[31]—that is, a 'society's *main* political social and economic institutions', considered as 'one unified system of social cooperation from one generation to the next',[32] completed by a set of basic rights[33] and liberties—are not open to *restrictive* amending, as Rawls argued in his example of a repeal of the First Amendment failing to count as valid law even if ratified in full respect of the provisions of Article V. What Rawls has in mind here, is called by Schmitt, in a different vocabulary, 'the fundamental political decisions that constitute the substance of the constitution',[34] or the joint commitments that define a given polity. In the case of the Weimar republic these commitments included: a parliamentary democracy, a republic and not a monarchy, and a federal state protective of certain rights. In the case of Italy, the same could be said of the idea of a democratic republic 'founded on labour' (Article 1) whose duty is 'to remove those obstacles of an economic or social nature which constrain the full development of the human person' (Article 3). A *second* subtype of 'structural unamendables' includes 'general legal principles' in Dworkin's sense ('non-retroactivity', 'no liability without fault', 'nemo judex in causa sua', 'one cannot benefit from one's own illicit act'), as well as other principles usually not explicitly stated in constitutions, but nonetheless presupposed: no amendment that introduces provisions inconsistent with these principles can be legitimate.[35] In this second group

---

[29] Constitution of the Czech Republic, Article 9.
[30] See n 26, above.
[31] The sense in which the phrase 'basic structure' is used by the Supreme Court of India is broader. It includes aspects that in our list are included in the second and third subtypes.
[32] Rawls, *PL* 11.
[33] Within the set of basic rights, a whole separate treatment would have to be dedicated to 'natural rights' as unamendable. 'Natural rights', regardless whether semantically equivalent to 'basic rights', are part of comprehensive philosophical doctrines, unsuitable to be the focal point of an overlapping consensus. The rights mentioned within these doctrines, however, may become 'unamendable' when included, explicitly or implicitly, in a constitutional text. For example, the present Constitution of France incorporates the Declaration of the Rights of Man of 1789, and the Constitution of the United States 'explicitly sets the establishment of justice as one of the polity's goals'. Furthermore, 'insofar as American tradition implants the nation's founding document, the Declaration of Independence, into the larger Constitution, natural rights impose binding standards on public officials', Walter F Murphy, 'Merlin's Memory: The Past and Future Imperfect of the Once and Future Polity', in Levinson, *Responding to Imperfection* (n 3) 180 (hereafter Murphy, 'Merlin's Memory').
[34] Carl Schmitt, *Constitutional Theory* (1928), translated and edited by J Seitzer, Foreword by E Kennedy (Duke University Press 2008) 79.
[35] See Dworkin, *Taking Rights Seriously* (Harvard University Press 1977) Ch 2, § 3. Within this group also fall, at least partially, what Yaniv Roznai calls 'supra-constitutional limits' to amendment power, though his category encompasses very heterogeneous 'limits', ranging from principles of natural law to binding

we can also include general presuppositions related to the rule of law: the principles of publicity and of the desirable consistency of the *corpus juris*. Again, obvious though it might sound, amending power cannot legitimately enact provisions that implicitly undermine these principles. A *third* subtype of structural limits, that obviously holds only for liberal-democratic polities, includes implicit democratic principles, such as 'majority rule', 'periodic elections', and 'plurality of parties'. Again, although these principles need not be explicitly stated, they operate in the background, so to speak, and make invalid any constitutional amendment that directly or indirectly negatively affects them. A *fourth* subtype of 'structural unamendables' includes provisions rooted in binding international law and treaties, elements of global constitutionalism such as the UN Charter, and in regional supranational law such as, for example, EU law in relation to member states. For the first time in history, the amending power exercised by the living segment of a demos meets supra-constitutional limits of a *positive* kind: not moral notions or customary norms, but *positive supranational law*. A *fifth* and final subtype of 'unamendables' often goes unmentioned, possibly on account of its extralegal or pre-legal nature. All human activities, including law, take place against a shared background of assumptions, a holistic layer of non-exhaustible propositions that everyone can trust to be held true by everyone else—a shared background variously called the *life-world* (Husserl, Schutz), a *form of life* (Wittgenstein), a *universe of meaning* (Berger and Luckmann), or simply a *background* (Searle). Law, like any other human practice, always unfolds against one such backdrop, made of expectations that locally 'everybody knows that everybody knows to be shared'. These expectations manifest interesting properties. They cannot be enumerated piecemeal in propositional form. Rather, they amount to a non-propositional holistic habitus, and cannot be changed at will, though they do change according to the pace of cultural evolution. They are not rules, but what makes it intelligible whether a rule has been followed. In that sense these aspects of the life-world are supra-constitutional limits to amending power. For example, no amending power can legitimately turn every workday into a holiday, abolish all taxation, or prolong forever the mandate of legislative institutions. Just as the ungrammatical sentences of a natural language are infinite and not reducible to a list, and yet remain (with varying margins of uncertainty) identifiable to any native speaker, in the same way this category of 'unamendables' cannot be condensed in a list, yet does not suffer from more indeterminacy than the 'unamendables' anchored to the interpretation of a standard or principle. In this sense, all constitutions partake of the normative intuition embedded in the British form of unwritten constitutionalism—namely, the intuition that the internalized, tacit standards of a practice, when sufficiently shared by enough participants, can operate as a functional substitute for a written constitution.

Finally, a *third* larger set of 'unamendables' includes constitutional provisions that suffer from a 'constructive imperviousness' to being amended, not because they are explicitly declared unamendable or fall into any of the five preceding subtypes, but because the thresholds required to amend them 'are so onerous that reformers cannot

---

transnational positive law, which perhaps are best kept separate, see his *Unconstitutional Constitutional Amendments* (n 24) 71–102. See also Otto Bachof, *Verfassungswidrige Verfassungsnormen?* (Mohr 1951).

realistically (though they could theoretically) satisfy the standard'.[36] As Richard Albert points out, constructive unamendability rarely derives from intentional design, which would have taken other forms to achieve its ends. It is most often the result of political fragmentation and division, and the prudential setting of thresholds so high that subsequently, under changed political conditions, the outcome is practical unamendability.

An important example of this kind of unamendability is offered, according to Albert, by the 'equal suffrage' clause of Article V of the Constitution of the United States: 'no State, without its Consent, shall be deprived of its equal Suffrage in the Senate'. The constructive unamendability of the clause follows from its implicitly requiring, due to the phrase 'equal Suffrage', the unanimous consent of *all* the States. Assuming that a formally correct proposal to reduce, for instance, Maine's representation in the Senate to one Senator met with the consent of Maine, all the other forty-nine States would also have to accept their newly modified representation, now *unequal* relative to Maine's. According to this interpretation, 'Vermont's failure to consent to [Maine's] reduced representation in the Senate would doom the proposal, since otherwise one would be foisting an "*un*equal Suffrage" on Vermont, relative to [Maine's], without its consent'.[37] The Constitution of Taiwan offers another example of constructive unamendability, given the demanding requirements for proposing and ratifying amendments.[38]

All constitutional matters—rules, standards, principles, programmatic or declaratory statements—*not* comprised within any of these three larger categories are at the disposal of the amending power, direct or delegated, of the living segment of the people. However, once the diverse kinds of constitutional provisions normatively shielded from amending power are identified, an argument is needed for justifying *why* they are so unmodifiable. In and of itself, a typologically differentiated list of unamendables cannot answer the following question:

> Why does the power to amend the Constitution *not* comprise the power to change fundamental political decisions? If the foundation of the constitution is only a contingent social fact, namely, the result of a political decision, why should it be impossible to change the essential elements of the constitution by means of *another contingent social fact*, that is, a political decision made by means of a constitutional amendment?[39]

A separate justification is needed.

---

[36] Richard Albert, *Constitutional Amendments: Making, Breaking, and Changing Constitutions* (Oxford University Press 2019) 158 (hereafter Albert, *Constitutional Amendments*).

[37] Sanford Levinson, 'The Political Implications of Amending Clauses' (1996) 13 Constitutional Commentary 122, n 32, quoted in Albert, *Constitutional Amendments* (n 36) 160. For a contrary interpretation, according to which the States' equal suffrage clause would allow amendment 'in accordance with the ratifying principle of Article VII', see Harris, *The Interpretable Constitution* (n 22) 191.

[38] See Albert, *Constitutional Amendments* (n 36), 158.

[39] Carlos Bernal, 'Unconstitutional Constitutional Amendments in the Case Study of Colombia: An Analysis of the Justification and Meaning of the Constitutional Replacement Doctrine' (2013) 11 International Journal of Constitutional Law 343, cited in Roznai, *Unconstitutional Constitutional Amendments* (n 24) 118 (emphasis added).

b. Why are implicit unamendables unamendable?

A number of justificatory arguments for the implicit limits of amending power can be found in the literature.

i. The coherence argument
The most frequently encountered justification for implicit limits to amending power is the coherence argument. It comes in different versions, which all converge on understanding illegitimate, non-valid amendments as those substantively inconsistent with the core, the basic structure, or the defining decisions embedded in the constitution. The difference is in the nuances. Richard Albert, citing Thomas Cooley's argument that an amendment 'must be in harmony with the thing amended, so far at least as concerns its general spirit and purpose' and, if not, is 'inoperative',[40] reconstructs a 'conventional theory' of amendment consisting of four propositions:

> First, the binary proposition: a constitutional alteration results either in an amendment or conceptually in a new constitution. Second, the substantive proposition: constitutional alterations formalized using the rules of amendment do not always result in a proper amendment. Third, the illegitimacy proposition: constitutional changes using the rules of amendment but resulting in something other than an amendment are illegitimate under the existing constitution. Fourth, the implicit limitations proposition: even where a constitutional text does not identify which kinds of constitutional alterations would qualify as either an amendment or a new constitution, this distinction is implicit in the very nature of an amendment.[41]

The intrinsic requirement of consistency, posited by Cooley, is here corroborated by citing Schmitt's point that lack of consistency with the core identity of the constitution transforms the amendment into a component of *a new constitution*, for the enactment of which the proponents of the amendment then lack the appropriate authorizing level of constituent power.

The coherence argument comes in several variations, which differ only in the tenor of the metaphor.[42] Some variants use the metaphor of the 'pillars' that sustain a building, as opposed to disposable parts that do not affect stability if removed— imagery that has influenced the doctrine of the Basic Structure in India.[43] Other variants draw on the image of an organic body and its vital, as opposed to secondary,

---

[40] Thomas M Cooley, 'The Power to Amend the Federal Constitution' (1893) 2 Michigan Law Journal 117, quoted in Albert, *Constitutional Amendments* (n 36) 70. In that renown article, Cooley identified, as examples of unamendables, hypothetical amendments aimed at detaching a certain part of the Union, at applying different tax rules to certain states, at establishing a nobility, or creating a monarchy. On this point and other points of Cooley's argument, see Vile, 'The Case against Implicit Limits' in Levinson *Responding to Imperfection* (n 3) 193 (hereafter Vile, 'The Case Against Implicit Limits').

[41] Thomas M Cooley, 'The Power to Amend the Federal Constitution' (1893) 2 Michigan Law Journal, 117, quoted in Albert, *Constitutional Amendments* (n 36) 71.

[42] Roznai, *Unconstitutional Constitutional Amendments* (n 24) 146–50.

[43] See Dietrich Conrad, 'Constituent Power, Amendment and Basic Structure of the Constitution: A Critical Reconsideration' (1977–78) Delhi Law Review 6–7.

organs, or of a tree, that depends on its roots for nourishment and stability.[44] Another group of coherence theories of unamendability uses the notion of *identity* as a normative core that is subject to change over time but usually resists its own destruction if adequately buttressed by an interpretation of its basic features.[45] Finally, the constitution has been compared by Joseph Raz to a house that over the centuries needs repairs, renovation, additions but remains the same house: change should not be confused with loss of identity.[46] Nevertheless the constitutions of several countries do include the possibility of undergoing a 'total revision'.[47]

Deeming the conventional theory inadequate, Albert proposes a 'content-based approach for defining an amendment'. Taking his cue from recent attempts at extensive constitutional amendments in Belize, Brazil, Canada, Ireland, Italy, and Japan, he calls them 'dismemberments', in that they 'have the effect of transforming their constitutions' and aim 'to destroy and to remake the core of the present constitution'.[48] Amendments, instead, should be 'corrective, elaborative, reformative, or restorative', but the feature that distinguishes them from 'dismemberments' is that legitimate amendments still 'cohere with the existing constitution and must keep the constitution consistent with its pre-change form'.[49] This formulation, if taken literally, would leave little leeway for amending a constitution: the point of an amendment is after all to *change* the previous constitution in some non-irrelevant way. The Twenty-First Amendment, abrogating 'prohibition', which certainly was not integral to the basic structure of the United States, would not pass the test set by Albert, in that it obviously collided with the Eighteenth Amendment, 'establishing prohibition', already incorporated in the Constitution. Even an amendment requiring government to run a balanced budget would not pass the test insofar as the newly resulting constitution would prohibit what the previous one allowed: running up unlimited public debt. The criterion that distinguishes amendment from dismemberment can neither be solely quantitative—the proportion of constitutional text subjected to amending—nor just the factual inconsistency of the amended and the previous constitutional text: then all possible amendment would be either illegitimate or irrelevant.

The crux of the matter lies in the nature and the *salience* of the inconsistency between the amended text and the extant constitution. The coherence argument in its plain version, if charitably interpreted, must be taken as suggesting that the only relevant inconsistency is the one that opposes the proposed amendment and the *defining* normative commitments, Schmitt's 'existential decisions', embedded in the constitution. Still, it must be noted, an argument is needed for *why* such inconsistency is unacceptable. The argument from coherence seems to rest on the implicit assumption

---

[44] Carl Joachim Friedrich, *Man and His Government* (McGraw-Hill 1963) 272, and Vicki C Jackson, 'Constitutions as "Living Trees"? Comparative Constitutional Law and Interpretive Metaphors' (2006–07) Fordham Law Review 75.

[45] Gary Jeffrey Jacobsohn, *Constitutional Identity* (Harvard University Press 2010) 325–26 and Sudhir Krishnaswamy, *Democracy and Constitutionalism in India: A Study of the Basic Structure Doctrine* (Oxford University Press 2010) 118.

[46] Joseph Raz, *Between Authority and Interpretation* (Oxford University Press 2009) 370.

[47] For example, see the Constitutions of Spain (Section 168), Austria (Article 44), Switzerland (Articles 192 and 193), Ecuador (Articles 441–444), and Bolivia (Article 411.1).

[48] Albert, *Constitutional Amendments* (n 36) 78.

[49] ibid 82.

that we are witnessing the degrading or dismembering of a liberal-democratic constitution at the hands of regressive forces. But the coherence view, unless properly refined, seems to also block the opposite direction of change: namely, constitutional amendments aimed at democratizing constitutions with an authoritarian core.

ii. The teleological argument
This unwelcome consequence is what Rawls tries to avoid with his *teleological* variant of the coherence argument, focused on a hypothetical amendment aimed at re-establishing religion in the United States, thereby subverting a consolidated practice and a trend towards the expansion of rights. In Rawls's view, it is the fact that the three Amendments related to the Civil War and the Nineteenth Amendment were all meant to bring 'the Constitution more in line with its original promise',[50] and not just the mere fact of inconsistency, that would enjoin the Supreme Court to reject 'an amendment to repeal the First Amendment' as invalid.[51] Thus, Rawls's defence of implicit entrenchment is different from Albert's coherence approach: unconstitutional are those amendments that are not simply inconsistent with the extant constitution, but that are regressively so.

Having said that, Rawls's argument appears equally fraught with difficulties as Albert's reliance on coherence alone. First, how should we understand the temporal line that separates (i) a consolidated constitutional practice that places legitimate restrictions on amendments running against the spirit of a constitution from (ii) a burgeoning constitutional practice which instead still allows for a multiplicity of options? Should one conclude that a newly enacted constitution has no entrenched core at all? Second, the 'original promise' of the Constitution may itself be a *contested* concept, that gives rise to a plurality of conflicting reasonable ways of understanding what contributes to, and what detracts from, the coherence of the constitution. Third, in what sense is the strategy of justifying entrenchment in terms of a vectorially oriented philosophy of history, with its attendant dimension of substantive progress or regression, consistent with the project of political liberalism?

Walter Murphy offers a teleological version of the coherence argument similar to Rawls's. After having surveyed his own catalogue of 'unamendables', Murphy addresses the question: does the bulwark of unamendables that limit the will of the electorate carry the implication that 'once a people have adopted constitutional democracy, they as well as future generations are forever trapped in that sort of political system?'.[52] Murphy's answer dovetails with Rawls's point. In his words,

> A plenary commitment to reason does not, however, permit *every* sort of systemic transformation, only that which will, at least equally as well as constitutional democracy, protect the capacity of humans to reason about basic values and political change and an opportunity to carry out changes that reason indicates. Thus, constitutional democracy would allow a transformation to another system that would enlarge reason's empire or strengthen its reign. But a move from constitutional democracy

---
[50] Rawls, *PL* 238–39.
[51] *PL* 239.
[52] Murphy, 'Merlin's Memory' (n 33) 188.

to dictatorship, again except in true emergencies and then for only limited periods, would restrict reason's ambit for all citizens except the ruler and his coterie; worse, such a system would not even push that elite to rule by reason.[53]

iii. The principal–delegate argument: a moderate version

A third argument for justifying implicit unamendability, put forward by Samuel Freeman, turns on the principal–delegate relation that in his opinion connects the holders respectively of constituent and amending power. Amending power arguably acts as 'representative' of the entire people. It is this 'principal–agent' dimension of their relationship that accounts for the subordination of the delegated amending power to the principal power of 'the people' from which it draws legal authorization. Even if the holder of amending power acts as 'trustee of the people' and may nominally have a 'supreme' amendment power, it is only a *fiduciary power* to act for *certain ends*, in alignment with the principal's will.[54] Here Freeman has in mind mainly the constituted legislative power when it acts in its amending capacity, pursuant to the amending provisions of the constitution.

Yaniv Roznai also anchors his account of the limits of amending power to the principal–delegate relation:

> Being a delegated authority, the amendment power may be explicitly limited both procedurally and substantively.... However, even if the amendment power is not explicitly limited, this is not a case of a 'blank cheque' where everything is left to the judgement and discretion of the constitutional amendment authority, as it must achieve a certain objective—that being *amending* the constitution and not destroying it or replacing it with a new one. It is thus implicitly limited by its nature.[55]

However, Roznai develops the principal–delegate argument in the direction of the 'spectrum theory' of constituent power mentioned above in Section 2.c. In lieu of a rigid distinction of primary constituent power and delegated amending power, Roznai outlines a gradient of constituent power on the basis of a comparative analysis of actual amending processes. Echoing Harris, Roznai argues that the closer the amending subject to the constituted powers, legislative and (if applicable) executive, the more stringent the limits legitimately imposed on it should be. At the opposite end of the spectrum, the closer the amending subject resembles the people, the more unimpeded its action should be. In between lie several intermediate institutional possibilities.

Some empirical corroboration of Roznai's view comes from the existence of jurisdictions in which the amending power of the electorate is equated with that of the people and thus is subjected to no limits and no review. In Chapter 2, the 1962

---

[53] ibid 189. For an opposite line of reasoning, holding that 'courts should steer clear of imposing implicit limits on the substance of amendments, even in the extreme circumstances Murphy mentions', see Vile, 'The Case against Implicit Limits' (n 40) 197.

[54] Samuel Freeman, 'Constitutional Democracy and the Legitimacy of Judicial Review' (1990) 9(4) 'Law and Philosophy' 348–49. In fact, Freeman's focus on institutional amending power allows him to combine his view of the limits of such power as derived from the principal–agent relation to 'the people', with a *serial* conception of popular sovereignty, discussed in Chapter 5, Section 3.b.

[55] Roznai, *Unconstitutional Constitutional Amendments* (n 24) 156.

pronouncement of the French Conseil Constitutionnel was mentioned, which validated de Gaulle's irregularly convened referendum on the direct election of the President of France on the basis of the amendment being approved through a direct popular vote, supposedly reflective of the will of the nation. Along similar lines, an amendment endorsed directly by 'the people' is understood as above judicial review and subject to no limits in two pronouncements of the Supreme Court of Ireland. In 1996 the Court found that 'No organ of the State, including this Court, is competent to review or nullify a decision of the people ... The will of the people as expressed in a referendum providing for the amendment of the Constitution is sacrosanct and if freely given, cannot be interfered with'.[56] In 1999, the Court stated that 'There can be no question of a constitutional amendment properly placed before the people and approved by them being itself unconstitutional'.[57] Similarly, an amendment passed via referendum is deemed beyond questioning by the Constitutional Court in Romania, because it is understood as issuing from the 'will of the people'. This understanding of the electorate's amending power incurs the difficulty of leaving the transgenerational people somehow 'unrepresented' in the process: strictly speaking, all that can be observed is a fraction of the transgenerational people, that is, the electorate, that claims to speak for the whole.

iv. The principal–delegate argument: a radical version
This delegate–principal argument is radicalized by Akhil Amar and William Harris. Limits to amending power are reputed to hold when that power is vested in representative officials, but Article V of the Constitution of the United States does not affirm that its institutional path for amending the Constitution is the only admissible one. Thus, according to Amar,

> Article V nowhere prevents the *People* themselves, acting apart from ordinary government, from exercising their legal right to alter or abolish government, via the proper legal procedures. Article V presupposes this background right of the People, and does nothing to interfere with it. It merely specifies how ordinary government can amend the Constitution *without* recurring to the People themselves, the true and sovereign source of all lawful power.[58]

Amar revisits important pronouncement by Jefferson and Madison that corroborate his thesis. According to Amar's rendition, Jefferson held as a 'self-evident truth' that, over and beyond the path specified by Article V for officials to amend the constitution, 'a simple majority of the People themselves—members of the polity—had a legal right to alter government and amend constitutions'.[59] Likewise, in a controversy over whether Maryland's sole legitimate pathway for enacting amendments was the one provided by its Constitution, Madison in Philadelphia defended the point that

---

[56] *Hanafin v Minister of the Environment* [1996] 2 ILRM 61, 183, quoted in Roznai, *Unconstitutional Constitutional Amendments* (n 24) 80.
[57] *Riordan v An Taoiseach* [1999] IESC 1, 4, quoted in ibid.
[58] Akhil R Amar, 'Popular Sovereignty and Constitutional Amendment', in Levinson, *Responding to Imperfection* (n 3) 90.
[59] ibid 91.

The difficulty in Maryland [over how exactly the Constitution provided for amendments] was no greater than in other States, where no mode of change was pointed out by the Constitution.... The people were in fact, the fountain of all power, and by resorting to them, all difficulties were got over. They could alter constitutions as they pleased. It was a principle in the Bills of Rights that first principles might be resorted to.[60]

On the basis of these authoritative sources, and arguing that the language of the Preamble ('We the People ... do ordain and establish this Constitution') and of Article VII ('The Ratification of the Conventions of nine States, shall be sufficient for the Establishment of this Constitution between the States so ratifying the Same') stands on a higher plane than the countermajoritarian terminology of other parts of the Constitution,[61] Amar concludes that Article V must be read in a 'non-exclusivist' way and that the amending pathway that it outlines does not preempt the enduring right, on the part of 'the people', to step in (via a referendum or other initiatives) and change the Constitution without being subject to the limits applicable to constituted powers. Much as in the cases of the de Gaulle- and the Erdogan-instigated referendums, the argument is that the amending power of the living segment of the people is on as equal a footing, and is as boundless, as that of the transgenerational people. Further evidence for this claim comes from Amar's observation that contemporary 'improvements in communication and transportation technology—radio, television, cable, fiber-optics, electronic town meetings, etc'—allow for 'ways to retain the deliberation of the convention while providing for even more direct popular participation, akin to referenda'.[62] In Amar's version, then, amending power comes in two versions: the constituted version, subject to limits, and the popular version, on a par with the original constituent power. In sum, the living segment of the people is no less a principal than the founding people.

A germane line of argument can be found in Harris's *The Interpretable Constitution*. Harris starts from the assumption that because a national convention is

> better able to formulate an overall design as its purpose than a legislature entrusted with many other governmental roles, then the national convention should be entrusted with the deliberative conception and formal initiation of large-scale revisions of changes with broad ramifying effects. Such a product can more likely be the result of a convention's focused intentions, in terms of institutional capacity, whereas a legislature may have extraneous intentions as well as duties.[63]

Harris then provides examples: a 'balanced budget amendment' would be suitable for the Congress-proposes/legislatures-ratify sequence, a 'human-life amendment' for a Congress-proposes/conventions-ratify sequence, an amendment banning flag-burning 'would have to be approved by popular conventions because it would take

---

[60] ibid 97.
[61] ibid 109.
[62] ibid 111.
[63] Harris, *The Interpretable Constitution* (n 22) 199–200.

away rights now interpreted as given by the Constitution to the people', and a possible rethinking of the 'one man, one vote' principle, in the direction of John Stuart Mill's 'plural voting',[64] would need a convention-proposes, conventions-ratify scheme.

These modalities of amending power should be taken, Harris continues, as indicators of a deeper distinction, waiting to be unearthed, between two notions of 'the people' cohabiting *inside* and *behind* the constitution: the 'constitutional people' and the 'sovereign people'. The former comes into existence 'simultaneously with the constitutional authority of the document'. In Harris's words,

> the constitutional writers and their authorization of the text are self-referentially made to be who they are by the thing written and authorized. Like the characters in a play who are also its collective playwright, what they speak makes them who they are even as they say it. In its Preamble, the text literally creates, and then refers to (*as if* already in existence) its author.[65]

This 'constitutional people' possesses an identity codified by the constitutional text: 'its sovereignty is a function of the Constitution, created by it for its own enactment and sustenance'. Although we may think of this people as the author of the Constitution, it is 'also a bounded creature of its own constituent act ... constrained to act in ways that preserve and fulfill its collective identity, the core of its character as solemnly announced now in its self-revealing text'.[66] The constitutional people is 'always under law', to use Michelman's phrase.

The 'sovereign people', instead, 'is a wild and natural people, a potentially new constitution maker outside the bounds of the constitutional order'.[67] 'Wholeness and deliberateness' mark and identify the sovereign people's 'unlimited power' as '*potential remaker of the constitutional order*, posited outside the text'[68]—a power bound solely by the need to safeguard the persistence of its sovereignty. While the constitutional people is 'the *interpretive* People of the Text', the '*imaginative* popular sovereign' is pure potentiality, a constituent power of the first order that could be reactivated any time and could reshape the terms of cooperation. Such reactivation may never happen, especially in liberal democracies that seek to respect the ideals of the rule of law and government under law but, not differently from Amar, Harris believes that alongside domesticated amending power, vested in the constituted powers and in the electorate, there exists an untamed, unbound, albeit largely virtual, primary constituent power that could take over the helm and reshape the polity at any time.

Both Amar's and Harris's accounts fail to explain why a couple of generations of 'the people', coinciding with the electorate, could defensibly claim to be reshaping the

---

[64] See John Stuart Mill, *Considerations on Representative Government* (1861) (The Floating Press, online edition, https://archive.org/stream/cu31924014292829?ref=ol#page/n293/mode/2up) 205–09. For a contemporary revisiting of the issue, see Dennis F Thompson, 'Representing future generations: political presentism and democratic trusteeship' (2010) 13(1) Critical Review of International and Political Philosophy 17.
[65] Harris, *The Interpretable Constitution* (n 22) 201.
[66] ibid 202.
[67] ibid.
[68] ibid 203 (emphasis added).

whole polity in the name of the whole transgenerational people rather than *in their own*. Just as the 'truth of tomorrow', supposedly always susceptible to undermine the truth of today, is an empty concept unless its propositional content is specified, likewise the 'sovereign people' hovering over the constitution, waiting to run the present regime aground and start a new one, is an empty concept, unless some new constitutional principle, not yet in sight, is specified.

Unlike these views that, in a train of thought now hijacked by populist forces, transfer a supposed boundlessness of primary constituent power to the electorate acting through referendums or constitutional conventions, one of the merits of Roznai's delegation theory of amending power is that it never falls into this trap. Aware of the tension arising between the democratic will and the constitutional idea of government under law, Roznai correctly identifies the substantive limits of amending power and the legitimacy of a judicial identification and enforcement of these limits, while strongly rejecting the charge of endorsing a juristocratic curtailing of democracy. In the end, one could not agree more with Roznai's thesis that 'the phrase "unconstitutional constitutional amendment" does not entail a paradox, but merely a misapplication of presuppositions. Once the theory of constitutional unamendability is correctly construed, the alleged paradox disappears'.[69]

However, Roznai argues that primary constituent power is bound solely by positive supranational law, of either a regional or a global kind. The only non-positive constraint taken into consideration by him is natural law, and natural law is rightly declared 'inadequate to function' as a contemporary source of unamendability.[70] These strategic choices, along with the problems linked with imagining that the currently living segment of the people acts as a representative and not out of an autonomous will, lead us to search for another justification of the limits to amending power.

In the footsteps of Rawls's implicit constitutionalism and of Michelman's 'always under law' thesis, in the next section I outline a view of amending power that does not reduce its limits to positive supranational law and yet does not fall back onto natural law. These limits, as we shall see, rest on the idea of a conception of justice most reasonable for the self-same charterers and chartered participants in a polity regulated by a constitution and respectful of a duty of reciprocity among all the generations that co-author the constitution.

c. Vertical reciprocity and implicit unamendability

On the basis of *Political Liberalism*, an alternative argument for implicit unamendability can be developed that does not draw on a problematic philosophy of history or on a somewhat conservative-leaning coherence view. This alternative argument vigorously rejects the extreme form of the delegate–principal view and also takes distance from the moderate versions, differently articulated by Freeman and Roznai. The delegate–principal view reduces the living segment of the people to a representative of the transgenerational people, thereby generating two problematic consequences. *First*,

---

[69] Roznai, *Unconstitutional Constitutional Amendments* (n 24) 233
[70] ibid 100.

the electorate becomes a competitor of the constitutional court as interpreter of 'the will of the people'. Second, the constitutional will of the living segment of the people becomes a mere projection of the will of another actor.

My political-liberal understanding of the implicit limits of amending power pivots around the notion of *reciprocity*, embedded in the practical component of reasonableness, as the leading normative concept through which we can capture the relation of the different generations of the same people. Vertical reciprocity is the normative core of sequential sovereignty.

Amending power should be barred from altering the constitutional essentials (basic structure, basic rights and liberties) in any way that would make it *less reasonable* for the other generations, past or future, of the people to be imagined as willing to live their political lives within that newly generated constitutional order. This threshold of reasonability—to be legally enforced by an institution that represents the transgenerational people—is binding on amending power not because this power, while drawing its authorization from being part of the peoples' generational sequence, acts on a mandate to execute a principal's will, but because the living segment of the people—a principal to itself endowed with an autonomous political will—nonetheless is under the obligation to relate on the basis of reciprocity to *all* the free and equal generations of the people. As a link in an intergenerational chain, and no differently from an individual citizen living within a fair scheme of social cooperation, the electorate is under the obligation, also applicable to future generations acting on a basis defined by the constitutional commitments, to abide by terms of cooperation that *all* generations of the same people as free and equal can accept. This idea of *vertical reciprocity* among the generations of a people can and should be clarified in relation to the question of limits to amending power.

Intergenerational reciprocity is not a new idea. One formulation of it can be found in the section on 'The Problem of Justice Between Generations' in *A Theory of Justice*:

> all generations have their appropriate aims. They are not subordinate to one another any more than individuals are and no generation has stronger claims than any other. The life of a people is conceived as a scheme of cooperation spread out in historical time. It is to be governed by the same conception of justice that regulates the cooperation of contemporaries.[71]

Rawls developed this view with regard to distributive justice under the heading of a principle of just savings. In *Political Liberalism*, after defining society as 'a system of co-operation between generations over time', Rawls identified the correct principle of just saving as 'that which the members of any generation (and so all generations) would

---

[71] J Rawls, *A Theory of Justice* (1971). Revised edition (Harvard University Press 1999), § 44, 257. On the problems imported into the contractarian framework of *A Theory of Justice* by introducing the problem of intergenerational justice, and especially on the problem of rethinking the original position, see Brian Barry, *Theories of Justice* (University of California Press 1989) and also his 'Justice Between Generations' in PMS Hacker and J Raz (eds), *Law, Morality, and Society* (Clarendon Press 1977) 268. For an insightful discussion of intergenerational justice within *A Theory of Justice*, see also Ferdinando G Menga, *Etica intergenerazionale* (Morcelliana 2021), 63–74 and C Dierksmeier, 'John Rawls on the rights of future generations' in Joerg C Tremmel (ed), *Handbook of Intergenerational Justice* (Elgar 2006), 72.

adopt as the one their generation is to follow and as the principle they would want preceding generations to have followed (and later generations to follow), no matter how far back (or forward) in time'.[72]

When it comes to the constitution, however, matters are more complex. Its 'perpetuity', to use Jefferson's term, or transgenerational cogency has been justified on the basis of the adverse consequences incurred by the model of serial sovereignty (discussed in Chapter 5, Section 3), but we need to clarify what the principle of reciprocity means. Drawing on a suggestion by Dennis Thompson, we can think of the relation between the present and future generations of a people as enjoining present citizens to take responsibility for preserving 'a democratic process that gives future citizens at least as much competent control over their collective decision-making as present citizens have'—echoing Locke's famous saying, 'present sovereigns should leave their successors "enough and as good" sovereignty as they themselves enjoy'.[73]

A more demanding, indeed supererogatory version of the principle of reciprocity could 'stipulate that current majorities should seek, up to the point that competent control over their own decision making begins to decrease, to maximize the competent control that future majorities will enjoy'.[74] The first version of this principle of intergenerational reciprocity, however, suffices to ground the notion that current generations of citizens are under the obligation to safeguard not the full range of interests and ideas of the good of future generations (future generations will define them by themselves), but simply to preserve the future generations' capacity to self-determine these interests and ideas of the good on the basis of a public autonomy not inferior to that of the present citizens.

On this basis, the implicit unamendability of constitutional essentials can be defended without recourse to notions as coherence, progressive expansion, or the principal–delegate relation. While the relation of reasonable individual citizens is *horizontal*, insofar as they all live and act within the same scheme of fair cooperation based on reciprocity, the relation of reasonable of citizens belonging to subsequent generations of the same people is *vertical*. When some generations live, others are no longer or not yet there. These not-living generations cannot *directly* agree that the reciprocity undergirding fair terms of intergenerational cooperation has been respected, but must be represented by an institution other than the electorate or its representatives,[75]

---

[72] Rawls, *PL* 274. On the difference between this formulation and the one propounded in *A Theory of Justice* 128 and 291, see footnote 12, *PL* 274. For an enlightening discussion of three distinct models (and related principles) that can justify an intergenerational requirement of distributive reciprocity (descending model, ascending model, and double reciprocal model), see Axel Gosseries, 'Three Models of Intergenerational Reciprocity' in Axel Gosseries and Lukas H Swaine (eds), *Intergenerational Justice* (Oxford University Press 2009) 119–46.

[73] Dennis Thompson, 'Democracy in Time: Popular Sovereignty and Temporal Representation' (2005) 12(2) Constellations 249 (hereafter Thompson, 'Democracy in Time'). See also Axel Gosseries, 'The Intergenerational Case for Constitutional Rigidity' (2014) 27(4) Ratio Juris 528–39; P. Häberle, 'A Constitutional Law for Future Generations—The 'Other' Form of Social Contract: the Generation Contract' in Joerg C Tremmel (ed), *Handbook of Intergenerational Justice* (Elgar 2006) 215, and J C Tremmel 'Establishing intergenerational justice in national constitutions', ibid 187.

[74] Thompson, 'Democracy in Time' (n 73).

[75] For a critique of the idea that rights and autonomy of the future generations of a people should be safeguarded by *representing* these future constituencies, see Andre Santos Campos, 'Representing the Future: The Interests of Future Persons in Representative Democracy' (2020) 1-2 British Journal of Political Science https://doi.org/10.1017/S000712341900067X|

because the electorate is, not necessarily but conceivably, self-interested and to that extent may become *judex in causa sua*. A rich literature has developed, over the past few years, concerning desirable institutional solutions for representing the interests of future generations. Proposals range from the appointment of ombudspersons, to the creation of *ad hoc* parliamentary chambers, to the enfranchisement of new constituencies or the modification of existing ones, to the establishment of parliamentary quotas for representing future generations, or to the creation of a 'heritage fund'.[76]

However, an important distinction needs to be drawn between (i) representing future generations for the purpose of policy-making, in order to avoid or limit policies foreseeably detrimental to future citizens' general wellbeing, and (ii) representing them for the purpose of protecting their equal rights and political autonomy. For this second purpose, a judicial institution could be better positioned for assessing the alignment of the rights of past, present, and future citizens who live under the same constitution. Judgments about the fulfilment of duties of reciprocity are to be applied to the possibly contested amendability of constitutional essentials. And the normative ground of the prohibition to infringe, *qua* individual, on what is dictated by fair terms of cooperation and, *qua* living segment of the people, to pass amendments that disfigure the constitutional essentials, lies in the same requirement to which any reasonable political subject, individual or generational, voluntarily adheres for the sake of free and equal membership in a larger social unit.

Finally, when reasonability in the service of reciprocity induces citizens to refrain from implementing their will, there they experience 'the so-called strains of commitment', understood as strains that arise in a society 'between its requirements of justice and citizens' legitimate interests its just institutions allow'.[77] Similarly, generations whose transformative will is curbed by the judicial review that enforces the implicit unamendability of constitutional essentials experience 'strains of commitment' in relation to their political will. But those strains, in all respects real, do have their normative justification in the principle of reciprocity that binds *all* the free and equal generations of the same people and excludes the very idea, central for populism, that the presently living generations might be—to use Orwell's phrase—'more equal than others'.

d. Amendments, permissible and impermissible: how to sort them?

The above considerations leave one more task to be accomplished: a procedure should be outlined for sorting amendments into legitimate and illegitimate or non-valid ones. The legal literature on the formal procedures for constitutional amendment is immense. Modern constitutions often adopt 'an escalating structure of variable amendment difficulty that reflects a hierarchy of constitutional values',[78] or impose temporal constraints on legitimate amending processes, in the form of 'safe harbours'

---

[76] These and several others institutional possibilities are documented and discussed in Iñigo González-Ricoy and Axel Gosseries (eds), *Institutions for Future Generations* (Oxford University Press 2016).
[77] Rawls, *PL* 17.
[78] Albert, *Constitutional Amendments* (n 36) 177.

(a special time during which no legitimate amending can take place),[79] time floors (eg minimum periods required to separate multiple votes in parliament, as in the case of Italy), or time ceilings (not to be exceeded in order to preserve a homogeneous context for deliberation, as in the case of Costa Rica).[80] Scandinavian countries connect the formal legitimacy of amendments with 'intervening elections': two successive parliaments need to endorse an amendment, with an election in between—a model that Ackerman has adopted for his Popular Sovereignty Initiative.[81] While no constitution formally requires 'intergenerational ratification', the American model allows it. Article V imposes no minimal time floor and no ceiling, and at the moment four proposals for amendment are still pending, since 1789, 1810, 1861, and 1924.[82]

However, the difficulty of outlining a political liberal criterion or principle for the legitimate exercise of amending power rests on issues that include but also exceed the timing of deliberation. There may be amendment proposals that receive attention in the public sphere for an extended period of time and are indeed corroborated by a widespread popular support, and yet leave the crucial conceptual conundrum still entirely unsolved: under what conditions can it legitimately be stated that the will of the electorate counts as the will of the people?

The teaching of political liberalism can be summed up in a twofold thesis. The will of the electorate can never be *directly* equated with the will of people, except at the inaugural stages of new polities, when the same generations have ratified the constitution and still live under it. Only at that point does Michelman's 'self-sameness of the people as charterers and chartered' find embodiment in the same set of living citizens.

When instead, as it often happens, a temporal gap of decades or centuries separates the people as charterers and as chartered, a falsificationist perspective should be adopted: the will of the electorate can boast the title of 'will of the people' only in the absence of contrary evidence. The function of a constitutional or supreme court is then to clear the ground from the suspicion that the will undergirding the proposed amendment might be at odds with that of the author of the constitution. For all the arguments developed above,[83] the function of ascertaining such consistency cannot be left entirely to the electorate or its representative institutions without violating the *nemo judex* principle. At the same time, the intergenerational people as a whole is not possessed of agency. Rawls's example concerning the implicit unamendability of the First Amendment illustrates this point: to repeat, the Supreme Court, in its capacity as representative of the entire transgenerational people, should legitimately invalidate a correctly approved new amendment that establishes a religion upon finding that its

---

[79] See ibid 203.
[80] See ibid 204.
[81] See ibid 205. Ackerman envisages a special statute called the *Popular Sovereignty Initiative* designed to involve the Presidency in proposing constitutional amendments, and designed to supplement and not to suppress Article V. His proposal links amendment ratification with electoral cycles. In his words, 'proposed by a (second-term) President, this Initiative should be submitted to Congress for two-thirds approval, and should then be submitted to the voters at the next two Presidential elections. If it passes these tests, it should be accorded constitutional status by the Supreme Court', Bruce Ackerman, *We the People*. Vol 2, *Transformations* (Harvard University Press 1998) 415.
[82] See Albert, *Constitutional Amendments* (n 36) 206–07.
[83] See Chapter 5, Section 3.a.

substance, albeit reflective of the electorate's will, clashes with 'the will of the people', as derivable from the ratification of the First Amendment.[84]

The implicit entrenchment of the First Amendment, however, is a relatively easy case: it is ideal theory of amending power, so to speak. Two further complications, one of a *temporal*, the other of a *substantive* tenor, need to be considered. These hypothetical cases are formulated with reference to the context of the United States, but *mutatis mutandis* they apply to any other context.

Concerning the *temporal* complication, let us recall that Rawls discusses the legitimacy of a one-shot attempt at the re-establishment of religion. Things begin to look different if we change that assumption. Imagine that *each generation* down a pluricentennial line, from the initial enactment of the First Amendment in 1791 to the present, successfully got a proposed amendment re-establishing religion underway and had it ratified in full compliance with Article V, only to then meet with an iterated invalidation on the part of the Supreme Court, staffed by different justices of course. Temporality is essential to law and constitutional adjudication, and even more to legitimacy. As Ronald Dworkin famously put it, if hypothetically formulated in 1903 rather than 1803, the argument of *Marbury v Madison* would not have proved convincing and judicial review could not have been established on its basis.[85] Similarly, a recurring 'will of the electorate' that consistently concentrated on re-establishing religion for two centuries after the ratification of the First Amendment cannot as easily be dismissed as running against 'the constitutional tradition of the oldest democratic regime in the world', a tradition 'validated by long historical practice',[86] for the simple reason that the iterated reappearance of such anti-anti-establishment 'will of the electorate' would attest the contested nature of both that tradition and that practice. Such 'will of the voters' could not be described as a sudden bout of populism in centuries of liberal democracy.

Rawls had his response to this hypothetical predicament: 'in the long run a strong majority of the electorate can eventually make a constitution conform to its political will. This is simply *a fact about political power as such*. There is no way around this fact, not even by entrenchment clauses that try to fix permanently the basic democratic guarantees'.[87] Thus judicial review, even if extended to assess also amendments and not only statutes, should not be expected to provide a kind of metaphysical bulwark against the assault of illiberal majorities on the constitution. The will of the people is an open-ended (re)-construction, but ultimately it remains anchored to historical realities. That is what makes constitutionalism different from a secular, rational theology of rights.

One corollary of this teaching of political liberalism is that the longer a constitutional democracy has kept faith in its own defining commitments—thanks, among

---

[84] For an excellent defence of the twin ideas that, in the case of the United States, Article V (i) does not contain explicit provisions that limit to Congress alone the overview of when the propriety, substantive and procedural, of the ratification of an amendment is respected, and (ii) allows for a legitimate reviewing role of the Supreme Court, see Walter Dellinger, 'The Legitimacy of Constitutional Change: Rethinking the Amendment Process' (1983) 97 Harvard Law Review 386.
[85] Ronald Dworkin, *A Matter of Principle* (Harvard University Press 1985) 38.
[86] Rawls, *PL* 239.
[87] Rawls, *PL* 233.

other things, to the tireless activity of judicial review and the flawless representing of the will of the people on the part of its highest interpreter—the more impervious it will be to stray political forces unsettling its course. The flip-side of the coin, for newly democratizing countries, is that a long and perilous path to stabilization may await democratic institutions, and no short cuts exist other than the cultivation of the democratic ethos and an unflinching resolve, on the part of constitutional courts, to protect the core of the constitution through their reviewing activity, and to nip in the bud all deviations from its spirit. Far from undermining democracy, when exercised within the limits of interpretation and directed both at statutes and at proposed amendments, judicial review is the strongest preserver of democracy.

Let us now consider the *substantive* complication. Again, with reference to the United States—but equivalents can readily be found in other constitutional contexts—Rawls and many liberals with him consider the First Amendment implicitly entrenched. Would he, and we, be prepared to consider the Second Amendment equally entrenched?

The question is debatable. The Second Amendment—'A well regulated Militia, being necessary to the security of a free State, the right of the people to keep and bear Arms, shall not be infringed'—has been interpreted along two different lines. As Jack Balkin observes, the interpretation of the Amendment historically has always been twofold: 'one [interpretation] that makes the right to bear arms a privilege or immunity of national citizenship, and one that does not'[88] and interprets it as individual right to bear arms for self-protecting one's person, family, and property from individual lawbreakers. The temporal watershed between the prevailing of either interpretation is the Reconstruction. Before the Civil War the right to bear arms was predominantly understood along civic republican lines, as the right of people, organized as a militia, to 'check potential federal tyranny and help preserve republican government' on a local basis.[89] Afterwards, it came to be understood as a liberal individual right to protect oneself from disbanded aggressive gangs of Southern veterans and Klansmen terrorizing the local community.[90] During the last two decades of the twentieth century, a 'Standard Model' came to prevail, that understands the right to bear arms as an unconditional individual right.

Mark Tushnet offers a distinction of three diverse versions of the now prevailing Standard Model. *First*, a 'pure individual-rights model', that understands the right to keep and bear arms as a right 'held by each of us as an individual, to be exercised for whatever reasons each of us might have (recreation, self-defense, whatever), and subject only to rather limited forms of government regulation when there's some truly pressing social need served by the regulation'.[91] *Second*, a 'citizen-militia individual right' model, that also considers the right to keep and bear arms as a right held by individuals, 'but for reasons related to the maintenance of a militia, understood not as

---

[88] Jack M Balkin, *Living Originalism* (Harvard University Press 2011) 205.
[89] ibid 206.
[90] 'Congressional Republicans believed that the freedmen and their political allies needed to bear arms to protect themselves from Klansmen and members of southern militias that were now terrorizing them', ibid 206.
[91] Mark Tushnet, *Out of Range: Why the Constitution Can't End the Battle over Guns* (Oxford University Press 2007) 4.

the state-organized National Guard but as the term militia was understood when the Second Amendment was adopted—the entire body of the people organized on their own to ensure that the government remains faithful to our national principles'.[92] *Third*, a version of the Standard Model according to which individuals have the right to keep and bear arms in their capacity as citizens: 'the right might include the citizen-militia right, but goes beyond it so that each of us has a right and indeed a duty to keep and bear arms for purposes of self-defense when the government fails to perform its side of the social contract and protect us against criminals who would deprive us of our life, liberty, or property'.[93]

Be that as it may, given the fierce controversy over the proper scope of the right to keep and bear arms, an implicit entrenchment—should a supermajority in favour of curtailing that right materialize—appears hard to justify. A distinguished constitutional scholar as Tushnet has come to acknowledge that 'disputes over gun policy have become deeply enmeshed in the culture wars between liberals and conservatives, between people who live in cities and people who live in the country' and that, far from being a clear expression of the 'will of the people', the Second Amendment becomes one of the contested terrains over which electoral majorities fight their battles. If gun control and gun rights constitute 'one of the arenas in which we as Americans try to figure out who we are',[94] then almost by definition no interpretation of a will of the people still largely under formation is possible.

If the contest of interpretation is that wide open—as indeed it might be on many other matters of constitutional significance—that means that the will of the people is *undecided*. In such a case, the 'will of the people' can only be *usurped* by cohorts of voters. Under such conditions it is then safe to assume that constitutional amendments approved in full respect of the provisions for amending the constitution are certified expressions of the will of the electorate, and have met the necessary conditions for counting as a *tentative anticipation* of the will of the author of the constitution. Only time can tell whether that anticipation will consolidate into an actual will of the people. Only time can let the uncontested will of one generation be accepted by the subsequent ones, in a path different from the Eighteenth Amendment about prohibition in the United States. The will of the electorate, once cleared from the suspicion of contradicting the constitution, becomes the will of the people only by lack of rejection 'over time'.

Constitutionalism is an open-ended process and an unfinished task. It is not the preservation of a constitutional ark per se, nor the adapting of the constitution to the sentiment prevailing at a given time, which would spell an end to the constitution's regulatory function. The process of amending a constitution entails, not differently from the process of transforming any other authentic identity, both fidelity and change. As with all individual or collective identities, there is no telling in advance where change will go, or whether temporary turns will stick and modify for good the original identity. The amending of a constitution is a process open to plurality because it is not preordained, responds to a pattern that itself evolves, is marked by uniqueness

[92] ibid.
[93] ibid.
[94] ibid xiv.

and at the same time overlaps with the constitution-making process of *other* liberal-democratic peoples on fundamental rights, the separation of powers, publicity, the rule of law, and majority rule. The judgment of apex courts can never impose a positive development, only block distorting ones.

A consideration of the teaching of nazism and fascism is still highly instructive. Both these regimes grew as tumours, at a time when only enlightened minorities prized constitutional democracy, without needing to repeal the formal shell of flexible liberal constitutions like that of the Weimar Republic or the Statuto Albertino of the Kingdom of Italy. It is far from certain that judicial review, even if it existed and hypothetically invalidated, for example, the *Enabling Law* of March 23 1933[95] or the fascist so-called plebiscitary electoral law, applied in the 'elections' of 1929 and 1934,[96] could have stopped powerful anti-democratic and anti-liberal forces. However, what is beyond question is that in those historical times the 'Italian people' and the 'German people' were not represented, whereas the respective electorates were the only voices represented by charismatic anti-democratic leaders. That tragic mistake has left deep traces in the constitutional identities of the peoples involved. Both embraced liberal-democratic constitutions afterwards and have learned where the tragic conflation of the people and the electorate can lead: their constitutions are then understood, with different nuances in the two cases, primarily as a safeguard against the return of the past.

4. The Liberal Principle of Amending Legitimacy

To conclude, it is worth condensing the above discussion into the form of a liberal principle of the 'legitimacy of constitution-amending'. In one passage of 'The Idea of Public Reason Revisited', Rawls briefly touches on the issue of the legitimacy of the constitution. Differently from previous formulations of the liberal principle of legitimacy,[97] he now anchors political legitimacy directly to 'the criterion of reciprocity':[98] 'our exercise of political power is proper only when we sincerely believe that the reasons we would offer for our political actions—were we to state them as

---

[95] The 'Gesetz zur Behebung der Not von Volk und Reich' (*Law to Remedy the Distress of People and Reich*), commonly known as *Ermächtigungsgesetz* (*Enabling Act*) of March 23 1933 allowed the government to enact laws that might 'deviate from the constitution as long as they do not affect the institutions of the Reichstag and the Reichsrat' (Article 2). The law was renewed twice in 1937 and 1941. See Anson Rabinbach and Sander L Gilman, *The Third Reich Sourcebook* (University of California Press 2013) 52.

[96] After gaining a 65 per cent majority in Parliament (thanks to the Acerbo-electoral law) in the last multi-party elections of 6 April 1924, marked by the assassination of prominent socialist leader Giacomo Matteotti, the Mussolini government had Parliament reform the electoral law after a so-called plebiscitary model. Institutions, unions, and various social and cultural associations would nominate 1,000 candidates for the 400 seats in Parliament. Then the *Grand Council* of the Fascist Party (the only legal party) would select 400 out of that pool: electors were provided with two ballots, one (marked with the Italian flag) for approving, the other (with no distinctive markings) for rejecting such list of 400 nominees. Secrecy was far from guaranteed, given that electors were to hand the ballot of choice to the scrutineers. Based on this electoral law, elections were held on 24 March 1929 and 25 March 1934, before being formally abolished in 1939. See Robert O Paxton, *The Anatomy of Fascism* (Knopf 2004).

[97] Rawls, *PL* 137 and 217.

[98] Rawls, 'The Idea of Public Reason Revisited', *PL* 446.

government officials—are sufficient, and we also reasonably think that other citizens might also reasonably accept those reasons'.[99] The term 'accept' is here clearly used as synonymous with 'endorse' or 'share' and not simply with 'understand'—ironically, he observes, 'Servetus could understand why Calvin wanted to burn him at the stake'.[100] Rawls then adds that his reciprocity-based criterion of legitimacy 'applies on two levels: one is *to the constitutional structure itself*, the other is to particular statutes and laws enacted in accordance with that structure. To be reasonable, political conceptions must justify only constitutions that satisfy this principle'.[101]

Elegant and parsimonious though it might be—and tempting though it may be to adopt it for capturing the justifiability of exercises of amending power—this new formulation suffers from three shortcomings. *First*, compared with the previous liberal principle of legitimacy, applicable to ordinary exercises of constituted authorities, the new wording lacks the function of reducing the range of reasonable disagreement by relocating the source of legitimacy from the unlikely consent on policies or provisions to the constitutional essentials. It seems to lead us back to the classical liberal notion of legitimacy as resting on the 'consent of the governed'.

Second, compared with the 'liberal principle of constitutional legitimacy', propounded in Chapter 3, this new formulation risks blurring the nexus, emphasized by Rawls in *Political Liberalism*, of the constitution to one political conception of justice, 'most reasonable' among the 'at least reasonable' political conceptions. The idea of reasonability cannot by itself compensate for the waning of the nexus of the constitution to a political conception of justice.

Third, Rawls's reciprocity-based principle of legitimacy, if applied to the assessment of exercises of amending power, suffers from an additional drawback: the reasonability of a proposed constitutional amendment is not distinguished sharply enough from the amendment's mere satisfying the requisite of respecting the (explicitly or implicitly) unamendable aspects of the constitution.

In order to avoid these three shortcomings, I propose the following liberal principle of 'amending legitimacy':

Liberal principle of amending legitimacy
Amending power is justifiably exercised when it modifies the constitution in full respect of the (explicitly and implicitly) unamendable essentials and of ideals and principles acceptable to present citizens as rational and reasonable, as well as compatible with vertical reciprocity among all the generations of the people.

As in the case of the liberal principle of constitutional legitimacy, the original phrase 'in accordance with a constitution' is excised because the purpose of exercising amending power is to *change* parts of the constitution, including some of its principles and standards. The legitimacy of the use of amending power depends on full abidance by those parts of the constitution which must be considered entrenched, explicitly or implicitly, for the reasons specified in Section 1.b. It is assumed that the judgment

---

[99] ibid 446–47.
[100] ibid 447.
[101] ibid (emphasis added).

concerning whether the unamendable aspects of the constitution have remained sufficiently unaffected by the given exercise of amending power cannot be left to the holders of amending power, whether officials or voters, but needs to be rendered by an institution that impartially represents the whole transgenerational people *qua* author of the constitution.

At the same time, the proposed principle does not reduce legitimacy to mere respect of explicit or implicit unamendability. As in the case of the liberal principle of legitimacy, the exercise of authority must offer evidence of being motivated not by strategic political calculation—for example, the modification of the constitutive rules of politics in order to gain a competitive advantage over political rivals—but by principles reputed to meet the fellow citizens' consent for their being 'rational and reasonable'. However, in addition to the formula used by Rawls for his principle of legitimacy, the legitimacy of exercises of *amending power* requires that the living citizens' sense not only of the rational and the reasonable, but also of the ideal of intergenerational reciprocity, be duly considered.

The formulation of the liberal principle of amending legitimacy completes the task of reconstructing Rawls's constitutional theory. To summarize: From his scant references to the constituent power of the people, evocative of Locke's normative framework, and from the main concepts of political liberalism, a distinct account of constituent power, its self-constituting subject, and the conditions for its legitimate exercise have been outlined above in Chapters 3 and 4. Amending power has then been distinguished from both constituent power, on one hand, and from the powers of the electorate and the separated powers vested in the institutions of the basic structure, on the other. The subject matter, object, temporal coordinates and constraints, institutional venues, but above all the limits of amending power have been elucidated and contrasted with the normative constraints that bind primary constituent power. A specific principle that orients our judgment about the legitimate exercise of amending power has then been formulated for the purpose of supplementing the liberal principle of legitimacy and the newly formulated principle of constitutional legitimacy.

It is my hope that this work of analysis and construction may strengthen Rawls's argument for the implicit unamendability of constitutional essentials and contribute to fulfilling the potential of *Political Liberalism*, unequalled among the contemporary paradigms of political philosophy and constitutionalism, for bringing all facets of the exercise of political power (constituent, amending, and constituted) under one coherent normative framework regardful of the plurality of our political worlds.

Bibliography

Ackerman B, *We the People*, vol 1, *Foundations* (Harvard University Press 1991).
Ackerman B, 'Higher Lawmaking' in S Levinson (ed), *Responding to Imperfection: The Theory and Practice of Constitutional Amendment* (Princeton University Press 1995) 63–87.
Ackerman B, *We the People*, vol 2, *Transformations* (Harvard University Press 1998).
Ackerman B, 'The New Separation of Powers' (2000) 3 Harvard Law Review 634.
Ackerman B, *The Decline and Fall of the American Republic* (Harvard University Press 2010).
Ackerman B, *We the People*, vol 3, *The Civil Rights Revolution* (Harvard University Press 2014).
Ackerman B, *Revolutionary Constitutions: Charismatic Leadership and the Rule of Law* (Harvard University Press 2019).
Ackerman B and JS Fishkin, *Deliberation Day* (Yale University Press 2004).
Agamben G, *The Coming Community* (1990) (University of Minnesota Press 1993).
Albert R, 'Nonconstitutional Amendments' (2009) 22(1) Canadian Journal of Law & Jurisprudence 5.
Albert R, 'The Expressive Function of Constitutional Amendment Rules' (2013) 59 McGill University Law Journal 226.
Albert R, 'Constitutional Amendment by Constitutional Desuetude' (2014) 62 American Journal of Comparative Law 641.
Albert R, *Constitutional Amendments: Making, Breaking, and Changing Constitutions* (Oxford University Press 2019).
Albert R, M Nakashidze, and T Olcay, 'The Formalist Resistance to Unconstitutional Constitutional Amendments' (2019) 70 Hastings Law Journal 22.
Amar AR, 'Popular Sovereignty and Constitutional Amendment', in S Levinson (ed), *Responding to Imperfection: The Theory and Practice of Constitutional Amendment* (Princeton University Press 1995) 89–115.
Anderson P, *The H-Word: The Periphery of Hegemony* (Verso 2017).
Anscombe GEM, *Intention* (Blackwell 1957).
Anselmi M, *Populism: An Introduction* (Routledge 2018).
Arato A, 'Multi-Track Constitutionalism Beyond Carl Schmitt' (2011) 18(3) Constellations 324.
Arato A, *The Adventures of Constituent Power. Beyond Revolutions* (Cambridge University Press 2017).
Arato A, 'Revolution on a Human Scale: Liberal Values, Populist Theory?' in R Albert (ed), *Revolutionary Constitutionalism: Law, Legitimacy, Power* (Hart 2020) 91.
Archibugi D, *The Global Commonwealth of Citizens: Toward Cosmopolitan Democracy* (Princeton University Press 2008).
Arditi B, 'Populism as an Internal Periphery of Democratic Politics' in F Panizza (ed), *Populism and the Mirror of Democracy* (Verso 2005) 72.
Arendt H, *The Origins of Totalitarianism* (1950). New edn with added prefaces (Harcourt 1976).
Arendt H, *The Human Condition: A Study of the Central Dilemmas Facing Modern Man* (1958) (Doubleday Anchor 1959).
Aristotle, *The Politics* (TA Sinclair tr, Penguin 1992).
Ashbury H, *The Great Illusion: An Informal History of Prohibition* (Greenwood Press 1968).

Bachof O, *Verfassungswidrige Verfassungsnormen?* (Mohr 1951).
Balkin JM, *Living Originalism* (Harvard University Press 2011).
Balkin JM, 'History, Rights, and the Moral Reading' (2016) 96(4) Boston University Law Review 1434.
Barber BR, *Strong Democracy: Participatory Politics for a New Age* (University of California Press 1984).
Barry B, *Theories of Justice* (University of California Press 1989)
Barry B, 'Justice Between Generations' in PMS Hacker and J Raz (eds), *Law, Morality, and Society* (Clarendon Press 1977) 268.
Beales D and EF Biagini, *The Risorgimento and the Unification of Italy* (Routledge 2002).
Beccaria C, *Of Crimes and Punishment and Other Writings* (Cambridge University Press 1995).
Beck H and G Vankeerberghen, 'The Many Faces of "the People" in the Ancient World' in H Beck and G Vankeerberghen (eds), *Rulers and Ruled in Ancient Greece, Rome and China* (Cambridge University Press 2021) 1.
Bellamy R, *Political Constitutionalism: A Republican Defence of the Constitutionality of Democracy* (Cambridge University Press 2007).
Bellamy R, *A Republican Europe of States: Cosmopolitanism, Intergovernmentalism and Democracy in the EU* (Cambridge University Press 2019).
Bellamy R and Castiglione D (eds), *Constitutionalism in Transformation: European and Theoretical Perspectives* (Blackwell 1996).
Bellamy R and Castiglione D, *From Maastricht to Brexit* (Rowman and Littlefield 2019).
Benhabib S, 'The multivariate polity or democratic fragmentation: On Alessandro Ferrara's *The Democratic Horizon: Hyperpluralism and the renewal of political liberalism*' (2016) 42(7) Philosophy & Social Criticism 649.
Beran H, *The Consent Theory of Political Obligation* (Croom Helm 1987).
Berger S, 'Germany in Historical Perspective: Between Theory and Practice' in S Berger and H Compston (eds), *Policy Concertation and Social Partnership in Western Europe: Lessons for the 21st Century* (Berghahn 2002) 125.
Berlin I, *The Crooked Timber of Humanity* (Random House 1992).
Bernal C, 'Unconstitutional Constitutional Amendments in the Case Study of Colombia: An Analysis of the Justification and Meaning of the Constitutional Replacement Doctrine' (2013) 11(2) International Journal of Constitutional Law 11.
Bernstein R, 'The Aporias of Carl Schmitt' (2011) 18(3) Constellations 402.
Bhabha H, *The Location of Culture* (Routledge 1994).
Bickel A, *The Least Dangerous Branch: The Supreme Court at the Bar of Politics* (1962) (2nd edn, Yale University Press 1986).
Blanchot M, *The Inavowable Community* (1983) (University of Minnesota Press 1988).
Blokker P, 'Varieties of Populist Constitutionalism: The Transnational Dimension' (2019) 20 German Law Journal 343.
Blokker P and M Anselmi (eds), *Multiple Populisms: Italy as Democracy's Mirror* (Routledge 2020).
Bobbit P, *Constitutional Interpretation* (Blackwell 1991).
Bohman J, *Democracy Across Borders: From Dêmos to Dêmoi* (MIT Press 2007).
Brilmayer L, 'Secession and Self-Determination: A Territorial Interpretation' (1991) 16 Yale Journal of International Law 177.
Buchanan A, *Secession: The Morality of Political Divorce from Fort Sumter to Lithuania and Quebec* (Westview Press 1991).
Buchanan A, 'Theories of Secession' (1997) 26(1) Philosophy & Public Affairs 31.
Buchanan A, *The Heart of Human Rights* (Oxford University Press 2013).

Buchstein H, 'Reviving Randomness: for Political Rationality: Elements of a Theory of Aleatory Democracy' (2010) 17 Constellations 435.
Calamandrei P, *La Costituzione e le leggi per attuarla* (1955) (Giuffrè 2000).
Campos AS, 'Representing the Future: The Interests of Future Persons in Representative Democracy' (2020) 1-2 British Journal of Political Science 1-15, https://doi.org/10.1017/S000712341900067X.
Canovan M, *Populism* (Junction Books 1981).
Canovan M, *The People* (Polity Press 2005).
Canovan M, 'Trust the People! Populism and the Two Faces of Democracy' (1999) 47 Political Studies 14.
Cartabia M, 'The Italian Constitution as a Revolutionary Agreement', in R Albert (ed), *Revolutionary Constitutionalism: Law, Legitimacy, Power* (Hart 2020) 313.
Castiglione D, 'Giving Pitkin her due: What the "representative claim" gets right, and what it risks missing' (2012) 11 Contemporary Political Theory 1.
Castiglione D and M Warren, 'A New Ecology of Democratic Representation? Eight Theoretical Issues' (2013) 2(2) Intrasformazione: Rivista di Storia delle Idee 155.
Christiano T, 'Democratic Legitimacy and International Institutions', in S Besson and J Tasioulis (eds), *The Philosophy of International Law* (Oxford University Press 2010) 119-38.
Claviez T, 'Traces of a Metonymic Society in American Literary History' in W Fluck et al (eds) American Studies Today (American Studies Monograph Series 2014) 299.
Claviez T, 'A Metonymic Community? Toward a Poetics of Community' in T Claviez (ed), *The Common Growl: Toward a Poetics of Precarious Community* (Fordham University Press 2016) 39.
Claviez T, 'Where are Jacques and Ernesto when you need them? Rancière and Laclau on populism, experts on contingency' (2019) 9-10 Philosophy & Social Criticism, Special Issue on Populism 1132.
Cohen JL, 'Populism and the Politics of Resentment' (2019) 1(1) Jus Cogens 5.
Cohen J, 'Taking Democracy Seriously: Review of Ronald Dworkin, *Is Democracy Possible Here?*', online publication, downloaded at https://www.academia.edu/26733113/Review_of_Ronald_Dworkin_Is_Democracy_Possible_Here.
Colón-Ríos JI, *Weak Constitutionalism: Democratic Legitimacy and the Question of Constituent Power* (Routledge 2012).
Colón-Ríos J, *Constituent Power and the Law* (Oxford University Press 2020).
Conant JB (ed), *The Overthrow of Phlogiston Theory: The Chemical Revolution of 1775-1789* (Harvard University Press 1964).
Condorcet M de, August 30, 1789. *Lettre de M de Condorcet à M le compte Mathieu de Montmorency*. See https://gallica.bnf.fr/ark:/12148/bpt6k41732k/f12.item.texteImage.
Congressional Record, 62d Congr, 3d Session, 11 December 1912.
Conniff ML (ed), *Populism in Latin America* (University of Alabama Press 2002).
Connolly W, *The Ethos of Pluralization* (University of Minnesota Press 1995).
Connolly W, *Pluralism* (Duke University Press 2005).
Conrad D, 'Constituent Power, Amendment and Basic Structure of the Constitution: A Critical Reconsideration' (1977-78) 6-7 Delhi Law Review 1-23.
Cooley TM, 'The Power to Amend the Federal Constitution' (1893) 2 Michigan Law Journal 109.
Cover RM, 'The Supreme Court, 1982 Term—Foreword: Nomos and Narrative', Faculty Scholarship Series. Paper 2705, http://digitalcommons.law.yale.edu/fss_papers/2705.
Crisp R (ed), *Griffin on Human Rights* (Oxford University Press 2014).
Cristi R, 'Carl Schmitt on Sovereignty and Constituent Power' in D Dyzenhaus (ed), *Law as Politics: Carl Schmitt's Critique of Liberalism*. With a preface by Ronald Beiner (Duke

University Press 1998) 179–95.Croce M and A Salvatore, *The Legal Theory of Carl Schmitt* (Routledge 2013).

Croce M and A Salvatore, *Carl Schmitt's Institutional Theory: The Political Power of Normality* (Cambridge University Press 2022).

Cronin C, 'On the Possibility of a Democratic Constitutional Founding: Habermas and Michelman in Dialogue' (2006) 19(3) Ratio Juris 342.

de la Torre C, *Populist Seduction in Latin America* (Ohio State University Press 2010).

Dellinger W, 'The Legitimacy of Constitutional Change: Rethinking the Amendment Process' (1983) 97 Harvard Law Review 386.

Derrida J, *Of Hospitality: Anne Dufourmantelle Invites Jacques Derrida to Respond* (Stanford University Press 2000).

Dewey J, *The Public and Its Problems* (1927) (Alan Swallow 1954).

Dewey J, 'Creative Democracy—The Task Before Us' in J Dewey, *The Later Works: 1925–1953. Volume 14: 1939–1941. Essays, reviews and Miscellany.* Edited by JA Boydston, with an introduction by RW Sleeper (Southern Illinois University Press 1988) 224.

Dierksmeier C, 'John Rawls on the Rights of Future Generations' in Joerg C Tremmel (ed), *Handbook of Intergenerational Justice* (Elgar 2006), 72.

Disch L, 'The "constructivist turn" in political representation' (2012) 11(1) Contemporary Political Theory 6–10.

Disch L, 'The "Constructivist Turn" in Democratic Representation: A Normative Dead-End?' (2015) 22(4) Constellations 487–99.

Dixon R, 'Creating dialogue about socioeconomic rights' (2007) 5 International Journal of Constitutional Law 391.

Dryzek J and S Niemeyer, 'Discursive Representation' (2008) 102(4) American Political Science Review 481.

Dworkin R, *Taking Rights Seriously* (Harvard University Press 1977).

Dworkin R, *A Matter of Principle* (Harvard University Press 1985).

Dworkin R, *Law's Empire* (Harvard University Press 1986).

Dworkin R, 'Liberal Community' (1989) 77(3) California Law Review 479.

Dworkin R, *Freedom's Law: The Moral Reading of the American Constitution* (Harvard University Press 1996).

Dworkin R, *Is Democracy Possible Here? Principles for a New Political Debate* (Princeton University Press 2006).

Dworkin R, *Justice in Robes* (Harvard University Press 2006).

Dworkin R, *Justice for Hedgehogs* (Harvard University Press 2011).

Dyzenhaus D and M Thorburn, *Philosophical Dimensions of Constitutional Law* (Oxford University Press 2016).

Eatwell R and MJ Goodwin, *National Populism: The Revolt Against Democracy* (Pelican Books 2018).

Eberhard DM, GF Simons, and CD Fennig (eds), *Ethnologue: Languages of the World*. Twenty-third edition. (SIL International 2020). Online version: http://www.ethnologue.com.

Eskridge WN jr and J Ferejohn, 'Super-statutes' (2001) 50 Duke Law Journal 1215.

Esposito R, *Communitas: The Origin and Destiny of Community* (1998) (Stanford University Press 2010).

Esposito R, *Third Person: Politics of Life and Philosophy of the Impersonal* (2007) (Polity, 2012).

Fabbrizi V and L Fiorespino (eds), *The Persistence of Justice as Fairness: Reflections on Rawls's Legacy*. With a preface by F Çullhaj (UniversItalia 2022).

Farrand M (ed), *The Records of the Federal Convention of 1787* (Yale University Press 1927).

Federalist Papers. By Alexander Hamilton, James Madison, John Jay (1788). With an introduction, table of contents, and index of ideas by Clinton Rossiter (Penguin 1961).

Ferrajoli L, *La logica del diritto: Dieci aporie nell'opera di Hans Kelsen* (Laterza 2016).
Ferrara A, *Modernity and Authenticity: A Study of the Social and Ethical Thought of Jean-Jacques Rousseau* (SUNY Press 1993).
Ferrara A, *Justice and Judgment: The Rise and the Prospect of the Judgment Model in Contemporary Political Philosophy* (Sage 1999).
Ferrara A, 'Of Boats and Principles: Reflections on Habermas's "Constitutional Democracy"' (2001) 29(6) Political Theory 782.
Ferrara A, *The Force of the Example: Explorations in the Paradigm of Judgment* (Columbia University Press 2008).
Ferrara A, 'Authenticity Without a True Self' in P Vannini and JP Williams (eds) *Authenticity in Culture, Self, and Society* (Ashgate 2009) 31.
Ferrara A, 'Ferrajoli's Argument for Constitutional Democracy and Structural Entrenchment' (2011) 17(4) Res Publica 377.
Ferrara A, 'The Idea of a Charter of Fundamental Human Rights' in C Corradetti (ed), *Philosophical Dimensions of Human Rights* (Springer 2012) 173.
Ferrara A, *The Democratic Horizon: Hyperpluralism and the Renewal of Political Liberalism* (Cambridge University Press 2014).
Ferrara A, 'The Absolute Power of Disembedded Financial Markets' in A Azmanova and M Mihai (eds), *Reclaiming Democracy: Judgment, Responsibility and the Right to Politics* (Routledge 2015) 110.
Ferrara A, 'Political liberalism revisited: A paradigm for liberal democracy in the 21st century' (2016) 42(7) Philosophy & Social Criticism 681.
Ferrara A, *Rousseau and Critical Theory* (Brill 2017).
Ferrara A, 'Exemplarity in the Public Realm' (2018) 30(3) Law & Literature 387.
Ferrara A, 'The Dual Paradox of Authenticity in the 21st Century' in T Claviez, K Imesch, and B Sweers (eds), *Critique of Authenticity* (Vernon Press 2019) 3.
Ferrara A, '"Most Reasonable for Humanity": Legitimation Beyond the State' (2019) 1(2) Jus Cogens 111.
Ferrara A, 'Social freedom and reasonable pluralism: Reflections on *Freedom's Right*' (2019) 45(6) Philosophy & Social Criticism 639.
Ferrara A, 'A Crypto-Liberalism of Collective Self-Restraint? On H Lindahl's *Authority and the Globalization of Inclusion and Exclusion*' (2019) 21(3) Etica & Politica/Ethics & Politics 371.
Ferrara A, 'Further Thoughts on A-Legality, Exemplarity and Constituent Power: Responding to Hans Lindahl' (2020) 22(2) Etica & Politica/Ethics & Politics 461.
Ferrara A, 'Unconventional Adaptation and the Authenticity of a Constitution' in R Albert (ed), *Revolutionary Constitutionalism* (Hart 2020) 157.
Ferrara A, 'Sideways at the entrance of the cave: a pluralist footnote to Plato' in V Kaul and I Salvatore (eds), *What is Pluralism?* (Routledge 2020) 81.
Ferrara A, 'Capitalism in neoliberal times: Rethinking the Left' (2021) 11(2) Philosophy and Public Issues (New Series) 19.
Ferrara A, 'What the controversy over "the reasonable" reveals: on Habermas's *Auch eine Geschichte der Philosophie*' (2022) 48(3) Philosophy and Social Criticism 313.
Ferrara A and FI Michelman, *Legitimation by Constitution: A Dialogue on Political Liberalism* (Oxford University Press 2021).
Finchelstein F, *From Fascism to Populism in History* (University of California Press 2017).
Fiorespino L, *Radical Democracy and Populism: A Thin Red Line?* (Springer 2022).
Fishkin JS, *The Voice of the People: Public Opinion and Democracy* (Yale University Press 1997).
Fishkin JS, *When the People Speak* (Oxford University Press 2009).
Fishkin JS, *Democracy: When the People are Thinking* (Oxford University Press 2018).

Fleming JE, *Fidelity to Our Imperfect Constitution: For Moral Readings and Against Originalisms* (Oxford University Press 2015).
Floyd J and M Stears (eds), *Political Philosophy versus History? Contextualism and Real Politics in Contemporary Political Thought* (Cambridge University Press 2011).
Forst R, *The Right to Justification* (Jeffrey Flynn tr, Columbia University Press 2012).
Frankfurt H, *The Importance of What We Care About: Philosophical Essays* (1988) (Cambridge University Press 2007).
Fraser N, 'Toward a Discourse Ethic of Solidarity' (1986) 5(4) Praxis International 425.
Fraser N, 'Against Progressive Neo-liberalism/A New Progressive Populism' (2017) 28 *Dissent Magazine*, 28 January 2017, https://www.dissentmagazine.org/online_articles/nancy-fraser-against-progressive-neoliberalism-progressive-populism.
Fraser N and R Jaeggi, *Capitalism: A Conversation in Critical Theory*. Edited by Brian Milstein (Polity Press 2018).
Freedom House Report 2020, accessed at https://freedomhouse.org/report/freedom-world/2020/leaderless-struggle-democracy on 15 May 2020.
Freeman S, 'Constitutional Democracy and the Legitimacy of Judicial Review' (1990) 9(4) Law and Philosophy 327.
Freeman S (ed), *The Cambridge Companion to Rawls* (Cambridge University Press 2002).
Freeman S, *John Rawls* (Routledge 2007).
Friedrich CJ, *Constitutional Government and Democracy* (Little, Brown and Co 1941).
Friedrich CJ, *Man and His Government* (McGraw-Hill 1963).
Galston W, 'Realism in Political Theory' (2010) 9(4) European Journal of Political Theory 385.
Gardbaum S, 'Uncharismatic Revolutionary Constitutionalism' in R Albert (ed), *Revolutionary Constitutionalism: Law, Legitimacy, Power* (Hart 2020) 133.
Gargarella R, 'Bruce Ackerman's Theory of History' in R Albert (ed), *Revolutionary Constitutionalism: Law, Legitimacy, Power* (Hart 2020) 55.
Gaus G, *The Order of Public Reason: A Theory of Freedom and Morality in a Diverse and Bounded World* (Cambridge University Press 2011).
Gaus G, 'Sectarianism Without Perfection? Quong's Political Liberalism' (2012) 2(1) Philosophy and Public Issues 7–15.
Gerald G, 'The Subtle Vices of the Passive Virtues' (1964) 64(1) Columbia Law Review 1.
Geuss R, *Philosophy and Real Politics* (Princeton University Press 2008).
Ginsburg T, 'Written Constitutions Around the World' (2015) 15(4) Insights on Law & Society.
Ginsburg T, 'Charismatic Fictions and Constitutional Politics' in R Albert (ed), *Revolutionary Constitutionalism: Law, Legitimacy, Power* (Hart 2020) 115.
Giovanola B and R Sala, 'The Reasons of the Unreasonable: Is Political Liberalism Still an Option?' (2022) 48(9) Philosophy & Social Criticism 1226–46.
Goldoni M *La dottrina costituzionale di Sieyès* (Firenze University Press 2009).
Goldoni M, 'At the Origins of Constitutional Review: Sieyes' Constitutional Jury and the Taming of Constituent Power' (2012) 32(2) Oxford Journal of Legal Studies 211.
González-Ricoy I and A Gosseries (eds), *Institutions for Future Generations* (Oxford University Press 2016).
Gosseries A, 'Three Models of Intergenerational Reciprocity' in A Gosseries and LH Swaine (eds), *Intergenerational Justice* (Oxford University Press 2009) 119.
Gosseries A, 'The Intergenerational Case for Constitutional Rigidity' (2014) 27(4) Ratio Juris 528.
Gray J, *Two Faces of Liberalism* (Polity Press 2000).
Griffin J, *On Human Rights* (Oxford University Press 2008).
Grimm D, *Constitutionalism: Past, Present, and Future* (Oxford University Press 2016).

Häberle P, 'A Constitutional Law for Future Generations—The "Other" Form of Social Contract: the Generation Contract' in JC Tremmel (ed), *Handbook of Intergenerational Justice* (Elgar 2006) 215.

Habermas J, 'Postscript to *Faktizität und Geltung*' (1994) 20(4) Philosophy & Social Criticism 135.

Habermas J, 'Reconciliation through the Public Use of Reason: Remarks on John Rawls's Political Liberalism' (1995) 92(3) Journal of Philosophy 109.

Habermas J, *Between Facts and Norms: Contributions to a Discourse Theory of Law and Democracy* (William Rehg tr, MIT Press 1996).

Habermas J, '"Reasonable" versus "True," or the Morality of Worldviews' in *The Inclusion of Other: Studies in Political Theory*, ed Ciaran Cronin and Pablo De Greiff (MIT Press 1998) 75.

Habermas J, 'Constitutional Democracy—A Paradoxical Union of Contradictory Principles?' (2001) 29(6) Political Theory.

Habermas J, 'Hermeneutic and Analytic Philosophy: Two Complementary Versions of the Linguistic Turn' (1999), reprinted in J Habermas, *Truth and Justification*, tr Barbara Fultner (MIT Press 2003) 51.

Habermas J, 'Religion in the Public Sphere: Cognitive Presuppositions of the "Public Use of Reason" by Religious and Secular Citizens' in J Habermas, *Between Naturalism and Religion* (Polity Press 2008) 114.

Habermas, J., 'Reply to my Critics' in JG Finlayson and F Freyenhagen (eds), *Habermas and Rawls: Disputing the Political* (Routledge 2011) 296.

Habermas J, *Auch eine Geschichte der Philosophie*. Vol 2. (Suhrkamp 2019).

Hamm F, *Shaping the Eighteenth Amendment: Temperance, Reform, Legal Culture and the Polity (1880–1920)* (University of North Carolina Press 1995).

Harel, A and A Shinar, 'Two Concepts of Constitutional Legitimacy'. Global Constitutionalism (2022 Forthcoming), Hebrew University of Jerusalem Legal Research Paper No. 22-13, available at SSRN: https://ssrn.com/abstract=4122333

Harris WF II, *The Interpretable Constitution* (Johns Hopkins University Press 1993).

Hart HLA, 'Self-Referring Laws' in HLA Hart, *Essays in Jurisprudence and Philosophy* (Clarendon Press 1983) 170.

Hassan Claudia G, 'Populism, Racism and Scapegoat' in Alfredo Alietti and Dario Padovan (eds), *Clockwork Enemy. Xenophobia and Racism in the Era of Neo-populism* (Mimesis International 2020) 221–39.

Held D, *Democracy and the Global Order: From the Modern State to Cosmopolitan Governance* (Stanford University Press 1995).

Held D and M Koenig-Archibugi (eds), *Taming Globalization: Frontiers of Governance* (Cambridge University Press 2005).

Heller H, *Sovereignty: A Contribution to the Theory of Public and International Law* (1927), edited and introduced by David Dyzenhaus (Oxford University Press 2019).

Herder Johann G, *Another Philosophy of History and Selected Political Writings*. Translated, edited, and with notes by Ioannis D Evrigenis and Daniel Pellerin (Hackett 2004).

Hobbes T, *Leviathan* (1651), edited and with an introduction by CB Macpherson (Penguin 1985).

Holmes S and CR Sunstein, 'The Politics of Constitutional Revision in Eastern Europe' in S Levinson, *Responding to Imperfection: The Theory and Practice of Constitutional Amendment* (Princeton University Press 1995) 275.

Honneth A, *Freedom's Right: The Social Foundations of Democratic Life* (J Ganahl tr, Polity Press 2014).

Ingram D, 'The Role of Recognition in Kelsen's Account of Legal Obligation and Political Duty' (2022) 51(3) OZP—Austrian Journal of Political Science 52–61.

Ionescu G and E Gellner, *Populism: Its Meaning and National Characteristics* (Garden City Press 1969).
Jackson VC, 'Constitutions as "Living Trees"? Comparative Constitutional Law and Interpretive Metaphors' (2006-07) 75 Fordham Law Review 921-60.
Jacobsohn GJ, *Constitutional Identity* (Harvard University Press 2010).
Jaklic K, *Constitutional Pluralism in the EU* (Oxford University Press 2014).
Jefferson T, *The Portable Thomas Jefferson*. Edited and with and introduction by Merril D Peterson (Penguin 1979).
Jellinek G, *Verfassungsänderung und Verfassungswandlung* (1906) (Adamant Media Co 2005).
Kant I, *Critique of the Power of Judgment* (1790). Edited by P Guyer (Cambridge University Press 2000).
Kelly E and L McPherson, 'On Tolerating the Unreasonable' (2001) 9 Journal of Political Philosophy 38.
Kelsen H, 'The Nature and Development of Constitutional Adjudication' (1929) in L Vinx (ed), *The Guardian of the Constitution: Hans Kelsen and Carl Schmitt on the Limits of Constitutional Law*. Translation, introduction, and notes by L Vinx (Cambridge University Press 2015) 22-78.
Kelsen H, *General Theory of Law and State* (Harvard University Press 1949).
Kelsen H, 'Foundations of Democracy' (1955) 66 Ethics 1.
Kelsen H, 'Derogation' in RA Newman (ed), *Essays in Jurisprudence in Honor of Roscoe Pound* (American Society for Legal History 1962) 155.
Kelsen H, *Pure Theory of Law*, translation from the 2nd (revised and enlarged) German edn by M Knight (University of California Press 1967).
Kelsen H, *General Theory of Law and State* (1949). With a new introduction by AJ Treviño (Transaction 2006).
Kelsen H, *The Essence and Value of Democracy*. Edited by N Urbinati and C Invernizzi Accetti (Rowman & Littlefied 2013).
Kelsen H, 'The Nature and Development of Constitutional Adjudication' in L Vinx (ed), *The Guardian of the Constitution: Hans Kelsen and Carl Schmitt on the Limits of Constitutional Law* (Cambridge University Press 2015) 22-78.
Kennedy E, *Constitutional Failure: Carl Schmitt in Weimar* (Duke University Press 2004).
Kohl H, 'Zehn-Punkte-Programm zur Überwindung der Teilung Deutschlands und Europas' ['Ten-Point Program for Overcoming the Division of Germany and Europe'] (28 November 1989) in V Gransow and K Jarausch (eds), *Die Deutsche Vereinigung: Dokumente zu Bürgerbewegung, Annäherung und Beitritt* (Verlag Wissenschaft und Politik 1991) 101.
Korsgaard C, *The Sources of Normativity* (Cambridge University Press 1996).
Korsgaard C, *Self-Constitution* (Oxford University Press 2009).
Kramer L, *The People Themselves: Popular Constitutionalism and Judicial Review* (Oxford University Press 2004).
Krishnaswamy S, *Democracy and Constitutionalism in India: A Study of the Basic Structure Doctrine* (Oxford University Press 2010).
Kumm Mattias, 'The Best of Times and the Worst of Times: Between Constitutional Triumphalism and Nostalgia' in P Dobner and M Laughlin (eds), *The Twilight of Constitutionalism?* (Oxford University Press 2010) 201-19.
Laclau E, *On Populist Reason* (Verso 2005).
Laclau E and C Mouffe, *Hegemony and Socialist Strategy* (Verso 1985).
Lafont C, *Democracy Without Shortcuts: A Participatory Conception of Deliberative Democracy* (Oxford University Press 2020).
Lara MP, 'The term "Populism" as a combat-concept and a catchword' (2019) 9-10 Philosophy & Social Criticism, special issue on populism 1144.

Larmore C, 'The Moral Basis of Political Liberalism' (1999) 96 Journal of Philosophy 12.
Larmore C, *Les pratiques du moi* (PUF 2004).
Lawson G, *Politica Sacra et Civilis* (1657) (Cambridge University Press 1992).
Lefort C, *Democracy and Political Theory* (Polity Press 1988).
Levinson S, 'How Many Times Has the United States Constitution Been Amended? (A) < 26; (B) 26; (C) 27; (D) > 27: Accounting for Constitutional Change' in S Levinson (ed), *Responding to Imperfection: The Theory and Practice of Constitutional Amendment* (Princeton University Press 1995) 13–36.
Levinson S, 'The Political Implications of Amending Clauses' (1996) 13 Constitutional Commentary 32.
Levinson S, 'How the United States Constitution Contributes to the Democratic Deficit in America' (2006–07) 55 Drake Law Review 859.
Levitsky S and D Ziblatt, *How Democracies Die* (Crown 2018).
Lindahl H, 'Constituent Power and Reflexive Identity: Towards an Ontology of Collective Selfhood' in M Loughlin and N Walker (eds), *The Paradox of Constitutionalism* (Oxford University Press 2007).
Lindahl H, *Fault Lines of Globalization: Legal Order and the Politics of A-Legality* (Oxford University Press 2013).
Lindahl H, 'Constituent Power and the Constitution' in D Dyzenhaus and M Thorburn, *Philosophical Dimensions of Constitutional Law* (Oxford University Press 2016) 141.
Lindahl H, *Authority and the Globalisation of Inclusion and Exclusion* (Cambridge University Press 2018).
Lindahl H, 'Inside and Outside Global Law', Julius Stone Address, in (2019) 41(1) Sydney Law Review.
Lindahl H, 'A-Legality, Representation, Constituent Power. Reply to Critics' (2019) 21(3) Etica & Politica/Ethics & Politics 417.
Locke J, *Two Treatises of Government* (1690), with an introduction and notes by Peter Laslett (New American Library 1965).
Loughlin M, The Idea of Public Law (Oxford University Press 2003).
Loughlin M, *Foundations of Public Law* (Oxford University Press 2010).
Mack Smith D, *Victor Emanuel, Cavour, and the Risorgimento* (Oxford University Press 1971).
Madison J, *The Papers of James Madison*. Edited by William T Hutchinson et al (University of Chicago Press 1962–77).
Maffettone S, *Rawls: An Introduction* (Polity Press 2010)
Mansbridge J, 'Rethinking Representation' (2003) 97(4) American Political Science Review 515–28.
Mansbridge J, 'Should Blacks Represent Blacks and Women Represent Women? A Contingent "Yes"' (2003) 61 The Journal of Politics 628.
Mansbridge J, 'The Fallacy of Tightening the Reins', Keynote Address to the Austrian Political Science Association, Vienna, 10 December 2004.
Mansbridge J, 'Recursive Representation' in D Castiglione and J Pollak, *Creating Political Presence: The New Politics of Democratic Representation* (University of Chicago Press 2019) 298.
March A, *Islam and Liberal Citizenship: The Search for an Overlapping Consensus* (Oxford University Press 2009).
Margalit A and J Raz, 'National Self-Determination' (1990) 87(9) The Journal of Philosophy 439.
Matravers D and JE Pike (eds), *Debates in Contemporary Political Philosophy: An Anthology* (Routledge 2003).
McConnell M, 'Originalism and the Desegregation Decisions' (1995) 81 Vermont Law Review 947.

Menga FG, *Potere costituente e rappresentanza democratica: Per una fenomenogia dello spazio istituzionale* (Editoriale Scientifica 2009).
Menga FG, *Ausdruck, Mitwelt, Ordnung: Zur Ursprünglichkeit einer Dimension des Politischen im Anschluss an die Philosophie des frühen Heidegger* (Fink 2018).
Menga FG, 'Contextualizing Hans Lindahl's Legal-Philosophical *Oeuvre*' (2019) 21(3) Etica & Politica/Ethics & Politics 363.
Menga FG, 'Political Conflicts and the Transformation of Legal Orders: Phenomenological Insights on Democratic Contingency and Transgression' (2019) 5(2) The Italian Law Journal 549.
Menga FG, *Etica intergenerazionale* (Morcelliana 2021).
Michelman FI, 'The Subject of Liberalism' (1994) 46(6) Stanford Law Review 1807.
Michelman FI, 'Always Under Law?' (1995) 12(2) Constitutional Commentary 227.
Michelman FI, 'Thirteen Easy Pieces' (1995) 93(6) Michigan Law Review 1297.
Michelman FI, 'Review of *Between Facts and Norms*' (1996) 93 Journal of Philosophy 307.
Michelman FI, 'Can Constitutional Democrats Be Legal Positivists? Or, Why Constitutionalism?' (1996) 2(3) Constellations 293.
Michelman FI, 'How Can the People Ever Make the Laws? A Critique of Deliberative Democracy' in J Bohman and W Rehg (eds) *Deliberative Democracy* (MIT Press 1997) 145.
Michelman FI, 'Morality, Identity, and "Constitutional Patriotism"' (1999) 76(4) Denver University Law Review 1009.
Michelman FI, 'Human Rights and the Limits of Constitutional Theory' (2000) 13(1) Ratio Juris 63.
Michelman FI, 'Legitimacy, the Social Turn, and Constitutional Review: What Political Liberalism Suggests' (2015) 98(3) Critical Quarterly for Legislation and Law 183–205.
Michelman FI, 'A Constitutional Horizon?' (2016) 42 Philosophy & Social Criticism 240.
Michelman FI, 'Political Liberalism's Constitutional Horizon: Some Further Thoughts' (2017) 4 Rivista internazionale di filosofia del diritto 599.
Michelman FI, "'Constitution (Written or Unwritten)": Legitimacy and Legality in the Thought of John Rawls' (2018) 31(4) Ratio Juris 379.
Michelman FI, 'Human Rights and Constitutional Rights: A Proceduralizing Function for Substantive Constitutional Law?' in S Voneky and G Neuman (eds), *Human Rights, Democracy, and Legitimacy in a World of Disorder* (Cambridge University Press 2018) 73–96.
Michelman FI, 'Political-Liberal Legitimacy and the Question of Judicial Restraint' (2019) 1(1) Jus Cogens 59.
Michelman FI and A Ferrara, *Polemika o ústavě* (CAS, Institute of Philosophy 2006).
Mill JS, *Considerations on Representative Government* (1861) (Floating Press 2009)
Montaigne M, *Essais* (Garnier-Flammarion 1969).
Montesquieu, *The Spirit of the Laws* (1748). Edited by Anne M Cohler, Basia Carolyn Miller, and Harold Samuel Stone (Cambridge University Press 1989).
Moore M, *The Ethics of Nationalism* (Oxford University Press 2001).
Moreso JJ, 'Kelsen on Justifying Judicial Review' in G Ramirez (ed), *Ecos de Kelsen: Vidas, obras y controversias* (Editorial Universidad Externado de Colombia 2012) 354.
Mouffe C, *The Return of the Political* (Verso 1993).
Mouffe C, 'Carl Schmitt and the Paradox of Liberal Democracy' in D Dyzenhaus (ed), *Law as Politics: Carl Schmitt's Critique of Liberalism*. With a preface by Ronald Beiner (Duke University Press 1998) 159.
Mouffe C, *The Democratic Paradox* (Verso 2000).
Mouffe C, *Agonistics: Thinking the World Politically* (Verso 2013).
Mouffe C, 'The Populist Moment' *DemocraciaAbierta*, 5 December 2016, https://www.opendemocracy.net/democraciaabierta/chantal-mouffe/populist-challenge.

Mouffe C, *For a Left Populism* (Verso 2018).
Mounk Y, *The People vs. Democracy: Why Our Freedom Is in Danger and How to Save It* (Harvard University Press 2018).
Mudde C and CR Kaltwasser, *Populism: A Very Short Introduction* (Oxford University Press 2017).
Müller JW, '"The People Must Be Extracted from Within the People": Reflections on Populism' (2014) 21(4) Constellations 483–93.
Müller JW, *What is Populism?* (University of Pennsylvania Press 2016).
Muñoz-Fraticelli V, 'The Problem of a Perpetual Constitution' in A Gosseries and LH Meyer (eds), *Intergenerational Justice* (Oxford University Press 2009) 377.
Murphy WF, 'Merlin's Memory: The Past and Future Imperfect of the Once and Future Polity' in S Levinson, *Responding to Imperfection: The Theory and Practice of Constitutional Amendment* (Princeton University Press 1995) 163.
Murphy WF, JE Fleming, and WF Harris, II, *American Constitutional Interpretation* (Foundation Press 1986).
Nancy J-L, *The Inoperative Community* (1986) (University of Minnesota Press 1991)
Nancy J-L, *Being Singular Plural* (1996) (Stanford University Press 2000).
Näsström S, 'The Legitimacy of the People' (2007) 35(5) Political Theory 624.
Näsström S, *The Spirit of Democracy: Corruption, Disintegration, Renewal* (Oxford University Press 2021)
Nielsen K, 'Secession: The Case of Quebec' (1993) 10(1) Journal of Applied Philosophy 29.
Norman W, 'Ethics of secession as the regulation of secessionist politics' in M Moore (ed), *National Self-Determination and Secession* (Oxford University Press 2003) 34.
Offe C, 'An "Empty Signifier"?' (2009) 16(4) Constellations 550.
O'Gorman R, 'Environmental Constitutionalism: A Comparative Study' (2017) 6(3) Transnational Environmental Law 435.
Paine T, 'Rights of Man' (1791), in *The Life and Major Writings of Tom Paine*, ed Philip Foner (Citadel 1961) 243–458.
Patberg M, *Constituent Power in the European Union* (Oxford University Press 2020).
Paxton RO, *The Anatomy of Fascism* (Knopf 2004).
Pettit P, *Republicanism: A Theory of Freedom and Government* (Clarendon Press 1997).
Pettit P, 'A Republican Law of Peoples' (2010) 9(1) European Journal of Political Theory 70.
Pettit P, *On the People's Terms: A Republican Theory and Model of Democracy* (Cambridge University Press 2012).
Philpott D, 'In Defense of Self-Determination' (1995) 105(2) Ethics 352.
Pitkin HF, *The Concept of Representation* (University of California Press 1967).
Plato, *The Republic*. Tr Desmond Lee, introduction by Melissa Lane (Penguin 2007).
Pogge T, *World Poverty and Human Rights: Cosmopolitan Responsibilities and Reforms* (2002) (Polity Press 2008).
Posner E and A Vermeule, *The Executive Unbound: The Post-Madisonian Republic* (Oxford University Press 2011).
Privitera W, 'La critica in sfere pubbliche populiste' (2012) 12 Quaderni di Teoria Sociale 5.
Privitera W, *The Public Sphere and the Populist Challenge* (Mimesis 2017).
Putnam H, *The Collapse of the Fact/Value Dichotomy* (Harvard University Press 2002).
Quong J, *Liberalism Without Perfection* (Oxford University Press 2011).
Quong J, 'Liberalism Without Perfection: A Précis by Jonathan Quong' (2012) 2(1) Philosophy and Public Issues 6.
Rabinbach A and SL Gilman, *The Third Reich Sourcebook* (University of California Press 2013).
Raskin JB, *Overruling Democracy: The Supreme Court versus the American People* (Routledge 2003).

Rasmussen D, 'Reflections on the nature of populism and the problem of stability' (2019) 9–10 Philosophy and Social Criticism, Special Issue on Populism 1058–68.
Rawls J, 'Two Concepts of Rules' (1955) 64 Philosophical Review 3.
Rawls J, *A Theory of Justice* (1971). Revised edn (Harvard University Press 1999).
Rawls J, 'Kantian Constructivism in Moral Theory' (1980) 88 The Journal of Philosophy 515.
Rawls J, 'The Domain of the Political and Overlapping Consensus' (1989) in D Matravers and J Pike (eds), *Debates in Contemporary Political Philosophy: An Anthology* (Routledge 2003) 160.
Rawls J, *Political Liberalism* (1993) expanded edn (Columbia University Press 2005).
Rawls J, 'Reply to Habermas' in J Rawls, *Political Liberalism* (1993) expanded edn (Columbia University Press 2005), 372.
Rawls J, 'The Idea of Public Reason Revisited' (1997), in J Rawls, *Political Liberalism*, expanded edn (Columbia University Press 2005), 440.
Rawls J, *The Law of Peoples* (Harvard University Press 1999).
Rawls J, *Justice as Fairness: A Restatement*, ed Erin Kelly (Harvard University Press 2001).
Rawls J, *Lectures on the History of Political Philosophy*, ed S Freeman (Harvard University Press 2007).
Raz J, *The Authority of Law: Essays on Law and Morality* (Oxford University Press 1979).
Raz J, *Between Authority and Interpretation* (Oxford University Press 2009).
Rehfeld A, 'Representation Rethought: on Trustees, Delegates, and Gyroscopes in the Study of Political Representation and Democracy' (2009) 103(2) The American Political Science Review.
Resnik J and Dilg L, 'Responding to a Democratic Deficit: Limiting the Powers and the Term of the Chief Justice of the United States' (2005–06) University of Pennsylvania Law Review 1575.
Ricoeur P, *Oneself as Another* (University of Chicago Press 1992).
Rorty R, 'The Priority of Democracy over Philosophy' in R Vaughan (ed), *The Virginia Statute of Religious Freedom: Two Hundred Years After* (University of Wisconsin Press 1988).
Rosanvallon P, 'A Reflection on Populism' (2011), Books&ideas.net accessed at http://www.booksandideas.net/IMG/pdf/20111110_populism.pdf.
Ross A, *On Law and Justice* (University of California Press 1959).
Rousseau J-J, *The Social Contract* (1762). Translated and with an introduction C Betts (Oxford University Press 1994).
Roznai Y, *Unconstitutional Constitutional Amendments: The Limits of Amendment Power* (Oxford University Press 2017).
Roznai Y, 'The Newest-Oldest Separation of Powers' (2018) 14(2) European Constitutional Law Review 430.
Rubinelli L, *Constituent Power: A History* (Cambridge University Press 2020).
Russell B, 'On Denoting' (1905) 14 Mind 479.
Ryle Gilbert, *The Concept of the Mind* (Harper & Row 1949).
Sadurski W (ed), *Constitutional Justice, East and West: Democratic Legitimacy and Constitutional Courts in Post-Communist Europe in a Comparative Perspective* (Kluzer 2002).
Sambhashan Quarterly, special issue on *Justice and Public Reason: With Rawls and Beyond* (2021) 2.
Sandel M, 'Moral Argument and Liberal Toleration: Abortion and Homosexuality' (1989) 77(3) California Law Review 521.
Savigny FK von, *The Vocation of Our Age for Legislation and Jurisprudence*, tr A Hayward (Lawbook Exchange 2002).
Saward M, *The Representative Claim* (Oxford University Press 2010).
Scanlon TM, *What We Owe to Each Other* (Harvard University Press 1998).
Scheppele KL, 'The opportunism of populists and the defense of constitutional liberalism' (2019) 20 German Law Journal.

Scheuerman W, 'The Realist Revival in Political Philosophy, or: Why New Is Not Always Improved' (2013) 50(6) International Politics 798.
Scheuerman W, *The End of Law: Carl Schmitt in the Twenty-First Century* (2nd edn, Rowman & Littlefield 2020).
Schlesinger AB, *The Imperial Presidency* (Houghton Mifflin 1973).
Schmitt C, *Political Theology: Four Chapters on the Concept of Sovereignty* (1922). Translated by G Schwab, foreword by Tracy B Strong (University of Chicago Press 2005).
Schmitt C, *Constitutional Theory* (1928). Translated and edited by J Seitzer, Foreword by E Kennedy (Duke University Press 2008).
Schmitt C, 'State Ethics and the Pluralist State' (1930) in AJ Jacobson and B Schlink (eds), *In Weimar: A Jurisprudence of Crisis* (University of California Press 2000) 300.
Schmitt C, *The Concept of the Political* (1932) expanded edition. Translated and with an introduction by G Schwab, with a foreword by TB Strong and with notes by L Strauss (University of Chicago Press 1996).
Shoemaker S, *The First-Person Perspective* (Cambridge University Press 1996).
Schupmann BA, *Carl Schmitt's State and Constitutional Theory: A Critical Analysis* (Oxford University Press 2017).
Searle J, *Speech Acts: An Essay in the Philosophy of Language* (Cambridge University Press 1969).
Seligman A, 'Ritual and Sincerity' (2010) 36(1) Philosophy and Social Criticism, special issue on *Ritual and/or Sincerity* 11.
Sieyès EJ, 'What is the Third Estate?' (1789), in *Political Writings*. Including the Debate between Sieyès and Tom Paine in 1791. Edited, with an introduction and translation of "What is the Third Estate?" by M Sonenscher (Hackett 2003).
Simmel G, 'Das individuelle Gesetz' (1913) in G Simmel, *Das Individuelle Gesetz: Philosophische Exkurse* (Suhrkamp 1987).
Simons GF and CD Fennig (eds) *Ethnologue: Languages of the World*. Twenty-first edn (SIL International 2018). Online version: http://www.ethnologue.com, accessed on 11 November 2018.
Spencer H, 'Progress: Its Law and Cause' (1857), in *Herbert Spencer on Social Evolution*. Edited and with an introduction by JDY Peel (University of Chicago Press 1972).
Strauss DA, 'The Irrelevance of Constitutional Amendments' (2001) 114 Harvard Law Review 1457.
Strawson PF, 'On Referring' (1950) 59 Mind 320.
Sunstein CR, *On the Expressive Function of Law* (1996) 144(5) University of Pennsylvania Law Review 2021.
Sutherland K and A Kovner, 'The Democratic Diarchy: Isegoria and Isonomia: Election by Lot and the Democratic Diarchy', paper read at the Association for Political Thought Conference, Exeter, 2020.
Swaine L, *The Liberal Conscience: Politics and Principle in a World of Religious Pluralism* (Columbia University Press 2006).
Taylor C, *Sources of the Self: The Making of the Modern Identity* (Harvard University Press 1989).
Taylor C, *A Secular Age* (Harvard University Press 2007).
Thompson DF, 'Democracy in Time: Popular Sovereignty and Temporal Representation' (2005) 12(2) Constellations 245.
Thompson DF, 'Representing Future Generations: Political Presentism and Democratic Trusteeship' (2010) 13(1) Critical Review of International and Political Philosophy 17.
Tremmel JC, 'Establishing intergenerational justice in national constitutions', in JC Tremmel (ed), *Handbook of Intergenerational Justice* (Elgar 2006), 187.
Troper M 'The Development of the Notion of Separation of Powers' (1992) 26(2) Israel Law Review 1.

Tucker N, 'Loving Day Recalls a Time When the Union of a Man and a Woman Was Banned' (2006) Washington Post, 13 June 2006, online at http://www.washingtonpost.com/wp-dyn/content/article/2006/06/12/AR2006061201716.html.
Tugendhat E, *Selbstbewusstsein und Selbstbestimmung* (Suhrkamp 1979).
Tully J, *Strange Multiplicity: Constitutionalism in an Age of Diversity* (Cambridge University Press 1995).
Tully J, *Public Philosophy in a New Key.* Vol 1: *Democracy and Civic Freedom* (Cambridge University Press 2008).
Tushnet M, *Taking the Constitution Away from the Courts* (Princeton University Press 1999).
Tushnet M, 'The Jurisprudence of Constitutional Regimes: Alexander Bickel and Cass Sunstein' in KD Ward and C Castillo (eds), *The Judiciary and American Democracy: Alexander Bickel, the Countermajoritarian Difficulty, and Contemporary Constitutional Theory* (SUNY Press 2005).
Tushnet M, *Out of Range: Why the Constitution Can't End the Battle over Guns* (Oxford University Press 2007).
Tushnet M, *Weak Courts, Strong Rights: Judicial Review and Social Welfare Rights in Comparative Constitutional Law* (Princeton University Press 2009).
Tushnet M, 'Varieties of Populism' (2019) 20 German Law Journal 382–89.
Urbinati N, 'Representation as Advocacy: A Study of Democratic Deliberation' (2000) 28 Political Theory 758.
Urbinati N, *Democracy Disfigured: Opinion, Truth, and the People* (Cambridge University Press 2014).
Urbinati N, *Me the People: How Populism Transforms Democracy* (Harvard University Press 2019).
van der Walt J, *The Concept of Liberal Democratic Law* (Routledge 2020).
van der Walt J, *The Horizontal Effect Revolution and the Question of Sovereignty* (de Gruyter 2014).
Van Reybrouck D, *Against Elections: The Case for Democracy* (Random House 2016).
Vergara C, 'Populism as Plebeian Politics: Inequality, Domination, and Popular Empowerment' (2020) 28(2) The Journal of Political Philosophy 222.
Vile JR, 'The Case against Implicit Limits on the Constitutional Amending Process' in S Levinson, *Responding to Imperfection: The Theory and Practice of Constitutional Amendment* (Princeton University Press 1995) 191.
Vinx L, *Kelsen's Pure Theory of Law: Legality and Legitimacy* (Oxford University Press 2007).
Vinx L (ed), *The Guardian of the Constitution: Hans Kelsen and Carl Schmitt on the Limits of Constitutional Law* (Cambridge University Press 2015).
Waldron J, *Law and Disagreement* (Oxford University Press 1999).
Waldron J, *The Dignity of Legislation* (Cambridge University Press 1999).
Waldron J, 'Legislatures Judging in their own Cause' (2009) 3(1) Legisprudence 125.
Waldron J, 'Freeman's Defense of Judicial Review' (1994) Law and Philosophy 13.
Waldron J, 'What a Dissenting Opinion Should Have Said in *Obergefell v Hodges*' (2016) http://papers.ssrn.com/sol3/papers.cfm?abstract_id=2844811).
Walzer M, 'Governing the Globe' (2000) in M Walzer, *Arguing about War* (Yale University Press 2004) 171.
Weber M, *Economy and Society*, edited by G Roth and C Wittich (University of California Press 1978).
Weithman P, *Why Political Liberalism: On John Rawls's Political Turn* (Oxford University Press 2010).

Wendt A, 'Why a World State is Democratically Necessary?', transcript of a presentation given by Alexander Wendt at Hiram College, 2 July 2015, online at http://wgresearch.org/why-a-world-state-is-democratically-necessary/.
Wingenbach Edward C, *Institutionalizing Agonistic Democracy: Post-Foundationalism and Political Liberalism* (Ashgate 2011).
White SK, *The Ethos of a Late-Modern Citizen* (Harvard University Press 2009).
White SK, *A Democratic Bearing: Admirable Citizens, Uneven Injustice, and Critical Theory* (Cambridge University Press 2017).
Williams B, 'A Fair State'. Review of Rawls's Political Liberalism (1993) 15(9) London Review of Books.
Williams B, *In the Beginning Was the Deed: Realism and Moralism in Political Argument*, selected, edited, and with an introduction by G Hawthorn (Princeton University Press 2004).
Winter SL, *A Clearing in the Forest: Law, Life, and Mind* (University of Chicago Press 2001).
Winter SL, 'Bridges of Law, Ideology, Commitment' (2022) 37 Touro Law Review 1981–2010.
Worsley P, 'The Concept of Populism' in G Ionescu and E Gellner, *Populism: Its Meaning and National Characteristics* (Garden City Press 1969) 212.
Wortman R, *The Crisis of Russian Populism* (Cambridge University Press 1967).
Young Iris M, *Justice and the Politics of Difference* (Princeton University Press 1990).
Young Iris M, *Inclusion and Democracy* (Oxford University Press 2000).
Zakaria F, *The Future of Freedom: Illiberal Democracy at Home and Abroad* (Norton 2007).
Zurn CF, *Deliberative Democracy and the Institutions of Judicial Review* (Cambridge University Press 2007).

Index

For the benefit of digital users, indexed terms that span two pages (e.g., 52–53) may, on occasion, appear on only one of those pages.

Ackerman, Bruce 11n.20, 14, 19, 21, 22–23, 22nn.17–19, 63n.2, 75n.39, 82–83, 173, 179nn.3–4, 180n.8, 224n.26
   and 'authenticity of a constitution' 163n.79
   on 'constitutional moments':
   Civil Rights Revolution 246
   New Deal 246, 254–55
   Reconstruction 252
   and dualist conception of democracy 22–23, 31, 101, 101n.34, 175
   on 'landmark statutes' 91n.108, 135n.157
   on 'Popular Sovereignty Initiative' 276n.81
   on 'revolutionary constitutions' 157–58nn.65–68, 158n.68
   on separation of powers 68n.19
   on 'unconventional adaptation' 43n.82, 157–58n.67, 233, 252
Adams, John 179n.1
African National Congress (South Africa) 158
African Union 174n.99
Agamben, Giorgio 56, 58n.132, 59
Albert, Richard 43n.82, 76n.44, 157–58nn.66–67, 160n.71, 162n.76, 163n.80, 205n.89, 263–64, 264n.36, 264nn.37–38, 265, 266, 267, 275n.78
Alito, Samuel 74n.36
Alternative für Deutschland 65
Althusser, Louis 86
Amar, Akhil Reed 13n.23, 252–53n.11, 269, 269n.58, 270, 271–72
amending power 3–7, 11, 12, 13, 15–16, 17–18, 22–23, 68, 71, 98–99, 112, 123, 135, 146, 167, 204, 204n.87, 215, 216, 247–48, 253–55, 259, *see also* 'constituent power'; 'liberal principle of amending legitimacy'; 'unamendability'

   and ameliorative amendments 256
   and corrective amendments 255
   as intermediate between constituent and constituted power 248, 249
   limits of, including three sets of 'unamendables' 260n.26, 261–64
   Roznai's 'spectrum theory' of 257, 257n.24
   in Schmitt's constitutional theory 109
   and vertical reciprocity 272–75
Anscombe, G.E.M. 153n.57
Anselmi, Manuel 73n.30, 74n.33
Arato, Andrew 79n.60, 104n.43, 109n.62, 124n.121, 157n.66
Arditi, Benjamin 63n.5
Arendt, Hannah. 39, 47, 79n.59, 155nn.62–63
Aristotle 39, 44n.87, 59, 212
Articles of Confederation 43, 259n.25
ASEAN (Association of Southeast Asian Nations) 173n.97
Austin, J.L. 67n.14
Australia 165–66
authenticity 9, 57, 152–53, 152n.48, 154, 157–63, 234–37
Ayer, Alfred Jules 189–90
Azmanova, Albena 137n.1

Bachof, Otto 262–63n.35
Balkin, Jack 8, 17, 214, 224n.26, 227n.39, 229–30, 232n.55, 232n.56, 234, 239, 278
   on 'framework originalism' 230
   as distinct from 'skyscraper originalism' 230–31
   on 'redemptive constitutionalism' 235
Barker, Ernest 182n.15
Barry, Brian 273n.71
Basso, Lelio 161

Beccaria, Cesare 240n.86
Beck, Hans 145n.25
Beiner, Ronald 113n.77
Belgium 65
Bellamy, Richard 14–15, 31, 39–44, 75n.38, 217, 217n.1, 219n.6, 222, 222n.19, 243
Ben-Gurion, David 158
Beran, Harry 165–66n.84
Berger, Peter 262–63
Berlin, Isaiah 29n.37, 39
Berlusconi, Silvio 82
Bernal, Carlos 264n.39
Bernstein, Richard 104n.44, 120–21n.110
Bhabha, Homi 56, 58
Bianchin, Matteo 144n.23
Bickel, Alexander 9, 205n.88, 218n.4
Bill of Rights (1689) 148
Bill of Rights (Constitution of the United States) 270
Blanchot, Maurice 56, 58, 59
Blokker, Paul 63n.2, 73n.30
Bobbit, Philip 239n.81
Bohman, James 24n.23, 225n.29
Bolsonaro, Jair 82
Bosnia-Herzegovina 166–67
Bossi, Umberto 84–85
Bozdag, Bekir 76
Brazil 253, 266
Brilmayer, Lea 165–66n.84
Brown v. Board of Education 135n.157, 161, 226, 226n.36, 227, 227n.38, 228, 230, 254
Brunei 70n.26
Buchanan, Allen 165n.82, 167, 167nn.86–87, 168, 169
Buchstein, Hubertus 179n.5
Burke, Edmund 186–88, 186n.29, 193–94, 202, 204–5
Bush, George W. 203n.83, 221
Butler, Judith 59

Calamandrei, Piero 162–63n.77
Campos, Andre Santos 274n.75
Canada 165–66, 169, 173–74, 257, 266
Canovan, Margaret 63n.5, 64–65n.9, 66n.12, 68n.20, 145, 145nn.25–26, 146
Cartabia, Marta 160n.71, 162–63n.77
Casey v. *Planned Parenthood* (1992) 227n.40

Castiglione, Dario 44n.88, 193n.51, 198n.71, 199n.73
Cavour, Camillo Benso, Count of 171
Charles I (Stuart) 71
Chávez, Hugo 65, 84, 201–2
China 70, 145n.25
Chisholm v. Georgia (1793) 246n.97
Churchill, Winston 202–3
Cicero 39
Civil Rights Act (US) 91, 135n.157
Claviez, Thomas 56, 58n.132, 59–60, 59nn.137–38, 63n.5
Cohen, Jean L. 63n.3
Cohen, Joshua 38, 38n.65
Colombia 204–5
Colón-Ríos, Joel I. 77n.48, 99n.27, 106n.49, 123n.120, 130n.145
Conant, James B. 138n.4
Condorcet, Marquis de 210, 210n.105
Congress of Vienna (1815) 170–71
Congress Party (India) 158
Conniff, Michael L. 84n.73
Conrad, Dietrich 265n.43
Conseil Constitutionnel (France) 76n.44
Constant, Benjamin 23, 46, 118–19
constituent power 1–3, 4, 5, 6–7, 14–16, 19, 22, 71, 72, 76–77, 78–79, 86, 90–91, 94, 95, 130–31, 137, 139, 143–44, 146, 148–49, 152, 153–54, 155, 204, 207, 209, 221–22, 247–49, 260, 270, 271–72, 282
as bound by the 'most reasonable' 132–34
in Locke's political philosophy 77, 93n.3, 94, 122
manifesting itself as constitution-amending (amending power) 174–76
manifesting itself as merging of a demos in a larger one 170, 171, 173
manifesting itself as regime-change 157–59, 160, 161–62
manifesting itself as secession 163–64, 166–67, 168–69
as not unbound 31, 122, 127–29
paradox of 139, 140, 141–42, 150–51
as rib of constituted power, for Kelsen 96, 102
in Schmitt's constitutional theory 109, 110–11
as vested in 'the people' 21, 61
see also 'amending power'; 'people (the)'

constitution
  as basis for political justification (*see* 'liberal principle of legitimacy')
  and future generations 4, 5, 7, 167, 201, 205, 209, 215–16, 232, 236, 249n.6, 267, 273, 274–75
  integrative function of 9n.18, 235nn.69–70
  as political project 215–16, 242
  proceduralizing function of 229
  regulatory function of 9, 22, 43–44, 161, 212–14, 229, 235
  and self-constitution 141, 159
Constitution of Brazil 253n.12
Constitution of Canada 257
Constitution of Costa Rica 275–76
Constitution of the Czech Republic 262n.29
Constitution of Ethiopia 166–67
Constitution of France 98, 137–38, 253n.12, 261n.28
Constitution of Germany (*Grundgesetz*) 137–38, 139–40, 173, 261–62
Constitution of Greece 253n.12
Constitution of India 204
Constitution of Italy 98, 106–7n.52, 137–38, 159–60, 161, 162–63, 181, 202n.82, 232–33, 238–39, 243n.93, 255n.15, 261n.28, 275–76
Constitution of the Netherlands 255n.15
Constitution of Portugal 137–38
Constitution of South Africa 257, 257n.23
Constitution of Spain 137–38, 253n.12, 266n.47
Constitution of Switzerland 266n.47
Constitution of Taiwan 264
Constitution of the United States 7, 12, 17–18, 97, 99, 106, 137, 213, 226, 232–33, 238, 243n.93, 251, 252, 253, 258–59, 262n.33, 266, 267, 269–70, 278
  Article V of 97, 128, 252–53n.11, 258–59, 262–63, 264, 269–70
  Article VII of 270
  First Amendment 7, 12, 17–18, 22, 97, 99, 109, 243n.93, 259–60, 262–63, 267, 276–77, 278
  Second Amendment 99, 213, 278–79
  Fourteenth Amendment 22, 38, 226, 227n.39, 228, 232n.55, 243, 246n.97

  Eighteenth Amendment 12, 251, 266, 279
  Nineteenth Amendment 12, 97–98, 267
  Twenty-First Amendment 12, 251, 266
  Twenty-Fourth Amendment 252
  Twenty-Seventh Amendment 253
  (hypothetical) Twenty-Eighth Amendment 99
constitutional authenticity 9, 154, 157–63, 234–37
Conte, Giuseppe 72–73
Cooley, Thomas 265, 265n.40, 265n.41
Corbyn, Jeremy 89
Correa, Rafael 84
Council of State (Turkey) 76
Cover, Robert M. 227n.40, 249n.7
Cristi, Renato 113n.77
critical theory 56, 89
Croatia 149, 166–67
Croce, Mariano 113, 115n.90, 116–17n.92
Cromwell, Oliver 148
Çullhaj, Florian 20n.1
Cummings v. Missouri (1867) 260n.26
Czechoslovakia 166–67

Dahl, Robert 178
Dansk Folkeparti 65
D'Azeglio, Massimo 149, 171
Declaration of the Rights of Man and Citizen (1789) 262n.33
Descartes, Renée 153
De Gasperi, Alcide 158
De Gaulle, Charles 75–76, 158, 204, 260–61, 268–69, 270
De La Torre, Carlos 84n.73
deliberative democracy 31, 32–35, 87–88
  and 'democratic dualism' 31
  discursive view of 33
Dellinger, Walter 277n.84
Democratic Party (Italy) 82
democratic sovereignty 1, 2–3, 207, 220
  sequential conception of 9–10, 11–12, 209–10, 259–60
  serial conception of 13, 209–16
    three consequences thereof:
      'the indistinct republic' 214–15
      'the underdetermined republic' 215
      'the wanton republic' 211–14
  and tension with government under law 129

Destri, Chiara 79n.60
Dewey, John 57–58, 60n.139, 151n.47
Dierksmeier, Claus 273n.71
Di Maio, Luigi 72–73
Disch, Lisa 198n.71, 198n.72
Dobbs et al. v. Jackson Women's Health Organization 74n.36
Dobner, Petra 140n.9
Dreben, Burton 20n.1
Dred Scott v. Sandford (1857) 246n.97
Dryzek, John 187n.30
Durkheim, Émile 3, 57–58, 120
Dutch Party for Freedom 65
Duterte, Rodrígo 65
Dworkin, Ronald 1–2, 14, 31, 35–39, 35n.47, 35n.50, 37n.56, 52, 53, 60, 94, 143n.20, 219, 223, 230n.50, 277n.85
  on legal principles as unamendable 262–63n.35
  on limits of public reason 37–38
  on 'making the most' 239n.83, 240, 242
  on Rawls's second principle 37–38
Dyzenhaus, David 99n.29, 102n.36, 113n.77, 114n.86, 119n.100, 150n.41

Eastern Europe 142
Eatwell, Roger 70n.24
Enabling Law (1933, German Reich) 280n.95
Erdogan, Recep Tayyp 76, 260–61, 270
Eskridge William N., jr. 91n.108
Esposito, Roberto 56, 58n.132
Estonia 168
EU (European Union) 12, 44, 147–48, 173–74, 262–63
exemplary normativity 55, 131n.148, 133, 151
  as connected with Kant's notion of the 'promotion of life' 244n.94

Fabbrizi, Valerio 20n.1
Fair Housing Act (US) 91, 135n.157
Fanfani, Amintore 159–60
Farrand, Max 180n.10
Fennig, Charles D. 147n.31
Ferejohn, John 91n.108
Ferrajoli, Luigi 97n.16
Fidesz (Hungary) 65, 72
Finchelstein, Federico 84n.73
Finns Party (formerly the '*True Finns*') 65

Fiorespino, Leonardo 20n.1, 43n.84, 70–71n.28, 87n.90
Fishkin, James 179nn.3–4
Five Star Movement (Italy) 65, 69, 72–73, 84, 90n.107, 202
Fleming, James E. 239n.81
Floyd, Jonathan 49n.104
Fluck, Winfried 58n.132
Forst, Rainer C3P78 n.83
Foucault, Michel 47
France 51, 65, 72, 75–76, 79, 105, 107–8, 145, 149, 157–58, 171, 204, 214, 268–69
Frankfurt, Harry 152n.48, 153n.53, 191–92
Fraser, Nancy 84, 89–90, 89n.100
Freedom House 70n.27, 99
Freeman, Samuel 13n.22, 16–17, 20n.1, 203, 206n.93, 207, 207n.95, 208, 208n.101, 209, 209n.103
Friedrich, Carl J. 184n.23, 266n.44

Galston, William 49n.104
Gardbaum, Stephen 157n.66
Gargarella, Roberto 157n.66
Garibaldi, Giuseppe 170–71
Gellner, Ernest 65n.10
Germany 139–40, 171–73, 172nn.94, 95, 202–3
  Federal Republic of 171–73
  German Democratic Republic 172–73
  German Reich 105, 106n.51, 107–8, 112, 113, 123–24
Geuss, Raymond 49n.104
Gierke, Otto von 183–84
Gilman, Sander L. 280n.95
Ginsburg, Tom 148n.36
Giovanola, Benedetta 120n.106
Glaucon 27, 30–31
Glorious Revolution 145
Golden Dawn (Greece) 65
Goldoni, Marco 79n.59
González-Ricoy, Iñigo 275n.76
Goodwin, Matthew 70n.24
Goodwyn, Lawrence 64–65n.9
Gorbachev, Mikhail 171–72
Gore, Al 203n.83, 221
Gosseries, Axel 216n.122, 274n.72
Gramsci, Antonio 84–85
Gransow, Volker 172n.94
Gray, John 14, 31, 49–52, 53, 55–56

INDEX   303

Great Reform Bill (1832) 42
Grimm, Dieter 9n.18, 235–36, 235n.69
Grotius (Hugo de Groot) 144n.24

Häberle, Peter 274n.73
Habermas, Jürgen 1–2, 14, 28n.33, 31, 32–35, 32n.40, 33n.44, 56–58, 68, 81–82, 81n.66, 89, 113–14, 117n.93, 132, 139n.6, 143, 174, 174n.101, 175n.104
   on co-originality thesis 32n.40
   and legitimation by constitution 32–33
   overlooking Rawls's standard of 'the most reasonable' 35
   on pluralism 33, 34–35
   on rational consensus as resting on the same reasons 34
   and the uncoercive force of the better argument 247
Hacker, P.M.S. 273n.71
Hamilton, Alexander 208
Hanafin v. Minister of the Environment (1996, Ireland) 269n.56
Harel, Alon 162n.76
Harlan, John Marshall 226n.37
Harris, William F. II 13n.24, 239n.81, 257, 257n.22, 259n.25, 260n.26, 264n.37, 268, 270–72, 270n.63
Hart, Herbert L.A. 260n.26
Hassan, Claudia G. 63n.5
Hawthorn, G. 49n.104
Hegel, Georg Wilhelm Friedrich 57–58, 114, 125
Heidegger, Martin 59, 227n.40
Heller, Hermann 99n.29, 103–4n.39, 123n.117
Herder, Johan G. 147n.33
Hobbes, Thomas 49–50, 52, 53–54, 55, 76nn.46–47, 78, 80n.62, 102–3, 110, 122, 138, 143, 148, 156n.64, 170, 174, 182, 183, 183n.17, 184
Holmes, Stephen 248, 248n.3
Honecker, Eric 171–72
Honneth, Axel 56–58, 56n.127, 57n.129, 60
Hugo, Victor 12–13
Hume, David 67n.14
Husserl, Edmund 262–63

ICC (International Criminal Court) 67–68
Imesch, Kornelia 58n.133

inauspicious conditions for democracy (*see also* 'Michelman') 24n.23, 33,
   additional 24n.24
   encompassing an occlusion of democratic authorship 8, 11, 206, 225–26, 228, 243, 244, 246
   encompassing a shortfall of agreement 8, 225–26
India 65, 157–58
   Supreme Court of 109, 204–5, 204n.87, 205n.89, 238–39, 259–60, 262n.31, 265–66
Indignados (Spain) 84
Ingram, David 101n.32
Instrument of Government (1653) 228
Invernizzi Accetti, Carlo 94n.6
Ionescu, Ghita 65n.10
Iran 157–58
Israel 157–58
Issacharoff, Samuel 70–71n.28
Italy 65, 68–69, 72–73, 90n.107, 105, 149, 157–58, 159–60, 161, 170–71, 181, 202, 214, 238, 266, 275–76 (*see also* 'Constitution of Italy')
   Chamber of Deputies of 160n.70
   Constitutional Court of 160n.71, 237n.76
   Italian Republic 142, 159–60, 238, 242
   Italian Risorgimento 171
   Kingdom of 170–71, 280

Jackson, Vicki C. 266n.44
Jacobsohn, Gary Jeffrey 266n.45
Jacobson, Arthur J. 116–17n.92
Jaeggi, Rahel 89n.100
James II (Stuart) 145
Japan 266
Jarausch, Konrad 172n.94
Jefferson, Thomas 3, 4, 122, 175n.105, 210, 210n.106, 212, 213, 214n.118, 216, 248–49, 261, 269, 274
Jellinek, Georg 104n.41, 183–84, 250n.9
Jesus Christ 181
Johnson, Boris 82
judicial restraint *see also* 'Michelman'
   as adopting weak-form judicial review 206
   as quiescence 205
   as tolerance 205

judicial review 9, 11, 16–17, 22–23, 43, 91, 98, 111, 112, 124, 135n.157, 157, 206, 207, 208–9, 220, 237, 260–61, 268–69, 275, 277
 as contributing to the democratic process 222–24, 247, 277–78, 280
 as contributing to invigorate 'constitutional authenticity' 234, 236
 as distinct from judicial supremacy 217–18
 as imposing costs to democratic self-determination 9, 218–20
 as leaning toward originalism if the court's mandate aims at remedying occlusion of democratic authorship 8n.13, 225
 as leaning toward reaching philosophically non-rejectable conclusions if the court's mandate aims at remedying shortfall of agreement 8n.13, 225–26
 as possibly combining the two understandings of the interpreter's mandate 226–28

Kaltwasser, Cristobal Rovira 64n.7
Kant, Immanuel 46, 55n.126, 56–57, 113–14, 118–19, 132, 173, 238
 on pleasure of the beautiful connected with a feeling of the promotion of life 243–44
 on 'purely reflective judgment' 240, 243–44
Kelly, Erin 23–24n.22, 93n.1, 119n.104
Kelsen, Hans 15–16, 93–94, 94n.6, 95–97, 95n.8, 95n.9, 95n.10, 97nn.16–17, 98–99, 103, 105, 108, 111, 113–14, 125–26, 141, 142, 148–49, 174
 on the basic norm 95–96
  as groundless 102–3
  as unrelated to justice 100
 on constituent power 94–96, 249n.6
 on implicit unamendability 98–99
 on judicial review 124
 on spirit of compromise as basic to law-making 100–2, 124–25
Kennedy, Ellen 113, 115n.90
Kesavananda Bharati Sripadagalvaru v. State of Kerala ((1973) 4 SCC 225) 109n.64, 204, 238–39
Khomeini, Ayatollah 158

King, Martin Luther 231–32
Kohl, Helmut 171–72, 172n.94, 172n.95, 202–3
Korsgaard, Christine 152, 152nn.48–49, 152nn.50–52, 153n.53
Kovner, Alex 179n.6
Krishnaswamy, Sudhir 266n.45
Kumm, Mattias 140n.9
Kymlicka, Will 148n.35

Laclau, Ernesto 84n.75, 85, 86, 87–88, 197n.64, 198n.71
 on expulsion of the population from the people 87
Lafont, Cristina 9n.17, 179n.2, 219n.11
 on judicial review as contributing to democracy 222, 222n.18, 222n.20, 223–24, 223n.23
landmark statutes 19, 91, 135n.157
Lara, María Pía 63n.2
Larmore, Charles 20n.1, 29, 152n.48, 153, 153nn.53–54, 154
Latvia 168
Laughlin, Martin 140n.9
Law and Justice (Poland) 65
Lawson, George 77n.48
League (Italy) 65, 69, 72–73, 84–85, 90n.107, 154
Lefort, Claude 68n.18, 87
'legitimation by constitution' 23–25, 33, 36, 38–39, 142–43n.18, 237
 and dualist democracy 31
Le Pen, Jean-Marie 68
Le Pen, Marine 72, 73
Levinson, Sanford 13n.23, 243n.92, 246n.97, 248n.3, 252–53n.11, 262n.33, 264n.37, 265n.40, 269n.58
Levitsky, Steven 64n.7
liberal principle of amending legitimacy 4–5, 13–14, 280–82
liberal principle of constitutional legitimacy 15–16, 126–36, 281–82
liberal principle of legitimacy 4–5, 23–25, 32–33, 41–42, 54–55, 94, 134–35, 206, 237, 280–81, 282
 different formulations of 23–24n.22
Lincoln, Abraham 42
Lindahl, Hans 6n.11, 16, 67–68nn.15–17, 98n.26, 123n.117, 139–42, 141n.12, 141n.13, 150–51, 153n.54, 155, *see also* 'constituent power: paradox of'

on the paradox of constituent power 139, 140, 141, 141n.12, 141n.13, 150–51
Lithuania 168, 173
Locke, John 1–2, 3, 21, 23, 40n.75, 53–54, 102–3, 126, 138, 146, 148, 156n.64, 159–60, 170, 247–48, 274, 282
 on constituent power not evaporating after creation of the commonwealth 77, 77n.48
 on constituent power not unbound 122n.114, 122n.115
Loewenstein, Karl 130n.145
Louis XIV 71, 210
Louis XV 210
Loving v. Virginia, (1967) 135n.157
Luckmann, Thomas 262–63
Luther, Martin 152, 241

MacDonagh, Oliver 42
Macedonia 166–67
Machiavelli, Niccolò 39, 54–55, 145, 159
Mack Smith, Denis 171n.93
Madison, James 186, 188–89, 202, 210, 212–13, 236, 269
Maduro, Nicolás 72, 82
Maffettone, Sebastiano 20n.1
Magna Carta (1215) 148
Mandela, Nelson 158
Mansbridge, Jane 16–17, 180n.9, 193–96, 193n.51, 199
Marbury v. Madison (1803) 135n.157, 205n.88, 208, 277
March, Andrew 120n.106
Margalit, Avishai 165n.82
Matravers, Derek 116n.91
Matteotti, Giacomo 280n.96
McConnell, Michael 227n.39
McCormick, John P. 79n.60
McPherson, Lionel 119n.104
Mélenchon, Jean-Luc 89
Menga, Ferdinando 140n.11, 273n.71
Metternich, Klemens von 170–71
Meyer, Lukas H. 216n.122
Michelman, Frank I. 23–24n.22, 94, 99n.27, 114n.83, 124n.123, 142–43n.18, 144n.22, 226–28, 249n.6, 252–53n.11, 276, *see also* 'constituent power as always under law'; 'inauspicious conditions'; 'judicial review';
 'legitimation by constitution'; 'sovereignty as jurisdiction'
 on 'always under law' thesis 2–3, 127–29, 130n.146, 271, 272
 on inauspicious conditions for democracy 24n.23, 33
 on 'legitimation by constitution' 24n.23, 25n.25
 on 'sovereignty as jurisdiction' 130, 130n.146, 131
 on three facets of a constitutional court's mandate 16–17, 205–6, 205n.90, 224–25
 on two ways of understanding the mandate of a constitutional court 8n.13, 225–26
 and a possible way of reconciling them 229
Mihai, Mihaela 137n.1
Mill, John Stuart 23, 46, 67n.14, 118–19, 189–90, 271n.64
Minerva Mills Ltd. v. *Union of India* (1980) 109n.64, 204n.87, 238–39
Modi, Narendra 65
Montaigne, Michel de 150n.38, 152, 156, 162
Montesquieu 23–24, 57–58, 78–79, 83, 111, 116–17, 147
Moore, Margaret 166n.85
Morales, Evo 65, 84, 201–2
Moreso, José Juan 98n.25
Morley, Imogen 172n.95
Moro, Aldo 161
Mouffe, Chantal 14, 31, 45–49, 45n.90, 45n.91, 45n.92, 47nn.97–99, 84, 87–88, 87n.91, 88n.98, 89, 113n.77, 114n.84, 119n.100
Mounk, Yascha 64n.7
Mudde, Cas 64n.7
Müller, Jan-Werner 64n.8, 65n.11
Muñoz-Fraticelli, Víctor 216n.122
Murphy, Walter F. 239n.81, 262n.33, 267, 267n.52, 268n.53
Mussolini, Benito 159, 162, 280n.96

Nakashidze, Malkhaz 76n.44
Nancy, Jean-Luc 56, 58, 59
Näsström, Sofia 138n.5, 139n.7
National Assembly (France) 75–76
National Rally (France) 65

Nehru, Jawaharlal 158
Nenni, Pietro 158
Neuman, Gerald 124n.123
Newman, Ralph A. 98n.24
Nielsen, Kai 168–69, 169n.91
Niemeyer, Simon 187n.30, 199n.73
Norman, Wayne 166n.85, 167n.86
  Norway 166–67

Obergefell v. Hodges 576 U.S. 644
  (2015) 73n.31, 74–75
Occupy Wall Street (USA) 84
O'Gorman, Roderic 256n.17
Olcay, Tarik 76n.44
oppression 14, 20, 27–29, 34, 53–54, 96–97, 245
  defined 27–28
  and 'reasonable pluralism' 28, 34–35, 58
Orbàn, Viktor 72, 82
Oregon v. Mitchell (1970) 246n.97
originalism 8, 151, 229–32
  conservative 230
  framework (Balkin) 230–31
  living (Balkin) 230
  political 9
  skyscraper 230–31
Orwell, George 275

Paine, Thomas 78n.50, 210, 211, 211n.111
Panizza, Francisco 63n.5
Patberg, Markus 203n.84
Paxton, Robert O. 280n.96
people (the) *see also* 'constituent power' and 'populism'
  as bearer of constituent power 1–2, 3, 110–11, 134, 249
  as construction 102, 177, 277
  as *demos* 147–48, 155, 170–74
  emerging from an *ethnos* through a 'commitment to share commitments' 6–7, 16, 110–11, 155, 156
  as deriving from populus 145
  as distinct from the electorate 1, 250–51, 260, 276–77
  as distinct from the population 68, 87
  as ethnos 147–48, 155, 170–74
  as transgenerational entity 202–3
  represented by a constitutional court 203–5, 224, 245–46
  legitimacy of 138
  'political conception' of 5–7, 142–56, 165
  representing the 8–10, 11, 16–17, 61, 201–6
  as self-constituting 139–42
  as self-governing 128
  through higher lawmaking 127, 225
Perón, Juan 65, 84–85
Pettit, Philip 14, 31, 39–44, 39n.66, 39n.68, 40n.72, 222n.17, 223
Philadelphia 43, 146, 180, 269
Philpott, Daniel 165n.83
Pike, Jonathan 116n.91
Pitkin, Hanna F. 9–10, 16–17, 178–93, *see also* 'representation'
  on contemporary value pluralism as favouring descriptive representation 191–93
  on descriptive representation 178–80
  on formalistic representation 182–84
  on substantive representation 184–86
  on symbolic representation 181–82
  on the 'trustee/delegate' dilemma of substantive representation 186–90
Plato 2–3
  allegory of the cave 1–2, 25–26, 132–33, 154, 227n.40
  as foil for grasping innovativeness of Rawls' public reason and standard of the 'most reasonable' 26–31
  political-philosophical significance of 26
Plebiscitary electoral law (1928, Italy) 280n.96
Plessy v. Ferguson, 163 U.S. (1896) 226n.36, 226n.37, 227n.40, 254
pluralism 24–25, 45–46, 47, 56–57, 58, 69, 80–81, 90–91, 116–17n.92, 241
  fact of (Rawls) 26
  hyperpluralism 33, 41–42, 225
  justification for respecting 25, 30–31
  reasonable (Rawls) 8, 28–30, 119–20, 131, 191–93
Podemos (Spain) 65, 72, 84, 87–88, 89
Poland 65, 157–58, 173
political constitutionalism 31, 43–44, 74, 217
political liberalism 1, 2–4, 12, 14–18, 19–61, 63–92, 94, 100, 102, 103–22, 124, 127, 134–36, 137–76, 206, 217, 224, 226, 242, 246, 247–82

and dualist (constitutional) democracy 19, 21, 22–23, 31, 101–2, 207
embedding 'legitimation by constitution' 23–24, 237
embedding a non-foundationalist anchoring of normativity and limit to liberal toleration 115–16, 119
and reasonable pluralism 29, 30–31, 101, 122, 192, 239–40, 267, 277–78
Pollak, Johannes 193n.51
Pollock v. Farmers' Loan & Trust Company (1895) 246n.97
populism 3, 14–15, 60–61, 63–92, 209, 216, 217, 220, 275, 277
 and attribution of full constituent power to the electorate 66, 68–69, 75
 and conflation of 'the people' and the electorate 66
 as determinant of *enfeebled* and *hollowed out* democracies 81–83
 non-populist sources of the attribution of full constituent power to the living segment of the people 77–80
 non-populist sources of conflation of people and electorate 73–75
 non populist sources of populist questioning of checks and balances 83–84
 and presumptively justified intolerance 67
 rightwing and leftwing not significantly different 84–90
 six inadequate concepts of populism 64–66
 three-pronged definition of 66–69
Posner, Eric 83–84, 83n.72
Privitera, Walter 82n.67, 82n.68
Prohibition 12, 251, 255
Putnam, Hilary 229n.46

Qatar 70n.26
Quong, Jonathan 115n.88, 119nn.102–3

Rabinbach, Anson 280n.95
Ramirez, G. 98n.25
Rancière, Jacques 56, 58
Rasmussen, David 70–71n.28
Rawls, John 1–4, 8, 12, 14–16, 17–18, 20, 28, 32–33, 34–35, 36–38, 40, 41–42, 45–46, 47, 50, 53, 54–57, 58, 60, 61, 127, 129, 130–33, 138–39, 141, 154, 160, 165–66, 174–75, 192, 217–18, 228, 230, 231, 235, 245, 260–61, 272, 273–74, 280–81, 282, *see also* 'legitimation by constitution'; 'liberal principle of legitimacy'; 'oppression'; 'political liberalism'
 and burdens of judgment 28, 46, 50, 81, 118–19, 127, 217, 247
 on constituent power 221
  as not unbound 122, 126, 133–34, 247–48
 on dualist conception of democracy 19, 22–23
 on five principles of constitutionalism 5–6
 on implicit unamendability 7, 12–13, 17–18, 22, 97, 109, 259–60, 262–63, 267, 276–77, 278
 on justice as fairness as most reasonable political conception of justice for us 50, 129, 241
 on 'liberal principle of legitimacy' 5, 24–25, 38–39, 134–35, 206
 and supposition of 'reasonable' pluralism 192
 and points of convergence with Kelsen's paradigm 96–97, 124–25
 and points of convergence with Schmitt's constitutional theory 108, 109, 113–16, 123, 233
 and points of divergence with Kelsen's paradigm 97–103
 and points of divergence with Schmitt's constitutional theory 116–22, 123–24, 125
 on political conception of the person 6, 142–43
 on public reason 26–27, 30, 219
 on rejecting both parliamentary and judicial supremacy 22
 on rejecting serial view of democratic sovereignty 7
 on the standard of 'the most reasonable' 10, 31, 132–33, 239–41, 281
Raz, Joseph 95n.10, 165–66, 265–66, 273n.71
reciprocity 23–24n.22, 37, 43, 46, 273, 281
 horizontal 274–75, 280–81
 as integral to reasonability 118–19
 vertical 3–4, 5, 11–14, 17–18, 247–82

Rehfeld, Andrew 16–17, 193, 194n.54, 199–200, 202, 205
Rehg, William 24n.23, 225n.29
Renzi, Matteo 82
representation 16–17, 139–40, 141, 150, 151, 152, 159, 168, 177–80, 181–90, 191–200, 201–16, 218, 247, 264, *see also* Pitkin, Hanna F.
  anticipatory (Mansfield) 193–94, 195–96
  constructivist turn in 178, 193, 198n.71, 199
  descriptive (Pitkin) 178–80, 182
  direct (Urbinati) 69n.22
  discursive (Dryzek) 199
  formalistic (Pitkin) 182–84
  Goldilocks dilemma of 191–92
  gyroscopic (Mansfield) 193–94, 199
  promissory (Mansfield) 193–94, 195–96
  as representative claim (Saward) 196–98
  substantive (Pitkin) 9–10, 184–86, 194, 247
    delegate version of 188–90
    trustee version of 186–88
  surrogate (Mansfield) 193–94, 199
  symbolic (Pitkin) 181–82
Republic of San Marino 51
Ricoeur, Paul 152–53, 154
Riordan v. An Taoiseach, (1999, Ireland) 269n.57
Roberts, John G., Chief Justice of the Supreme Court of the United States 73n.31
Roman Republic 146, 215
Rome 3
Roosevelt, Franklin D. 202–3
Rorty, Richard 25, 30n.38
Rosanvallon, Pierre 68n.19, 82n.69, 83
Ross, Alf 260n.26
Rousseau, Jean Jacques 4, 23, 190, 206, 247–48
  as endorser of serial sovereignty 14–15, 77–79, 80, 102–3, 109–10, 122, 126, 138, 139n.7, 174–75, 210, 248–49, 261
  and the *legislator* 133, 151, 241n.91
  and the riddle of 5–6, 16, 142, 144, 146, 148–51, 152, 155–56, 170
  and the tribunate 208
Roznai, Yaniv 98n.24, 257, 260n.26, 262–63n.35, 264n.39, 265n.42, 268–69, 272–73
  on delegation approach to amending power 272nn.69–70

Rubinelli, Lucia 79n.59
Russell, Bertrand 138n.4
Russia 64–65n.9, 70, 86, 146, 173
Ryle, Gilbert 153n.56

SAARC (South Asian Association for Regional Cooperation) 174n.98
Sala, Roberta 120n.106
Salvatore, Andrea 52n.114, 113, 115n.90
Salvini, Matteo 68, 72–73
Sandel, Michael 37n.60
Sanders, Bernie 89
Saragat, Giuseppe 159–60
Saudi Arabia 70n.26
Saussure, Ferdinand de 47, 48, 84–85, 181
Savigny, Friedrich K. von 151n.46
Savoy, Victor Emmanuel II (first king of Italy) 159
Saward, Michael 16–17, 193, 196–98, 196n.59, 198n.72
Scalia, Antonin 73–74
Scheppele, Kim 71
Scheuerman, William 49n.104, 123n.117
Schlesinger, Arthur B. 83n.71
Schlink, Bernhard 116–17n.92
Schmitt, Carl 15–16, 89, 99, 103–22, 125–26, 130–31, 137, 141, 142, 146, 179–80, 233, 262–63, 265
  on constituent power 116–17, 121–22, 123, 129
    and its fundamental existential decisions 106, 123, 266–67
    and its two variants 109–10
  on the constitution and different concepts of 105–8
  on the 'guardian of the constitution' 111–13
  on implicit unamendability 79–80, 106, 123–24
  on the people 93–94, 110–11
  on the political 104, 117–18, 119–20
  on the sovereign and the exception 104–5, 121–22, 130
Schumpeter, Joseph 52, 88
Schupmann, Benjamin A. 104n.41, 107n.53, 111n.71, 113, 114–15, 124n.122
Schutz, Alfred 262–63
Searle, John 96n.14, 262–63
Seligman, Adam 56, 58n.132

separation of powers 232–33, 234, 238–39, 246, 279–80
Shklar, Judith 49
Shoemaker, Sydney 153n.58
Sieyès, Emmanuel J. 3, 14–15, 77–79, 110, 122, 129, 210, 261
Simmel, Georg 241n.91
Simons, Gary F. 147n.31
Skinner, Quentin 47
Slovakia 166–67
Socrates 27
South Africa 142, 157–58, 165–66, 257
Soviet Union (URSS) 168
Spain 65, 69, 72, 105, 137–38, 142, 173–74, 253
Statuto Albertino 159, 162, 280
Stears, Marc 49n.104
Strauss, David A. 254n.14
Strawson, Peter F. 138n.4
Sunstein, Cass R. 162n.76, 166n.85, 248
Sutherland, Keith 179n.6
Swaine, Lukas H. 274n.72
Sweden 166–67
Sweden Democrats 65
Sweers, B. 58n.133
Syriza (Greece) 65

Taiwan 204–5
Thomas, Clarence, Justice of the Supreme Court of the United States 73–74
Thompson, Dennis F. 271n.64, 274
Thorburn, Malcolm 102n.36, 150n.41
Tocqueville, Alexis de 23
Togliatti, Palmiro 158
Tremmel, Joerg Ch. 273n.71
Trump, Donald 60–61, 65, 68, 69–70, 73, 82, 201–2
Tugendhat, Ernst 153n.59
Tully, James 14, 31, 45–49, 47n.100
Turkey 68–69, 76
Tushnet, Mark 84n.74, 162n.76, 218, 219, 219n.7, 219nn.8–9, 243, 278–79, 278n.91

UK Independence Party 65
unamendability (of constitutional essentials)
 explicit 259–60, 261–62
  Hart-Ross debate on circumventing explicit 260n.26

implicit (or structural entrenchment) 3, 12–13, 123–24, 233, 259–60
justification of implicit
 in teleological terms 97–98, 267–68
 in terms of coherence 12–13, 106, 265–67
 in terms of the principal-delegate relation (moderate version) 13, 268–69
 in terms of the principal-delegate relation (radical version) 13, 269–72
 in terms of vertical reciprocity 13, 17–18, 272–75
unamendables, three sets of 261–64
United Kingdom 79–80, 109, 168, 173–74
United Nations 164
United Socialist Party (Venezuela) 72
United States 11, 64–65, 68, 113–14, 128, 157, 165–66, 178–79, 211–12, 235, 238, 267, 277, 278, 279
 Congress of 113–14, 253–54, 256
 Presidency of 83, 232, 238, 246, 251, 276n.81
 Supreme Court of 22–23, 73–74, 83, 91, 97, 98, 99, 109, 203n.83, 204–5, 208, 218, 219, 221, 226–27, 246, 254–55, 260n.26, 267, 276–77
Urbinati, Nadia 63n.4, 66n.12, 69nn.21–22, 85n.82, 86n.87, 88, 89n.99, 181–82, 199n.73
USAN (Union of South American Nations) 174n.100

Van der Walt, Johan 95–96, 95n.10, 96n.12, 99n.27
Vankeerberghen, Griet 145n.25
Vannini, Philip 212–13n.114
Van Reybrouck, David 179n.5
Vaughan, R. 30n.38
Vergara, Camila 84n.73
Vermeule, Adrian 40n.72, 83
Vile, John R. 246n.97, 265n.40, 268n.53
Vinx, Lars 95n.8, 98n.24, 111n.71
Vlaams Belang Party 65
Voneky, Silja 124n.123
Voting Rights Act (US) 91, 135n.157, 254n.14
Vox (Spain) 65

Waldron, Jeremy 13, 74–75, 74nn.34–35, 203n.83, 207n.94, 217n.1, 218n.5, 219n.8, 220, 221, 221n.15, 223n.22, 243
Walesa, Lech 158
Walker, Neil 5n.8, 6n.11, 141n.12
Warren, Mark 199n.73
　Washington, D.C. 65, 73
　Weber, Max 52, 53, 104n.41, 108, 183–84, 191–92, 199–200
　Weimar
　Constitution 105, 106, 108, 113, 123–24
　Republic 111, 235, 262–63, 280
Weithman, Paul 20n.1
　Wendt, Alexander 147n.34
Westminster (UK Parliament) 79–80, 186–87, 211–12

White, Stephen K. 45n.90
Williams, Bernard 14, 31, 49, 52, 52–56nn.115–121, 123
Williams, Patrick J. 212–13n.114
Wingenbach, Edward C. 45n.90
Winter, Steven L. 213n.116, 215n.120, 226n.37, 227n.40
Wittgenstein, Ludwig 47, 262–63
Worsley, Peter 65n.10
Wortman, Richard 64–65n.9
WTO 67–68

Young, Iris M. 180n.9, 199

Zakaria, Fareed 64n.7
Ziblatt, Daniel 64n.7
Zurn, Christopher F. 179n.4, 207n.94